P9-DFC-966

WITHDRAWN

The Coming Age of Scarcity

CUMBERLAND COLLEGE LIBRARY
PO BOX 517
VINELAND, NJ 08362-0517

Syracuse Studies on Peace and Conflict Resolution
Harriet Hyman Alonso, Charles Chatfield, *and* Louis Kriesberg,
Series Editors

WITHDRAWN

The Coming Age of Scarcity

Preventing Mass Death and Genocide in the Twenty-first Century

EDITED BY

Michael N. Dobkowski AND
Isidor Wallimann

WITH A FOREWORD BY JOHN K. ROTH

 SYRACUSE UNIVERSITY PRESS

99-480

Copyright © 1998 by Syracuse University Press
Syracuse, New York 13244-5160

All Rights Reserved

First Edition 1998

98 99 00 01 02 03   6 5 4 3 2 1

The paper used in this publication meets the minimum requirements of American National Standard for Information Sciences—Permanence of Paper for Printed Library Materials, ANSI Z39.48–1984. ∞

Library of Congress Cataloging-in-Publication Data
The coming age of scarcity : preventing mass death and genocide in the
    twenty-first century / edited by Michael N. Dobkowski and Isidor Wallimann. — 1st ed.
        p.   cm. — (Syracuse studies on peace and conflict resolution)
    Includes bibliographical references and index.
    ISBN 0-8516-2744-0 (pbk. : alk. paper)
        1. Scarcity.   2. Natural resources.   3. Economic development.
    4. Sustainable development.   I. Dobkowski, Michael N.
    II. Wallimann, Isidor, 1944–   .   III. Series.
    HB199.C635   1998
        333.7—dc21   97-18715

Manufactured in the United States of America

Contents

Maps

Table

Foreword

Despair Is No Solution

John K. Roth

> The genocides of the 20th century have unveiled the true heart of human-
> ity. At our center lies an ability to commit evil of an almost unimagined
> degree. . . . The unthinkable has already happened; the idea of future catas-
> trophes is therefore not unthinkable.
>
> —Michael Dobkowski and Isidor Wallimann

The Coming Age of Scarcity scares me. Perhaps you will feel the same.
The reasons are not far to find. They are summed up in this foreword's
epigraph, which comes from the introductory essay that Michael
Dobkowski and Isidor Wallimann, the editors of this volume, have
provided.

Showing how scarcity and surplus populations can lead to disaster, *The Coming Age of Scarcity* is about evil. It documents "ethnic cleansing" and excavates the world's expanding killing fields. Sadly, it
anticipates mass death and genocide in the twenty-first century even
while trying to prevent them.

The writers who have contributed to these pages know evil when
they see it. They intend that their readers see it, too. They succeed—
so much so that this book does more than scare me. It leaves me
depressed, almost to the point of despair.

To understate the case, this book discourages me. Perhaps it will
do the same for you. How could it not? The world's expanding
megacities and refugee hordes, as well as pressures for and protests

against immigration, are only the latest signs of an unrelenting global population crunch, which increasingly leaves the world with more people than anyone needs. A world with more people than anyone needs is a deadly place. It is a stage set perpetually for mass death and genocide.

Surplus people are only one of the preconditions for mass death and genocide. Roger Smith's essay rightly argues that scarcity is another. As this entire book suggests, moreover, the specter of scarcity is likely to be even worse in the twenty-first century than it has been in the twentieth. That judgment is credible even though the late-1996 World Food Summit will have taken place in Rome before this book appears. Sponsored by the Food and Agricultural Organization (FAO) of the United Nations, the summit meeting intends to renew the commitment of world leaders to eradicate hunger and malnutrition and to ensure lasting food security for the world's people.

The word *renew* bears watching. A similar World Food Conference in 1974 had already committed—supposedly—the world community to such worthy aims. Two decades later, however, the FAO reports that 800 million people in developing countries face chronic malnutrition. Eighty-eight countries, forty-two in sub-Saharan Africa alone, are in low-income, food-deficit conditions. Meanwhile, with the figures calculated in 1985 U.S. dollars, external aid for such places declined from $10 billion in 1982 to $7.2 billion in 1992. The daunting problems faced by the 1996 World Food Summit are made even more so by the fact that the meeting has no binding effects on anyone. Each participating country remains free to do as much, or as little, as it sees fit.

Sociologist Gil Elliot rightly identified the twentieth century as the most devastating in history as far as human-made deaths are concerned. No updating of Elliot's 1972 calculations would do anything to change that judgment. To the contrary, although "Never again!" still resounds after Auschwitz, post-Holocaust history has nearly turned that cry into an all-too-hollow cliché. The fact is that genocidal killing has taken more lives since the Holocaust ended than it did in the first half of the twentieth century. The arrival of a new century, moreover, will unlikely bring relief. There is every reason to think that the twenty-first century will feature even more human-made death than the twentieth.

At least thus far, attempts to prosecute those who have been accused of genocidal crimes in Rwanda and the former Yugoslavia do not inspire confidence that the threat of arrest and punishment will do much to deter genocide's fury. Nor can one take heart from the opening of John Cobb's essay, which observes that projections about the future are uncertain because history is always full of surprises. As his analysis helps to make depressingly clear, more often than not history's surprises are lethal to the point of catastrophe.

In every contribution to this book, there are plenty of reasons for despair. Joseph Tainter shows how competition and expansion—long the boosters for "progress"—exacerbate conflict that can turn genocidal. John Gowdy measures the biophysical limits to industrialization, creating a nasty surprise for those who think that the future will be benignly open forever. Ted Trainer sees present society as unsustainable, Virginia Abernethy wonders about the bloody divisiveness that accompanies resurgent tribalism, and Chris Lewis analyzes the necessary collapse of modern industrial civilization.

The list could go on and on, but this book's impact drives home the point that, in one way or another, we are approaching the end of the human world as we have known it. Do not misunderstand: an apocalyptic doomsday is not at hand. The world is not going to end anytime soon, but the times are changing decisively nonetheless.

Sometimes the ending of an era is cause for celebration. Ironically, in an age of mass death and genocide, such a conclusion would be unrealistic. The conditions accounting for our deadly age will die hard. Whatever happens, including even the corrective and constructive changes that this book's authors recommend, the shifts are likely to be wrenching and violent. Things will get worse before they get better—if they do get better.

One reason is that for too long too many of us, including even people who have the means to buy this book and the time to read it, have enjoyed the world that is too much with us. Much as we deplore mass death and genocide, we will still find it extremely difficult to bring about the global changes that are needed to check it. Even while trying to prevent mass death and genocide in the twenty-first century, we may also resist the changes that are really needed to eliminate them.

The many beneficiaries of existing circumstances will not set aside their privileges easily any more than the wretched of the earth will placidly accept their desperate conditions of scarcity. As the pressures mount, and they will, parties on all sides will defend their interests. In too many cases, moreover, the defense will be by any means—wrenching and violent—that are perceived as necessary. History may prove such judgments wrong, but that outcome would be so surprising that only the foolish would bank on it.

This book calls forth dark moods within me. And yet it evokes other moods as well. Perhaps it will do the same for you. At least in my case, these "and yet" moods are neither removed from nor located beyond the darkness with which this book engulfs me. Their movement is a stirring within that darkness, but the movement is not easily named. What I feel is *not* captured by words like *hope* or *conviction*, and even less do my feelings involve much that a glib word like *optimism* contains.

The stirring aroused within me by *The Coming Age of Scarcity* is best expressed in the negative. It is reflected in this foreword's title: *despair is no solution*. Those words also come from the introduction that Michael Dobkowski and Isidor Wallimann have written, which ultimately urges people to work against despair within and despite the darkness.

As I explore these feelings and write the words that they have provoked here, I do so as a philosopher and teacher who has spent most of a thirty-year academic career studying the damage that the Holocaust and other forms of genocide have done. In particular, I have written these words right after completing the syllabus for my current course on the Holocaust and genocide and just before the 1996–97 academic year begins. Reflecting on the essays in this book while I have been preparing again to teach young college students about the subjects it addresses, I have been reminded once more that teachers are constantly stalked by despair. How could we not be?

Most teachers are idealists. However jaded we may become, most of us became teachers because we wanted to mend the world. That hope, however, encounters discouragement aplenty. History, especially genocide's history, provides it. So does teaching, which is a less-than-reassuring activity when humankind's future is at stake.

We are all beginners every day. No matter how hard we teachers try, indifference persists, prejudice remains, ignorance endures, and no place on earth guarantees safety from the destruction that such forces can unleash. Education's gains take place against stiff odds; learning is not evolutionary progress. Every year, every class, means starting over because wisdom does not accumulate.

Teaching about the Holocaust and genocide makes me more melancholy than I used to be. It makes me realize how much despair lurks around every classroom door. Even more, however, such teaching makes me understand that those recognitions are not the conclusion, but they must be the stirring amid darkness, the insistence affirms that despair is not the solution. To let despair have its way would be to give every genocidal act a victory that it does not deserve and must not have.

Where mass death and genocide are concerned, however, what is the solution? Is there such a thing? Perhaps, but if so, what ingredients does it contain? Responses to those questions—good and thoughtful ones—are found in this book's pages. As they draw to a close, I would add only two words of recapitulation: a warning and then a fact.

The warning: "If we stop remembering," says Holocaust survivor Elie Wiesel, "we stop being." The memory and analysis of mass death and genocide found in this book warn against despair. The effect of that warning can be to sensitize us against indifference, which is despair's best friend and evil's welcome accomplice.

As for the fact, the essays in this book can sensitize us against despair and indifference because history shows that human-made mass death and genocide are not inevitable and no events related to them ever will be. We know this because human-made mass death and genocide emerge from decisions and institutions that depend on ordinary human beings who are responsible for their actions and who could act differently and better than they often do.

If we heed the warning and do not deny the fact—especially in an age of scarcity, mass death, and genocide—we will keep working to mend the world's broken heart. Despite much of its content, then, this book awakens, haunts, and challenges me in ways that I ignore at everyone's peril. I trust it will do the same for you.

Acknowledgments

The two of us came to the study of scarcity and conflict from different disciplines and from different sides of the Atlantic Ocean. That we could produce this joint effort is a tribute to the centrality of the issue, to the respect we have for each other, both personally and professionally, and to our commitment to multidisciplinary work and interchange.

We have spent more than a decade studying genocide, fascism, and other forms of human cruelty. Those of us who study mass death do so in the hope that it will preserve life. We don't want our subject to become commonplace and even familiar; we want to bring it to the forefront of public discourse.

We wish to thank colleagues in our respective institutions and other friends and students who have provided an intellectual environment that was conducive to productive work. We are particularly grateful to the contributors for the prompt submission of their essays and the high quality of their work. We benefited from several reviewers whose comments helped make this a better book and from the advice and counsel of Louis Kriesberg, who, as always, offered honest and insightful critique and support. We are, of course, responsible for any errors that remain.

A special acknowledgment goes to Judy Mahoney, who typed, retyped, formatted, merged, and otherwise helped prepare the final manuscript for submission. Thanks also to Cynthia Maude-Gembler, executive editor of Syracuse University Press, who encouraged this project from its conception and to John Fruehwirth, managing editor.

Finally, there are our students and colleagues at our respective institutions, friends and families who sustained, distracted, and encouraged us. To Karen, who fills my life with joy and meaning; to my mother, Bronia, who continues to be a source of strength and guidance; to my children, Batsheva, Jonathan, and Tamar who also did their part by reminding me why the issues in this book are important and for getting me on occasion to leave my work to concern myself with what was taking place in the "real" world, such as college, the New York Knicks, Hillel School, high school basketball, friends, and fashion.

Contributors

Virginia Abernethy is a professor of psychiatry (anthropology) at Vanderbilt Medical School and edits the bimonthly journal, *Population and Environment*. She is author of several books, including *Population Pressure and Cultural Adjustment* and *Population Politics: The Choices That Shape Our Future.*

John B. Cobb, Jr., is professor emeritus of theology of the School of Theology at Claremont College and a director of the Center for Process Studies. He is author of *Sustainability* and *Sustaining the Common Good* and coauthor of *The Liberation of Life* (with Charles Birch) and *For the Common Good* (with Herman Daly).

Craig Dilworth is reader in theoretical philosophy at Uppsala University, Sweden. He is author of *Scientific Progress* (3d ed.) and *The Metaphysics of Science* (1996) and is completing a work in environmental research entitled "Sustainable Development and Decision Making."

Michael N. Dobkowski is professor of religious studies at Hobart and William Smith Colleges. He is author of *The Tarnished Dream: The Basis of American Anti-Semitism, The Politics of Indifference: Documentary History of Holocaust Victims in America,* and *Jewish American Voluntary Organizations*. With Isidor Wallimann, he is editor of several books, including *Genocide and the Modern Age: Etiology and Case Studies* and *Genocide in Our Time*. With Isidor Wallimann and Louis Kriesberg, Dobkowski edits the research annual, *Research in Social Movements, Conflicts, and Change.*

Kurt Finsterbusch is professor of sociology at the University of Maryland at College Park. He has written extensively on the impact of scarcity on politics and society and is author of *Understanding Social Impacts: Social Research for Policy Decisions* (with Annabelle Bender Motz), and *Organizational Change as a Development Strategy: Models and Tactics for Improving Third World Organizations* (with Jerald Hage).

John M. Gowdy is professor of economics at Rensselaer Polytechnic Institute in Troy, New York. His works include two recent books, *Coevolutionary Economics* and *Economic Theory for Environmentalists* (with Sabine O'Hara). In 1995 he was a Fulbright Scholar at the Institute for Environmental Economics and Management in Vienna.

Chris H. Lewis is an instructor in the Sewall American Studies Program at the University of Colorado at Boulder. An environmental and intellectual historian, he has recently completed *Ecology and the Human Future* and is presently writing a history of the global sustainable development movement.

Waltraud Queiser Morales is professor of international and comparative studies at the University of Central Florida. She is author of *Bolivia: Land of Struggle, Social Revolution: Theory and Historical Application,* and coauthor of *Human Rights: A User's Guide.*

Leon Rappoport is professor of psychology at Kansas State University. He is author of numerous research articles, a textbook on personality development, and is coauthor of *The Holocaust and the Crisis of Human Behavior.*

Craig A. Rimmerman is associate professor of political science at Hobart and William Smith Colleges and is author of *Presidency by Plebiscite: The Reagan-Bush Era in Institutional Perspective.* Author of articles on democratic theory and environmental policy, he is also editor of *Gay Rights, Military Wrongs: Political Perspectives on Lesbians and Gays in the Military.*

John K. Roth is Pitzer professor of philosophy at Claremont McKenna College. He has published more than twenty books, many of them focusing on the Holocaust and genocide. He serves on the United

States Holocaust Memorial Council, which governs the United States Holocaust Memorial Museum in Washington, D.C.

David Norman Smith is an associate professor of sociology at the University of Kansas. He is author of several books including *Marx's "Kapital" for Beginners* and *Who Rules the Universities?* and is editor of the first English-language edition of Karl Marx's *Ethnological Notebooks* (forthcoming).

Roger W. Smith is a professor of government at the College of William and Mary. He has written about the nature and history of genocide, language and genocide, ratification of the Genocide Convention by the U.S. Senate, and denial of the Armenian Genocide. He is currently writing a book on women and genocide.

Joseph A. Tainter is project leader of Cultural Heritage Research, Rocky Mountain Forest and Range Experiment Station, Albuquerque, New Mexico, and has taught anthropology at the University of New Mexico. His book, *The Collapse of Complex Societies,* develops a long-standing research interest in the evolution of socioeconomic complexity. He is also coeditor (with Bonnie Bagley Tainter) of *Evolving Complexity and Environmental Risk in the Prehistoric Southwest.*

Ted Trainer lectures on sociology within the School of Social work at the University of New South Wales. His most recent publications include *The Conserver Society; Alternatives for Sustainability* and *Towards a Sustainable Economy.*

Isidor Wallimann is senior lecturer in sociology at the School of Social Work in Basel, Switzerland, and a lecturer at the University of Fribourg. He is author of *Estrangement: Marx's Conception of Human Nature and the Division of Labor* and is coeditor (with Michael Dobkowski) of *Towards the Holocaust, Genocide and the Modern Age: Etiology and Case Studies,* and *Radical Perspectives on the Rise of Fascism in Germany, 1919–1945,* and *Genocide in Our Time.* With Michael Dobkowski and Louis Kriesberg, he edits the research annual, *Research in Social Movements, Conflicts and Change.*

The Coming Age of Scarcity

1. The Coming Age of Scarcity

An Introduction

Michael N. Dobkowski *and* Isidor Wallimann

The twentieth century can be characterized as the "age of genocide." The "progress" of this century has been constant along its journey of horrors—from the massacre of the Armenians, to Stalin's planned famine in the Ukraine, to the Holocaust, to the killing fields of Cambodia, to the ethnic massacres in Burundi and Rwanda, to the ethnic cleansing in the former Yugoslavia.

According to a number of scholars, the violence of past centuries pales before the violence and mayhem of the present one. In his pioneering work, *Twentieth Century Book of the Dead*, Scottish sociologist Gil Elliot estimated that more than 110 million people were killed by their fellow human beings between 1900 and 1972. Such findings led him to conclude that manmade death "is the central moral as well as material fact of our time" (Elliot 1972, 1–6). Sociologist Pitirim Sorokin, tracing quantitative trends in collective violence over the centuries, came to a similar conclusion. On the basis of his analysis, Sorokin concluded that "the curse or privilege to be the most devastating or most bloody war century belongs to the twentieth; in one quarter century it imposed upon the population a 'blood tribute' far greater than that imposed by any of the whole centuries combined." (Sorokin 1962, 342).

Although the literature on collective violence focuses predominantly on genocide and warfare, it is important to recognize that there are other forms of governmental mass killing. In several earlier studies, we attempted to broaden the discussion of genocide by including a consideration of structural violence—the violence created by social, political, and economic institutions and structures, or by benign neglect or demographic and environmental factors. Structural violence, by causing suffering and death as the result of structured social inequality, creates conditions conducive to the outbreak of overt violence, particularly as civil war and ethnic conflict. Once initiated, this violence usually exacerbates the socioeconomic conditions by destroying portions of the economic infrastructure, by overturning the delicate political balance, and by damaging the ecosystem thereby aggravating the economic and social conditions that cause structural violence. It can easily become a vicious circle of violence. We see that being played out in the Balkans, the former Soviet Union, and in Africa.

The enormity of the violence of our century is indicated by our almost schizophrenic attitude toward it. We move between attitudes of despair and numbing on the one hand and denial or avoidance on the other. These attitudes are mirror images of each other. They both seek to deny reality by avoiding any responsibility for the need to understand and confront the phenomenon. Our first obligation, however, is to face it squarely.

As we argued ten years ago in *Genocide and the Modern Age*, if scholarly efforts are to contribute to the improvement of the human condition by preserving life, in the case of genocide and mass deaths we can no longer conceive of them as random and rare historic phenomena. History and contemporary experience just won't allow such a conclusion. Instead, we are compelled to look for patterns and causation that lead to and are associated with these tendencies. We must look upon the history and nature of societies giving rise to mass death as human-made and thereby influenceable. Any other perspective would preclude the human agency necessary to act preventively. Thus, we postulate that the social, economic, and historic circumstances making mass death possible are largely the creations of human beings, are not random and may be associated with social patterns and structures that can be studied. Scholars have demonstrated that for past genocides. We should be able to bring these insight to bear on a consideration of the dangers we face in the future. As we approach the end of the millennium and the beginning of the twenty-first century, nothing is clear or certain except that the projection of present directions in population growth, land resources, energy consumption, and per capita consumption cannot be sustained and may lead to even greater catastrophe. These challenges are experienced and expressed by different social segments in ways that are likely to create fierce conflict within place and between place. Within place, producers, the state, and local groups are battling over the control of natural resources. Between place, communities and nations battle over who should produce and consume, and who should conserve.[1]

The problem facing us as we approach the twenty-first century is not how to reduce scarcity amid downsizing, but how to resolve the resulting conflicts without resorting to genocide either explicitly through warfare or implicitly through unequal burden sharing. We maintain, with the contributors to this volume, the conviction that the issues we face are very serious. However, we also believe that they are susceptible to analysis and that the problems are influenceable. We do not subscribe to rigid historical determinism—the future can be altered as long as we understand the forces that may be propelling it and have the individual and collective will to think beyond self-interest and narrow parochialism. We all have a stake in balancing economic and ecological needs, short- and long-term demand and individual and community interests, both local and global. If we realize that, we have the chance of devising strategies capable of allowing for diverse and divisive social segments to make peaceful decisions as socioeconomic and ecosystems contract. The alternative may be war and genocide. But before purposeful action can be taken to prevent potential disasters, we first have to understand what is at stake and what the issues are.

This book addresses one of the most pressing and significant issues that humanity has been confronted with so far. Yet, despite the compelling nature of the problem, only few attempts are under way—little effort is spent—to analyze the dangers we face and to develop strategies designed to avert the looming catastrophe. We would like to maintain that world industrialization and urbanization and its associated social system and techniques—such as the universal market system or centralized planning bureaucracies—cannot be sustained except

---

1. Isidor Wallimann and Michael N. Dobkowski, eds., *Genocide and the Modern Age: Etiology and Case Studies of Mass Death* (Westport, Conn.: Greenwood Press, 1987); Michael N. Dobkowski and Isidor Wallimann, *Genocide in Our Time: An Annotated Bibliography with Analytical Introductions* (Ann Arbor, Mich.: Pierian Press, 1992).

for a relatively few privileged people and at the cost of increased mass death, which may include genocide. The alternative, namely, to abandon the global industrialization project and to begin a move away from industrial society as it is known today, equally entails a risk of mass death on a tremendous scale.

It is true that modernization and industrialization have confronted us with many great problems before while millions have been forced into deprivation, poverty, wars, and premature death. In the course of modernization worldwide, however, the world population has nevertheless grown significantly. Therefore, one might be tempted to conclude that the social and economic systems that have laid the paths and been the engines for industrialization will again respond in time to avert the anticipated mass death and increasing spiral of human self-destruction on a scale never witnessed so far. However, this would indeed be a fateful attitude to assume.

If this is so, we are as social scientists and humanists well advised to speedily reconsider our priorities and to increasingly engage in a kind of scientific praxis that is *explicitly* directed toward the preservation of life, at home and elsewhere in our global society. Guided by the norm and the wish to preserve life, we have to increasingly ask the following questions:

1. What knowledge is required? Do we have necessary theoretical social science knowledge to guide us through the forthcoming great transformation that is to lead us away from today's modernity?

2. Whom does this knowledge serve? Do we have the type of knowledge that will both guide us through this transformation and serve humanity in that it is directed toward the preservation of life?

But what exactly is the problem that confronts us? What are the anticipated bottlenecks based upon which one could say that traditional modernization will come to an end? What are the bottlenecks that could lead to mass death? In an attempt to address these questions, let us first turn to a short discussion of industrialization.

Industrialization

It is important to recall that the great transformation from agricultural to modern, urban, and industrial societies has always been financed on the back of peasants both in the nineteenth century, in the area that is now known as the center, and in the twentieth century, in the area now known as the periphery. Whether this transfer of value from the agricultural sector has been achieved with political and bureaucratic means or through the indirect and anonymous coercion of market systems, the truth remains that the surplus value produced in agriculture alone financed industrial production and made urban and industrial life sustainable. This is not to deny that agriculture simultaneously became more productive owing, in part, to the very growth in the urban-based sciences and industrial production it had financed. However, much of this "great transformation" has always been associated with immense hardship on the peasantry, be it for the many who remained in rural areas or for those who migrated as wage laborers to the growing cities. Much premature death because of poverty, disease, and lack of medical attention went hand in hand with drastic improvements in the life expectancy, particularly for infants. Thus, the age structure of the population was shifted to a median age of twenty, or even below, while life expectancy at birth rose to about sixty years.

The most common techniques to bring about the transformation of agricultural society have been the market mechanisms associated with capitalism and the socialist central planning approach relying primarily on authoritarian bureaucratic methods. These methods can again be divided into those that encouraged urban formations (Eastern Europe) and those that tended to discourage large-scale, rural-urban migration. Thus, China has tended to promote the selective industrialization of rural communities. Despite these differences, however, the socialist approaches have one thing in common that clearly distinguishes them from the capitalist transformation technique: the idea, and the social contract, that modernity and industrial society can be attained while guaranteeing—in conjunction with the right and the obligation for men and women to work—a sociocultural existence minimum to all. Only from about 1795 to 1834, and only in England during the Speenhamland regulations, did the capitalist technique resort to a kind of guaranteed minimum-income policy. Even this phase can primarily be seen as a strategy to get the transformation going, to soften the blows dealt by enclosures, and to encourage enough persons to permanently participate as wage laborers outside agriculture. Once the transformation had gained sufficient momentum, the Speenhamland regulations were abandoned to make room for the poor laws, police and jails, utilitarianism and free markets, Manchester liberalism and social Darwinism, cyclically recurring economic crises, class struggle, and revolutionary activity.

By the time the modern welfare state was developed, the capitalist system had entered the ongoing imperialist phase. Its transformation technique had taken a firm grip of ever more distant agricultural populations whose surplus could be used to both expand the newly created industrial society in the center and to introduce large-scale urban life and rudimentary industrial production in the periphery. Class struggle and other conflicts may have been instrumental in bringing it about, but the welfare state, and the almost guaranteed existence minimum that we associate with this institution, particularly since World War II, has also been financed by the surplus transferred and appropriated from the periphery. Meanwhile, however, the half of the world's population still subject to transformation under capitalism is far from having an existence minimum guaranteed and, if at all, is only beginning to establish the first and most rudimentary social insurance schemes. Additionally, as the worldwide transformation proceeds, thus providing alternatives for industrial producers in the center, the center's welfare state guarantees to existence are also eroding, despite such normative documents as the United Nations human rights convention or the European social charter. Faced with the competing socialist alternative to modernization, these documents were once strongly promoted by the already transformed and modernized capitalist center.

Population Growth

All industrialization has been associated with significant population growth. The world's population roughly doubled from 1750 to 1900 and again from 1900 to 1950. In 1800 it still took far more than a hundred years for the world population to double. Today it takes only thirty-eight years. Some 1.7 billion people inhabited this planet in 1900. In 1990 it was 5.3 billion and in the year 2025 we shall have 8.5 billion. Only about one-fifth of the world's population lives in the fully transformed and industrialized part of the world including Eastern Europe. About two-fifths alone live in India and China, giving China a slightly larger population than India. Sixty percent of the world's population lives in Asia, about 9 percent in Latin America, and about 12 percent in Africa. The reasons for the ever faster population growth are well known. Although birthrates have tended to decline, they have not decreased fast enough to compensate for the gains owing to lower infant mortality and the general increase in life expectancy. These gains have not been made possible by high-tech medicine, but by relatively simple techniques, such as an improved diet, better control over bacterial environments (general hygiene, water supply, food storage, antibiotics), and by vaccinations against various contagious and other diseases. The world-wide knowledge of these techniques, the possibility for their widespread deployment at a low cost, world information on social and medical problems, political pressure, the need for social control, and human compassion have been major causes for the ever-accelerating population growth. Presently, it is not expected that AIDS or diseases such as cholera or tuberculosis, although growing, will significantly alter the rate of population growth in the near future.

One of the correlates of modernization has been that birthrates decrease with increased urbanization and a higher standard of living. Experience in the fully transformed industrial countries generally has shown that population growth tends to stabilize at a low positive rate and that some countries even have slightly negative growth rate. This experience leads to the notion that, once the world will be transformed into modernity, industrialized, and economically developed, the world population too will be stabilized in its growth. Of course, the crucial assumption made here is that it is possible to provide the world with the standard of living of industrial countries, irrespective of the economic systems—particularly capitalism, which chronically tends toward overproduction and crisis—and ecological considerations.

Experience shows that most campaigns to more swiftly reduce the birthrate are successful only in societies with a sufficiently high standard of living. However, they can also be successful in relatively poor societies with a low standard of living if, and only if, social and economic justice is simultaneously given a high priority. The more vulnerable people become economically, and the more they are threatened by modernization and industrialization, the more they are inclined to adhere to birthrates that enhance population growth. This pattern is often seen as an example of irrational behavior. Allegedly, it prevents families from accumulating the human, social, and financial capital needed for the family's economic improvement, and it is said to annul all productivity gains made on the macro level to improve the standard of living. However, as is well known among development workers and agricultural specialists, when people must live at the margins of existence, they tend to *minimize risks* and *not to maximize profits and accumulation*. By adhering to higher birthrates, they aim to spread severe existential risks to more people, which from their point of view is a reasonable thing to do.

However, it is also true that women often give birth to more children than they desire, and that the children are required for the family's survival and successful reproduction. Because this condition is usually induced by gender inequality, it follows that birthrates can also be reduced in part by strengthening the position of women in society. In sum, without sufficient equality on the micro and macro levels, there is little hope to reduce the birthrate sufficiently for population growth to level off.

Migration and Employment

Because the transformation reduces the percentage of the population employed in agriculture, and because insufficient alternative employment is available in rural areas, people have migrated to cities. Presently, some 45 percent of the world's population lives in urban spaces. In fully transformed countries, it is about 70 percent, while it is only about 35 percent in those areas still undergoing transformation. Latin America is an exception. About 70 percent of its population lives in cities.

Migrants tend to be young and not only male. In some economic environments and cultures, women tend to migrate even more often than men. Because of the volume of migration and the high fertility potential of the migrant population itself, the population grows at a much higher rate in urban as compared to rural areas.

The industrialized center has only about 7 percent of its population employed in the agricultural sector. The rest of the world (which accounts for about four-fifths of the globe's inhabitants) still employs about 60 percent of its population in agriculture. This corresponds to the situation in Europe and the United States in the middle of the nineteenth century, when Europe's industrialization was well under way. However, industrialization and urbanization then involved both a smaller population and extended over a larger time span than is true today. Therefore, new and old urban spaces contain considerably more people than nineteenth-century cities, and we have not even begun to imagine what it means to bring—besides the ongoing population growth—only half of the now remaining agricultural population into other forms of usually urban-based economic activities.

The nineteenth-century transformation of agricultural society channeled migrants into industrial work—to the extent that they found employment at all. The tertiary, mostly service, sector was developed later. Today just the opposite is true. The formal economy favors the expansion of services. In addition, the huge informal economic activity belongs itself more to the tertiary than to the secondary sector. This pattern seems to confirm the notion that we are far from growing into a true world industrial society. Displaced from agricultural occupations, people end up with few perspectives and no vision that can make them feel part of a new era, involving such things as the creation of nation states, industrial production, and mobility, which were characteristic of the nineteenth century. To the extent that they are taking part in the international division of labor, they mostly do so in dependency and with unequal terms of trade. And even though the standard of living in developing countries erodes further and poverty deepens, the population affected by industrialization and urbanization remains politically disenfranchised on an international level, where industrialization policies and world economic decisions are being made.

Energy and Other Resources

Thus far, all industrialization and urbanization has been associated with an increased use of energy, directly and indirectly replacing the human and animal energy used in production and distribution, expanding the sphere of unnecessary consumption, and allowing for world markets and their corollary, the world division of labor. This expansion of world trade and the world division of labor is, of course, again a precondition for world industrialization.

World energy consumption, although increasing, remained relatively low until 1950. From 1950 to 1990, however, the use of energy increased sevenfold, far outpacing the population, which approximately doubled during the same period. Most of this increase came from the use of fossil fuels, of which oil and gas constituted the largest share. The contribution of atomic and hydroelectric power to the world's energy supply is only about 15 percent.

As gross national product (GNP) per capita grows, so does the use of energy. Therefore, one-fifth of the world's population uses about four-fifths of the world's energy, most of it as industrial fuels. Traditional fuels (wood, peat, dung) supply about 5 percent of the world's energy and are almost entirely (85 percent) used in peripheral countries. At the present rate of use, it is estimated that the world has oil for another 40 years, gas for another 60, and coal for another 660 years. Coal supplies about a third of today's energy. The future supply of traditional fuels (particularly wood) depends on several factors, such as the need for drinking water, the need to reduce carbon dioxide levels, the amount of acid rain, and the damage from the destruction of ozone layers.

It is not possible here to address the future supply of all resources such as minerals and water. It is important, however, to mention that the arable land available for the production of food and fibers tends to shrink. Any expansion will be possible only at the expense of forests or grasslands, jeopardizing other resources, particularly water and topsoil. Any increases in the agricultural output would, therefore, have to come from different growing techniques, pest controls, irrigation, the use of fertilizers, plant breeding, and genetic engineering. During the 1980s, the growth in world grain production has decreased and, if measured per capita to correct for population growth, world grain production has tended to level off.

Bottlenecks: A Historically Unique Constellation

Impending bottlenecks, as can be deduced from the discussion so far, center in population growth, land resources, energy, and environmental constraints. What is most crucial is that we have never found ourselves in a situation in which all four factors are so closely linked. Sure, we have had a growing population and population pressures before, but there has always been more land to be cultivated. Sure, we have had large populations to care for before, but more energy-intensive agricultural production and improvements in plant breeding have always been possible. Sure, we have had the need for more energy before, but there has always been some new oil field just a few feet below the ground. Sure, we have had all these pressures before. But have we experienced them as impenetrable limits, as absolute deficiencies of land and energy? Have we experienced them all at the same time and as impenetrable limits? Certainly not. Have we ever simultaneously experienced such severe land and energy limits and also faced the real danger of an ecological collapse? Again, certainly not.

Today, this planet counts some 5.5 billion people. In 2025, it will contain 8.5 billion. Beyond 2025, we do not know how much the population will grow. Current opinion tends to assume that, as a result of economic development, the birthrate will "automatically" fall to about two children per family before 2050, a level now observed for transformed countries. This assumption is very unrealistic, however, since about 35 percent of the population under transformation already lives in poverty—although the transformation is far from having been completed and the number of children per family in industrializing countries under transformation is still about four. But even if the assumption should prove to be correct, the population is expected to reach 9.5 billion in 2050 and to level off at about 10 billion in 2075. However, by 2030, we shall also have exhausted the presently known oil reserves or about 30 percent of today's energy supply. And by 2050, we shall further have exhausted the presently known gas supply or (together with oil) about one-half of today's energy supply, although owing to population growth, we shall also have reduced the per capita energy consumption by about 40 percent.

The energy crunch is made worse by environmental limits. The degree to which we have been using fossil fuels is changing our ecosystem and the human, animal, and plant reproduction and survival patterns that have for centuries been built around it. The lives of millions are increasingly at risk if sea levels begin to rise and glaciers melt. It is estimated that 30 percent of the world's population lives in a thirty-mile-wide coastal strip and is concentrated in Asia and Europe. Millions of people would have to be relocated as environmental refugees, their lives would be threatened by floods and tidal waves, more fertile arable land would be lost, and the erosion inland would be more severe owing to increased rains.

As a result, the largest environmental organizations urge a 30 percent reduction of carbon dioxide levels by 2005, a 50 percent reduction by 2020, and an 80 percent reduction by 2050. These reductions would indeed necessitate a drastic change in our present energy-use patterns and amount to a drastic *absolute* cut in the amount of energy used—all this in times of significant population growth.

Finally, the tremendous food pressures must be reiterated. We can cultivate the land more intensively and turn our lawns into vegetable gardens, but how many millions more can be fed by such measures? We may resort to the oceans for protein, but oceans are already overfished. We may turn away from animal protein to feed more people with the same amount of grain, but this reserve applies only to the transformed world and becomes increasingly insignificant as the Third World population grows. We may resort to ocean farming, greenhouse and hydroponic production, but can we compensate for the destruction of agricultural lands because of overuse and overexposure to wind and water? Can we compensate for the loss in land because of urbanization and the increased demand for housing? Can we compensate for the loss in plant growth and crop yield because of increased ultra-violet radiation? We do not believe that these challenges will be met without bottlenecks that may cost the lives of millions.

It seems evident now that there will be a temporal conjunction of four sizable bottlenecks: population, land, energy, and environmental-carrying capacity. All of them are so intricately related that they form a system complexity whose very balance has never been so delicate and yet so important to our survival. Therefore, we must also distin-guish between bottlenecks that present continuous but stable chal-lenges and those that represent discontinuous and unstable challenges. Population growth, for example, is a challenge with great continuity. However, as we approach the question of energy and land, particu-larly if environmental pressures are included, we can increasingly expect challenges characterized by discontinuity. Even though energy resources may not be depleted, the supply of energy could for techno-logical, political, or economic reasons become highly discontinuous. Agricultural land may increasingly go out of commission in a discon-tinuous way, be it because of events such as droughts, floods, erosion, or drastic overuse. As the system reaches an ever-greater complexity, and as survival hinges ever more and with small margins on this complexity, any jolt to the system is bound to make survival more immediately a matter of life and death.

Furthermore, the jolts emitted by the economic system are also of importance, for production factors like population, land, energy, as well as many environmental constraints are mediated and coordinated by markets. Markets, however, are also known to have a great deal of discontinuity owing to the anonymous number of its participants and the unforeseeable outcome produced by their myriad market interac-tions. Thus, the capitalist market, the *very* technique chosen to *manage* survival, is itself a *threat* to survival, as is exemplified by speculation, recessions, and depressions, booms and busts. Market dynamics them-selves upset the delicate balance between land, energy, population, and the environment, and thereby directly determine survival and death rates.

Additionally, techniques to *assure* continuity in a world of random but significant disturbances may break down. Already insurance com-panies suspect that a number of recent weather-related events may have ceased to be sufficiently random or insignificant or both to be insured. The private market insurance system may soon prove to be unable to ensure against certain ecosystem risks. The instability would thereby increase, leaving politics as the last potential guarantor of continuity and stability, as is already the case with atomic power plants, where no private insurer is willing to cover the entire risk, *nor could such risk be covered*. However, how many big risks, should the event and the scarcity associated with them occur, can the political system handle before solidarity breaks down, instability increases, conflicts grow, and massive death results?

In times of growth and system expansion, potential conflicts can more likely be ignored, for their resolution is relatively easy. Everybody can come up with Pareto-type conflict resolutions. The going gets much tougher though, and more lives are at stake, when conflicts await resolution during system contraction, increased scarcity, and shrinking surpluses. First, the number and severity of conflicts tend to increase. Second, conflict potentials can no longer be as easily ignored, for, should they erupt, the disturbance would only augment the scarcity and make any resolution increasingly and unnecessarily more difficult. Third, resolutions to conflicts are politically and economically much *harder* to find in times of general scarcity and contraction.

Presently, our world still relies on expansion and Pareto-type conflict resolutions. International exchange and free trade is thus enhanced, as is evident by the North American Free Trade Agreement (NAFTA) and the General Agreement on Tariffs and Trade (GATT). Furthermore, Eastern Europe, once a highly self-sufficient economic and political system, is being dismantled and integrated with the world division of labor. China, while still self-sufficient, may because of its participation in international trade and communication also become more unstable and be pressured to further expand market relations. While Eastern Europe and China chose to bring about industrialization by the primacy of political priorities over market priorities and by politically distributing scarcity (also in the sphere of consumption), Eastern Europe is now joining the rest of the world by introducing social and political relations based on the primacy of markets. And China may soon follow and experience large-scale migration, increased inequality, poverty, higher birthrates, and destabilized population growth.

Capitalism, which is now the world's dominant political and economic system, thrives on market expansion. However, how compatible is capitalism with the long-term zero or negative growth environment of the future? It is incompatible! Not only does capitalism have great difficulty in handling such conditions, economically and politically, but it also has, for the same reasons, difficulty in preparing for them. Thus, markets, if left to themselves, cannot factor in long-term scarcity. Has the price of oil, for example, signaled that oil will soon be very scarce? On the contrary, oil markets have, if anything, signaled an ever-growing supply of oil. The same could be said for land, lumber, and many other natural resources in limited supply.

The ability of the capitalist market system to guide us through the next decades of increasing scarcity and downscaling of industrial production is very limited indeed, and if lives are to be preserved, the primacy of politics over markets will have to be introduced again, as was the case for practically all of human history except its bourgeois phase. In this context, it is ironic that, just when political control over the economy is especially needed, Eastern Europe is—with huge losses in productive capacity and means of production and at tremendous social and economic restructuring costs—reintroducing the primacy of markets.

Issues to Be Addressed

To enter an age of ever-increasing scarcity and downscaling is to enter an age of increased conflicts that contain a great potential for mass death and even genocide depending on the mechanisms by which scarcity is channeled to affect only certain groups and the mechanisms by which conflict is resolved, managed, or suppressed. If the analysis given here is correct or even plausible, and if the goal is to help humanity survive this tremendous challenge with no or minimal human loss, we must increasingly ask questions like the following:

1. Based on our knowledge, where and how can we warn the larger public of impending bottlenecks, and thus make the bottlenecks a legitimate focus of high priority discussion everywhere?

2. How does the capitalist system tend to react when it approaches a zero or negative growth environment? What are the economic and political mechanisms by which scarcity is distributed? What is the likelihood for fascism and other authoritarian political systems to arise to deal with scarcity while preserving class relations? What might be the cost in human lives if the distribution of scarcity were left to markets or to authoritarian and fascist politics?

3. What could we learn from societies at war or in an environment of war? How did they experience and deal with scarcity? What

forms of solidarity and other coping mechanisms (even under capitalism) did they adopt?

4. What conflict-resolution strategies can be pursued for conflicts in which all parties have something to *lose*?

5. What can be learned from the behavior of cooperatives and other mutual-help type social organizations pertaining to the management of *scarcity*?

6. To what extent is the broad social control over the means of production a *prerequisite* for increased solidarity and a more equal distribution of scarcity (or surplus), particularly since even a relatively perfect worldwide distribution of income alone would not come *close* to eliminating world poverty today?

7. To what extent can the impending bottlenecks be dealt with only by reestablishing basic self-sufficiency on a regional basis?

8. To what extent can basic regional self-sufficiency, if coupled with a democratic access to the means of production, inhibit migration, decrease the birthrate, and reduce the surplus that is transferred from the periphery to the center?

9. What is the necessary kind and level of industrial production, and modern cultural and social life that *must* be retained to effectively and efficiently downscale while simultaneously meeting growing bottlenecks and needs?

10. To what extent should social scientists be engaged as catalysts and organizers of movements concerned with social justice and the preservation of human life? After all, it is well accepted that social scientists are involved in such things as human relations, quality of work life, and other "movements" to keep corporate organizations alive. Why should social scientists not be equally free and assertive in sharing their knowledge with organizations whose aim is to stop world industrialization, to downscale industrial society, and to preserve life?

These are but a few questions that must increasingly be addressed, and many of them are broached in this volume. Other important questions could be added. Moreover, the social science theory repertoire must, in anticipation of the issues ahead, also be reevaluated. Many classic and modern social science theories have their origin in the late-eighteenth and nineteenth centuries. Invariably, these theories are concerned with the dramatic social changes brought about by the opening, expansion, and differentiation of social and economic systems, and as a consequence, will soon prove to be grossly inadequate. As this analysis suggests, the severe bottlenecks that lie ahead will bring about an equally drastic social change owing to scarcity, system closure, and to the downscaling in industrial production, world markets, the world division of labor, urbanization, and so on. This transformation of society will not be just a 180-degree reversal of the ongoing world industrialization, but one of another kind. This all encompassing, fast, and drastic social change of the near future will ultimately also generate a new brand of "classic" social theory.

The Enlightenment of the eighteenth century bore two different and opposing conceptions of the human being. Hobbes argued that left to their own devices, people would descend to the level of the animal, so that without the proper ordering of society and civilization, human beings would be ruled by the law of the jungle. The contrary position is that of Rousseau, who argued that people are inherently good but society was the corrupting influence. Modernist faith has largely followed Rousseau's position: the self was thought of as ultimately good. What was needed was a societal revolution that allowed the natural goodness of the individual to emerge and flourish.

We have come to be highly skeptical of the belief in the inherent goodness of the self. Enlightenment, education, culture, and science will not necessarily produce individuals who will do what is right. The genocides of the twentieth century have unveiled the true heart of humanity. At our center lies an ability to commit evil of an almost unimagined degree. We have seen the nature of human beings and found that the most ordinary among us can transport millions to their death, can fill the earth and the sky with the victims of killing fields. The theory of the inherent goodness of the human being was daily disproved in Nazi Germany and in the other state-sponsored genocides and massacres.

But if Rousseau's argument was shown to be naive, so has Hobbes's been proved wrong, for what made Nazism possible was the use of state power for absolute evil ends. The near-total genocide of the Jewish people, for example, would not have been possible without, on the one hand, the ability to use all aspects of cultural transmission to reduce the Jew to nonperson and, on the other, the ability to mobilize the full weight of the modern bureaucratic state to carry out mass murder.

That dual ability is still with us. It would be a tragic error to think that what happened in Germany and Europe, for example, was a singular event that we cannot understand and that cannot be repeated;

we can and it already has. *Newsweek* reported on May 9, 1994: "As many as 200,000 people have been murdered, mutilated and dumped like garbage in the streets of Kigali, the capital, and in the verdant countryside of Rwanda during weeks of savage tribal warfare. Wielding machetes, knives, clubs, and grenades, Hutu government forces and paramilitary extremists have hunted down and slaughtered Tutsi civilians and sympathizers in . . . a campaign of 'genocide.' Refugee sites have become deathtraps" (24).

Even now, in Europe, in Africa, and elsewhere, specialists are selecting, exploiting, and concentrating new victims. Potentially, these measures are the precursors of a killing operation. As time passes, the destruction of European Jewry and the other genocides of the twentieth century will recede into memory. From this moment on, however, fundamental assumptions about human behavior and about civilization can no longer stand unchallenged, for though the occurrence is past, the phenomenon remains, as well as the causes exacerbated by the political, social, *and* economic bottlenecks outlined above. The unthinkable has already happened; the idea of future catastrophes is therefore not unthinkable.

When we look at our young students, we tremble for their future. We would like to be able to tell them that despite endless violence and disillusionment, one must maintain faith in people and in humankind and in our ability to solve problems. Despair is no solution. The solution lies in analysis, in hard thinking and questioning, and in purposeful and informed action. To that goal this book is dedicated.

The structure of the book is simple. The first part, including the essays by John B. Cobb, Jr., and Chris Lewis, analyze major forces having an impact on the survivability of civilization as we know it into the twenty-first century. Both authors outline the challenges we face, including overpopulation, pressure upon the land, migration, ecological damage, and social instability. They conclude that rates of growth in population and in per capita consumption cannot be sustained. They argue, therefore, that we are witnessing the collapse of global industrial civilization. The paradox of development is that within the tremendous success of modern industrial civilization lies the cause of its collapse and ruin. By recognizing that imminent collapse, however, we may also find a solution to the impending catastrophe. Instead of seeing the collapse as a tragedy, both authors see it as an opportunity to move away from a global, market-driven economy to more local and regional models.

In part two, we present more detailed discussion of the problem of scarcity and how it relates to conflict. The authors in this section powerfully argue that the current level of human activity is unsustainable. They demonstrate that population growth in particular affects the natural world and can affect the social order and international political systems. John Gowdy and Joseph Tainter remind us that there are historical dimensions to this problem that we need to be aware of. We can learn from past societies that the economy is a subsystem of a larger biophysical system and dependent upon it. Past civilizations collapsed because their leadership elites ignored this basic fact. There is a connection between power, environmental degradation, and social collapse. A demographic explosion not only hurts the hundreds of millions of people caught in it, but also does great damage to other spheres. Human activity, ecological damage, and social and political conflict are related, these authors contend. Their consensus, with some variation, is that the projected growth in the world's population cannot be sustained without social and political turmoil.

The earth is under a twofold attack from human beings—the excessive demands and wasteful habits of affluent populations of developed countries and the billions of new mouths to feed in the developing world. This leads Gowdy, Trainer, and Abernethy to portray the issues as a race against time. The main source of conflict and war is the ceaseless quest for greater wealth and power in a world with shrinking resources. Dilworth provides a theory that tries to explain how we got into this vicious-circle predicament, but he also believes that there can be no solution to the problems outlined above within an economy driven by market forces and capital accumulation. If we do nothing to stabilize the world's total population, curb the profligate use of energy and food, and control damage to the environment, before long we will have so overpopulated and ransacked the earth that we will pay a heavy price in regional, possibly global, conflict. As Abernethy suggests, even the United States is not insulated from this problem. Migration strains, illegal immigration, urban collapse, the growth of an urban underclass, social disintegration, and rampant crime are all related to illegal immigration, which is related to global overpopulation. This problem also has an impact on the developed world, which must find solutions; Abernethy suggests some that deal with population and immigration control. Finsterbusch proposes solutions that increase the ability of governments to macromanage the economy and allow for major value shifts in society away from consumption to simplicity and "conspicuous frugality."

It is clear that ideological rivalries, racial and religious hatreds, and historical factors also contribute to conflict. Nevertheless, the social effects of scarcity seem to form the context within which such struggles swiftly intensify. Although, as Tainter and Dilworth point out, this was as true in ancient Macedonia or in eighteenth-century Europe as it is today, what has changed is the momentum of population growth involving hundreds of millions of people, rather than the millions in Louis XIV's day. What sort of future do we face if social turbulence increases at the same pace as the world's population? That is the subject of the case studies in part three of the book.

The authors in part three go beyond the empirical and theoretical studies of the first two parts to examine how scarcity has already led to mass death and genocide in Rwanda, Bosnia, Somalia, and Haiti and to speculate on the likelihood that scarcities could be a more decisive factor in genocide in the future. Roger Smith, David Smith, and Waltraud Morales argue effectively that scarcity is not the only explanation for global wars, ethnic violence, and civil unrest within states or between them. However, the important conditioning and motivating factor of scarcity cannot be underestimated and probably will be more prevalent in the future given the convergence of resource scarcity, environmental depletion, human degradation, and ethnopolitical and religious discrimination. Furthermore, as Rappoport argues, "postmodern" people, unfortunately, will generally be tolerant of and perhaps indifferent to genocidal events. All the relevant cultural factors—the language, imagery, and climate of moral ambiguity—suggest that a growing desensitization is at work. To help break through this pervasive psychic numbing and political apathy, Craig Rimmerman calls for engaging students in a serious confrontation with the implications of doomsday thinking and its critique. We must find ways of encouraging students and ourselves to confront serious issues and their social implications. Otherwise, we may slide into the fragmentation of the postmodern personality that Rappoport believes facilitates the adoption of desensitizing or defense mechanisms when facing impending tragedy.

Against such seemingly persistent and powerful social, economic, demographic, and psychological forces, what can an individual or a polity do to forestall these destructive forces? In the modern world, events move at an outstanding speed, and our consciousness cannot keep pace. We remain trapped in the old, familiar modalities of thought and politics and economic organization. Yet, we have the ability, if not always the will, to change. We are, it seems to us, overdue to start this change and transformation. We have no alternative. As Primo Levi wrote more than a decade ago about the brave souls who stood up to oppression in the Warsaw Ghetto rebellion: "They have demonstrated that even when everything is lost, it is granted to man to save, together with his own dignity, that of future generations." (Levi 1989, 170–71). We still have that ability, but with every passing year and every new global tragedy, it becomes more difficult to grasp.

PART ONE

Statement of the Problem

Introduction

Why should affluent societies in Europe or the Americas care about the population explosion in the developing world, ecological disasters in the Mediterranean basin, and the spread of mass poverty and disease in the far-flung corners of the world? Of what practical concern is it for a banker in Tokyo, a businessman in Copenhagen, a farmer in Iowa, or a housewife in Alberta—who are busy trying to live their lives—that there is famine and civil war in Somalia, floods in Bangladesh, and genocide in Rwanda or Bosnia? There always have been enormous gaps between the rich and the poor nations. The reason people in the developed world should care is that it is absolutely in their self-interest to limit the exponential growth in population and resource depletion.

The demographic imbalance between rich and poor societies is producing a migratory flow from the poor to the rich societies, that is challenging the ability of the rich societies to absorb the poor without devastating conflict. It is certain that people have always inflicted damage upon their environment. Human beings have cut down, burned, overgrazed, and polluted their habitats since ancient times. But the environmental crisis we now confront is quantitatively and qualitatively different from anything we have faced before simply because so many people have inflicted so much damage to the world's ecosystem during the present century that the system as a whole—not simply its parts—may be in danger. We see this happening in world population growth, in increasing rates of resource depletion, in ecological damage, and in widening disparities of income and resource use between developing and developed nations. All of these tendencies strain the capacities of the world's ecosystem to sustain itself into the next century without regional or global disasters. That is the focus of the following section.

2. The Threat to the Underclass

John B. Cobb, Jr.

Projecting the future is very uncertain business. Nothing is more certain than that there will be surprises. History never moves smoothly along expected lines.

What can be said with some certainty is that projection of present directions leads to catastrophe. Current rates of growth in population and in per capita consumption cannot be sustained. Great expansion of both is still possible in principle, especially assuming increased efficiency in the use of resources, continuing technological advances, reduced warfare and military expenditures, and major social adjustments. Surprising developments can extend this possibility even further than can now be imagined.

The cost of this continuation of present trends will be enormous. Remaining wilderness will disappear, with great reduction of biodiversity. Agricultural production will be more and more dependent on high-tech methods. Increasing dependence on chemicals and bioengineering will have now-unpredictable effects on human health. Nuclear energy will be relied on regardless of the dangers involved. Higher levels of pollution will have to be tolerated.

Although this scenario seems more optimistic than its alternative of earlier collapse of the system, it is, in some respects, more frightening. By postponing adjustments for a long time, indeed, until the surface of the earth and human relations have all been adapted to high tech and to full global integration, they lead to a situation in which the eventual failure of the system will affect everyone catastrophically. Even the knowledge of how to survive apart from the expertise of the technocrats

25

will have been lost, and the sources for subsisting from nature will have been destroyed. Hence, although now-dominant forces will hold this course as long as possible, and most people are likely to support them, this may well be the most destructive of the possible scenarios.

The surprises in store for us may not be of this sort. They may instead be crises that strike us much sooner than we expect. Changes in weather may appear more abruptly than now anticipated, and they may prove more disruptive of agricultural production globally than now projected. These changes might lead to mass migrations to places where there is food, migrations that will be violently resisted. Bacteria and viruses may evolve faster than our devices for protecting ourselves from them, leading to population reduction through massive epidemics. People oppressed by the continual expansion of the present system may revolt in much larger numbers than in the past and may cause social chaos. The psychological stresses associated with the present system may overwhelm it as it continues to assault human community and demand the abandonment of all security. Fanatic political or religious movements may gain such power as fundamentally to disrupt the economic system.

I am making no such predictions. Surprises cannot be predicted. The likelihood is that what happens will not fit any pattern now imaginable to us. Perhaps some surprises will favor the continuation of growth and others will lead to major setbacks. The greatest surprise would be the emergence of a widespread recognition that the continuing pursuit of growth is a mistake. Such a surprise is not impossible, and to that possibility we will return.

Having acknowledged the likelihood that present trends will not simply continue into the future, I will nevertheless describe these as they now appear in the United States and point out some of the already emerging negative features that threaten to become steadily worse. These are the dark side of policies and procedures that are now almost universally accepted and affirmed. Basically these policies and procedures express the "economism" that is now the dominant spiritual force in the world, the belief that the economic sector is the one hope of salvation and that it affects this salvation through growth.[1]

1. My sources, other than general information and the article by Kaplan for which data are provided in the text, are not in regularly published documents. For my comments on Cuba I am indebted to a Food First Action Alert, spring 1994, entitled "The

Because of the victory of "economism" since World War II, national governments have relinquished power in favor of the Bretton Woods institutions and the transnational corporations. It is the decisions of these economic institutions that now determine the fate of the planet. Their primary goal is to facilitate the increase of gross world product through overcoming all remaining restrictions on the movement of capital and goods across national boundaries.

Because national boundaries still inhibit the movement of workers, the mobility of capital and goods puts the workers in each country into competition with those in others. This competitive situation exerts a downward pressure on wages in affluent countries. It also discourages standards of workplace safety and environmental safeguards, and it undercuts the bargaining position of labor unions. Unfortunately, because of the vast number of unemployed and underemployed persons in low-wage countries, it does not exert a comparable upward pressure on wages, standards, or empowerment of labor in the countries to which capital moves.

In sum, the globalization of the market restores the great advantage of capital over labor, which had been eroded during the later years of national markets. In those contexts, labor could organize and bargain with considerable success. Because corporations were competing with other corporations that had to make similar concessions to labor, their resistance to these concessions was limited. Governments were interested in the quality of life of their citizens and hence regulated business in its treatment of workers. The globalization of the market ended this relative equity. Labor unions cannot organize effectively across national boundaries, and no global governmental organizations enforce standards on transnational corporations.

The result is that the gap between those who live from capital and those who live from labor is growing steadily wider. Those who live from capital are not only the financiers themselves but also those dependent on lawyers, managers, technical experts, educators, and

Greening of Cuba" by Peter Rosset and Shea Cunningham. For my information on Kerala I am indebted to an unpublished essay by W. M. Alexander, 30 El Mirador Court, San Luis Obispo, Calif. 93401, entitled "Exceptional Kerala: Efficient and Sustainable Human Behavior." The statistics I cite are found on page 17. The data on the GPI are in a desktop publication of Redefining Progress, 116 New Montgomery, Room 209, San Francisco, Calif. 94105, dated September 1994. It is entitled "The Genuine Progress Indicator: Summary of Data and Methodology," and its authors are Clifford Cobb and Ted Halstead. The detailed statistics are provided on page 39.

specialists of many other kinds who are paid well for their services. In affluent nations perhaps 20 percent of the population enjoy the prosperity of capital.

The remainder of the population is divided between those whose labor is needed in the market and those who are not needed. The unneeded group exists because of surplus labor in general or because persons in the group lack the qualities or skills required to function effectively in the market. In the United States, as farming was displaced by agribusiness and unskilled factory work was sent overseas, this unneeded group grew. It has become a full-fledged underclass.

Such a class has always existed, but it has in the past been a minor element in society. As long as most people lived on farms, there was work for all. Small-scale production could employ persons of a wide range of education, skills, and personality types. Industrial society also provided innumerable unskilled jobs.

Now we have a society in which almost all persons are separated from all means of production. They have been removed from the land. Small-scale local production cannot compete with major industries. And major industries have found it more profitable to employ low-skilled and semiskilled labor in other countries. Because competition in the global market requires constant reduction of labor costs, and because technology can replace even highly skilled labor, the superfluous group grows, and competition for the remaining attractive opportunities intensifies. Reduced use of middle management threatens members of this class as well. Former members of the classes of skilled labor and management are forced to compete for fewer well-paying jobs. All of this makes an increasing segment of our society superfluous from the point of view of production for the market.

When the governments assumed some responsibility to feed, house, and clothe all citizens, programs were instituted to provide a minimum of income for all. As the underclass grows, it claims more from the government through these programs. The programs at the same time discourage the underclass from taking such unskilled, poorly paid positions as are still available. Because welfare pays as well as these jobs, and because these positions no longer lead to better ones, dependence on the government becomes the less unattractive choice for some.

The more enterprising members of the underclass turn to crime. The laws against drugs that are nevertheless in great demand make control of their distribution lucrative and the best chance to escape permanent poverty. Competition in the underclass for control of distribution contributes to the mutual killing that is so widespread. The crime within the underclass leads to near war between it and the police. At any given time a high percentage of the young males is in prison.

Meanwhile, the declining standard of living and reduced prospects of the working class make its members anxious and angry. Their anger is directed not at the wealthy but at the underclass. The underclass is depicted as being supported by the taxes of workers despite the unwillingness of the underclass to work. Its criminal activity is highlighted, and the need to be protected from it is exaggerated. Little attention is given to the causes of the growth of this unproductive, sometimes violent, and often self-destructive segment of society.

The climate now exists in the United States for withdrawal of governmental support of the underclass. The money saved will be used to strengthen law enforcement and build more prisons. Meanwhile, the economic system increases the size of the underclass, and the withdrawal of public support and concern lead to fewer alternatives to criminal activity and self-destruction. Fewer alternatives intensify the fear and hostility of workers and allow those in power to increase the barriers between the underclass and the remainder of society. Their self-destruction is now accepted so long as they do not disturb the rest of society.

I am here depicting a rapidly emerging situation. The residual compassion for the suffering of the underclass still prevents "the final solution." Those who decrease support for its members are careful in their public rhetoric. But the trend in public opinion and public policy is to abandon this class to its own devices. And if this leads to its self-destruction, few mourn! That most of the members of this class are black and brown makes it easier for the white majority to ignore their suffering and to blame those who suffer for their misery.

Globally, the population that is superfluous in relation to the needs of the market is much larger. It includes a considerable part of Africa, Latin America, and south Asia as well as selected populations in the Middle East. The Palestinian Arabs constitute an especially clear case.

The Jews would have preferred that the Palestinians leave as they conquered Palestine. They have not resorted to extreme measures to eliminate them. They have not practiced genocide. But they have taken most of the best land and, even more important, most of the water resources, thus drastically restricting the economic opportunities of the Palestinians. They have repressed resistance to these measures and generally allowed few political or civil rights. They have spread their settlements in such a way as to make a genuine Palestinian state unlikely. Although they do make use of some Palestinians as workers, they are reducing this dependence. Survival of Palestinians in the land left to them in the Gaza Strip, for example, will depend on an international largess that is very restricted. With few exceptions, Palestinian Arabs are being forced into underclass status.

This forced underclass status is happening on a much larger scale in Africa. R. D. Kaplan, in a shocking article, "The Coming Anarchy," published in the February 1994 issue of The *Atlantic Monthly*, describes the situation in West Africa. In Sierra Leone supplying timber for the global market led to deforestation, which in turn has caused erosion of much of the agricultural land. Much of the rural population has moved to shantytowns around the capital, where the water supply is not differentiated from the sewers. Swamps have appeared where forests once grew, and these breed malarial mosquitoes. Now most persons have a type of malaria that does not respond to standard treatment. AIDS is spreading rapidly. Political order has broken down.

The resources of Sierra Leone are no longer important for the global market. With the end of the cold war, strategic considerations are no longer relevant. The threat of malaria keeps foreigners out. Hence aid depends on charitable concerns, concerns that are not important in global circles. We may thus consider almost all of the population of this country as relegated permanently to the underclass. The world will pay little attention as civil war, hunger, and disease take their course.

Kaplan describes the global increase in shantytowns surrounding the urban centers of "developing" countries. He notes that they vary greatly in their ability to generate livable communities. But the conclusion is that an increasing portion of the vast population that becomes superfluous in rural areas because of modernization of agriculture cannot be absorbed in the industrializing cities. This underclass constitutes a threat to political stability. We may doubt that governments defending themselves against this superfluous population will be particularly hesitant to use near-genocidal means.

Some of the people who are superfluous from the perspective of the market cling to their land in rural areas. Peasant resistance to displacement by agribusiness occurs in many places. The major warfare that has developed in recent decades is low-intensity conflict by armies against peasant resistance. Because the labor of these peasants is not needed by the developing economy, and their presence hinders modernization, governments are rarely concerned with their political and human rights.

The threat to indigenous peoples is more extreme. In many situations their livelihood is bound up with the forests that are being destroyed in the name of the global market and economic progress. Their defense of these forests is often met with violence, and the destruction of the forests undercuts their way of life and their means of livelihood. The globalization of the market is accompanied by the decline of indigenous populations worldwide. They are not only superfluous but positively stand in the way of progress.

These comments are about the recent past and the present with limited projections into the future. The market creates an underclass, which has occurred nationally in the past as Joseph Tainter and Chris Lewis point out in subsequent chapters. As the market becomes more and more fully global, this underclass grows rapidly and comes to include whole peoples.

When we hear that a billion people in the world are hungry, we are usually told that we should promote economic development through the expansion of the global market to produce the food needed. We are less often told that it is the economic development and the expansion of the global market that has caused most of the hunger. Nor are we usually told that the increased agricultural production generated by modernization of agriculture does not provide food for these people because they have no means to pay for it. In short, we are rarely told that the policies supposedly justified by the needs of the poor are the policies that have made them poor and that add to their numbers year by year.

Because the policies do not tend to include these people in the productive economy but tend to increase the size of the underclass, and because members of this class are too poor to constitute a significant market for the increasing supply of goods, these people are, indeed, superfluous as far as the global economy is concerned. They are already suffering a none too benign neglect and sometimes active attack. When production can no longer keep up with demand because of resource shortages and pollution, we can be sure that it is they who will suffer first and most acutely. We can be sure of this because it is already happening and because the policies that lead to these results are becoming more fully dominant.

The one restraint on brutal treatment of the underclass is the moral teaching of humanism and of the major religious traditions. This moral restraint is losing its hold on the masses of workers, who think they are asked to make sacrifices for the sake of the underclass. Should significant sacrifices really be asked of them, it is clear that they will refuse.

In our essays for this book we are asked to consider not only the threats to human well-being implicit in present practices as they are projected into a future of real scarcity but also how the foreseeable suffering may be mitigated. In the sections that follow, I will consider, briefly, directions the underclass itself may adopt to reduce threats to its survival. I will then consider, at greater length, the possibility that the working class may call for changes in basic policies that would eventually reincorporate the underclass into the economy. These possibilities also involve changes that could enable society to adapt to growing scarcity in ways that would not be self-destructive.

The one generalization that can be made about the future of the underclass is that it cannot count on help from the dominant society as long as present policies are in force. In the inner cities of the United States and in the slums surrounding Third World cities, this class will be increasingly neglected and contained, even sealed off, from the rest of society. West Africa will be ignored. Resistant peasants and indigenous people will be harassed, will have their leaders imprisoned or killed, and will be forced off their remaining land. Their survival will depend on their own resources under extremely adverse circumstances.

What is astonishing is the extent to which, under such circumstances, many do find ways of surviving, which requires that they establish solidarity among themselves and self-reliance. Kaplan describes the great differences in slums in which new communities are created and in those where such community is absent.

In the inner cities of the United States, the most hopeful developments are those of local self-organization into more self-reliant neighborhoods. When such communities develop, the small sums of money that enter them can circulate internally rather than quickly leaving to pay for external goods and services. The more goods and services the members of such communities can provide for one another, the less dependent they are on gaining external money.

There are severe limits to the economic independence possible for many inner city communities. Nevertheless, far more can be done than has generally been realized. Even the quantity of food that can be produced locally in urban areas is surprising. Pooling of financial resources can lead to support of local, very small-scale entrepreneurs. Housing repair and maintenance can often be done by local people. Those who have such skills can teach others. When cash is scarce, services can be provided within the neighborhood by barter and labor exchange. As the community meets more of its members' needs, automobiles become less important.

This buildup of the local community contributes to survival not only by reducing reliance on unreliable external sources but also by improving the self-image of the members. Members of the underclass become self-destructive when they internalize the image held of them by the larger society. To whatever extent they become self-determining they also gain self-respect and respect for one another. Consumption of drugs, alcohol, and tobacco declines, while their costs in crime, money, and human ability become available for constructive use in the neighborhood.

These comments are vague, but they point in the only direction that offers hope. If the wider society involves itself at all, it is to tie the inner city more into the larger economy. This procedure does not work and will not last. The few who are benefited arc likely to leave the community. Only if such resources that the larger society is prepared to offer are brought under the control of the community will they benefit the neighborhood in an inclusive way. And this benefit will occur only to the extent that the resources are used to make the community less dependent on the larger society.

These comments are also idealistic. The extent to which they can be implemented in any neighborhood composed largely of the underclass is likely to be limited. To picture any such neighborhood as able to survive without strong ties to the outside seems absurd. Nevertheless, in my projections, it is the only hope. As outside support and positive involvement declines, drastic changes *will* occur. Where a strong sense of community exists in a neighborhood, these changes may be toward greater mutual support even in desperate conditions. Where it does not, we must expect mutual destruction by persons who are seeking their own survival at the expense of their neighbors.

The survival of whole nations that are superfluous in the global economy depends on similar principles. They will survive to the extent that they become self-sufficient economically. Their long-term survival will also depend on their sustainable use of their resources.

An interesting case study here is Cuba. Cuba never intended to become a self-sufficient economy. Its economy was long tied into that of the Soviet Union, and in typical market fashion it specialized in producing what it could export to Eastern Europe, chiefly sugar. It imported oil, fertilizer, insecticides, more than half of its food, and industrial equipment and supplies.

When the Soviet empire broke up, the problems with such "interdependence" became apparent. Because of Cuba's interdependence with the Soviet Union, it could not meet its own basic needs without this trade. This situation would not have been serious if Cuba had been admitted on reasonable terms into the new global trading system. But the price of admission was to abandon its socialist experiment and return to the capitalism from which it had freed itself. Unwilling to do this, it has been forced to move toward a much more self-sufficient economy. Its continued political independence depends on its success in making this difficult move.

The transition is extremely painful. Because Cuba produced less than half of its food, and because even that depended on imported fertilizers and insecticides, the nation was in very poor condition to go it alone. Despite heroic efforts to shift production, food consumption per capita may have dropped by 30 percent! From being a well-fed nation, Cuba has dropped to the level of the poorest of Latin American countries. The only difference is that what food there is is distributed equitably by rationing.

The question is whether Cuba can learn quickly to produce food organically and with human and animal labor. Fortunately, Cuban agronomists had done a great deal of research on alternative farming methods before the crisis, which has enabled Cuba to make relatively rapid progress. If Cuba succeeds in making this transition and feeding its people organically and sustainably, it will mark a first case of successful transition from unsustainable monoculture to sustainable agriculture.

It is far too early to say whether Cuba will succeed. It is being forced to make this transition under enormous hostile pressure from the United States, which is doing all it can to make the transition difficult and to encourage opposition to the government within Cuba. The Cuban people may decide they prefer subservience to the United

States to hunger. On the other hand, there is no clear sign that the will to political independence has died. What has been learned unequivocally is that such political independence is possible only if there is basic economic independence as well.

Even if Cuba succeeds in feeding itself sustainably, there will be many continuing economic problems. Becoming industrially self-sustaining may prove even more difficult. Doing so with a sustainable use of resources may not be possible. The whole experiment may fail. Even if it fails, it will have come close enough to success to suggest that under more favorable circumstances and with more time to make the transition, many countries could still attain relatively sustainable economic self-sufficiency.

It may be unrealistic to think that any country will voluntarily adopt this course. At present most countries have acquiesced in the structural adjustment policies of the International Monetary Fund designed to move them further away from self-sufficiency and to bind them more firmly to the global market. They have done so despite the obvious suffering this imposes on their people. Once they have taken these steps, extricating themselves from the market becomes more and more difficult—as difficult as it is proving for Cuba. Nevertheless, it is important to see that political and economic independence may not yet be impossible. And as the price of dependence on the global market to nations at its periphery becomes ever clearer, some of those that are most expendable from the perspective of the global market may follow Cuba's example.

A qualification is in order here. Cuba has been able to make its own decisions only because of the strength of an army that is loyal to the government. Invasion by the United States would be too costly in American lives to be supported by the American people, and the revolution has been too popular among the people for efforts at subversion to succeed.

These circumstances are unique. The Cuban is the only revolution in Latin America that the United States has allowed to continue for such a long time. Chile, Granada, Panama, and Nicaragua are more typical examples of revolutionary efforts and their destruction. Through direct intervention or through subversion, the United States may continue to prevent other nations from following the Cuban model, even if it continues to succeed. Probably this policy will continue for some time to be true in Latin America. But in Africa and in parts of Asia, where less is at stake for the United States and the global market, countries unimportant to the global market may be allowed in time to follow Cuba's examples.

For the underclass, I have argued, as long as the global market reigns supreme, the one hope is disengagement from it. Any neighborhoods or countries that have thus disengaged will have not only a better chance of surviving while the market reigns but also a better chance of surviving its ultimate collapse. Of course, they will not escape the global problems of pollution and weather change. And any resources they preserve for sustainable use may stir the envy of more prodigal neighbors when global shortages are acute. This is not an optimistic scenario.

The long-term hope of the underclass must be that the world's workers will awaken to the consequences for them of the global market system. This awakening would mean that the anger now directed against the underclass would be redirected against the system that produces this class and works against their own well-being. If this redirection happens widely enough and soon enough, the direction of the economy can still be changed—an occurrence that would be a surprise. It would be the one truly favorable surprise that I can now imagine.

To consider how such a change could occur requires us to consider how matters now stand. Most workers recognize that massive redistribution of existing wealth will not occur. Further, they do not want what little wealth they themselves possess to be redistributed to the underclass. In any case the communist experiment in redistribution is viewed as a total failure. Hence, economic solutions must not require such redistribution.

The solution to economic problems must therefore be economic growth. Growth enables all to gain at the expense of none. The capitalist system best promotes growth. It requires specialization in production, the more the better. The amount of specialization possible is proportional to the size of the market within which capital and goods flow freely. Hence, expanding the market to the entire planet gives maximum opportunity for that growth to occur.

This general picture is so deeply rooted in the common sense of modern culture that even the occurrence of massive counterevidence does little to raise questions about it. For example, during the past twenty years, while economic growth in the United States has continued unabated, wages have fallen dramatically. The growth of the economy has not benefited workers.

The standard response is that this is a temporary situation to be corrected by further growth and that this further growth requires globalization of the market. This, in turn, requires that U.S. producers become more efficient, and that means that they should employ fewer workers. Thus the downsizing of U.S. companies that directly reduces the number of well-paying jobs available is affirmed as the means of benefiting U.S. workers. In support of this argument economists point out how many new jobs have been generated in the U.S. economy. They rarely point out at the same time that these are less well-paying, less secure jobs, with less prospect for advancement.

This counterfactual defense of globalization as the way of improving the situation of workers is buttressed by blaming other countries for being less open to U.S. goods than the United States is to theirs. Japan is the target of this criticism. Certainly, Japan is internally far less committed to the free market than is the United States. The Japanese government and financial leaders still strive to order the economy to the benefit of the Japanese people as a whole. In this they have been remarkably successful. Of course, their economy as a whole benefits immensely from the openness of U.S. markets to their goods. But even if they surrendered to U.S. pressure and removed all formal restraint on imports, the benefits to U.S. workers would be minimal.

The truth is that the gains made by U.S. labor in a basically national economy are being rapidly eroded in its globalization. There is no reason to suppose that continued globalization will reverse this trend. On the contrary, the only hope for improvement in the conditions of labor is the return to a national economy.

The objection is immediately made that such a return would be less productive, meaning that it would reduce the gross national product (GNP) or the gross domestic product (GDP), or at least slow their increase. Because it is assumed that rapid growth as measured by these indices is of near-ultimate importance for the economic well-being of the nation and its people, this argument is taken as decisive.

Because of the widespread assumption that growth, measured in this way, is desirable, a few efforts have been made to ascertain the relation between such growth and the economic well-being of the people. All economists agree that the correlation is not perfect. Some things are counted in GNP and GDP that do not contribute to economic welfare, and some things that do contribute to economic welfare are not counted.

An example of the former are expenditures on crime that rise with the rate of crime and do not indicate that people are better off. For example, household activities, such as cooking, cleaning, and child care, are essential to the economic well-being of the community. However, while acknowledging that the GNP and GDP are imperfect indications of economic well-being, economists generally continue to use them to measure economic progress. Recently they have come to favor the GDP.

More careful study, however, reveals that the gap between what is measured by the GDP and real, sustainable economic well-being is sometimes very large. The most thorough study now available is being conducted by Redefining Progress, a San Francisco organization. It has developed what it calls the genuine progress indicator (GPI). According to this indicator, from 1950 to 1992, while the per capita GDP more than doubled (from less than $8,000 to more than $16,000), per capita GPI declined from nearly $6,000 to just over $4,000, or about 25 percent.

There is no exact measure of economic well-being. But if the best available figures indicate that the policies leading to doubling the GDP also lead to a massive decline in sustainable economic well-being, surely questions should be raised about the wisdom of continuing those policies! Because this decline in economic well-being, both current and anticipated, corresponds to the experience of most workers, it may be possible to persuade them to detach themselves from commitment to this destructive form of growth.

Not all the factors considered in the genuine progress indicator are of interest to all workers. Some of them deal with environmental deterioration. Those concerned for the well-being of the environment and with intergenerational equity constitute another group, overlapping with labor, who may be persuaded that continuation of current growth-oriented policies, especially the globalization of the market, is a mistake. These policies certainly intensify the assault upon the natural world.

The environmental community currently is more vigorous in articulation of its concerns than is labor. Also, although many of its members are strong supporters of economic growth and globalization, others have already recognized the inherent problem with this direction. Environmentalists and labor joined forces in criticizing the North American Free Trade Agreement and gained some concessions. Having done so, some of each group accepted the agreement. Others, especially among the environmentalists, opposed it on more funda-mental grounds.

Unfortunately, the tenuous alliance that was then forged was frag-mented by the outcome. Those who understand that growth and glo-balization are twin enemies of humanity remain a small element in society as a whole. Supporters of the present system are firmly in control of both political parties, the media, and the academy. They are currently recovering ground lost to environmentalists in the past two decades. At least in the United States and in the global power system, the sovereignty of the market has never seemed more secure.

On the other hand, pride might come before a fall. The arrogance with which everything is subordinated to a market that serves the rich at the expense of all others could elicit a reaction. Workers and envi-ronmentalists could once more join forces, and they could achieve greater persuasiveness among other citizens. I am not predicting this scenario; I am simply describing the only hopeful one I can imagine.

The question is what positive program could be proposed to pre-pare for the coming scarcities. The answer is that the program would have to be worked out by those who recognized its importance. Nev-ertheless, in this very speculative essay, my speculations about what should go into such a program can be included.

I have already made it clear that the first step would be the rever-sal of the move to the global economy. This step would be far from easy! Nevertheless, for the United States such a move would not entail the suffering that is now occurring in Cuba. For the United States to feed itself and meet its other basic needs would not be difficult. For it to shift massively to organic agriculture without serious disruptions would take time, but it is certainly possible. For it to shift toward more labor-intensive farming with more use of animals would also take time, but there are no fundamental obstacles once a popular decision to move in this direction was reached.

The goal would not be simply for the United States to feed itself but for most food for each region to be grown locally. Shortened sup-ply lines are another part of the move toward reduced use of scarce resources and reduced pollution. There would be no need abruptly to cut off all imports or to stop trading with other parts of the country, but as shortages become more critical, the regions most able to feed their residents will be most secure.

Even this kind of farming is not ultimately sustainable, for it does not end the erosion of soils. Further experiments in preserving and regenerating soils are urgent. The most interesting now are those of the Land Institute under the leadership of Wes Jackson. The institute is developing perennial plants that can be grown in combinations analogous to those of the prairie and attain yields comparable to today's annual grains. Success in this experiment could revolutionize farming and make it truly sustainable.

We now pay very little for our food, because the costs are passed on to society and to the future in other forms. This passing of costs is connected with the oil-intensive agriculture that has displaced so many farmers. Some of our payments to the unemployed are also part of the cost of food.

A society oriented to minimizing future crises resulting from shortages would pay the full cost of producing food sustainably. It would accept imperfections in vegetables and fruits. On the other hand, its produce would be fresher and more healthful.

Another change would be a shift from heavy emphasis on meat to more fruits, vegetables, and grains. Eating meat is an inefficient way to gain the calories and nutrients we need. Our current meat-oriented diet is, in any case, less healthful. Much of the increased cost in producing fruits, vegetables, and grains with fewer chemical fertilizers and insecticides and less oil-run machinery would be canceled by the reduced cost of eating grains directly in comparison with meat.

I have concentrated on food, because when we think of fundamental shortages and the risk of massive human suffering resulting from them, food comes first. A people who can feed themselves are likely to survive. "Food first" is the correct slogan.

The discussion of food also indicates how the society that can survive will involve more of its people in its economy. One major cause of the underclass is the displacement of farm labor by fossil fuels and the agribusiness these make possible. The development of a truly sustainable agriculture will require the reemployment of many people. Of course, the move from inner city to countryside will be just as difficult as the earlier move from countryside to inner city, but it can have a far more positive outcome. As necessary habits and skills are developed, society can again find means to help many become independent farmers with a secure and crucially important role in society.

Proposing a move in the United States from global dependency to national sufficiency as a means of readying itself for global shortages appears to many to be hard-hearted in relation to our trading partners. It is true that it will be highly disruptive, just as the shift from national economies to a global one has been disruptive. It is not true that in what matters most, it will harm these partners. If they are to survive the coming shortages without immense suffering, they, too, need to live close to the soil and be able to meet their basic needs. Encouraging them to stop producing food for themselves in order to export the products of agribusiness to us has not been good for their people. To reverse this process will benefit far more people than it will harm.

There is, however, a serious problem with which I have not dealt, or needed to deal, in my scenarios for Cuba or the United States. In much of the world, population growth has made it impossible to return to earlier economic patterns. The shift to independent farmers would enable many to return to the land, but many others would find no place there. And in some countries the agricultural base probably cannot support the existing population, much less the larger populations projected in the next century.

My judgment is that there is no way of preventing massive suffering that does not involve curtailment of population growth, sometimes drastic. At present, it is true, overconsumption is a greater problem for the planet than overpopulation. The difference is that consumption can be greatly curtailed without terrible suffering by policies such as I have outlined. But where a population already presses the limits of carrying capacity, it simply cannot continue to grow. One solution is emigration to other regions that are not so crowded. If countries like the United States and Canada agreed to take surplus populations, absolute global limits would be postponed—but not much. Meanwhile, the price in social and ecological disruption would be enormous. I do not believe that easing barriers to emigration from overpopulated countries is truly helpful. It is important for people in each geographical area to face the finitude of their land and to determine what they want to do. If birthrates continue high, death rates will rise. If they choose that maxim, they must accept the consequences. Populations will not reach the projected highs.

Nevertheless, changing policies in the United States will help even in these countries, especially if the policies are followed in other affluent countries. Many of the resources of impoverished countries are now annually transferred to the affluent world. Repayment of debts and the policies required to make these payments are a major factor.

In a world no longer committed to globalization of the market, these debts could and should be promptly forgiven. Poorer countries would be left with their own resources to use for themselves.

Furthermore, the abandonment of the global economic system need not mean the end of aid. Ambiguous as aid has been in the past, some forms have helped people. Aid in family-planning programs and in community development should be greatly increased, while massive projects geared to what has been called development in the past should end. In any case, people must develop their own solutions. Ones imposed from without will not work.

Kerala provides a hopeful indication of what a less-industrialized people can do for itself. Kerala is a state in India with per capita income about average for that country. It has operated with democratic processes and has come through open discussion to the adoption of a number of interesting social policies. Its remarkable success can be judged by the following statistics comparing Kerala with India in general.

1. In India 31 percent of women of high school age are in school; in Kerala, 93 percent.

2. In India the number of deaths per thousand live births is 91; in Kerala, 16.

3. In India the average number of children per family is 3.9; in Kerala, 1.9.

4. In India the life expectancy of women born today is 59; in Kerala, 73.

Again, it is important to understand that these results were not achieved by economic growth. In this respect Kerala is not ahead of India as a whole. They were achieved by social policies that have ensured that the basic needs of all are met and that have targeted the improvement of the condition of women as of special importance. These policies have not involved compulsion by an authoritarian government but shared decisions. Kerala's success is one of the unforeseeable surprises that make hope possible.

3. The Paradox of Global Development and the Necessary Collapse of Modern Industrial Civilization

Chris H. Lewis

> *Collapse is recurrent in human history; it is global in its occurrence; and it affects the spectrum of societies from simple foragers to great empires.*
> —Joseph Tainter
> *The Collapse of Complex Societies*

With the growth and expansion of a European market economy since the seventeenth century and the development of a global industrial economy in the twentieth century, science has recorded the rapidly accelerating human destruction of the earth (Turner et al. 1990). Since the 1950s, with the aid of modern science and technology, the human population has doubled, and scientists predict that the enormous transformations of the earth in the past three centuries will be doubled, trebled, or more in the centuries to come (Kates, Turner, and Clark 1990, 14). If we are to feed the projected 10 to 12 billion people by 2050, we will need to increase agricultural production three to four times and increase energy consumption six to eight times (Kates, Turner, and Clark 1990, 14). Can global, modern industrial civilization sustain this rapid rate of growth without destroying itself or really endangering the well-being of future generations? How can we support growing populations in the underdeveloped world and increasing affluence

43

in the developed world without destroying the earth and undermining modern industrial civilization? Tragically, the struggle to feed exploding populations and improve living standards throughout the world is only accelerating the global destruction of the environment.

Since its birth in sixteenth- and seventeenth-century Europe, the modern world, driven by the desire to accumulate wealth and control human and natural resources, has waged a brutal war against the earth. In *Extinction*, biologists Paul and Anne Ehrlich (1981, 8) note that "never in the 500 million years of terrestrial evolution has this mantle we call the biosphere been under such savage attack." In their 1993 World Scientists' Warning to Humanity, signed by more than 1,680 scientists worldwide, concerned scientists warned that "human activities inflict harsh and often irreversible damage on the environment and on critical resources" (Union of Concerned Scientists 1993, 3). Tragically, the modern world's relentless struggle to conquer and subdue the earth in the name of progress will bring its collapse and ruin. Its vain struggle to control and defeat the awesome power of nature will, in the end, destroy modern industrial civilization.

I will argue that we are witnessing the collapse of global industrial civilization. Driven by individualism, materialism, and the endless pursuit of wealth and power, the modern industrialized world's efforts to modernize and integrate the world politically, economically, and culturally since World War II are only accelerating this global collapse. In the late-twentieth century, global development leaves 80 percent of the world's population outside the industrialized nations' progress and affluence (Wallimann 1994). When the modern industrialized world collapses, people in the underdeveloped world will continue their daily struggle for dignity and survival at the margins of a moribund global industrial civilization.

With the collapse of the modern world, smaller, autonomous, local and regional civilizations, cultures, and polities will emerge. We can reduce the threat of mass death and genocide that will surely accompany this collapse by encouraging the creation and growth of sustainable, self-sufficient regional polities. John Cobb has already made a case for how this may work in the United States and how it is working in Kerala, India. After the collapse of global civilization, modern peoples will not have the material resources, biological capital, and energy to reestablish global civilization. Forced by economic necessity to become dependent on local resources and ecosystems for their survival, peoples throughout the world will work to conserve and restore their environments. For the societies that destroy their local environments and economies, as modern people so often do, will themselves face collapse and ruin.

Thus, the rapid expansion of modern industrial civilization since the 1600s, which modern peoples understand as progress, is destroying the earth and threatening the human future (Hauchler and Kennedy 1994). Since the birth of the modern world, we have witnessed accelerating global population growth, air and water pollution, destruction of forests, farmland, and fisheries, depletion of nonrenewable natural resources, loss of biodiversity, and increasing poverty and misery throughout the nonmodern world (Brown and Kane 1994). In *Worldwatch's State of the World 1995*, Hilary French (1995, 171) concludes: "The relentless pace of global ecological decline shows no signs of letting up. Carbon dioxide concentrations are mounting in the atmosphere, species loss continues to accelerate, fisheries are collapsing, land degradation frustrates efforts to feed hungry people, and the earth's forest cover keeps shrinking." And in his introduction to *State of the World 1995*, Lester Brown (1995) warns that eroding soils, shrinking forests, deteriorating rangelands, expanding deserts, acid rain, stratospheric ozone depletion, the buildup of greenhouse gases, air pollution, and the loss of biological diversity threatens global food production and future economic growth. How could this rapid growth in wealth, population, science and technology, and human control over the natural world have produced such catastrophic results?

Progress is proving to be a dangerous delusion, which modern peoples continue to support despite the overwhelming evidence that it has led to an escalating war against the earth. Ironically, the modern world's relentless pursuit of victory in this centuries-old war against nature will be the principal cause of its defeat and collapse. In *The Vanishing White Man*, Stan Steiner (1976, 277) argued: The ruins of the Roman Empire, and the Mayan and Byzantine and Ottoman and Inca and Islamic and Egyptian and Ghanaian and Nigerian and Spanish and Aztec and English and Grecian and Persian, and the Mongolian civilization of the great Khans are visible for all to see. Is it heresy to say that the civilization of the white man of Western Europe, which has dominated much of the earth for four hundred years, is about to become one more magnificent ruin? Not because it has failed to accomplish its goals, but because it has succeeded so well, its time on earth may be done. The paradox of development is that the tremendous success of modern industrial civilization will be the cause of its collapse and ruin. To understand this paradox, we need to understand how modern economic and political institutions are creating both the so-called developed and underdeveloped worlds, which I will refer to as the First and Third worlds (Escobar 1995).

By creating the specter of vast, untold wealth and freedom in the First World and massive, desperate poverty and despair in the Third World, global development is creating the contradictions that will undermine global industrial civilization. On the one hand, global economic integration is creating spectacular wealth and progress for the 20 percent who live in the developed world, but, on the other hand, it is creating massive poverty and social unrest for the 80 percent who live in the underdeveloped world (Barnet and Cavanagh 1994). Between 1960 and 1995, rather than shrinking, the income gap between the rich and the poor grew. In 1960 the richest 20 percent of the world earned thirty times as much income as the poorest 20 percent, while by 1991 the richest 20 percent was approaching sixty-one times as much wealth as the poorest (French 1995, 176). At the United Nations World Summit for Social Development in March 1995, James Speth, administrator of the United Nations Development Program, noting that the income gap between the rich and poor had doubled over the past thirty years, said: "This widening gulf breeds despair and instability. It imperils our world" (Crossette 1995, A6).

Despite this growing inequality between the developed and the developing worlds, aid to developing nations has been shrinking and will continue to do so. Industrial nations and the major international lending institutions are asking developing nations to invest more of their own money to meet basic needs (Crossette 1995, A6). But how can they afford to do this given the increasing burden of debt servicing? By 1993 the total external debt of developing countries was $1.7 trillion (French 1995, 178). To pay off that debt, developing countries paid $160 billion in debt-service payments in 1992—more than two and a half times total official development assistance (French 1995, 178). Instead of becoming developed, some Third World leaders charged that they were becoming even poorer, and even more dependent on shrinking foreign aid (Escobar 1995).

Most people in the world are living on the margins of development. Three-quarters of the world's population lives in the 130 poorer countries of Latin America, Africa, and Asia, and most of the population do not have either steady jobs or secure income (Barnet and Cavanagh 1994, 179). In *Global Dreams*, Richard Barnet and John

Cavanagh (1995, 22) argue that there is a growing struggle between "the forces of globalization and the territorially based forces of local survival seeking to preserve and to redefine community." Barnet and Cavanagh (1995, 429) conclude that "local citizens' movements and alternative institutions are springing up all over the world to meet basic economic needs to preserve local traditions, religious life, cultural life, biological species, and other treasures of the natural world, and to struggle for human dignity." This increasing conflict between the demands of global industrial civilization and diverse peoples and cultures to protect their way of life and local autonomy is further evidence that the modern world is collapsing.

The integration of the global economy after World War II caused the growth of neofeudalism in the Third World, and in parts of the First World. Outside the increasingly guarded and walled prosperity of the developed world lives an expanding global peasantry, struggling to survive the encroachment of the modern industrial world into their lives. Surrounded by impoverished masses, neofeudal city-regions are emerging as the new hubs of global economic activity (Gardels 1995). Today there are at least thirty city-regions that dominate international trade and commerce (Petrella 1995, 21). The wealthy in these city-regions (CR) share more economic and political interests in common than they do with the citizens of the nations they are located in (Petrella 1995, 21). Instead of the G-7 nations controlling the global economy, we are witnessing the rise of the CR 30. In an increasingly neofeudal world, these city-regions are islands of affluence, surrounded by a sea of global peasants, whose livelihoods have been undermined by global free trade, the mechanization of industry and agriculture, environmental degradation, and the growth of sprawling, deteriorating megacities in the Third and First Worlds (Petrella 1995).

This global peasantry faces increasing poverty, misery, and despair. According to the United Nations, "the world's poorest, in fact, got poorer in the 1980s and there is a great correlation between mounting instability . . . widespread unrest, turmoil and violence which is now affecting an unprecedented number of countries in the developing worlds" (Ihonvbere 1992, 8). In 1992 the head of the World Bank, Barbar Conable said, "Living standards in Latin America have fallen below those of the 1970s. In sub-Saharan Africa, parts of the region have suffered a veritable collapse of living standards, institutions, and infrastructure" (Ihonvbere 1992, 7). In its 1990 report, the youth commission warns about the political and economic threats created by "mass poverty, economic dislocation, deindustrialization, declining foreign aid, mass net transfer of resources of about $40 billion a year from the Third World to the developed world, decaying institutions, political tensions and instability and the general inability of poverty-stricken and debt-ridden countries to provide for the basic needs of the majority" (Ihonvbere 1992, 8). With the possible exception of some of the newly industrializing countries of east Asia, most of the rest of the Third World "is an economic, social, and ecological disaster zone" (O'Connor 1994, 171).

The increasing poverty and despair of the Third World was exacerbated in the 1990s by the First World's effort to rebuild Eastern Europe and help the countries of the former Soviet Union. Many Third World leaders complained that this diversion of resources and foreign aid has increased their suffering and desperate situation (Ihonvbere 1992, 10). In "The Continent That Lost Its Way," Victoria Brittain (1994, 150) describes Africa as a disintegrating continent: "Across Africa, nation-states are disintegrating under the pressures of economic, environmental, political, and social stress more acute than at any time since the slave trade. Hundreds of thousands of people are on the move." Amid this societal disintegration, AIDS is wreaking untold havoc on the African continent. What has caused the rapid growth of what political scientists refer to as failed or collapsed states in Africa?

Massive population growth, deforestation and soil erosion, air and water pollution, destruction of the environment, the growth of export agriculture, and mass migration to overpopulated, deteriorating cities is straining the ability of African nations to meet the needs of their people and increasing the spread of the AIDS virus. Besides the loss of vital foreign aid, African countries are facing increased economic competition, promoted by the World Bank, from Asia and Latin America, which has driven the prices of African exports lower and lower (Brittain 1994, 151). Faced with declining export earnings, increasing tariff barriers in the industrialized nations, and pressure from First World lending institutions to pay its foreign debt, Africa is sinking into poverty, starvation, and despair.

But this desperate situation faces not only Africa but increasingly the entire Third World. While many in the First World experience untold wealth and affluence, the Third World continues to sink into poverty and misery. According to the United Nations Development Program, between 1960 and 1989, the gap between the rich and the poor nations doubled (Chomsky 1994, 129). This growing economic inequality is created by the developed nations feeding off the wealth of the underdeveloped nations. According to Susan George, resource transfers from the Third to the First World amounted to "a much understated $418 billion from 1982 to 1990, which is the equivalent in today's dollars of some six Marshall Plans for the rich through debt service alone" (Chomsky 1994, 130). During these same years, besides the developed world's looting their resources, predatory loans from First World banks increased the Third World debt burden by 61 percent, 110 percent for the least-developed countries (Chomsky 1994, 130). And, finally, according to the World Bank, tariffs and protectionist measures of the industrial countries reduced national income in the Third World by about twice the amount of official aid (Chomsky 1994, 129). Thus, First World development depends on the underdevelopment of the Third World and the growth of neofeudalism.

In the 1990s increasing violence and societal decay is widespread throughout the underdeveloped world. Made superfluous—surplus population—by the global economy, young people, especially young men, from Kinshasa to Munich to Los Angeles act out by becoming brutal, violent criminals, "striking out blindly in all directions" (Enzensberger 1993, 39). This condition is most evident in the failed or collapsed states in Africa. In 1995 most states in Africa have either failed or are collapsing (Gruhn 1995). Civil wars and sporadic violence in failing states have produced enormous refugee populations throughout Africa (Gruhn, 1995).

Instead of seeing these collapsed states as the result of the failure of development, and the increasing economic marginalization of entire populations, the American foreign-policy elite sees these problems as the result of "ethnic, nationalist, and separatist conflicts, which they refer to as ENS wars" (Schwarz 1995, 58). According to Leslie Gelb, the president of the Council on Foreign Relations, these foreign civil wars are "the new core problem in post-Cold War politics" (Schwarz 1995, 67). Gelb concludes that "the main strategic challenge for the United States is to develop plans . . . to stem civil wars" (Schwarz 1995, 58). But Gelb and First World economic and political leaders fail to recognize the larger cause of these ENS wars, which is the economic, societal, and environmental ruin caused by development. These states fail because their citizens no longer believe they can solve the economic and political crises they face. Instead of looking to the state, they look to ethnic, religious, tribal, and social groups to end their poverty and restore social and political order. The increasing number of ethnic, nationalist, and separatist conflicts (ENS wars) throughout the world further demonstrates that global industrial civilization is collapsing.

Failed states and chaotic and lawless cities in Africa illustrate the growing contradictions confronting the modern world. In *Civil Wars*, Hans Magnus Enzensberger (1993) examines what he calls "molecular civil wars" created by the breakdown of the state. In molecular civil wars, which are raging out of control in many parts of Africa, the young and the desperate prey on the helpless masses and themselves. This violence further undermines the ability of the failed state and society to restore economic, political, and social order. Reflecting on the vicious, brutal, nihilistic nature of escalating urban violence in *Savages and Civilization,* Jack Weatherford (1994, 282) argues that "civilization has produced a savagery far worse than that which we once imputed to primitive tribes. . . . Civilization created and nourished [these urban savages], and the center of the city has become the new frontier." This savagery and the violence, disorder, and despair it generates is caused by global development and the underdevelopment it creates.

With the growth of a global industrial economy after World War II, First World political and economic elites found that to support continued economic growth and affluence of the developed world, they had to promote poverty, social disorder, and despair in the Third World. The irony, however, is that since the 1970s, these elites have been forced to create similar conditions in the First World. The economic and social crises created by this poverty, disorder, and despair in both the Third and increasingly the First World countries is causing the collapse of global industrial civilization.

In the early 1980s the so-called Third World debt crisis threatened to destabilize the global economy. Developing countries found that development and the creation of export industries paid for by First World loans could not solve the economic and social problems that development experts and global elites promised they would. Instead of ending poverty and improving the quality of life, development seemed to be creating more poverty, and even underdevelopment.

By the 1980s, because of the deterioration of terms of trade, falling commodity prices, tariff barriers, and extraction of economic surplus by transnational corporations and by the World Bank and First World banks, it was evident to many Third World peoples that their poverty and underdevelopment was caused by First World exploitation of their wealth, resources, and workers. In the 1980s, large parts of Asia, Africa, and Latin America saw their worst economic crisis in this century (Escobar 1995, 90). For example, in the 1980s Latin American nations paid the First World an average of $30 billion more each year than they received in new lending (Escobar 1995, 83). In Latin America the 1980s are known as the lost decade.

By the 1990s it was all too evident that the First World's prosperity was dependent on the continued underdevelopment of the Third World. While the 130-plus developing countries of the South (referred to as the Group of 77) already account for four-fifths of the world's people and one-sixth of its economic output, the industrialized countries (known as the G-7 industrial nations), with 26 percent of the population, account for 78 percent of world production of goods and services, 81 percent of energy consumption, 70 percent of chemical fertilizers, and 87 percent of world armaments (Escobar 1995, 212). In the 1990s the average per capita income in the developing countries is only about 6 percent of that of the developed countries (Speth 1992). While the First World celebrated the return of economic prosperity in the 1980s, more than fifty developing countries experienced a decline in per capita food production (Speth 1992). Moreover, since 1982, the food available to poor people in the Third World has fallen by about 30 percent. It has fallen because of the success of development and the growth of export markets. Without the wealth and affluence of the First World, Third World peoples found they could not afford to buy the food that development helped them produce. As a result, according to the United Nations, the number of people in absolute poverty is 1.3 billion (Crossette 1995). The debt crisis and increasing poverty and suffering in the 1980s led many Third World peoples to conclude that development, far from being a miracle cure for their growing problems, was just another form of neocolonialism.

By the early 1990s development experts were predicting that within the next fifty years, the human population would exceed 9 billion and global economic output may quintuple (Homer-Dixon, Boutwell, and Rathjens 1993). If the use of energy increased sevenfold between 1950 and 1990 to create our present development, what increase in energy would it take to develop the entire globe (Wallimann 1994, 47)? In addition, we must ask whether the global environment can support another sevenfold increase in energy use between 1990 and 2030. Could development, even sustainable development, provide the natural resources, ecosystem services, affluence, and freedom to support this growth without undermining the ability of the earth to meet the demands of modern industrial civilization? This was the central question participants at the 1992 United Nations Conference on the Environment and Development in Rio de Janeiro, which pretentious organizers called the Earth Summit, were confronted with (Sitarz 1994).

But despite the 1992 Earth Summit and international discussions about sustainable development by First World political and economic elites in the 1980s and 1990s, the relentless pursuit of wealth and profits and unsustainable development continues. The great modern myth supporting this development is the promise that global economic growth will eventually bring to all peoples the wealth and abundance enjoyed by a minority in the First World. But this myth is increasingly being questioned by the majority in the Third World, who have yet to see the cornucopia created by development.

In fact, First World claims about the emergence of a democratic, fully integrated, global industrial economy are clearly specious. Despite this so-called globalization, most people are outside the global industrial economy (Barnet and Cavanagh 1994). The transnational corporations (TNCs), which are the primary links in this global economy, are concentrated in the industrial world and in scattered enclaves throughout the underdeveloped world. Thus, globalization has created islands of affluence in a vast sea of underdevelopment in the Third World (Redclift 1987). In this emerging global industrial economy, development enables the First World to live off the resources and degraded environments of the Third World.

In *Sustainable Development: Exploring the Contradictions*, Michael Redclift (1987, 112) defines development as "the process through which the environment is transformed from a local cultural and ecological system . . . into a functioning element in the international system." Precisely because of this development, Redclift (1987, 45) concludes, "the ecological breakdown, forecast in the 1960s and 1970s, has already occurred in parts of the South." Billions of people in Latin America, Africa, and Asia are discovering that poverty, collapsing social institutions, and environmental degradation are the price of development.

The growth of failed states in sub-Saharan Africa is a measure of the true costs of development. Having borrowed billions of dollars to pay for this development, much of sub-Saharan Africa is now starving while debt interest is being paid (Redclift 1987, 69). In "The Coming Anarchy," Robert Kaplan (1994, 46) argues that "West Africa is becoming the symbol of worldwide demographic, environmental stress, in which criminal anarchy emerges as the real 'strategic' danger. Disease, overpopulation, unprovoked crime, scarcity of resources, refugee migrations, the increasing erosion of nation-states and international borders, and the empowerment of private armies, security firms, and international drug cartels are not the most tellingly demonstrated through a West African prism." Connelly and Kennedy (1994, 72) warn that West Africa "increasingly looks like strife-torn, plague-ridden medieval Europe." And Kaplan (1994, 58) concludes that in West Africa we are witnessing "the political and strategic impact of surging populations, spreading disease, deforestation and soil erosion, water depletion, air pollution. . . ." With its failed states and deteriorating environment, sub-Saharan Africa demonstrates the tragic impact of development in the Third World.

The 1992 Earth Summit and the promise of sustainable development promoted in Agenda 21, the United Nations' 1992 plan for creating a global sustainable society, were attempts to resolve the increasing doubts Third World peoples and politicians have about the promise of development (Chatterjee and Finger 1994). If Third World countries withdraw from the global economy to solve their increasing economic and societal problems, First World economic and political elites fear that this will deprive them of their source of cheap raw materials, export markets, and cheap labor required to maintain their profits in an increasingly competitive global economy. In the 1980s political and economic elites in the developed countries created the ideology of sustainable development in a desperate attempt to convince underdeveloped countries that only further global development and economic growth can solve the economic and political crises created by development (Chatterjee and Finger 1994).

But, ironically, just as First World countries compete to achieve increasing control over the global economy, they are discovering that they have less and less control over their own economies and resources. With the growth of a global economy since the 1960s, TNCs are limiting the ability of even the most powerful First World nations such as the United States, Germany, and Japan to control their own national economies. The only currently functioning global agents are TNCs, not First World national governments. TNCs conduct 70 percent of international trade and 80 percent of foreign investment (Chatterjee and Finger 1994, 112). According to the United Nations, the TNCs control 80 percent of cultivated land for export crops worldwide and a mere twenty of them control 90 percent of pesticide sales (Chatterjee and Finger 1993, 106).

If sustainable development and the further integration of the global economy are not the answers to the increasing problems confronting both the First and the Third Worlds, then what is the solution? The answer, as John Cobb has already argued, lies in the remarkable ability of peoples and cultures to adapt to constantly changing local and regional environments. Thus, if Third World peoples find that development and their dependence on the global economy is creating poverty, suffering, and political turmoil, it would, in fact, be very adaptive for them to withdraw from the global economy and refuse to accept First World efforts to develop them. This would further undermine the myth of development, the myth that human progress can be achieved only through modernization.

Whether we call it civilizing, progress, modernization, development, or now sustainable development, modern peoples have imagined that it is the developed world's "manifest destiny" to teach the rest of the world that modernity is the only course open to them. But this is simply not true. There are just too many diverse cultures, religions, and ways of life for modernization and global development to finally triumph. By refusing to disappear into history, despite innumerable attempts to civilize and teach them to be modern, nonmodern peoples demonstrate the resilience and strength of their cultures and societies to survive and adapt in a complex and chaotic world.

The First World's failure to modernize and civilize the world should not be seen as a tragedy, but as an opportunity. With the increasing recognition of the inability of development to resolve the economic and political contradictions it creates, whether you call it sustainable or not, peoples and communities will be once again forced to draw on their own cultures, histories, religions, and intimate knowledge of their local environments to improve their lives and ensure a "reasonable life" for their children. For most of history, successfully adapting to changing local and regional environments was the fundamental challenge facing human societies.

But how will First World political and economic elites react to these efforts by Third World peoples and others to withdraw from the global economy and to create a society and future not based on modernization and development? Third World peoples' refusal to pay their debts, to sell their resources to the developed world, and their refusal to allow the First World and TNCs to dominate their economies, societies, and politics will not come without global conflict and struggle.

There will be neocolonial wars, political and economic subversion, widespread suffering and turmoil, and social and political chaos. We witnessed some of this during the cold war, when the United States and Europe found more often than not that they had to force Third World people to accept development and the neocolonialism and tremendous poverty, suffering, and political unrest it created. The Somalis and Balkan nations' ability to use force to prevent continued First World domination are models for this future conflict. The process will not be easy. It will be like the wars and conflicts that brought the fall of the Mayan and Roman empires (Ponting 1991).

The successful collapse of global industrial civilization is, in part, dependent on the 80 percent not fully integrated with the global economy breaking free from their ties to modern industrial civilization. Faced with growing threats of economic and ecological collapse, many underdeveloped nations and regions should declare their independence from the global economy, recognizing that this economy is the larger cause of their poverty. After breaking free from the First World's economic and political hegemony, underdeveloped countries can then use their resources and people to feed themselves and improve their quality of life. Of course, we have been witnessing such attempts for the past fifty years after World War II as colonial and neocolonial struggles for independence. The wars in Vietnam, Cambodia, Afghanistan, Nicaragua, El Salvador, Angola, Mozambique, Somalia, and in the nations of the former Soviet Union were all struggles to win independence from foreign domination. The cold war was, in large part, a struggle between the United States and the Soviet Union over who would dominate the modern world and the so-called nonaligned nations of the Third World. With the global instability created by the end of the cold war, the collapse of the Soviet Union, and the decline of American hegemony, underdeveloped countries may find that they have the strategic opportunity to demand their independence from First World domination. They can refuse to pay their debts, withdraw from the global industrial economy, nationalize foreign corporations that are exploiting their wealth, and create local and regional economies to support their own people. But Third World independence from the First World-dominated global economy will not come without a heavy economic, political, and military price.

With the withdrawal of underdeveloped countries from the global economy within the next thirty to fifty years, the developed countries will face continual material, ecological, and energy shortages that will force them to downscale their economies. The First World will, ironically, be forced to follow the lead of the Third World and create local and regional economies that are sustainable and self-sufficient. In many instances, nations will break up, forming smaller polities tied together by ethnic, religious, or social bonds. If these polities and nations take responsibility for helping their peoples survive the hardship and suffering imposed by the devolution of the global industrial civilization and economy, they will be better able to reduce the real threat of mass death and genocide that will arise from the collapse of modern industrial civilization.

Most critics would argue, probably correctly, that instead of allowing underdeveloped countries to withdraw from the global economy and undermine the economies of the developed world, the United States, Europe, and Japan and others will fight neocolonial wars to force these countries to remain within this collapsing global economy. These neocolonial wars will result in mass death, suffering, and even regional nuclear wars. If First World countries choose military confrontation and political repression to maintain the global economy, then we may see mass death and genocide on a global scale that will make the deaths of World War II pale in comparison. However, these neocolonial wars, fought to maintain the developed nations' economic and political hegemony, will cause the final collapse of our global industrial civilization. These wars will so damage the complex economic and trading networks and squander material, biological, and energy resources that they will undermine the global economy and its ability to support the earth's 6 to 8 billion people. This would be the worst-case scenario for the collapse of global civilization.

It is also entirely possible that the global economy is already so fragile that developed countries cannot afford to engage in these neocolonial wars, especially if they do not do it as a global block of developed nations through the United Nations. The desperate struggle among competing modern empires to maintain their resource pipelines into the underdeveloped world will only further undermine global civilization. Warring nations' attempts to cripple their enemies by denying access to their economies and resources will only hasten the collapse of the global economy.

No matter how it collapses, through economic collapse and the development of local and regional economies or through a global military struggle by the First World to maintain its access to Third World resources, or both modern industrial civilization will collapse because its demands for energy, natural resources, and ecosystem services are not sustainable.

The current collapse of economies and states in Africa, Latin America, and the former Soviet Union demonstrate that this global collapse is already occurring. The inability of the United States and the United Nations in the 1990s to solve the economic and political problems that exacerbate conflicts in Africa, Latin America, Eastern Europe, and the former Soviet Union demonstrate that the developed countries might be under such economic and political stress that they cannot afford to use the political or military capital necessary to force recalcitrant nations and peoples to remain within the global industrial economy. Although many would argue that the massive death and suffering caused by these conflicts must be stopped, it could be that this death will be less than if the First World intervened and tried to force Third World countries to remain within global civilization. Attempts to intervene in these growing regional conflicts, on the basis of liberal internationalism and global civilization, will backfire and cause only more suffering. In fact, these interventions will further accelerate the collapse of global civilization.

The fundamental dilemma facing First World political and economic elites is that their efforts to create a global industrial economy by further integrating Third World countries into the global trade and economic system dangerously stresses the material, biological, and energy resources of the earth (Union of Concerned Scientists 1993). And this economic integration, based on past economic history, will create only more poverty in the underdeveloped world. The only way to sustain the standard of living of the 20 percent of the world's population in the First World is to continue to drain resources from the Third World, which even now supports 80 percent of the world's population.

However, there are those who would challenge my conclusions, arguing that Agenda 21 (Sitarz 1994) and United Nations' plans for a global sustainable society could resolve the growing economic and political contradictions that threaten the future of global industrial civilization. Agenda 21 calls for reducing the standard of living of developed countries and then raising the standard of living of the underdeveloped countries up to that sustainable level. Such a global sustainable society, however, is impossible because the earth cannot support 6 billion people at or anywhere near a modern, First World standard of living (Union of Concerned Scientists 1993). Second, the brutal destruction of global ecosystems, material resources, and energy stocks in the past four hundred years has so damaged the earth that there simply aren't the resources and ecosystem services to support a sustainable, modern global society. The irony and tragedy is that our very efforts to create a global economy based on high standards of living and progress in the last 400 years has so damaged the earth and torn apart the fabric of modern civilization that a global sustainable society is no longer possible. The fact is that our efforts to sustain an increasing standard of living for the 20 percent of the world's people in the developed world has created increasing poverty, despair, and political and economic chaos for the 80 percent of the global population that lives in the underdeveloped world.

I am not arguing, however, that human overpopulation and the resulting destruction of global resources will be the primary factor causing the collapse of global civilization. The global environmental crisis is the result of the expansion of modern industrial civilization and the development of the First World and the underdevelopment of the Third World since the 1600s. In *Sustaining the Earth*, John Young (1990, 107) argues that "people constitute an environmental problem, not because of their existence, but because of what they do, and the parts of the environment they use up or damage." The culture of the modern world—its individualism, materialism, scientism, and faith in progress—and the global expansion of that culture is the central cause of the collapse of modern industrial civilization (Ehrenfeld 1978). And surviving polities and nations must keep this firmly in mind if they are to avoid future collapses themselves.

The only alternative we now have is to recognize the very real imminent collapse of global industrial civilization. Instead of seeing this collapse as a tragedy, and trying to put Humpty Dumpty back together again, we must see it as a real opportunity to solve some of the basic economic, political, and social problems created and exacerbated by the development of modern industrial civilization. Instead of insisting on coordinated global actions, we should encourage self-sufficiency through the creation of local and regional economies and trading networks (Norgaard 1994). We must help political and economic leaders understand that the more their countries are tied to the global economic system, the more risk there is of serious economic and political collapse.

In the case of the collapse of Mayan civilization, the city-states and regions in Central America that were not as dependent on the central

Mayan civilization, economy, and trade were more likely to survive its collapse. The city-states that were heavily dependent on Mayan hegemony destroyed themselves by fighting bitter wars with other powerful city-states to maintain their declining economic and political dominance (Weatherford 1994). Like the collapse of Mayan and Roman civilization, the collapse of global civilization will cause mass death and suffering as a result of the turmoil created by economic and political collapse. The more dependent nations are on the global economy, the more economic, political, and social chaos they will experience when it breaks down.

Once global civilization collapses, humanity will not have the material, biological, and energy resources to rebuild it. This must be the real lesson that nations and polities learn from this global collapse. If they try to rebuild unsustainable regional or even international economies, it will only cause more suffering and mass death.

In conclusion, the only solution to the growing political and economic chaos caused by the collapse of global industrial civilization is to encourage the uncoupling of nations and regions from the global economy. Efforts to integrate the underdeveloped countries with this global economy through sustainable development programs such as Agenda 21 will only further undermine the global economy and industrial civilization.

Unfortunately, millions will die in the wars and economic and political conflicts created by the accelerating collapse of global civilization. But we can be assured, on the basis of the past history of the collapse of regional civilizations such as the Mayan and the Roman empires, that, barring global nuclear war, human societies and civilizations will continue to exist and develop on a smaller, regional scale. Yes, such civilizations will be violent, corrupt, and often cruel, but, in the end, less so than our current global industrial civilization, which is abusing the entire planet and threatening the mass death and suffering of all its peoples and the living, biological fabric of life on earth.

The paradox of global economic development is that although it creates massive wealth and power for modern elites, it also creates massive poverty and suffering for underdeveloped peoples and societies. The failure of global development to end this suffering and destruction will bring about its collapse. This collapse will cause millions of people to suffer and die throughout the world, but it should, paradoxically, ensure the survival of future human societies. The collapse of global civilization is necessary for the future, long-term survival of human beings. Although this future seems hopeless and heartless, it is not. We can learn much from our present global crisis. What we learn will shape our future and the future of the complex, interconnected web of life on earth.

PART TWO

Scarcity and Conflict

Introduction

In the light of the broad global trends discussed in the preceding section, we should not be surprised if there is a relationship between scarcity and internal and regional conflict. With population pressures building up in various parts of the globe, the struggle for resources intensifies and with the end of the cold war, we may expect to see old ethnic animosities and religious conflicts come to the surface with greater intensity, particularly in the poorer parts of the world. We have already seen this happening in Central America, Southeast Asia, Afghanistan, the Middle East, the Balkans, Africa, and the rimlands of the former Soviet Union.

The optimists argue that natural resources are not a finite entity that is steadily being depleted; they see the creation of new or modified resources that are the result of human inventions and labor, and they believe technology has an infinite capacity for solving the earth's problems. They also have abiding faith in the resiliency of the earth itself and its human inhabitants. Just as Malthus was wrong in his predictions, so are today's doomsayers. If the optimists are correct, the world will just be a more prosperous place with more "stuff" distributed to larger numbers of people. If they are wrong, as the contributors in this section argue, the human race may be in for more conflict and suffering if it does not change its course of the relentless pursuit of growth, accumulation, and waste.

4. Biophysical Limits to Industrialization

Prospects for the Twenty-first Century

John M. Gowdy

Human Beings and the natural world are on a collision course. Human activities inflict harsh and often irreversible damage on the environment and on critical resources. If not checked, many of our current practices put at serious risk the future that we wish for human society and the plant and animal kingdoms, and may so alter the living world that it will be unable to sustain life in the manner that we know. Fundamental changes are urgent if we are to avoid the collision our present course will bring about.

—Union of Concerned Scientists
"Warning to Humanity"

Among physical scientists, and among biologists and ecologists in particular, the view is widely held that the current level of human activity is unsustainable. Various biophysical indicators suggest that our species is pushing the limits of the ability of the planet to support us. According to calculations by Vitousek and others (1986), human activity, directly and indirectly, expropriates about 40 percent of the potential terrestrial products of photosynthesis. Exhaustive calculations by Kraushaar and Ristinen (1993), based on solar energy flow, conversion efficiencies, and many other factors, estimate that the planet has enough arable land to support a population of 10 billion. The human population is now approaching 6 billion and still growing rapidly. Economic activity, particularly burning fossil fuels and the destruction of forests, has pushed atmospheric CO_2 to the highest levels since a period of global warming some 125,000 years ago. Atmospheric CO_2 is expected to increase from its preindustrial level of 270 ppm to 600 ppm by the middle of the twenty-first century raising global temperatures by 3.5° to 7°C and raising sea levels by 1 to 2 meters by thermal expansion alone (Manabe and Stouffer 1993). Even if there are no surprises, such as a sudden climate flip from one steady sate to another, the rise in temperature caused by higher atmospheric CO_2 levels will have serious consequences for the ability of the human population to feed itself. In the view of many biologists, the most serious environmental problem is biodiversity loss. According to E. O. Wilson (1992) the current catastrophic loss of biodiversity represents the sixth major extinction of life on earth that has occurred during the 570-million-year history of complex life on the planet. He estimates that by the middle of the next century more than 20 percent of existing species will disappear.

Each of the above calculations and observations may be disputed. The likelihood, however, that they are all fundamentally wrong is virtually zero. From many different perspectives it is clear that we are pushing the limits of the ability of the biophysical world to support the continued expansion of the use of natural resources and of the assimilative capacity of the environment. Evidence from many sources leads us to the conclusion that industrial production will be drastically reduced because of constraints on energy and resource use arising from supply constraints and environmental limits. It is increasingly likely that sometime in the next century the "industrialization project" (Wallimann 1994) will come to a halt with unforeseen but probably negative consequences for our species. What are the prospects for getting off the industrial growth path before social disintegration and mass death is inevitable?

We who are alive today are in a unique position in human history. Not only do we exist at a critical instant in the biophysical history of the planet but we also have an unprecedented understanding of the details of this history. We are beginning to understand how the biophysical boundary conditions for human activity are irreversibly changing and to understand the human role in that process. Scientific advances in the past two decades have been truly astounding. Models designed to predict the consequences of climate change are being continually refined and are becoming more and more accurate. Ecological research showing the value of biodiversity to ecosystem stability is also being developed and refined. Even more important, perhaps, we are beginning to understand the connections between social phenomena, such as class differentiation and the generation of economic surplus, and environmental degradation.

Most of the global changes in the earth's support systems have occurred since World War II. The primary cause is the tremendous increase in world economic output, particularly in the northern countries. Economic indicators have shown vigorous growth while most biophysical indicators show an alarming decline. Understanding the conflict between economic and biophysical systems is essential to understanding our present predicament and in finding a way out of it.

The Importance of Economic Growth Within the World Sociopolitical System

It is becoming increasingly obvious that the promise of utopia through the creation of an ever-more-abundant array of material possessions is a hollow one. Not only is continued economic growth impossible in a finite world, opinion surveys indicate that, despite rapid economic growth in the past, people are becoming less, not more, satisfied with the quality of their lives (Schor 1991). Even the relatively small minority of the world's population who have reaped the benefits of an increasing material abundance are increasingly unhappy, less secure, and have less leisure time to enjoy their lives. Furthermore, the promise of extending northern prosperity to "developing" southern countries is a fading dream. An increasing number of countries are being added to the list of what are cynically termed "failed nations."

If it is physically impossible for economic growth to continue for much longer, and if this growth is evidently making its beneficiaries less happy, why then is the goal of economic growth accepted without question by every existing government? Two basic reasons are (1) economic growth does benefit the tiny minority who make the basic decisions about resource use and the distribution of economic surpluses and (2) economic growth is an essential feature of a self-organizing system whose existence depends on continual expansion.

From the international to the local level, the proponents of economic growth are those who directly benefit from it. These are the people most willing to sacrifice environmental quality and social security and stability for economic expansion. The people making investment decisions that will degrade the environment and the quality of life are those who can best insulate themselves from the adverse consequences of those decisions. World leaders of all stripes must be assured that "development" can continue before environmental issues are even discussed. Any interference with national sovereignty on ecological grounds is met with a self-righteous declaration of the "right to develop" (Sachs 1995). Who makes the decisions to develop and who reaps the benefits? Decisions to destroy collective goods, such as rain forests or climate stability, are made by a handful of people in the boardrooms of Tokyo, New York, or Zurich. These decisions are frequently subsidized by the institutions of international capital, such as the World Bank or International Monetary Fund. At the local level, economic growth at all costs is promoted by the most conservative growth-oriented segments of the economy as represented by local chambers of commerce. The side effects of economic growth at the local level, including increased congestion and higher taxes to pay for new services demanded, are borne by others. The blind march toward the increasing "rationalization" of economic activity and increasing privatization of markets is eliminating the last vestiges of social control over investment and resource-use decisions.

Economic growth seems to be indispensable to the world economy as it currently functions. Economic growth makes it possible to reap the benefits of technological advance by ensuring a more rapid turnover of capital stock, by alleviating the need to deal with questions of unequal income distribution, and by allowing firms to capture increasing productivity from increasing returns to scale (Gowdy 1994). When worker productivity increases, the resulting higher incomes generate a need for new products to absorb the increase in demand. Expansion due to increased demand enables producers to capture economies of scale, resulting in more productivity improvement, higher incomes, and so on ad infinitum. Positive feedback mechanisms such as these mean that economic growth perpetuates more economic growth and that socioeconomic and political features that promote growth are continually reinforced. The points of conflict between the prerogatives of economic growth and the prerogative of maintaining a planet suitable for continued human existence are clear:

1. Population increase is good for the economy because it increases the market for goods, but the human population level has reached the point where it is environmentally unsupportable.

2. Increasing per capita consumption is good for the economy but requires increasing amounts of resources and generates increasing amounts of waste products.

3. The expansion of markets is good for the economy but brings new parts of the natural world under the peculiar and shortsighted logic of market exchange.

When economic growth slows, income distribution becomes more unequal, as it has within the northern countries and between the north and the South, since the productivity slowdown that began with the energy crises of the 1970s. When economic output declines, as in the global and local economic depressions of this century, and today in much of the Third World, the result is usually social upheaval and mass destruction. Within the present world economic system, economic growth is essential to keeping the incomes of the wealthy high and keeping the lid on those at the bottom. The problem is that natural, biophysical laws will, sometime in the next century, halt the expansion of this human-created system.

Human Economy as a Self-Organizing System

Recent work applying entropy to economic systems has illuminated the fact that economic activity is possible only by extracting low entropy from the larger biophysical system. Thermodynamic analysis also shows clearly the potential for chaos in far-from-equilibrium self-organizing systems such as the modern economy. The pioneer of this approach to economic theory was Nicholas Georgescu-Roegen (1971), who twenty-five years ago published his monumental work, *The Entropy Law and the Economic Process*. Georgescu-Roegen used the entropy metaphor to develop an economic theory based in historical time and grounded within biophysical reality. Georgescu-Roegen called his theory "bioeconomics." He argued that bound energy and matter, low entropy, is not only the taproot of economic value but was also the ultimate source of social conflict. Georgescu-Roegen was born in Romania in 1906 and lived until 1994, giving him a historical and geographical perspective that fueled his intellectual contributions to economics and political economy.

> The idea that the economic process is not a mechanical analogue, but an entropic, unidirectional transformation began to turn over in my mind long ago, as I witnessed the oil wells of the Ploesti field of both World Wars' fame becoming dry one by one and as I grew aware of the Romanian peasants' struggle against the deterioration of their farming soil by continuous use and by rains as well. However, it was the new representation of a process that enabled me to crystallize my thoughts in describing for the first time the economic process as the

entropic transformation of valuable natural resources (low entropy) into valueless waste (high entropy). I may hasten to add . . . that this is only the material side of the process. The true product of the economic process is an immaterial flux, the enjoyment of life, whose relation with the entropic transformation of matter-energy is still wrapped in mystery. (Georgescu-Roegen 1976, xiv)

Georgescu-Roegen's great contribution was to show, with the entropy metaphor, that the economic process is not a reversible, self-contained circular flow as described by neoclassic economic theory, but is an irreversible system constrained by and dependent upon larger ongoing processes taking place in the biophysical universe. This simple fact means not only that economic activity is constrained by the larger systems but also that by degrading the enveloping biophysical system, we limit the future possibilities for human activity. Although these observations are self-evident to most natural scientists, they are ignored or even hotly contested by most neoclassical economists.

The application of thermodynamics to social and biological systems got a boost when Ilya Prigogine won the Nobel Prize for chemistry in 1977. He argued that far-from-equilibrium systems can achieve a high degree of self-organization by drawing low entropy from an adjacent environment (see the discussion in Foster 1995). The implications of Prigogine's work are (1) an economic system cannot exist without an open boundary between it and the outside world upon which it depends and (2) such a system is inherently unstable because the boundary conditions change as low entropy matter and energy pass into the system and as high entropy waste passes back across the boundary.

The extension of the work of Georgescu-Roegen and Prigogine shows not only the impossibility of continued economic expansion in a finite system but also the increasing instability of such a system as the limits to expansion are reached. Technological "improvements" cannot be relied upon to overcome biophysical limits, because technological change necessarily affects the boundary conditions between the economic system and the rest of the world. Perrings (1995) has developed a far-from-equilibrium model showing clearly that technological change is not independent of the economic growth process as mainstream economics argues. The law of conservation of mass implies that economic expansion must result in the material transformation of economic and ecological processes. Given the impossibility of prices to reflect changes in environmental attributes, such changes will be unanticipated by markets. Perrings (1995) concludes that "not only is the growth oriented economy itself an unstable system, it is directly responsible for destabilizing the global system of which it is a constituent part."

The history of the human species since the widespread adoption of agriculture some ten thousand years ago has been one of playing out a far-from-equilibrium-producing process of expansion and collapse. Cultures after cultures, in various climates, regions, and epochs, have temporarily escaped environmental constraints by tapping scarce low entropy only to collapse as the boundary conditions inevitably changed and as the biophysical processes upon which they depended could no longer support the unsustainable level of economic activity.

Ghosts from the Recent Past:
A Business-as-Usual Scenario

The information and scientific revolution in the past few decades has brought a better understanding of past civilizations. Better dating techniques, satellite imagery, and more sophisticated analysis of the climates and ecosystems supporting past civilizations have led researchers to increasingly appreciate the role of environmental degradation in social collapse. Human cultures moved to unsustainable technologies with the widespread adoption of agriculture some ten thousand years ago. The switch from hunting and gathering to agriculture was most likely triggered by a sudden climate change, namely, the global warming that continues today. The widespread ecological disruption triggered by this sudden warming caused a period of coevolutionary disequilibrium during which it became increasingly difficult to support the human population through hunting and gathering. Once agriculture and settled communities became established, the increase in human population and the formation of hierarchical class-based societies locked in the new agricultural way of life.

The transition to agriculture was the most profound change in human history in terms of our relationship to the natural world and in our relationships with one another. Rather than living off the day-to-day flows from nature, the new economic system depended upon stocks of natural resources and complex capital goods. Production was no longer for immediate use but was geared to creating an economic surplus. Not only were these new systems environmentally unsustainable, but production for surplus created a new and evidently unprecedented social system based on class division. As Malinowski succinctly put it, "Authority is the very essence of social organization" (quoted in Woodburn 1982). With the adoption of economies geared to the production of surpluses, and the resulting concentration of power in a few hands, the organizers of economic activity and the beneficiaries of environmental exploitation were those who could best insulate themselves from the negative effects of that exploitation.

Intensive agriculture was evidently adopted independently in three areas of the world about the same time: Mesoamerica, China, and southwest Asia. This new economic system quickly led to huge increases in population, highly stratified societies, and large-scale environmental disruption. In contrast to the highly stable hunting and gathering cultures, which in some cases lasted hundreds of thousands of years, the agricultural age has been characterized by rapid expansion and sudden collapse. In central Jordan, by 6000 B.C., less than one thousand years after the first adoption of agriculture, villages were being abandoned as deforestation led to soil erosion and declining crop yields (Ponting 1991, 69). The first literate society was that of the Sumerians, who kept detailed administrative records about crop yields. Analysis of these records show that increasing salinization from overirrigation was a problem early on. Wheat and barley were the two main crops grown by the Sumerians. Wheat is much more sensitive to soil salinity than barley and administrative records show a steady decrease in the percentage of wheat grown over the fifteen hundred year period beginning about 3500 B.C.. Written and archaeological evidence shows that by 2400 B.C. crop production began to decline rapidly. From that time on, there is evidence of a shrinking resource base, social unrest, and eventually external conquest by the Akkadian empire (Ponting 1991, 70–72). The Akkadian empire, in turn, repeated the pattern of expansion, environmental degradation, and social disintegration (Weiss et al. 1993). Ponting discusses this pattern for other cases, including the Mayan, the Indus Valley, and the Greek and Roman empires. Pollen records and other sources show that the present-day Greek landscape is a result of millennia of overgrazing, deforestation, and general land abuse (Runnels 1995).

The Mayan civilization, which expanded by an increasingly intensive system of cultivation until it collapsed about six hundred A.D., shows the typical overshoot and collapse. According to Ponting (83), by using the natural resources readily available to them, by finding ways of exploiting these more fully, and, in some cases, by creating artificial environments, the Maya were able to build a complex society capable of great cultural and intellectual achievements, but they ended up destroying what they had created. Perhaps the more complex the superstructure, the more difficult it was to retain an awareness of the connections or to alter course.

Recent evidence indicates that the Maya leveled their forests to make lime stucco used in their monumental architecture. The stucco was used on limestone palaces to make a smooth veneer on which to create bas-relief scenes of deities and Mayan rulers. According to archaeologist Richard Hansen, "The object was to display their wealth and power and to manipulate the ichnography so as to sustain the ruling class" (quoted by Honan 1995, 9).

One of the most incredible and yet most relevant examples of short-sighted environmental abuse and social dysfunction is that of Easter Island. Easter Island is one of the most isolated human habitations in the world lying thousands of kilometers from the nearest inhabited islands. It was first settled about A.D. 700 (Bahn and Flenley 1993, 81) probably by voyagers from Polynesia. When the first settlers landed, the island was forested with palm trees. The soil was rich enough to support an agricultural base for a population that peaked at about seven thousand. The diet of these settlers included chickens and Polynesian rats, which they brought with them, and sweet potatoes.

Despite the extreme isolation of Easter Island and its small size (it is possible to walk around the island in a day), its inhabitants stripped the island of almost all trees, overworked the soil, and in general created an environmental catastrophe for themselves. By the time Europeans arrived in 1722, the population was reduced to a few hundred impoverished residents living in squalor in caves. Apparently, the island was controlled by religious cults based on the construction and worship of the huge stone figures for which the island is famous. In a frequently recurring pattern, as the resource base of the island became more and more precarious, religious fanaticism intensified until even the most modest efforts at self-preservation were ignored. The huge statues were transported using trees as skids, which required tremendous amounts of timber as competition to erect statues increased among the island's clans. The resulting environmental devastation is described by Ponting (1991, 5).

From [the year] 1500 the shortage of trees was forcing many people to abandon building houses from timber and live in caves, and when the wood eventually ran out altogether about a century later everyone had to use the only materials left. They resorted to stone shelters dug into the hillsides or flimsy reed huts made from the vegetation that grew around the edges of the crater lakes. Canoes could no longer be built and only reed boats incapable of long voyages could be made. Fishing was also more difficult because nets had previously been made from the mulberry tree (which could also be made into cloth) and that was no longer available. Removal of the tree cover also badly affected the soil of the island, which would have already suffered from a lack of suitable animal manure to replace nutrients taken up by the crops.

One lesson to be learned from the history of past civilizations is that political pressure from elites bent on preserving their power at all cost will inevitably result in perpetuating unsustainable systems until it is too late, that is, until environmental degradation leads to social disintegration. Easter Island society collapsed even though there were no outside forces such as military threats, colonization, or social disruption through trade. The society used only local natural resources whose limits should have been obvious, although the evidence indicates that they acted as if they were oblivious to the impending resource exhaustion. Large stone heads were started in quarries but were left unfinished because there were no trees left to move them. If such obvious self-inflicted environmental collapse could happen in isolated island societies where environmental damage is immediate and obvious, this is certainly an indication that there are no "natural" mechanisms present in post-hunter-gatherer societies to ensure even short-run ecological sustainability. There is evidently no negative feedback mechanism in complex societies that limits environmental destruction even when that destruction threatens social stability.

In these past examples (except that of Easter Island), when a particular society disintegrated, the survivors could migrate to other areas and repeat the rapid expansion and collapse. Today the same thing is happening on a global scale and there will be no place to go when the current system repeats this well-established pattern. A comprehensive study led by Homer-Dixon, Boutwell, and Rathjens (1993, 38) involving a team of thirty researchers concluded that "scarcities of renewable resources are already contributing to violent conflicts in many parts of the developing world." The results of this study confirm the theoretical (thermodynamic) analysis discussed above, and show that the recurring pattern of expansion, resource exhaustion, and collapse of human societies during the past millennia is now repeating itself on a global scale. Homer-Dixon and others (1993, 38) conclude that (1) increasing resource scarcity can strengthen the hand of the social elite and exacerbate an unequal distribution of resources, (2) the parameters of the resource base, such as the depth of upland soil in the tropics, are a physical given, not a product of human institutions, and (3) environmental degradation may have passed, in much of the developing world, a threshold of irreversibility. Dasgupta (1995), drawing on empirical studies from a number of disciplines, comes to a similar conclusion. There are self-reinforcing links between population, poverty, and the degradation of local environments. Dasgupta also points out that power is shared unequally among classes and gender and those who make decisions about resource use and income distribution typically do not pay the environmental and social costs of their decisions. For example, in the decision to have more children, men in developing countries have more power, yet it is the women who bear the costs. Dasgupta (1995) found an unmistakable relationship between poverty, female illiteracy, and population growth. Data on the status of women from seventy-nine so-called Third World countries display an unmistakable pattern: high fertility, high rates of illiteracy, low share of paid employment, and a high percentage working at home for no pay—they all hang together.

Timothy Weiskel sees common patterns in the collapse of past civilizations and today's environmental and social crises. He argues that the history of past civilizations shows a common pattern of "gradual emergence, brief flowering, and rapid collapse of civilization, often taking the form in the final stages of devastating military struggles for the control of arable land or essential resources" (Weiskel 1989, 104). The most pronounced ecological and social breakdown is occurring in Africa where two-thirds of the countries are affected by famine to some degree (Goldsmith 1985). Kaplan (1994) argues what is happening in West Africa is a portent of things to come worldwide: West Africa is becoming the symbol of worldwide demographic, environmental, and societal stress, in which criminal anarchy emerges as the real "strategic" danger. Disease, overpopulation, unprovoked crime, scarcity of resources, refugee migrations, the increasing erosion of nation-states, and international borders, and the empowerment of private armies, security firms, and international drug cartels are now most tellingly demonstrated through a West African prism. West Africa provides an appropriate introduction to the issues, often extremely unpleasant to discuss, that will soon confront our civilization.

The pattern of burgeoning city populations, environmental degradation, and social unrest is not confined to the African continent. Even countries considered success stories, such as China, are facing the same problems. The Chinese economic miracle, according to Homer-Dixon, is an illusion. China's recent 14 percent economic growth rate indicates only that the cities of coastal China are joining the Pacific rim. China is still experiencing tremendous population growth and incredible environmental degradation (Smil 1993). A large-scale population movement from the rural areas to the cities is now under way, with the usual accompaniment of crime and growing income disparities. Homer-Dixon expects that China will fragment like West Africa. Mayumi (1993) also sees a disturbing pattern in the collapse of past civilizations and what is happening in the Third World. In the collapse of past civilizations, disintegration started first on the peripheries of power, then closed in on the center.

A look at past civilizations such as Easter Island shows that their institutions could not deal with the problem of long-run ecological sustainability. Faced with increasing environmental constraints, just before their final collapse, these societies intensified the very behavior that took them to the brink of collapse in the first place. Likewise, the usual solution suggested today for the problems caused by economic growth is yet more growth. For example, the Brundtland report on sustainable development began with a clarion call to protect the environment from further degradation. The proposed solution, however, was more economic growth to pay for environmental cleanup. A detailed analysis of the recommendations of the Brundtland report by Duchin and Lange (1994) concluded that even if all of its recommendations were implemented, the world economy would not achieve sustainability.

Ghosts from the Distant Past: Is There Any Hope?

Our species, *Homo sapiens*, is the last remaining member of a genus that first appeared some 3.5 million years ago. For almost all the time human beings have lived on earth, our economic and social institutions were based on a hunting and gathering life-style. This is the most successful way of life yet devised by human beings in social equality and ecological sustainability. An examination of the characteristics of hunter-gatherers can illuminate the connection between social equality and environmental integrity and give us some insights as to how we might change our existing institutions and get on the path toward a just and ecologically sustainable society.

James Woodburn (1982), based on field studies of the Hadza, a hunter-gatherer culture of Tanzania, describes some of the characteristics of hunter-gatherer societies that promote social equality:

1. Social groups are flexible and fluid.

2. Individuals are completely free to choose whom they associate with, reside with, and trade and exchange with.

3. Individuals are not dependent on specific others for access to basic requirements.

4. All relationships stress sharing and mutuality without requiring long-term binding commitments.

In these types of societies individuals have no real authority over one another. Furthermore, all of these characteristics are consciously protected as part of what Woodburn calls an "aggressively egalitarian" social strategy. He writes:

> In these societies equalities of power, equalities of wealth and equalities of prestige or rank are not merely sought but are, with certain limited exceptions, genuinely realized. But, the evidence suggests, they are never unchallenged. People are well aware of the possibility that individuals or groups within their own egalitarian societies may try to acquire wealth, to assert more power or to claim more status than other people, and are vigilant in seeking to prevent or limit this. (Woodburn 1982, 432)

Woodburn distinguishes between "immediate return" cultures, in which people obtain an immediate and direct return from their labor. Food is eaten soon after it is gathered or hunted, and technology is very simple. In "delayed return" systems, people hold some property rights over some assets. These assets include "capital" used in production, such as nets or boats, processed or stored food, and rights associated with wild products that have been improved by human effort, such as selectively culled wild herbs or wild plants that have been cared for. Although both types are much more egalitarian than agricultural- or industrial-based societies, the immediate return systems are the most egalitarian in wealth, status, and power. Inequalities of wealth are not tolerated and women have far more independence than in delayed return systems (Woodburn 1978).

The basic reason is that in immediate return systems, access to the means for making a living is free and open to all. Material technology is limited. The basic requirement to get along in these societies is the extensive knowledge about the specific ecosystems of which each society is a part. This knowledge is freely available and is given to all members of the group. With delayed return societies, although they are also very egalitarian, we see the beginnings of class differences based on access to technology and the resulting control of an economic surplus. With permanent surpluses, almost always associated with agriculture, came social divisions and the control of production and distribution by elites. To the Western way of thinking, the most remarkable thing about the distribution of the economic output among hunter-gatherers is that it is independent of who produces it. In societies like the Hadza and !Kung, most of the meat is provided by a few hunters. Woodburn notes that among the Hadza there are healthy, adult men who have scarcely killed an animal in their entire lives, yet are provided for just like everyone else and suffer no ostracism. The !Kung have elaborate formal rules disassociating the hunter from his kill (Woodburn 1982, 440). After the kill, the meat is shared among the members of the band according to strict rules that break the link between production and consumption. Woodburn writes of the Hadza:

> Among the Hadza the best portions (which differ depending on which species has been killed) belong to the initiated men and may not under any circumstances be eaten by the hunter on his own. For the Hadza this would be a particularly heinous offence which would be likely to result in violence toward the hunter; it would also, Hadza believe, cause him to become seriously ill and perhaps even die. (1982, 441)

Neoclassical economists would argue that such sharing among non-Western societies is merely an insurance policy for future lack of success in hunting. A hunter may give up some of his rights over a kill to receive a reciprocal exchange later. The evidence suggests that this interpretation is totally wrong. According to Woodburn (1982, 441): "Donors often remain on balance donors and may not receive anything like an equivalent return. Entitlement does not depend in any way on donation. Some men who are regular recipients never themselves contribute."

That there is no connection between production and distribution, nothing like a "marginal productivity theory of distribution," shows the fiction of the notion of "economic man." There is nothing inherently selfish and greedy about our species. Judging from historical hunting and gathering societies, the "natural" state of humankind may be much closer to Marx's "primitive communism" than to contemporary capitalism.

Another feature of hunter-gatherers is that there are frequently sanctions on accumulation of personal possessions. The lack of possessions is not merely due to the nomadic nature of hunter-gatherer life. There are sanctions that apply even to the lightest objects, such as bread or arrowheads. Woodburn (1982, 445) sees one central feature of the social organization of those societies that insures egalitarianism. People are disengaged from property and thus from the potential for property rights to create dependency. This idea could not be more subversive to the standard economic way of thinking, which equates "freedom" with an ever-greater expansion of "property rights."

Maintaining Options for the Twenty-first Century

What can we learn from past societies? Can we use the concepts and scientific evidence discussed above to prevent a repeat of history and the collapse of our civilization? Two simple facts follow from the above discussion:

1. The economy is a subsystem of a larger biophysical system and dependent upon it. Past civilizations collapsed because their institutions ignored this basic fact.

2. There is a connection between power, environmental degradation, and social collapse. Decisions about resource use are made by those whose power and prestige depends upon continued exploitation.

In environmental preservation what should we do? The recommendations of most natural scientists concerned about the environment are basically the same. Chief among the physical requirements of sustainability are these: (1) stop burning fossil fuels; (2) reduce the human population to a manageable level; and (3) protect biodiversity by protecting large wild areas from market exploitation. Only by quickly taking these steps can we prevent mass death and eventual social collapse and ensure that our species has a future when our economic and social systems change to a new, and unpredictable, form.

How can we achieve these goals? Gurr (1985) argues that both environmentalists and technological optimists have been naive in their assessments of the ability of human societies to adapt to change. Technological utopians fail to recognize the environmental limits that constrain human technology, and environmentalists fail to appreciate the policy constraints imposed by political realities. Growth proponents are guilty of technological optimism, and environmentalists are guilty of political optimism.

Gurr (1985, 53) writes: "[J]ust as there are ultimate ecological constraints on economic growth, political constraints weigh heavily on what might be achieved collectively in the face of serious scarcity." Gurr suggests that when relative scarcity increases, and the more rapidly it proceeds, the greater the negative political consequences. The main negative consequence is a move toward greater disparities in income distribution as those in power try to maintain their income growth when faced with increasing resource constraints. Thus scarcity induced economic decline is likely to result in redistribution from the bottom and middle to the top income groups. Such a widening of income differences has happened in almost every country since the energy crises of the 1970s. The United States now ranks first in income inequality among industrialized nations with the wealthiest 1 percent owning 40 percent of the nation's wealth (Bradsher 1995). The increasing concentration of economic and thus political power in the hands of a few makes environmentally destructive resource-use decisions more likely even if opposed by the majority. In a democracy the increased wealth at the top will be translated into growing political power for the most reactionary forces.

Is there any reason to hope that this process can be reversed? Gurr (1985, 68) suggests that future environmental crises will be large enough and come rapidly enough to convince people of the need for comprehensive solutions. The question is will these solutions take the form of policies to promote further growth at all costs (by attempting to increase the supplies of economic goods), or will policies recognize environmental limits (by decreasing the demand for economic goods)?

In Western democracies, particularly in the United States, we are seeing a desperate push by the most conservative forces to increase the income of the wealthy at the expense of other income groups and the environment. What potential is there for collective action against this retrenchment? First of all, the connection between reactionary social policies and environmental scarcity must be understood and articulated. As Breyman (1993) notes, knowledge truly is power. Time and a growing body of scientific information is on our side. Solutions emphasizing shared responsibility and a recognition of limits must be advanced in the political arena. The following groups are likely allies in a movement emphasizing frugality, redistribution, and shared responsibility:

1. social activists, the poor and lower-middle classes, who are feeling the brunt of elitist polices of redistribution,

2. environmentalists, an increasingly powerful lobby in the United States and Western Europe,

3. the young, who are most concerned with medium and long-term environmental crises and with social decay, and

4. segments of the business community that will be most adversely affected by scarcity.

Again, the connection must be carefully and explicitly made between reactionary social policies and increasing scarcity.

Paradoxically, it seems that the only hope of preventing a repeat of the overshoot and collapse pattern of the past is a sudden, severe, and unmistakable environmental shock. If the greenhouse researchers are correct, and they have been correct so far, we could see such a shock in the next decade or two. The predicted consequences of global warming, sea level rise, increasing severity of storms, and an increasing frequency of droughts and crop failure are already happening. The ranks of environmental organizations will swell as events such as global warming begin to hit with increasing force. Young people who may expect to live another fifty to sixty years will be most alarmed by the prospects of impending environmental degradation from global warming and biodiversity loss. Powerful economic interests will also be adversely affected by global warming. The insurance industry, for example, is already expressing concern about environmental issues, and certainly the real estate and tourism industries will be affected by sea level rise and severe weather.

A common theme in much of the new literature about environmental degradation and social conflict is that the nation-state as we know it will be of less importance in the future (Gurr 1985, Homer-Dixon 1991, Kaplan 1994). Kaplan argues that the central government as a unifying force is already being replaced in many regions of the world by religious and ethnic organizations. It may be that the best hope for preventing social breakdown in the next century is to develop collective institutions based on the middle ground between private individualism and national governments. Much of biodiversity preservation is being done by organizations such as the Nature Conservancy and by local land trusts. As inadequate as these current efforts are, they offer a blueprint for reasserting collective decision making regarding resource use.

Calls for a steady-state economy (Daly 1977) have done much to educate and mobilize those concerned about the environmental and social decay caused by economic growth. But we must now move beyond this simple idea. First of all, it is clear that human activity is well beyond an ecologically supportable level. We need to have a declining state before we reach sustainability. Second, a steady state means no growth, a condition incompatible with industrial capitalism and maybe incompatible with surplus-generating economies in general. The idea that we can substitute "nonmaterial" economic growth for resource-intensive growth does little to free us from the old growth-as-progress paradigm. We need to go beyond "limits to growth" and find "alternatives to growth." The difficulty of this task should not be underestimated, but we need to start developing comprehensive alternatives now to be ready with workable alternatives when most are ready to consider them.

5. Our Unsustainable Society

Basic Causes, Interconnections, and Solutions

Ted Trainer

The first purpose of this chapter is to summarize the reasons for seeing the quest for economic growth and affluent life-styles as the fundamental cause of the rapidly deteriorating global predicament. (For detailed argument see Trainer 1985, 1989, and 1995a and the Cobb, Lewis, and Gowdy chapters in this book.) This obsession largely explains many apparently unrelated problems, most notably the environment, resource scarcity, Third World deprivation, conflict between nations, and social breakdown.

Mineral Resources

Except for a very few items, to extract minerals from crustal rock, as distinct from ore deposits, would require prohibitive quantities of energy, for example, ten to a thousand times that required for the poorest ores. Estimates of the quantity of minerals that have been formed into ore deposits within the top 4.6-kilometer depth of the earth's continental crust have been derived by Skinner (1987). It would be optimistic to assume that 10 percent of these ore deposits can be retrieved (ignoring ore grades and energy costs) (Trainer 1995d). If we also assume that mineral consumption will increase from now until 2060 when it will have reached the level required to provide 11 billion with present rich-world per capita amounts, by 2060 43 percent of the thirty-six most commonly used mineral items would be exhausted. In other words, unless the resource estimates are grossly mistaken, it will be impossible for all people to rise to the per capita levels of mineral-resource consumption rich countries have now.

Food

It takes about 2 hectares (about 5 acres) to provide the diet for one person in a rich country (Rees 1992, 125). To provide such a diet for the 11 billion people likely to live on earth in 2060 would therefore require 22 billion hectares. However, there are only 13 billion hectares on the planet, and all available cropland in use is not likely to exceed 1.5 billion hectares. Obviously, it would not be possible for all *the present* world population of 5.5 billion to have rich world diets, let alone all the people soon likely to live on earth.

Biological Resources

The annual American per capita consumption of wood requires 1.3 hectares of forest (Pimentel et al. 1994, 369, 371). For 11 billion people, 14.3 billion hectares of forest would be required, which is 3.5 times total world forested land area.

Biological resources are more scarce than minerals or energy. The rich-world per capita consumption of most resources is fifteen to twenty times that averaged by the poorest half of the world's people. If all people expected late next century were to use timber, water, and other biologic resources at the rate people in rich countries do today, world annual production of these resources would be about ten times what it is today. Most biological resources would be exhausted in a few decades at most.

The Net Biological Productivity of the Planet

About 40 percent of all the biological production of the planet's land mass, that is, 40 percent of all plant and animal growth, is ultimately harvested by humans (Daly and Cobb 1989, 143). This figure includes the timber we take, the fields our animals graze, all crop and orchard lands, and so on. Yet, world population is likely to double. One species out of the possibly 30 million on the planet will not likely be able to gear 80 percent of the planet's land biological productivity to its purposes. Remember that if by 2060 all Third World people were to become as affluent as people in rich countries are now, annual demand on resources would be ten times what it is now, hence limits to growth. Theorists agree with Korten's general conclusion that "sustained economic growth is not possible because human economic activity already fills the available ecological space" (Korten 1990, 97).

The Environment

The way of life taken for granted in rich countries has damaging impact on the environment. Large quantities of resources are taken from the environment and dumped back into it as waste. The average American consumes twenty tons of new materials every year (U.S. Bureau of Mines 1985). The limits-to-growth position is that the environmental problem will not be solved until we move to ways of life that enable us to greatly reduce such figures. Those ways must involve far less production and consumption than we average now.

This point is clearly made with respect to the greenhouse problem. The Inter-governmental Panel on Climate Change (1990) concluded that to prevent the carbon content of the atmosphere from increasing any further, fossil fuel use must be *reduced by 60 to 80 percent.* (Brown 1991 p. 24). If it were cut by 60 percent and shared equally among 11 billion people, each person in a rich country would receive *only one-eighteenth* of the amount each uses now. In other words, enormous reductions in resource use and environmental impact must be confronted, and the basic implication of the limits-to-growth argument is that these reductions will not be achieved without radical change in life-styles and systems.

Possibly the most disturbing element in the limits-to-growth case is that several indexes of global agricultural and biological productivity that have grown rapidly in recent decades have tapered to plateau or declined in the 1980s. This is true for world meat production, irrigated land area, fertilizer use, fish production, grain land, and grain production. Grain production rose at about 3 percent per annum between 1950 and 1980, but in the 1980s averaged only 1 percent per annum growth. The total area of land for agriculture is not likely to increase. As new (and more costly) land is being brought into use, much the same area of productive land is lost through erosion and other forces. World fish catch has fallen below the level of the early

1980s. It appears, therefore, that after hundreds of years of constantly increasing production, we are in a decade when many crucial biological limits are being reached. The World Watch Institute concludes, "The earth's biological productivity is shrinking" (Brown 1990, 7).

The present levels of global output and consumption are inflicting unsustainable damage on the planet and they appear to be approaching limits; yet, high living standards are being provided for only 1 billion people and eleven times as many will probably have to be provided for soon. Similarly, if 3 percent per annum growth in world economic output is averaged until 2060, world output would be eight times present levels and would double every twenty-three years after that. Such multiples would not be achievable if we were already approaching limits for agricultural production.

Energy

If the most common estimates of potentially recoverable resources of oil, gas, coal, shale oil, and uranium are taken, and it is assumed that 11 billion people were to use energy at the per capita rate of people in the rich countries today, all these energy resources would be exhausted in about forty years (Trainer 1985, chapter 4; Trainer 1995a, chapter 8). This projection ignores the greenhouse problem, which implies that most of the remaining quantities of all of these sources except uranium should not be used.

It is very unlikely that present levels of world energy consumption can be maintained with nuclear or renewable energy sources. A world in which 11 billion people have present rich-world energy use per capita would require about 250,000 giant reactors—about a thousand times present capacity. Nuclear fusion is at best many decades away, and owing to the scarcity of lithium, the most likely process has potential similarly limited to that of fossil fuels. Therefore, for perhaps a century the reactors would have to be mostly "breeders," meaning about 1 million metric tons of plutonium constantly in use or being moved from reactors to reprocessing plants, and one worn-out reactor buried every hour, to say nothing of waste or accident problems (Trainer 1985, chapter 5; Trainer 1995a, chapter 8).

Solar, wind, and other renewable energy sources must eventually be the forms on which we entirely rely, but it is not plausible that they could sustain the present liquid fuel or electricity demand of the rich countries. (The reasons are detailed in Trainer 1995a, chapter 8; 1995c.)

The impressive figures now being published for solar and wind energy costs come from the world's few best sites of experimental projects. They do not take into account the huge losses that would be involved in the storage and transport of electrical energy from sunny regions to high latitudes where most rich-world people live. If photovoltaic cells producing hydrogen are used to do this, about 96 percent of the energy harvested is lost by the time electricity is delivered, because of the inefficiencies of conversion, storage, and transport. Plant construction and fuel costs for a plant to deliver a thousand megawatts would be near $65 billion (assuming $500 per meter total installed system cost, and 20 percent efficient cells). This is some thirty-three times the cost for a coal-fired plant, even ignoring all the other costs, such as for operation and maintenance, company profits, insurance, and the interest payments on borrowed capital. Interest costs would probably double or treble the construction cost. The best choice might be thermochemical, or hot rock, energy storage and transmission by long-distance high voltage lines. This choice might cut the construction cost to $26 billion, but formidable problems would have to be solved, such as how to store vast quantities of gas or heat. An industrialized society could not survive the at least twentyfold multiple of present electricity costs that would seem to be involved.

Wind energy will also contribute to a sustainable world economy, but is not likely to support present electric demand. Only 0.6 percent of the United States is suitable for efficient wind generation of electricity, although this area might produce electricity equal to 20 percent of present demand, ignoring the storage problem (Elliott, Wendel, and Gower 1991). Europe (except for the United Kingdom) has poorer wind resources than the United States. Even in the United Kingdom, wind might at best meet less than 10 percent of electric demand (Department of Trade and Industry [U.K.] 1993, 2). The main problem with wind energy is that even in a good region, there is a good probability that all mills will be idle at the same time. This probability is generally taken to limit the contribution of wind to a system to 5 to 20 percent of demand.

There is too little land to fuel present world road transport by biomass, let alone a fleet ten times as large, which is what we would need if 11 billion people had as much transport per person as we in rich countries have now.

These have been some of the main reasons for not accepting the common assumption that affluent industrial societies can be sustained simply by switching from fossil fuels to renewables. (Again, for detailed argument see Trainer 1995c.)

In view of these considerations regarding crucial mineral, biological, and energy resources, it is difficult to escape the conclusion that it *will be impossible for all people to rise to the life-styles people in rich countries have today.* These life-styles exist essentially because the rich countries are consuming 75 to 80 percent of world-resource output. The main implication has been appropriately summarized by the statement that "the rich must live more simply so that the poor may simply live." In other words, if the limits-to-growth argument is basically valid, rich countries should face up to major reduction in their average per capita use of resources.

Limitless Growth Is the Supreme Goal

The limits-to-growth argument is that *present* levels of production, consumption, and resource use in rich countries are unsustainable. Yet, the fundamental and unquestioned goal of almost all economists, politicians, journalists, and ordinary people is to increase "material living standards,"—per capita consumption and the GNP—as much as possible and without limit.

Growth advocates are unconcerned about the multiples of present output that their commitment will soon lead to. If output grows at 3 percent per annum, then in seventy years the economy will be producing eight times as much every year. For a 5 percent growth rate, the multiple is thirty-two. In the 1980s Australia averaged 3.2 percent per annum economic growth. This average was clearly insufficient for economic health, because virtually all economic problems became more serious. Let us then assume that 4 percent growth would be sufficient to make our economy healthy. (Prime Minister Keating has said at least 4 percent growth is required to start bringing unemployment down.) If there is 4 percent per annum growth in an economy, in seventy years it will be producing sixteen times as much each year as it does now. If we assume that by 2060 all the world's people will have risen to the living standards we in rich countries would have by then, total world economic output would be 220 times what it is today.

Even if we assume that the rich countries will have 3 percent per annum growth to 2060 while the Third World rises to the present rich-world living standard, total world economic output would be twenty times as great as it is now.

These multiples are absurdly impossible. Yet, this is the path current social and economic policies commit us to. There are strong grounds for concluding that *present* levels of resource use and environmental impact are totally unsustainable, yet we have an economic system that will seek to multiply them many times in coming decades. It is difficult to understand the mental processes that enable all mainstream economists and politicians to proceed as if there were no need whatsoever even to consider possible limits to growth.

The Third World

The foregoing argument has been about the limits that exist to growth. We must also face up to the claim that pursuing growth is *causing* the major global problems facing us. This claim is most evident when Third World "development" is analyzed (Trainer 1989, 1995a).

Development has been conceived of primarily in doing what will stimulate the maximum increase in GNP, that is, stimulating as much business activity, sales, exports, investment, and so on, as possible. This "growth and trickle down" approach has failed to solve the problems of most Third World people. The real living conditions of the poorest one-third of the world's people have deteriorated over the past decade. Possibly a billion people have an insufficient diet. Hundreds of millions are constantly hungry. Perhaps 2 billion do not have safe drinking water. Third World debt has risen to impossible levels. More than thirty-five thousand infants die every day from avoidable causes.

The basic reason for the failure of conventional development theory and practice is the unequal distributions of wealth and resources that inevitably result when market forces and growth are the guiding principles. If increasing sales and business turnover is one's development goal, one will facilitate the flow of resources to those who can pay most for them and into those investments likely to generate most sales and income. The result will be that the relatively rich take most of the scarce oil and other resources for sale while poorer people must do without them. Hence, rich-world people average seventeen times the energy consumption averaged by the poorest half of the world's people, and one-third of all world grain production is fed to animals in rich countries (World Bank 1990, Trainer 1989).

Why do these appallingly unjust distributions occur? The answer is simple. The rich countries take most of the world's resource output simply by bidding more for it in the global marketplace. They also take many of the things produced by Third World land, labor, and capital (including the coffee, tea, and cocoa produce on 16 million hectares of Third World land). Many plantation and mine workers are hungry, while we enjoy the luxuries they produce. The appalling distribution and deprivation are therefore direct consequences of the way the global market economy functions. A market will always enable the relatively rich to take what they want and thus deprive those in most need.

The development that takes place will also be inappropriate to the needs of most people, because returns on investment are not maximized by investing in the production of cheap goods for poor people. More important, the resources the poor once had will be drawn into producing items for export. Possibly the worst illustrations of this are the millions of hectares of the best Third World land now growing crops to export to the rich countries while some of the world's most impoverished people work in those plantations.

There is therefore a contradiction between developing things that are most urgently needed and developing what will most maximize returns to investors and add most to the GNP. The most appropriate development strategies would reduce the GNP, for example, by taking land out of export cropping and enabling people to plant it with Permaculture "edible landscapes," a system of agriculture emphasizing the use of renewable resources, to supply themselves with food and materials outside the cash economy.

Living standards in rich countries could not be anywhere near as high as they are if the global economy were more just; it delivers most of the world's wealth to us while it ignores the poor. What would your coffee cost if those producing it were paid decent wages? The rich countries often support brutal dictatorships willing to keep their economies to the policies that benefit the rich countries. When any move has been made by poor people in the Western sphere of influence to an approach to development that would primarily benefit the poor, we have branded it as communist subversion and sent military aid to stamp it out.

Above all, the limits-to-growth analysis makes clear that the conventional conception of development is totally mistaken about goals. It is not possible for all Third World people to rise to the living standards of the rich countries. Yet, that goal is still taken for granted in almost all official development theory and practice.

Peace and Conflict

Some of the most disturbing implications of the limits-to-growth analysis of the global situation arise regarding the problems of peace and conflict. The foregoing argument has been that only a few can have the life-styles that we in rich countries have, and we can have them only for a historically short period, because there are not enough resources for all to rise to anything like the living standards we take for granted. But we who have per capita incomes averaging sixty times those of the poorest half of the world's people are obsessed with getting richer as fast as possible and without end. Now, if we and all others continue to pursue that goal, as population doubles, and resources become scarcer, there can be no other conceivable outcome than increasing levels of conflict in the world.

Much of the foregoing argument has been that we have an empire, a sphere of influence, without which our living standards could not be as high as they are. We have to be extensively involved in military activity to secure our lines of supply from the empire. We could not be sure of getting all that oil from the Middle East if we did not have aircraft carriers in the Mediterranean, rapid deployment forces specially trained and ready to fly into trouble spots, minesweepers able to clear vital shipping lanes, the military presence that stands as a warning to others that they had better not interfere with "our" oil fields, and the contingency plans for dealing with any rebel tribesmen or any sectional uprising that might cut the pipelines. We must be able to protect our allies, interests, trading arrangements, and clients.

United States Army Gen. M. D. Taylor said that "U.S. military priorities must be shifted . . . towards insuring a steady flow of resources from the Third World." He referred to "a fierce competition among industrial powers for the same raw materials markets sought by the United States" and "growing hostility displayed by have-not nations towards their affluent counterparts" (Cypher 1981). Speaking to American soldiers at Camp Stanly, Korea, President Johnson said, "Don't forget, there are two hundred million of us in a world of three billion. They want what we've got—and we're not going to give it to them!" Ashley says that "expansion is a prime source of conflict. War is mainly explicable in terms of differential growth in a world of scarce and unevenly distributed resources" (1980, 3, 126). Nettleship makes the same point: "War is an inevitable result of the struggle between economies for expansion" (1975, 497). Chase-Dunn says that "warfare appears as a normal and periodic form of competition within the capitalist world economy. . . . World wars regularly occur during a period of economic expansion" (1989, 108, 163).

In other words, the main source of conflict and war in the world is the ceaseless quest for greater wealth and power. We have no chance of achieving a peaceful world until nations stop being greedy and work out how to live without constantly striving to grow richer. Yet, the supreme commitment in our economy is to rapid and ceaseless growth!

The Basic Problem: The Economy

There can be no solution to the problems outlined above within an economy driven by the profit motive, market forces, capital accumulation, and economic growth (Trainer 1995b). The problems are being generated by these factors, most obviously by the obsession with constantly increasing production and consumption in a world with finite and scarce resources. (Nevertheless, a satisfactory economy could have an important place for market forces and free enterprise; see below.) If the limits-to-growth analyses are at all valid, it is clear that not only must we eventually arrive at a zero-growth or steady-state economy but also we in rich countries must first undergo a long period of negative growth in which per capita production and consumption measured in cash must be drastically reduced.

The second major fault built into the foundations of this economy is the very mechanism its advocates are most proud of: the market. As has been explained, the more freedom that is given individuals to maximize their profits in a market, the more effectively will resources flow to those who are richest, and the more surely will there be development of the industries that produce for the rich. More importantly, the more scope that is given the market to determine what is done, the less influence will be exercised by considerations of morality, social benefit, or ecological sustainability. A glance at the Third World problem or the situation in rich-world urban ghettos or the ecological problem shows that all too often the right policies require action *contrary* to market forces. It requires action that free enterprise will not take because it would not maximize profits and it would either require increased government expenditure and therefore taxation, or the return of control to local people so that they could collectively develop solutions to their problems largely outside the cash economy.

It is difficult to understand why faith in growth and the freedom of enterprise remains almost unchallenged despite its extraordinarily bad record of achievement. Consider the fact that although Australia's GDP per capita in real terms has more than doubled since 1950, and increased by one-third in the 1980s, in the 1980s various indexes show that inequality increased 25 percent, poverty increased 70 percent, the unemployment rate almost doubled, the rural debt multiplied by nine, and the foreign debt multiplied by ten (Trainer 1995b, chapter 4)! The picture would be worse if we could add numerical indexes for environmental quality and the quality of life. For instance, the Australian rate of youth suicide has doubled in a generation and problems of stress anxiety and depression are reported to be ten times as prevalent as they were a generation ago. Extensive evidence indicates that as GNP per person has more than doubled in rich countries in recent decades, measures of the quality of life have not increased or have fallen. Easterlin came to this conclusion after reviewing more than thirty studies (1976). Daly and Cobb's detailed Measure of Sustainable Economic Welfare in the United States declined for two decades despite continued economic growth (Daly and Cobb 1989, 420). Douthwaite's *The Growth Illusion* (1992) deals at length with evidence and argument supporting his claim that growth has not been accompanied by improvement in the experienced quality of life.

It requires little sociological insight to understand how the obsession with narrow economic goals has contributed to social breakdown. To facilitate the maximum rate of increase in economic activity, resources have been predominantly allocated, not to helping the most disadvantaged and needy, nor to developing the facilities most likely to build cohesive and supportive communities, but to enabling more goods and services to be marketed profitably. All impediments to this end, set by social structures, customs, or traditions, must be removed. Hence, the accelerated atrophy of community and the elimination of the informal and noneconomic factors that once supported people, plunging everyone further into an individualistic competitive struggle in an economy that will not provide for all. It is no surprise therefore that the social wreckage of homelessness, suicide, and violence rises higher and higher. These are direct consequences of making growth the supreme goal, and of refusing to challenge the trickle-down myth claiming that growth, the profit motive, and the freedom of enterprise are the best principles for enriching all in the long run.

Possibly most disturbing are the effects of the economy on bonding, mutual concern, civility, social responsibility, and citizenship. A satisfactory society is not possible unless its members have a good degree of concern for the welfare of others and of the society as a whole. Yet, our economy is founded on the principle that the best outcomes for all will follow if all individuals seek to maximize their individual advantage and wealth.

Economic theory is largely responsible for the predicament we are in (Trainer 1995b, chapter 11). It pretends to be the theory of economics in general, but it is only the theory of capitalist economics; that is, it is only about the form and functioning of the production, distribution, and exchange mechanisms evident within an economy where the overriding goal is to maximize production for sale and freedom of enterprise. This theory can say nothing whatsoever about the perhaps half of the real economy, which does not involve cash: the household sector. Many other realms of value are crucial for production and distribution decisions that have little or nothing to do with cash value, such as morality, justice, quality of life, work experience, personal growth, culture and tradition, community, and, above all, ecological values. Yet, in the past twenty years we have entered an era in which all considerations other than the maximization of cash benefits are being deliberately and energetically swept aside. Public assets are being sold off, protection is being eliminated, the last remote areas of the Third World are being drawn into the market system, all barriers to "trade" (that is, impediments to the access of transnational corporations to new resources and markets and profitable business opportunities) are being removed—all in a desperate effort to "get the economy going again." The conventional economist knows no other solution to problems of recession and unemployment than to facilitate more business turnover, regardless of how great the volume of unnecessary and wasteful production might already be.

Since the 1970s the global economy has entered a period of serious crisis that is essentially due to the inability to sell all that can be produced. This crisis has generated a frantic effort to find profitable investment outlets for all the capital that is constantly accumulating (in the United States the amount available for investment per capita is estimated to double each twenty years [U.S. Bureau of Mines, 1985, 6]. This effort explains the "casino capitalism" evident in speculation on commodities, takeovers, stock markets, and foreign exchange dealings, where more than 90 percent of the deals are gambles on changes in exchange rates. It also explains the radical global restructuring that is going on, especially the privatization and elimination of arrangements that once protected people, regions, industries, and nations from the ravages of market forces. Hence, the new orthodoxy enforced by supranational agencies such as the World Bank through the General Agreement on Tariffs and Trade and now the World Trade Organization, which prevent governments from taking action against patently unjust, environmentally destructive, or socially damaging practices, on the grounds that there must be no interference with the freedom of trade. Why do governments go along with these policies, which literally entail the destruction of their societies and the further impoverishment of their poorest people? Because they have learned their orthodox economics well; they know that the supreme goal and the only conceivable solution to our problems is to generate more business turnover, more production for sale, more growth.

It should be obvious that even if there were no limits-to-growth problems, this economic system cannot solve the problems it now generates at an accelerating rate. It provides well for perhaps only 10 percent of the world's people, that is, the richest half of those who live in the rich countries. It is dumping more and more of the people in those countries into poverty and a poor quality of life. And it has been rapidly burning up its resource and ecological capital; from here on, those bills will start flooding in. The recent emergence of much critical literature and many alternative economics organizations, such as the New Economics Foundation and the Human Economy Network, testify to the increasing recognition that a radically different economic system is required.

The Form a Sustainable Society Must Take

If the limits-to-growth analysis of our global predicament is valid, there are four crucial and inescapable implications for the nature of a sustainable society: (1) it must have materially simple life-styles; (2) there must be a very high level of local economic self-sufficiency; most of the things people need must be produced by local labor, land, expertise, and capital; (3) there must be much more cooperation and much less competition than there is in present society; and (4) above all, there must be no economic growth; it must be a steady-state economy. These principles mean fundamental change in life-styles, in the geography of settlements (that is, we must mostly build villages), and in the economy. Some elaboration on these key themes follows. (For a detailed account see Trainer 1995a.)

Simple Life-styles

Living simply does not mean being deprived of anything that matters. It means being content with what is *sufficient*—for example, sufficient for comfort and hygiene. Often the difference between a sufficient and a normal standard in consumer society is great. For example, normal housing typically costs ten to twenty times as much as perfectly adequate and aesthetically pleasing housing built from mud brick (Trainer 1995a, chapter 4).

Self-Sufficiency

Most crucial for the development of sustainable settlements is the need for small-scale local economies that are highly self-sufficient. First, households could produce much more for themselves than they do at present, through home gardening, knitting, bottling and preserving, sewing, construction, and homemade entertainment. Second, there must be far less transport and trade.

However, it is the town, suburban, and neighborhood levels that are most important here. These must become thriving local economies, producing many of the things people need for a high quality of life from resources that exist locally. This means much decentralization, with many small places of employment, enabling most people to get to work on foot or by bicycle. Some of these enterprises could be the usual types, such as bakeries, but many could function as part-time hobby production. It would make sense to retain some big mass production factories, but many of the things we need could come from small local craft production, thus minimizing factory work.

Many market gardens could be located throughout suburbs within cities, for example, on derelict factory sites and beside railway lines. This would reduce the cost of food by 70 percent, especially by cutting its transport costs. More important, having food produced close to where people live would enable nutrients to be recycled back to the soil through garbage-gas units. Two of the most unsustainable aspects of our present agriculture are its heavy dependence on energy inputs and the fact that it extracts nutrients from the soil and does not return them.

Houses on each block could become a neighborhood workshop, recycling store, meeting place, barter exchange, and library. We could dig up many roads, thereby increasing urban land area by one-third or more, because there will be far less need for them when we reduce production and decentralize. When we have dug up those roads, we will have much communal property, so we can plant community orchards and forests and put in community ponds for ducks and fish. Most of the neighborhood could become a Permaculture jungle, an "edible landscape" crammed with long-lived, largely self-maintaining productive plants, such as nut trees.

There would also be many varieties of animals living in our suburbs, including an entire fishing industry based on tanks and ponds. Many materials can also be freely available from communal woodlots, fruit trees, bamboo clumps, ponds, and meadows. Many areas could easily supply themselves with the clay to produce all the crockery needed. Similarly, just about all the cabinetmaking wood needed could come from those forests, by means of one small saw bench in what was a garage.

There is much scope for deriving materials from plants that could be grown in our suburbs, such as bark for tanning. Dyes from plants, tar and resins from distilled flue gases, wool, wax, leather, feathers, paint from oil seeds like sunflowers, and many medicines are all possible. Small local businesses and hobbyists could make use of such locally produced materials.

Most all neighborhoods have all the capital they need to develop the things that would most enrich them, yet this never happens when savings are put in conventional banks. The solution is to form small town banks in which the savings of local people will be lent only to firms and projects that will improve the local region. Many neighborhoods and towns are now starting their own banks and moneyless trading systems (such as LETS).

More Cooperation, Less Competition

The third necessary characteristic of the alternative neighborhood is that it must provide a much more communal way of life. We must share more things. We could have one stepladder, one electric drill, and so on in the neighborhood workshop rather than one in every backyard. We would be on various voluntary rosters and committees and on working bees to carry out most of the child minding, nursing, basic educating, and care of aged and handicapped people, as well as perform most of the functions that councils now carry out for us, such as maintaining our parks and streets. We would therefore need far fewer bureaucrats and professionals and we would need to earn less money to pay the taxes now needed to support them. Each of us might contribute half a day a week to community work projects, such as maintaining the orchards and woodlots that provide our "free" goods.

If we lived more simply, eliminated much unnecessary production, and shifted much of the necessary production to backyards, local small businesses, cooperatives, and the noncash sector of the economy, we might need to work in an office or a mass production factory only one or two days a week. We could spend the other five or six working and playing in the neighborhood doing many varied, interesting, and useful things.

We would live in leisure-rich environments. Suburbs at present are leisure deserts. The alternative neighborhood would be full of interesting things to do, familiar people, common projects, animals, gardens, forests, and landscaping. People would be less inclined to go away on weekends and holidays, greatly reducing national energy consumption.

Most important of all, there would be far more community than there is now. People would know one another and interact on local projects. One could certainly predict a huge decrease in social problems. It would be a much healthier and happier place to live, especially for older people.

There would be genuine participatory democracy. Most of our local policies and programs could be worked out by elected nonpaid committees, and we could all vote on the important matters concerning our small area. The kibbutz settlements in Israel are good examples of this kind of self-government. There would still be important functions of state and national governments, but relatively few.

No Economic Growth

There would be no chance of making these changes while we retained the present economic system. Market forces and the profit motive might have a place in an acceptable alternative economy, but they cannot be allowed to continue as major determinants of economic affairs. The basic economic priorities must be planned according to what is socially desirable (democratically planned, mostly at the local level, not dictated by huge and distant bureaucracies). However, much of the economy could remain as a (carefully monitored) free enterprise carried on by small firms, households, and cooperatives, using local markets, so long as their goals were not profit maximization and growth.

The new economy would have a number of overlapping sectors. One would still use cash. In another, market forces would be allowed to operate. One sector would be fully planned. Another would be run by cooperatives. Another would involve barter and gifts (that is, just giving away surpluses). In one sector there would be totally free goods (for example, from the roadside fruit and nut trees).

Most of us would live well without much need for cash incomes, because we would not need to buy very much. Consequently, we might work only one day a week for money and spend the rest of the week working and playing in our neighborhoods in a wide variety of activities. Production would be greatly reduced, as would the GNP. There would be no unemployment and no poverty (there are none in Israel's kibbutzim). We would have neighborhood work-coordination committees, who would make sure that all who wanted work had a share of the work that needed doing.

The alternative economy is being thought of as a "third way"— quite different from free enterprise and big-state socialism but combining some aspects of both within a context of decentralization and small scale, with no concern to increase production and consumption over time; indeed, the supreme goal for decades would be to reduce production and consumption throughout.

This vision does not imply any reduction in research or sophisticated technology. We could still have all the high-tech and modern ways that made sense, for example, in medicine, windmill design, public transport, and houschold appliances. We could have far more resources for science and research, and for education and the arts, because we would have liberated all the resources presently being wasted in the production of unnecessary items, including arms.

The past two decades have seen the emergence of much literature and many groups working on the general limits-to-growth analysis of the global crisis summarized above. More recently there has been the beginning of practical ventures aimed at building alternative settlements outlined. There is now a global ecovillage movement, which includes hundreds of long-established rural intentional communities and more being planned and built in the hope of becoming influential examples of sustainable settlement (in Context Inst. 1995a, chapter 17).

Many would regard the account of the required alternative society given here as naively utopian and impossible to attain. The point of this chapter has been to make clear that this is *the general form a society must take if it is to be sustainable, whether we like it or not,* and whether or not we think it is achievable. We will either make it to a society characterized by simple life-styles, cooperative arrangements, and zero economic growth and local economic self-sufficiency—or we will not achieve a sustainable society. There are persuasive reasons for concluding that we will not have the collective sense to take this path, given the gross irrationality, indifference, and irresponsibility now characteristic of affluent-consumer society.

The most important research tasks now have to do with working out how best to assist country towns and city suburbs to grasp the need for transition and to begin working on their salvation. Many country towns are dying, many people are suffering the boredom of unemployment in cities. The problem is how to develop the procedures by which the vast but idle personal, material, and financial resources can be applied to building new social and economic systems that will enable these people to provide one another with most of the things they need.

The Rocky Mountains Institute's Urban Renewal Program is an example of the pioneering action we urgently need on a large scale. A team goes into a town to work with local people on questions such as: Are residents paying money that could be reduced, for example, by insulating houses to cut fuel bills? What things are being imported that the town could set up small firms to produce? What resources, such as idle land, buildings, retired people, and sources of capital, does the town have that could be applied to development that would enrich people's lives? Can there be a market and festival day each month? Can we put some of our savings in a fund to facilitate the start-up of much-needed little firms that would give incomes to more of our people? Can we plant fast-growing woodlots to save money on heating fuel? Can we start a cooperative poultry, rabbit, and fish group to give us good fresh and cheap meat? What town developments might be carried out by weekly voluntary working bees? What leisure, entertainment, and cultural activities could we organize?

Despite the alarming magnitude of global problems and the virtually complete failure of governments, bureaucracies, mainstream economists, and journalists to attend to the limits-to-growth analysis or the radical-conserver alternative, there are now grounds for optimism. There is much literature agreeing on the form that a sustainable society must take, and for two decades small groups have been pioneering the experimental development of ecovillages. The outcome is anything but certain and immense dangers loom on all sides, but at least the general path to sustainability is now clearly evident.

6. Defining the New American Community

A Slide to Tribalism?

Virginia Abernethy

Doubters that rapid population growth drives poverty, inequality, re-source overconsumption, and polluting emissions that overwhelm nature's restorative capacity do, of course, exist. Denial lives. The blithe ones, unaware and unafraid, enjoy the free-fall from the penthouse roof—until everything changes.

All may indeed (seems likely to) change. But if a soft landing remains possible, clear sight and a long view of population pressure on resources should pay off. Former Secretary of State Warren Christopher addressed the fundamentals at a December 1994 State Department conference on population and development. "When population grows too quickly," he said, "it strains resources, it stunts economic growth, it generates disease, it spawns huge refugee flows, and ultimately it threatens [U.S.] stability" (Dickinson 1995, 1). The process that threatens is insidious: drizzles and drops. Crises may be staggered and localized; oases may remain.

Constructive strategies are within reach, but first one must recognize elements that darken the horizon. Namely, the rapid increase in the population and labor force and the associated depletion of re-sources are propelling the United States toward shrinking shares per capita and toward widening inequality between rich and poor. The economic effects of population growth are adding to fiscal imbalances, which already have burdened the American people with $5 trillion of federal debt. The feedback loops that link population growth to the nation's carrying capacity and the economy are accelerating a downward spiral.

Recognition of limits is neither new nor unique. Great Britain's 1949 Report of the Royal Commission on Population stated, "We have no hesitation in recommending . . . a replacement size of family . . . in Great Britain at the present time" (cited in Willey 1994, 3). Similarly, the 1972 report of the Presidential Commission on Population Growth and the American Future concluded that no national interest is served by continuing population growth. Addressing common economic and quality-of-life values, commission members said that ordinary Americans would be better off if population growth stopped immediately; conversely, *almost every social, economic, and environmental problem would be made worse by continuing growth* (President's Commission 1972).

Disillusionment with the American dream and fragmentation along ethnic or religious lines could precipitate a breakdown in civil society. Crime, riots, and incipient vigilantism today may escalate to worse riots, kangaroo courts, scapegoating, and separatism tomorrow. If such conditions were to occur, a government seeking to keep control might be expected to resort to unpleasantness, in violation of civil rights. Here we examine the relationship between (1) scarcity, diversity, and conflict, (2) population growth and carrying capacity, and (3) population growth and disquiet in America.

Scarcity, Diversity, and Conflict

The underlying issue in much domestic and international conflict is the incapacity of natural systems to support the resident population. Nevertheless, violent upheavals are often reported as class, ethnic, and religious conflicts because regions and societies fracture along these fault lines. Reports of political and social stresses and associated individual pathology (for example, Kleinman 1995) often inappropriately omit mention of the causal role of rapid population growth (Bouvier 1995).

Homer-Dixon, Boutwell, and Rathjens (1993) explicitly reject attempts to gloss over population/resource imbalances in the genesis of conflict. Their analysis of civil and international wars on several continents shows how resource scarcity makes direct contributions to conflict and feeds back into political and social alignments in ways that exaggerate unequal distribution of wealth. The synergistic effects of overpopulation and scarcity occur as impoverishment breeds competition; and competition turns into resource grabs where sociopolitical alignments (tribes, gangs, economic cartels, political factions) provide both the cover of legitimacy and the sheer power of numbers and organization.

Journalist R. D. Kaplan (1994) also observes that environments collapsed by the "impact of surging populations" are the frequent root cause of political chaos. As overtaxed environments fail, Kaplan expects to see "re-primitivized man: warrior societies operating at a time of unprecedented resource scarcity and planetary crowding. . . . Crime and war become indistinguishable" (73–74) and security of sorts is found only in private guards and armies. West Africa may be "*the* symbol of worldwide demographic, environmental, and societal stress, in which criminal anarchy emerges as the real 'strategic' danger" (46). However, collapsing or invaded nations on every continent are potentially threatened by sociopolitical disintegration, refugee migrations across international borders, ethnic mixing, and loss of a cultural center.

Milton Esman (1994) focuses on the risks, sources of conflict or accommodation, and likely channels of protest that accompany the presence of several minorities together or, alternately, a minority residing alongside a majority group within one territory. Permutations include whether one minority regards the shared territory as its homeland. Noel Malcolm (1995, 66) suggests that "aggressive nationalism is typically a syndrome of the dispossessed, of those who feel power has been taken from them." Kaplan finds that ethnic diversity where wealthier minority populations can be demonized spawns the most vicious conflicts.

Esman's thesis is that the presence of minorities invariably creates strain, so the implicit or explicit goal of a vigorous society is the minimization of diversity. He writes, "The classic approach to depluralization is the encouragement of individual assimilation" (255). Schwarz (1995) also argues that accommodation to diversity is a false political myth and that until recently, and although more slowly with African-Americans, diversity in America has been systematically erased through assimilation. An example (see Kaplan 1994, 75–76) is Saul Bellow's description of his immigrant family in turn-of-the-century Chicago: "The country took us over. It *was* a country then, not a collection of cultures." An expanding economic pie makes assimilation easier because competition is muted.

Failing assimilation, conflict-management strategies depend on the strength of the state that mediates between parties. But, as Kaplan and Esman both point out, a state is fatally weakened by environmental collapse. The legitimacy of a state is further affected by whether minority or majority interests are in control. Schwarz (1995) suggests that unicultural dominance is a precondition of national stability; that is, claims made by diverse elements in a society cannot be resolved by "reasonable" divisions of resources and power, because minorities are seldom satisfied by distributions that do not entail significant (therefore unacceptable) losses to the dominant group.

Diversity becomes problematic if a nation's institutions allow, even encourage, the mobilization of minorities by "ethnic entrepreneurs" (Esman 1994, 245). Illustratively, the judicial construction of "affirmative action" in the United States has created resentment on all sides. Affirmative action programs—now widely viewed as a perversion of an ostensibly race-neutral civil rights policy—are being rejected in proposals and ballot initiatives to affirm the language of the 1964 Civil Rights Law, which forbids discrimination on the basis of race, creed, or ethnicity. Dismantling affirmative action exacerbates grievances in sectors that acquired a sense of entitlement and now stand to lose (Roberts and Stratton 1995).

Esman warns that diversity is intrinsically antagonistic to democracy, because "where the state loses control of ethnic relations, the result is likely to be protracted violence and civil war, as in Bosnia, Sri Lanka, and Sudan" (255). Containing violence among ethnic groups tends to entail increasingly authoritarian state measures. An embattled state will prefer an unarmed citizenry; but individuals and groups rightly fear losing the capability of self-defense, needed if the state were (1) unable to keep order or (2) captured by a hostile faction.

The United States, which sometimes defines itself as a "nation of immigrants," at first appears as a contrary example to Esman's principal themes. Yet diminished shares and a diversifying national profile complicate unity and democracy. Alexis de Toqueville observed that the roots of American liberty are planted in the natural wealth of our continent: "The chief circumstance which has favored the establishment and maintenance of a democratic system in the United States is the nature of the territory that the Americans inhabit. Their ancestors gave them a love of equality and freedom; but God Himself gave them the means of remaining equal and free by placing them upon a boundless continent" (cited in Potter 1954, 92).

Indeed, American history is congruent with the Esman-Kaplan-Schwarz analysis. Recent multiethnic riots in Los Angeles—where, significantly, some businesses escaped being burned out because owners (mostly Korean) engaged in self-defense—involved newly arrived immigrant groups who compete with citizens for jobs, housing, and education (Miles 1992). Esman's observation that authoritarianism becomes indispensable to control of ethnic relations foreshadows the use of police and national guard to quell the Los Angeles disturbances, gun control legislation, and questionable, it is claimed, violent activities against citizens by law enforcement agencies (the FBI and Bureau of Alcohol, Tobacco, and Firearms [BATF]). Law-abiding citizens have reason to fear both injury from extremists and loss of constitutionally guaranteed liberties as, once empowered, authoritarian institutions expand their mission.

In the slide to social disintegration, states Kaplan, democracy becomes "less and less relevant to the larger issue of governability. . . . [I]t is not clear that the United States will survive the next century in exactly its present form. Because America is a multiethnic society, the nation-state has always been more fragile here than it is in more homogeneous societies. . . . " (Kaplan 1994, 75–76).

Liberty, tolerance, and democracy are fragile. Civil virtues may not survive population growth and shrinkage of the ordinary person's portion. But unwanted trade-offs between liberty and order can be resisted. Much of the population growth results from immigration, a de facto population policy that, to many Americans, appears arbitrary and unnecessary.

Population Growth and Carrying Capacity

Carrying capacity refers to the number of individuals who can be supported without degrading the environment, that is, without reducing the ability of the environment to sustain the population at the desired quality of life over the long term. A degraded environment produces less. Exceeding the carrying capacity today reduces tomorrow's productivity, so that smaller and smaller numbers can be supported without further damage (Arrow et al. 1995). Population growth combined with the high consumption levels to which all Americans and immigrants aspire is the ultimate threat to carrying capacity—the topsoil, forests, energy, clean air and water, and other resources—of our national home.

One cannot predict which of several factors will ultimately become limiting, because technological and market adjustments alter pressure points in the system. David Pimentel and others (1995) show, for example, that topsoil is being eroded fifteen to thirty times faster than its natural formation rate and that 3 million acres annually are being paved over or made useless for agriculture. No known technology creates or substitutes for topsoil, although its loss is temporarily masked by petroleum-intensive technology. If present trends continue, arable land will shrink from the 1.8 acres per person now available in the United States to only 0.6 acres per person by 2050 (but 1.2 acres per person is needed to provide a diverse diet).

Similarly, major aquifers are being depleted 25 percent faster than their replenishment rate. Transport of water from ever-more distant sources and desalination are energy-intensive and expensive. Competition between urban and agricultural users of water is intensifying and, foreseeably, water-short areas (much of the U.S. West) will cease to be agricultural.

Agriculture accounts for 17 percent of U.S. petrochemical use. Domestic oil is expected to be effectively gone in twenty-five years (meaning that the energy recovered will be less than the energy used to get, refine, and distribute the oil). Some uses for oil have no substitute (Gever, Kaufmann, Skole, and Vorosmarty 1986).

Already 60 percent of oil is imported. Reliance on foreign sources could greatly impact food production, domestic food prices, the $40 billion per year income from agricultural exports, and policy options vis-à-vis oil-producing nations, including Russia, Iran, Iraq, Egypt, Libya, Kuwait, and Saudi Arabia.

Demography explains America's insatiable thirst for oil and energy. Nearly all (93 pecent) of a 25 percent increase in energy use between 1970 and 1990 was driven by population growth. That is, consumption per capita leveled off, but increased efficiency and conservation efforts were, and continue to be, overwhelmed by growing numbers (Holdren 1990).

Population growth is also endangering whole U.S. ecosystems. Thirty systems have declined over 98 percent of their natural area, imperiling habitat for countless animal and plant species (Stevens 1995). Five hundred species have vanished already as humans encroach on habitat (Ling-Ling 1995). The 40 percent loss of Staten Island's original species is attributed to population growth. Man and Biosphere (MAB) reserves in New Jersey, the outer islands of the Chesapeake Bay, and southern Florida are similarly at risk. The critical shift is from agricultural to more intensive uses of land as population density increases (Long 1995).

Losses in biodiversity have economic as well as moral and esthetic implications. Biodiversity contributes in uncounted ways to productivity and income, for example, honeybees pollinate billions of dollars worth of crops and we have no substitute! Unseen microorganisms restore (albeit over decades or even centuries) eroded topsoil; theirs is an essential contribution because "about 10% of all the energy [all types] used in U.S. agriculture today is spent just to offset the losses of nutrients, water, and crop productivity caused by erosion" (Pimentel et al. 1995, 1120).

Other factors (deforestation, pollutants, infrastructure, traffic congestion) could be chosen to illustrate carrying-capacity limits. Resources are being depleted even at the present rate of use; more people demand more resources; in using them, people create more pollution. Some systems have no substitute and, once used up or degraded, the loss is irretrievable. Other systems are remediable but at a cost, for example, $25 billion is the estimated annual cost of implementing the Clean Air Act. Such programs compete with other economic and fiscal uses for money.

Population Growth and Disquiet in America

As a country grows poorer in natural capital, the hardship that citizens endure depends on the population growth rate, the distribution of wealth, and economic competitiveness.

The United States has the fastest population growth rate in the industrialized world. At more than 1.1 percent per year, the U.S. rate approaches that of some Third World countries and puts the population on track to double in less than sixty years. Every increase yields a less favorable natural resource/per capita ratio than enjoyed today. Yet, few alarms have been sounded over the no-end-to-growth-in-sight scenario (Stycos 1995).

Historically, the U.S. Census Bureau's projections have been too low. Their series were revised upward in 1989, 1990, and 1992, because assumptions about immigrant numbers and subsequent fertility had to be raised. A 1995 series escaped upward revision by altering assumptions about departures from the United States each year. Moreover, asylum claimants (those in the United States but not yet processed by the Immigrant and Naturalization Service [INS]), estimated at 150,000 per year, are overlooked; this omission resulted in a greater than 10 percent underestimate of immigration in the 1995 Report of the U.S. Commission on Immigration Reform.

A population of one-half billion was "the most likely" variant projected for the United States in the year 2050 by demographers Ahlburg and Vaupel (1990). Their number might now be raised in contemplation of high immigrant fertility, an increased annual flow of legal immigrants (to 1 million including refugees and asylees), and the conservatively estimated net 300,000 illegal immigrants including the many who overstay visas (aircraft passenger manifests show several hundred thousand more persons arriving than leaving each year) (Grant 1992).

The distribution of wealth is second in importance for determining national well-being. How is the manmade and (inherently limited) natural wealth divided up?

The question is fraught with political ideology, but what is desirable ought not be confounded with what seems likely. Historical and contemporary societies, and principles of market economics, suggest that distributional equity is incompatible with shrinking resources per capita. Government can alter for a time the identity of "winners," but equality of results is probably not—nor ever has been—achievable. As an anthropologist, I conclude that every society that experiences population growth without commensurate growth in resources arrives at an advanced state of social stratification. The late Mayans and Aztecs preyed upon their neighbors and developed elaborate class systems of nobles, religious functionaries, military leaders, and commoners. The Incas had the same, with the probable added features of vassalage and slavery. Neolithic peoples in Great Britain evolved from egalitarian to stratified social structures as their communities became more densely populated. Stratification became prominent in both India (Davis 1951) and Algeria (Baer 1964) about the time that these societies became more crowded (Abernethy 1979). Women became chattel property in Europe's overpopulated late Middle Ages. The overpopulated New Guinea Enga victimized women, unlike neighbors with a generous land-to-people ratio. So it goes through the ancient and modern world. The gap between privileged and powerless appears to enlarge as overpopulation and poverty become more profound.

Growth in the labor force is one mechanism by which population growth widens the gulf between rich and poor. Labor is a commodity with respect to production. Thus, a large supply of labor relative to demand (availability of jobs) drives down the price (wage) that employers are willing to pay. The larger the supply of labor, the more that the compensation for labor falls.

Ronald Lee documents the inverse relationship between population size and wages. Time series for western Europe beginning in A.D. 1260, show how "a 10 percent increase in population relative to its long-run trend . . . depressed wages by 16 percent" (Lee 1987, 448). Individual countries were characterized by 25 percent (Austria), 24 percent (Germany and Spain), and 22 percent (France) declines in wages in response to 10 percent surges in the labor force. The population effect on working persons in preindustrial England was equally dramatic: "[R]eckoning in terms of agricultural goods, a 10% increase in population depressed wages by 22% and lowered labor's share of national income by 14%" (Lee 1980, 547). Emphasizing that "population-induced changes in the preindustrial [English] economy were not trivial," Lee adds that "the segment of society dependent primarily on wage income was comfortably off at the end of the fifteenth century; [but] after a century of population growth their wages had fallen by 60% and their situation was desperate" (Lee 1980, 519).

The population effect on wages is predictable regardless of the source of growth. Claudia Goldin examines the 1897–1917 period during which 17 million Europeans immigrated to the United States. Men's clothing and foundries preferentially employed foreign labor, and displacement of less-skilled workers of the native-born population caused ripple effects so that across industries, states Goldin, "a 1 percentage point increase in the fraction of a city's population that was foreign born decreased wages by about 1.5 to 3 percent" (1993, 21–22).

Effects were probably more far-reaching than Goldin imagines, because the large labor supply stifled internal migration toward new industrial jobs. In his well-remembered "Put Down Your Buckets Where You Are" speech at the 1895 Atlanta Exposition, Booker T. Washington pleaded for an end to immigration because it contributed to continuing underemployment in rural and small-town America. Indeed, African-Americans began to take advantage of industrial job opportunities in the north only after immigration was effectively ended in the early 1920s (Morris 1990; Briggs 1992).

Current U.S. data again show deterioration in both wages and the conditions of work (Bernstein 1994; Mishel and Bernstein 1995). Real wages stagnated for up to 80 percent of the population beginning in the early 1970s, a period coincident with a one-time surge from women and the baby-boom generation bursting simultaneously onto the labor market. Continuing growth in the supply of workers is driven by immigration. About three-quarters of immigrants enter the labor force, nearly doubling the annual demand for net new jobs. Underemployment (the unemployed plus involuntarily part-time workers) rose from 9.8 percent of the labor force in 1989 to 12.6 percent in 1993 (Morris 1995), and is an obstacle to the absorption of a probable 10 million discouraged workers, the many welfare recipients whose benefits may end, and the 900,000 a year more young Americans entering than older workers leaving the labor force.

By 1990 immigrants were 10 percent of the total U.S. labor force and a quarter of all workers without a high school diploma. Vernon Briggs, Jr. (1990) testified before the Congressional Judiciary Subcommittee on Immigration, Refugees, and International Law that immigration victimizes the lower end of the U.S. labor pool, including both citizens and established, earlier immigrants whose labor force characteristics resemble those of newcomers. Frank Morris (1990), dean of graduate studies at Morgan State University (Baltimore), testified in the same hearings that "the black community . . . may find that any encouraging assumptions we had about opportunities for young black workers and prospective workers have been sidetracked by hasty immigration policies. . . . It is clear that America's black population is bearing a disproportionate share of immigrants' competition for jobs, housing and social services." Richard Estrada, of the *Dallas Morning News,* concurs. "Apologists for massive immigration appear to blame the large-scale replacement of black workers by Hispanic immigrants in the hotel-cleaning industry of Los Angeles on the blacks themselves, instead of acknowledging the obvious explanation that the immigrants depressed prevailing wages and systematically squeezed thousands of citizens out of the industry" (1991, 25). Earlier immigrants also lose, even when an influx is their own ethnic group. Estrada (1990) attributes unemployment among established Hispanics to new arrivals from Mexico and elsewhere who undercut wages, that is, will work for less and with fewer benefits. He adds,

> In sum, the evidence shows that Hispanic-Americans have emerged as the greatest victims of U.S. immigration policy since 1965, instead of its greatest beneficiaries. The notion that Hispanics in this country favor more immigration, while the rest of America favors less, is a

false one that has poisoned the debate for too long. This distortion must be corrected, especially by those who explicitly claim to represent Hispanic-Americans. (1991, 28)

George Borjas and Richard Freeman (1992) attribute the deterioration in economic position of high school–educated U.S. workers to competition from immigrants and net imports of goods manufactured by unskilled labor outside of the United States. High school dropouts are still more affected: immigration and the trade imbalance together raised the 1988 effective labor supply by 28 percent for men and 31 percent for women, accounting for up to half of a ten-percentage-point decline in the wages of unskilled labor between 1970 and the late 1980s.

Recent labor market studies show further net negative impacts. Estimating that immigration accounts for as much as one-third of the 1980s relative income decline among lower-paid workers, Borjas (1995) sees it costing working Americans more than $133 billion annually in job opportunities, depressed wages, and deteriorating conditions of work. Symmetrically, immigration puts $140 billion into the pockets of employers. The net $7 billion added to the aggregate economy comes at the cost of increasing polarization between rich and poor.

Steve H. Murdock's testimony on March 22, 1995, before the U.S. Commission on Immigration Reform also suggests that immigration adds to aggregate income but without corresponding benefit to individual American families. By 2050, states Murdock, "average per-household annual income (in 1990 dollars) would be approximately $600 lower because of immigration."

Jobs are systematically downgraded by labor competition so that the nostrum, "There are some jobs that Americans won't do," becomes a self-fulfilling prophecy. Bring in fresh Third World labor and the wage, benefit, and safety conditions to which jobs devolve attract neither native-born Americans nor established immigrants (Marshall 1995). Wages and conditions of work are competed down so that jobs in whole industries—construction, meat packing, and hotelery, for example—become less attractive. Meat packing, formerly unionized and characterized by adequate wages and working conditions, is now said to be the most dangerous job in the United States (Browne 1995). Supply and demand operating in the labor market means that "a surge in immigration guarantees that the less skilled service-sector jobs remain low paid" (Whitmore 1992, 1E).

In testimony on March 22, 1995, before the U.S. Commission on Immigration Reform, a representative of the Arizona restaurant owners association made a telling admission when asked how the industry had coped with the temporarily smaller flow of illegal alien labor after passage of the 1986 Immigration Reform and Control Act (IRCA). He replied, "We made the jobs more attractive by increasing wages, improving working conditions, and establishing promotion tracks." Queried as to how the industry might cope with new legislation that restricted immigrant labor, this same spokesman could not think of one single way.

Some newcomers are entrepreneurial (but at no higher rate than the native-born) and upgrade communities. Nevertheless, Americans may not benefit because immigrants tend to hire others of their own ethnic group, and some businesses are not new but only displace American-owned operations. In 1960 blacks owned 25 percent of the gas stations in Florida's Dade County (encompassing Miami). By 1979 black ownership had dwindled to 9 percent and Cuban ownership accounted for 48 percent of the total (Abernethy 1993).

Low-skill black and white Americans flee states that are heavily affected by immigration (Frey 1994; 1995), so data from local labor markets understate the extent to which Americans are displaced. Rejecting early econometric models that purport to show that legal and illegal immigration have little, if any, negative effect on U.S. labor, Donald Huddle asks if models and field studies that do show "significant wage depression and job displacement [are] ignored and distorted . . . treated as taboos, because immigration as a win-win situation is such a powerful myth?" (1992, 3). Huddle (1993) estimates that more than 2 million Americans unemployed in 1992 were displaced by immigrants, for a public sector cost of $11.9 billion in social safety net programs.

American skilled labor is also under pressure, particularly in fields where fluent English is not required (Coping 1994; Nelson 1994). The national security implications are not trivial (Wiarda and Wiarda 1986). Displacement of specialized professionals by immigrants who often will work for much lower wages threatens the viability of U.S. engineering schools and science departments. Is it wise for the United States to cede preeminence in mathematics, physical sciences, and engineering education?

International competitiveness, meaning the ability to sell goods and services abroad, is the final factor affecting the resource/population balance. Exports pay for natural resource imports while leaving, ideally, a balance-of-payments surplus. A positive trade balance enables countries to afford imported carrying capacity (Teo 1995). The Netherlands imports carrying capacity.

Japan, Singapore, and other so-called Asian tigers have increased competitiveness through large gains in labor productivity. Rising productivity depends, in turn, on investment in technology, equipment, and plant (McCracken 1991).

The United States, although competitive in many sectors, may be overtaken because of its slower productivity gains: 0.8 percent average annual increment compared with 2.8 percent in Japan. Neoconservatives explain the variation in productivity trends in the effect of capital gains tax rates on savings and investment (Rubenstein 1995). But the difference between the 28 percent U.S. maximum tax rate and the 20 percent Japanese rate seems insufficient to fully explain the disparate rates of capital investment.

A likely contributor to the differential is the cheapness of American labor. Continuing rapid growth in the U.S. labor force (against almost no growth in Japan) drives down the relative cost of American labor and probably encourages reliance on labor in place of investment in labor-saving technology. Preference for creating new jobs rather than investing to raise the productivity of existing workers tends to dilute the average amount of capital backing each job. This is a drag on productivity gains and, thus, on international competitiveness in the long run.

Never to be forgotten as one heads down this road is the widening gulf between rich and poor. In a democracy, the benefit of cheap labor to employers may be transient, because it fosters the rhetoric of class warfare and demagoguery. The electoral process can result in tax and regulatory policies designed to redistribute wealth; but these also stifle wealth-creating business activity (for example, Sweden) so the "remedy" is self-defeating. Amelioration of conditions by a debt-ridden government is unrealistic in the long run. No one wins as government debt grows and underemployment worsens.

Lower compensation and heavier taxation both eat at the middle class, which is the bulwark of the domestic consumer market, political stability, and democracy. Not only dissatisfaction among ordinary Americans but also pathological behavior can spread. Despair of ever joining (or remaining in) the mainstream fosters crime, riots, vigilantism, intolerance, scapegoating, and other signs of disappointment and anger. All erode civil society and generate instability.

Conclusion

Population growth underlies many of the serious environmental, economic, cultural, and political tendencies that threaten to engulf America.
Many Americans are resentful, having believed for so long that their
birthright is the opportunity for honest work that will produce a good
living.

The people are far ahead of their leaders in trying to stop population growth. Native-born Americans limit family size to 1.8 children.
(The average national rate of 2.1 reflects the significantly higher fertility of the immigrant sector.) A cross-section of Americans also affirms
that "controlling immigration [is] a very important goal" [73 percent
of public versus 28 percent of leaders]; and that "immigrants [are] a
critical threat" [74 percent of public versus 31 percent of leaders] (Rielly
1995, 6). Similarly, the 1988–90 Latino National Political Survey—
released by the Ford Foundation in December 1992, two months after
passage of legislation that raised legal immigration by 40 percent—
suggests that more than 75 percent of Mexicans and Puerto Ricans
residing in the United States agree or strongly agree that "there are too
many immigrants" (LNPS 1992).

The general public is not xenophobic in its rejection of immigration, but a growing number perceive a link between worsening conditions, population growth, and the large inflow of aliens. Two-thirds
believe that "the American Dream of equal opportunity, personal
freedom, and social mobility [have] become harder to achieve in the
past 10 years" and 74 percent expect that the struggle will intensify
in the coming decade (Rielly 1995, 8). If current trends continue,
resentment could rise sharply, redefining who is unwanted and what
is unAmerican.

Perception of being cheated out of what is commonly seen as an
American citizen's birthright will enrage many. Democracy and mutual tolerance may not survive the realization that government, the
media elite, and multinational corporations have governed in their
own interests, in disregard for the well-being of the average, loyal
citizen. The less sophisticated will sense mainly their own alienation
from society and a near-total absence of a stake in its peaceful continu-
ance. Demagogic leaders could mobilize this mass in the usual way—
scapegoating, myths, promises—and the America we honor would
become history. A descent into genocide as gangs, tribes, and factions
war over spoils seems farfetched except in the context of history.

The further tragedy would be that the sacrifice is based on self-delusion, a persistent belief that open-arms immigration policies help countries from which immigrants come. They do not help. On the contrary, holding out the promise of rescue promotes false perceptions. Believing that local limits will not apply, foreign governments and people conclude that reproductive self-discipline can be disregarded. This miscommunication is devastating because societies cannot, without limiting natural increase, bring population into balance with the carrying capacity of their environment (Abernethy 1979, 1993, 1994a, 1994b).

Stopping the momentum of population growth in the United States is daunting. Albert Bartlett and Edward Lytwak (1995) explain that attaining zero population growth immediately means that the total of deaths and emigration must equal (or be greater than) the total of births and immigration. Given the 1992 estimates for the United States of 2.2 million deaths and 0.2 million emigrants per year, the total of births and immigration should not exceed 2.4—a problem to say the least, because births alone were 4.1 million in 1992!

The array of zero-population-growth scenarios can be represented by the two most diverse possibilities. One gives the whole allowance (2.4 million) to births while placing immigration at zero (42.5 percent and 100 percent reductions respectively). At the other extreme, immigration remains at the estimated 1992 level of 1.3 million, leaving room for just 1.1 million births (a 73.2 percent reduction in U.S. fertility).

The preceding exercise reveals the strength of the force producing population growth and the corresponding risks of delay in formulating and implementing policy. Delay now could contribute to crisis later, a high-stakes gamble. Never (one hopes) will individual decisions about childbearing be overruled by government, but China, of necessity, provides precedent.

Immigration numbers, unlike childbearing, are historically and appropriately within the public-policy arena. An all-inclusive cap of 100,000 annually, say, might give continuing priority to America's valued role as a refuge of last resort. One-quarter, or 25,000 places, could be reserved for refugees. Asylum claimants (who apply for resident status only after entering the United States) "jump the line," and so need not be rewarded with any significant quota. Skilled immigrants and citizens' nuclear families (but not collateral relatives) complete the list of those who should be admitted under a reformed immigration policy.

Americans could be proud of this policy. It is sensitive and restrained and, given the population growth to which we are unavoidably already committed, is congruent with "the interests, and limitations of our country" (Kennan 1995, 116). This policy would produce a gradual decline in population size (through attrition) beginning in about 2050. It would come none too soon to mitigate the very likely social and political sequelae of overpopulation that could be increasingly upon us.

7. The Vicious Circle Principle

A Contribution to the Theory of Population and Development

Craig Dilworth

As humankind moves into the twenty-first century, probably few among us believe that it may well be our last. And the response to such a suggestion is most often to say that there have been prophets of doom in the past, and their prophecies have not come true. But their prophecies, unlike the present warning, have not been based on an extrapolation of accepted fact.

The facts supporting such a bleak view of the future are themselves easily accessible to most people, and are already known to many. They include a combination of global warming, the thinning of the ozone layer, nonrenewable resource depletion, increasing pollution of air, soil, and water, decreasing fresh-water stocks, accelerating erosion and desertification, drastically decreasing biological diversity, and exponential population growth.

But it is not the intention of this chapter to prophesy, doom or otherwise. The intention rather is to provide an understanding of how we got into this predicament, and against the background of this understanding to offer some suggestions as to how we might best deal with the situation. To obtain such an understanding, we must have

Support for research used in this article was provided by the Swedish Environmental Protection Agency.

before us a picture of the whole of the development of humankind, and should therefore begin with a consideration of human prehistory.

Human Development

According to the archaeological evidence, the life-form that evolved into human beings branched off from other life-forms some 6 to 8 million years ago. Our nearest living relatives are the chimpanzees, who are genetically more like us than they are like the gorillas, their and our next nearest kin. And we may still be considered a type of ape, one going under the name of hominid.

The first hominids, the *Australopithecus* (southern ape) appeared 4 to 5 million years ago, and differed from other apes primarily in their upright stance. Their brain size was still relatively small, and their similarity to modern humans has not been considered sufficient to include them in the genus *Homo*.

The first members of the genus *Homo* appeared some 2.5 million years ago; and the earliest named species of the genus, *Homo habilis* (handy human), lived from about 2 to 1.5 million years ago. The first recognizable stone tools were manufactured by *Homo habilis*, if not by a somewhat earlier form of *Homo*.

The next major step in human genetic development was the evolution of the larger-brained *Homo erectus* from *Homo habilis*, some 1.8 million years ago. *Homo erectus*, who may be considered a true human, learned to control (if not create) fire some 1.5 million years ago, and about the same time began producing hand axes, a practice that continued more than a million years. From their production of hand axes of different sizes but the same proportions, it has been suggested that *Homo erectus* may have used language. There is archaeological evidence that this species of humans hunted elephants, horses, rhinoceroses, and giant baboons. By 1 million years ago both *Australopithecus* and *Homo habilis* had become extinct, and *Homo erectus* were the only living hominids.

The first *Homo sapiens* (wise humans) evolved from *Homo erectus* about 400,000 years ago. They too used hand axes, but also developed the wooden thrusting spear, as well as wooden containers and canoes. Although all early human beings were hunters and gatherers, hunting rather than scavenging continually became of greater importance over the years. *Homo sapiens* were almost certainly capable of speech some 300,000 years ago, a skill that may have been acquired in ritual activities performed around the fire, and would have been an aid in hunting big game on a large scale.

The Human Revolution

A view over the whole of the development of humankind shows cultural changes to have occurred at an ever-accelerating pace from its beginning some 6 million years ago right up to the present. This development took a particular spurt some 100,000 years ago, which was some 30,000 years after the appearance of the Neanderthals and about the same time as the arrival of the Cro-Magnons, or *Homo sapiens sapiens*—our own species. After this time human life became increasingly sophisticated, particularly in the case of the new biologic species the Cro-Magnons, with the creation of purely aesthetic objects, the use of bone for tools, the making of tools with built-in handles, and probably the use of skin clothing. These various developments have led many authors to speak of a "human revolution" as occurring at this time.

Both the Neanderthals and the Cro-Magnons had brains at least as large as ours. But where the Neanderthals were heavily built, with large teeth and a jutting brow, the Cro-Magnons were physiologically much like modern humans, though of a more athletic build. Both lived during the last glacial period, which stretched from about 115,000 to 10,000 years ago; and both engaged in big-game hunting on the large steppe-tundra areas of that time. About 35,000 years ago the Neanderthals, some of whose blood we may share, became extinct.

The average human life expectancy during this period was slightly over 30 years for men and slightly under 30 for women (Lenski et.al. 1995, 109). Despite what we would consider short life spans, however, these people suffered relatively little from communicable diseases (Hole 1992, 373).

Starting about 40,000 years ago there occurred another spurt in human cultural development, as well as an increase in population size, within the hunting-and-gathering life-style. This included the systematic hunting of selected animals, the development of cave art, the widespread use of blade tools, the ability to create fire, and the invention of lamps, needles with eyes, spoons, pestles, axes, the spear thrower, and, about 12,000 years ago, the first machine: the bow and arrow. In comparison with a spear hurled with the aid of a spear thrower, an arrow could be shot twice the distance, at more than double the speed, and with greater accuracy.

Somewhat before 12,000 years ago, but after the arrival of human beings, all megafauna in Australia, including the giant kangaroo, became extinct. And shortly after 12,000 years ago, in Eurasia and America, such large mammals as the mammoth, the mastodon, the woolly rhinoceros, the giant deer, the saber-toothed tiger, the giant wolf, the native American horse and the giant ground sloth all became extinct. All in all, by 10,000 years ago, more than fifty genera of large mammals had become extinct over a few thousand years, a greater number of extinctions than during the preceding 4 million years.

The Horticultural Revolution

Human beings could not live on meat alone, and much of their diet depended on plants. During the last glacial period the men hunted big game; the women gathered edible roots, fruit, and wild cereals. By the end of that period, however, not only had much of the big game disappeared, but the warming climate meant an increase in the distribution of edible plants, particularly wild cereals. Ten thousand years ago the climate was as warm as today, and at that time began what may be termed the second great revolution in human development, though a purely cultural rather than biological one, the horticultural revolution.

The primary tool that may be associated with the horticultural revolution is the digging stick, or hoe. Rather than forage after sparsely distributed roots in the wild, tubers were planted, normally by women, in a garden near the place of domicile. This would often take place in an area whose vegetation had previously been removed by fire, the whole process being known as swidden, or slash-and-burn, cultivation.

Starting about 10,000 years ago, the horticultural life style became human beings' primary means of subsistence, hunting and gathering playing a more peripheral role. At that time the earth's human population was between 5 and 10 million, after which it began to increase markedly. The domestication of crops began in marginal areas in the tropics, and among the first were yams, potatoes, taro, and cassava. Tree-borne crops, such as bananas, coconuts, olives, and various nuts, also began to be cultivated about this time. Along with the domestication of plants there also occurred a domestication of animals, first in western Asia, starting with the dog, some 12,000 years ago or earlier, and succeeded by goats and sheep about 9,000 years ago, then cattle, pigs, and bees, and then the horse and donkey about 6,000 years ago.

Domesticating animals can be seen as going through the stages of taming, in which a few young animals are raised, herding, in which the animals are essentially wild but are rounded up for slaughter, and proper domestication, which requires the feeding of the animals and may include, for example, their being milked or sheared. Domesticated animals were probably poorly fed and were almost invariably smaller than their wild ancestors. The domestication of animals led for the first time in human development to situations of ownership, domesticated animals rather than, say, land, being the first instance of somethings being considered the property of a particular person.

A major impact of the horticultural revolution upon the human life-style was that for the first time human societies became sedentary, the first human settlements coinciding with the beginning of the horticultural period. At this time such fortified towns as Jericho, with a population of about two thousand, were built. Where hunter-gatherer societies on the average consisted of some forty people, horticultural societies consisted of some fifteen hundred at the beginning of the era, and about five thousand by the end. Horticultural food production was able to support about twenty times as many people per unit area as hunting and gathering.

Because human beings no longer needed to move about carrying all their possessions with them, many more possessions could be accumulated. Also, such heavy articles as pottery, first produced some 9,000 years ago, could be put to use. In connection with pottery the second machine was invented, the potter's wheel, about 6,500 years ago.

The beginning of the horticultural era also coincided with that of the Neolithic era, or New Stone Age, which involved the grinding and polishing of stone tools. This phase in human development was eventually replaced by the use of metals, the first being copper about 7,000 years ago, and then bronze, in what may be termed the advanced horticultural period. Technological innovations during the horticultural period included sickles, cloth, basket making, sailboats, fishnets, fishhooks, ice picks, and combs. Throughout the development of the horticultural era, there was an increase in the specialization of human activities.

Interaction between different societies also became notable with the horticultural revolution. This interaction took the form of commerce and warfare, both of which increased with time, as did female infanticide. Hunter-gatherers, in conflicts with horticulturalists, were invariably outnumbered, and their only defense was to retreat to less desirable areas. The result of conflicts between horticulturalists themselves may have largely been determined by the quality of the respective parties' weapons, the use of bronze weapons providing a distinct advantage.

The horticultural life-style provided human beings for the first time with an economic surplus, and excess food became the first medium of exchange.

The Agricultural Revolution

Where the horticultural revolution consisted in the transformation to the cultivation of small vegetable and fruit gardens by women using the digging stick or hoe, the agricultural revolution can be described as the transformation to the growing of cereals in large fields by men using plows. Both involved cultural rather than biological or genetic changes.

The agricultural revolution can be considered to have begun with the invention of the plow in Mesopotamia or Egypt somewhat before 5,000 years ago. Compared to the hoe, the plow was more effective in killing weeds and, by turning them into the soil, in returning nutrients to the soil and keeping them near the surface, where they could be of use to crops. Thus, with crop rotation, the same area of land could be used for longer periods, and the amount of food produced per unit land was greatly increased. Also, where hoeing could be done only by human beings, it was soon realized that a plow could be drawn by oxen, leading to the cultivation of larger areas and therefore to even greater productivity. This productivity was further enhanced by irrigation and the use of manure from the oxen to fertilize the fields.

The first plows were made of wood; later the plowshares on some were made of bronze—though this metal was relatively scarce—and not before about 2,750 years ago were they generally made of quench-hardened iron, that is, steel. Since then, steel has remained the primary material for making tools and weapons used for cutting. The plow was not used in sub-Saharan Africa or America until introduced there by Europeans.

The agricultural revolution was contemporaneous with "the dawn of civilization" in Egypt and Mesopotamia. The size of the population once again began to increase dramatically, particularly in the valleys of such large rivers as the Nile and the Tigris and Euphrates, leading to the appearance of cities with over 100,000 inhabitants and empires with their divine hereditary rulers. Although the first irrigation canals were constructed some 7,500 years ago (in Mesopotamia), their use became widespread during the agrarian era. Megalithic structures were built, the most notable being the Egyptian pyramids, and writing was introduced to record economic transactions.

At first, as in the horticultural era, food products constituted the medium of exchange, but the products were more particularly various kinds of grain, which could be stored longer than, for example, tubers. Nevertheless, owing to the bulkiness and perishability of grains, metals such as silver and copper began being used as currency early in the agricultural period. Trade, in which metal currency allowed the rise of a class of merchants or middlemen, increased throughout the agrarian era.

Technological innovations during this period included, more than 5,000 years ago, the plow, the wagon wheel, animal harnesses, writing and numerical notation, and the calendar. Later inventions include the catapult, the crossbow, gunpowder, horseshoes, stirrups, the lathe, the screw, the wheelbarrow, the clock, the spinning wheel, printing, water mills, and windmills. By the eighteenth century, agrarian societies could support cities with as many as 1 million inhabitants.

Life expectancy during the agrarian period generally varied between twenty and twenty-five years, longer for men than for women, and shorter in cities than in the country. The spread of disease was even more of a problem than during the horticultural era, because of increased population density and interaction between societies, as well as worsening sanitary conditions in cities as they grew larger. Warfare was also common throughout this era.

Art, music, architecture, and learning also developed markedly through this period, as is witnessed by, for example, Greek sculpture, Gothic cathedrals, and the birth and development of philosophy and science.

The Industrial Revolution

Just before and at the beginning of the industrial revolution, which occurred first in Britain between 1750 and 1850, came a number of inventions, including the Neilson hot blast stove, the Newcomen engine, Watt's steam engine, the flying shuttle, the spinning jenny, and the water frame. The main inventions at this time were directly or indirectly associated with coal, Newcomen's and later Watt's engine first being used to pump water out of ever-deepening coal mines.

With the industrial revolution came a huge increase in economic activity, including the building of systems of rails and canals, largely for the transportation of coal, and the use of the new inventions for the production of ever-more products. At the same time the population of Britain and Wales, for example, increased tremendously, tripling in the 110 years from 1751 to 1861 (Stevenson 1993, 232). More people married, marriages were on the average earlier, and there were more illegitimate children. Life expectancy also increased during this period, averaging about thirty-two years in the 1670s and almost thirty-nine in the 1810s (Laqueur 1993, 105).

Wars have been larger and more destructive since the industrial revolution, because of the invention and use of more powerful weapons, the latest on the list being nuclear weapons. There have of course been other inventions during this period, some of the best known being the telephone, the electric light, the radio and television, the automobile and the airplane. The automobile and airplane were dependent on the prior invention of the internal combustion engine. Rather than coal as its source of energy, this engine uses oil (gasoline); the first oil well was drilled in the United States in 1859.

Since the beginning of the industrial revolution, about 1750, the population of the world has increased from about 730 million to 5.7 billion, an increase of about 780 percent, and has more than doubled in the past forty years. This increase has been accompanied by an increase in urbanization, some cities now containing as many as 20 million people, as well as an increase in the problems of resource depletion and pollution mentioned at the beginning of this chapter. Industrialization has spread to areas supporting about 20 percent of the world's population, these people accounting for about 80 percent of world resource use. The consequent difference in the standard of living between the two groups is huge and constantly growing.

Economic activity has also been constantly increasing, as has the movement of people over large distances, which has been accompanied by an increase in the spread of communicable diseases, such as AIDS. Furthermore, at present, about 13 million people die each year of malnutrition or starvation. Nevertheless, world life expectancy has increased dramatically during the past fifty years, the average now being sixty-five years, slightly higher for women than for men (Johnson 1994, 224, 364).

The Demographic Transition Model

The present population of the world is far beyond what is sustainable in the long run, and it is still growing at an alarming rate. What has been the driving force behind the increasing size of the human population, and what could possibly make it level off or decline in the future, with as little suffering as possible?

The generally accepted and seldom questioned view of population growth versus stability has been the "demographic transition" model. According to it, populations grow when people believe that having many children will benefit them, particularly in old age; to stabilize population size, the society must reach a stage where the standard of living is sufficiently high to make such a reliance unnecessary. Thus, according to this view, the improved medical and sanitary conditions and pesticide use that have led to a marked decrease in infant mortality in the world, and a consequent lengthening of life expectancy, will also lead to a decrease in fertility and an eventual leveling off of the world's population. Politically, this view has had the effect of supporting continued economic growth as a goal for both industrialized and nonindustialized countries, as well as a laissez-faire policy in dealing with the problem of overpopulation: increase economic growth and the population problem will solve itself.

What is not being questioned here is the fact that in many societies, before the implementation of medical and other technologies from industrial societies, high infant mortality was at least partly responsible for low population growth. What is being questioned is the purported causal link from improved material standard of living to decreased fertility. As has been pointed out by Virginia Abernethy, the demographic transition model arose in the 1930s, when Third World countries had higher fertility rates than industrialized countries (Abernethy 1993, 33). But, as she says, the problem is that this situation was taken to be evidence of a *causal* relation,[1] a relation that moreover did not apply just at that time but generally! Are we expected to think that the size of the population of *Homo sapiens sapiens*, which has been increasing at an accelerating rate over the past 40,00 years, should level off when and only when each family unit of the species is equipped with a refrigerator, car, and television?

At this point we might pause, however, to note that, even if the demographic transition model were absolutely correct, its being

---

1. In this regard the demographic transition model may be seen as yet another expression of the positivism that has influenced so much thinking in this century, one characteristic of which is to take relations of uniformity to be causal relations. As pointed out by Herman Daly (1992, 164), in the present case lower fertility might just as well be the *cause* of higher per capita income, rather than the *effect*. For a critique of positivistic thinking as applied to modern science, see Dilworth 1995.

followed politically would by no means solve the problems to which global overpopulation is giving rise, namely, resource depletion and pollution. Even if the size of the population of the poorer 80 percent of the world's inhabitants would become constant when these people had attained the standard of living of the wealthier 20 percent, rather than having decreased, the rate of resource depletion and pollution in the world would have increased tremendously. For this reason alone, the aim of stabilizing population through global economic growth is untenable.

But, in any case, Abernethy has succeeded in raising grave doubts about the viability of the demographic transition model itself. She cites periods in human history where, contrary to the model, either a worsening standard of living has gone hand in hand with decreasing fertility, or an improved standard of living has gone hand in hand with increasing fertility. These examples include the fact that the transition to lower fertility in Germany and France preceded or was at least simultaneous with declining infant mortality and the situation in the United States after the Second World War, when massive economic growth was coincident with a baby boom. Other examples are the fertility declines in China, Costa Rica, and Sri Lanka despite people's low incomes and the high fertility rates in Brazil and Mexico despite increasing industrialization and per capita economic growth, as well as high fertility rates in several Middle Eastern countries despite high income levels (Ehrlich and Ehrlich 1990, 215; Meadows et al. 1992, 29). Abernethy's argument, which has the merit of being supported by common sense, is that it is just when people expect good times ahead that they have *more* children, not fewer.

As for high fertility rates in Third World countries, alternative explanations to that of the demographic transition model have been put forward by others. There seems to be a consensus that the high population growth in the Third World is largely a result of the impact of European culture. As argued by Richard G. Wilkinson, "many primitive societies, particularly before contact with Europeans disrupted their cultural systems, prevented population growth and managed to live in equilibrium with their resources without threat of hunger" (Wilkinson 1973, 6). The growth rate of the poorer 80 percent of the world's population is *twenty to thirty times* higher now than it was before contact of these cultures with those of industrialized nations (Lenski et al, 1995, 380). As for contributing to the solution of the overpopulation problem, economic growth is certainly getting off to a bad start!

Even advocates of the demographic transition view would admit that decreasing mortality is a result of European intervention, but that preindustrial cultures often could keep their population size in check is seldom mentioned. One of the ways in which this was effected was through infanticide.

Among the Tapirapé Indians of Brazil, couples could raise two children of one sex, three in all. Tapirapé culture banned parents from raising more, because additional mouths would siphon resources needed by other families. The Tapirapé considered it selfish and immoral to try to keep a surplus baby. The death of the infant, who was not defined as human, was considered morally necessary for other members of the group to survive (Kottak 1994, 250).

According to Wilkinson, the issue at stake involves throwing out the whole popular idea of primitive societies as societies in a perpetual state of hardship, scarcely able to scrape up a bare minimum of subsistence, with large families, children suffering from malnutrition, and a low life expectancy. Insofar as this *is* the situation in parts of the underdeveloped world, it is a comparatively recent phenomenon. Contact with Europeans, and with their alien values and practices, has led to the abandonment of customs such as abortion and infanticide that once helped prevent overpopulation. As early as the third quarter of the eighteenth century a missionary in Paraguay claimed that Christianity had led to the abolition of abortion and infanticide among the Abipones. Ironically, the same missionary also remarked on how plentiful food had been, as if the fact was unrelated to the existence of these practices (Wilkinson 1973, 32–33).

Such arguments add to the reasons for strongly questioning the political goal of economic growth as a route to population stability. In the following, we shall attempt to give views such as those of Abernethy and Wilkinson a broader theoretical underpinning by suggesting the mechanism responsible not only for human population growth but also for technological development, economic growth, resource depletion, and environmental destruction, throughout the development of humankind.

The Vicious Circle Principle

Just as the demographic transition model fits well in a worldview that gives high priority to economic growth, so does the view that technological change is an expression of human progress. This view is, prima facie, easy to understand, for most technical change appears to lighten people's work loads or add to their enjoyment of their leisure time. Though this view is attractive, it does not take account of whether the technological change in question is accompanied by an increase in the size of the population affected by the change.

In the view presented here, in keeping with Wilkinson's, the essence of technological change consists in human beings' development of new methods of relating to their environment so that more can be extracted from that environment to support a growing population. Thus, technological change is seen here as paradigmatically being a defensive move by human beings in reaction to a worsening life situation resulting from an increase in the number of people living on a particular area of land. The words *essence* and *paradigmatically* are intended to convey the idea that technological change may well occur for reasons other than the one given, but that the reason given, more than any other, constitutes the basic driving force behind the technological development human beings have brought about, beginning already with the invention of the first stone tools.

A secondary driving force behind technological development, however, is technological development itself. Thus, just as we might say with Hume, Malthus, and others, that necessity is the mother of invention, we might also say that invention can be the mother of necessity. In other words, once a new invention has been adopted in a society, it tends to create pressure within the society to make other innovative changes. Once telephones come into use, telephone cable technology and switchboard technology have to be developed, and the results manufactured and put into use; the invention and use of cars demands an improvement in road technology and the development of a huge system of highways and service stations.

A tertiary driving force behind technological development is a result of the efforts of the mercantile or business class in society. Already with the influx of gold and silver from the New World in the sixteenth century, more of the economic resources of European societies wound up in the hands of people who were interested in, and knew something about, both economics and technology. More than that, these were people oriented to rational profit making (not a typical orientation in agrarian societies) and therefore motivated to provide financial support for technological innovations that would increase the efficiency of people and machines (Lenski et al, 1995, 242). Thus, capitalists' interest in maximizing their profits also tends to spur technological development.

This having been said, our theory, based on the vicious circle principle, suggests that human technological and economic development are essentially part of a recurring phenomenon consisting of population growth, which increases consumption, which leads to a scarcity of resources, which creates a demand for technological development, which when employed enables previously inaccessible resources to be drawn from the environment. These developments trigger economic growth, which increases the use of energy, which in turn increases the production of waste while creating conditions for an even greater number of humans to occupy a given area of land, which leads to further population growth, which again results in increased consumption, and so on.

Note that no suggestion is being made here as to the inevitability of this process. It is possible, and has been the case in many societies, that the size of a particular population be under control, so that the vicious circle need not get started. Nor need it be the case that, once started, the vicious circle cannot be stopped. Furthermore, the present view does not exclude the possibility of technological developments taking a new turn, so that rather than leading to an extraction of *more* from the environment, it leads to an extraction of *less*.

To investigate the viability of our theory, we might return to consider how far our earlier sketch of human development can be understood in its light.

Human Development Revisited

Though one might be inclined to see the invention of early stone tools, such as the hand ax, as a response to population pressure, we lack sufficient information about the size and living conditions of the human population at that time to warrant the making of such a connection. In any case, the possibility of applying the vicious circle principle to human development becomes of greater relevance with the appearance of our own species, *Homo sapiens sapiens*, in conjunction with what we have termed the human revolution.

The Human Revolution

As has been emphasized by a number of authors, at this time, about 100,000 years ago, cultural evolution replaced biological evolution as the primary form of human adaptation to the environment. To this we might add that, in our theory, the very innovativeness of our species, evident already at this time, is responsible for the ecological and demographic predicament in which we find ourselves today.

Perhaps what is most notable about cultural evolution during the last glacial period was the improvement in weapons, particularly the development from the wooden thrusting spear, to the stone-pointed throwing spear, to the throwing spear that could be hurled a greater distance with the aid of a spear thrower, and finally to the bow and arrow. The demise of the Neanderthals may have been a direct result of these latter weapons' developments occurring already with the Cro-Magnons. Whether the extinction of the Neanderthals was at the hands of the technologically more developed Cro-Magnons, there is little doubt that increased hunting as compared to scavenging was at least partly a result of impovements in human weapon technology; moreover, humans with their weapons were responsible for the extinctions of many if not all of the megafauna that disappeared at the end of the last glacial period. The size of the human population began to increase about forty thousand years ago, at the same time as a number of technological inventions were made; and the disappearance of many of the megafauna may have resulted from the invention of the bow and arrow.

There have been attempts to explain the extinction of megafauna at this time that do not see the reason in human technological inventiveness. The most common is that these animals, adapted to ice-age conditions, could not survive changes associated with the warming climate. This explanation, however, does not account for the fact that they had survived earlier interglacial warm periods. Nor does it account for the fact that no smaller animals or plants became extinct at this time. Further evidence for the extinctions being caused by human beings is the disappearance of many large mammals both on Madagascar and in New Zealand about a thousand years ago, directly after the arrival of humans.

> One wonders, if extinction was due to climatic change, why Madagascar extinctions were not coincident with those of Africa 220 miles away; and why European and Ukrainian mammoths became extinct 13,000 years ago while in North America they survived another 2000 years. Previous great extinction waves had affected plants and small animals as well as large animals, but the late Pleistocene extinctions are concentrated on the large, gregarious, herding, or slow moving animals—the ideal prey of human hunters (Smith, 1992, 5).

Another aspect of this phenomenon is that although many megafaunal extinctions occurred in America, Eurasia, and Australia, none occurred in Africa. The best explanation of this aspect seems to be that it was when human beings entered new areas, where their prey had not had the time to adapt to human beings' evolving predatory prowess, that they were driven to extinction. This effect would have been heightened if the newly arriving human beings were equipped with the bow and arrow.

A further point is that in our theory virtually every technological advance at this time, no matter how minor, can be seen as directly or indirectly increasing the number of human beings who could occupy a particular area of land. Thus, developments that may seem minor, such as the invention of needles with eyes, or even bowls and spoons, contributed to creating an environment that could support a greater number of people at that time.

The Horticultural Revolution

The horticultural revolution is generally seen as a response to the warming climate at the beginning of the Holocene, which led to a focus on gardening rather than hunting as an easier way to obtain a livelihood. One might ask, however, why gardening was not introduced at the end of the previous glacial period. One answer might be that the more highly evolved *Homo sapiens sapiens* had yet to inhabit larger areas of the world. On the other hand, the members of many hunter-gatherer societies understood and occasionally applied the basic principles of plant cultivation thousands of years before horticulture became their primary mode of subsistence (Lenski et al. 1995, 135–36).

As to why horticulture as a means of subsistence began at all, archaeological evidence suggests that food production developed in response to problems caused by the undue success of the hunter-gatherers, whose rate of food extraction came to exceed the carrying capacity of the environment. It also suggests that some people resisted the introduction of horticulture for centuries after first making its acquaintance (van der Merwe 1992, 370).

Here we see, then, a clear case for the application of the vicious circle principle. Technological advance—the invention of weapons such as the bow and arrow—made sources of food available that were previously unavailable, paving the way for an increase in population at the same time it led to resource depletion. The greater population coupled with the diminished resources created the need for new technology—horticulture—capable of extracting even more from the environment.

This view is further supported by another source.

> To explain the origin of food production (and economic change in general), many scholars now assume that the people most likely to adopt a new subsistence strategy are those who are having trouble following the subsistence practices that are common to their group. Thus, ancient Middle Easterners who lived outside the zone where wild foods were most abundant would be the most likely to experiment—leading to new subsistence strategies. Recent archaeological finds support the hypothesis that domestication began in marginal areas rather than in the optimal zones, such as the Hilly Flanks, where traditional foods were most abundant.
>
> Early cultivation began as an attempt to copy, in a less favourable environment, the dense stands of wheat and barley that grew wild in the Hilly Flanks. (Kottak, 1994, 202–3)

Regarding the idea that technological advance leads to an improvement in standard of living, as is part of the modern ethos that includes both the demographic transition model and economic growth as a political goal, both archaeological and anthropological evidence indicate that the opposite occurred in the revolution from the hunter-gatherer period to the horticultural. Human life expectancy at birth fell from about thirty years for hunter-gatherer peoples to less than twenty years during this period, despite the resultant change from hand-to-mouth feeding to the storing of food (Clark 1989, 84–85). Apart from the effects of war, the dependence on specialized food production meant a lack of flexibility that could lead to starvation when crops failed, for example, because of drought. Higher population density and trade links also contributed to the increase in the spread of infectious diseases, and the sedentary life-style led to more unsanitary conditions and the spread of parasites.

The horticultural revolution also meant a lower standard of living in other respects.

> One was that food producers typically work harder than foragers do— and for a less adequate diet. Diets based on crops and dairy products

tend to be less varied, nutritious, and healthful than foragers' diet, which are usually higher in proteins and lower in fats and carbohydrates. With the shift to food production, the physical well-being of the population often declines. Communicable diseases, protein deficiency, and dental caries increase, while average stature tends to decrease. By contrast, most foragers are, compared with farmers and herders, relatively disease-free, stress-free, and well-nourished. Other disadvantages accompanied food production. Social inequality increased, as elaborate systems of social stratification replaced the egalitarianism of the past. Slavery was invented. Poverty, crime, war, and human sacrifice became widespread, and the rate at which human beings degraded their environments increased. (Kottak 1994, 216)

Concerning, for example, the time required to meet daily needs, a study of modern hunter-gatherers, the !Kung San of the Kalahari desert of southern Africa, shows that they are engaged in sustenance-related activities between twelve and nineteen hours per week, much less than is required in a horticultural society. Furthermore, their intake of calories and protein during the third year of a severe drought was above the recommended daily allowance for people of their stature— despite their being forced to sustain themselves in a semi-arid environment. Furthermore, their life expectancy compares favorably to that of industrialized populations (Reader 1988, 144, 148). It might also be mentioned that the fertility level among the !Kung is low relative to other contemporary African peoples, a possible cause being a long lactation period, which also tends to increase resistance to infection for both mothers and children.

Another notable aspect of the lowering of the human standard of living with the coming of the horticultural life-style, as mentioned in the previous quote, is the drudgery it involves. The development of the Neolithic culture that accompanied the revolution to horticulture meant an increasing division of labor. While women worked in gardens, a task involving a good deal of drudgery itself, men worked grinding, polishing, and boring holes in stone tools for use in the gardens—as Mumford suggests, the beginning of boring work and the daily grind.

But this is not all. Further in keeping with the vicious circle principle we see that horticulture not only allowed for the sustenance of a population that had overexploited its environment with the aid of weapon technology but it also allowed the size of that population to increase. During the horticultural period the human population, despite undergoing a lowering in its standard of living, grew from some 10 million to about 80 million.

At this point we might emphasize the distinction between societies that for some period managed to keep their population size within the carrying capacity of their environment and societies that did not. When technological change has been very slow or nonexistent, it is possible for a society to maintain a constant population size through checks of its own. These can be preventive, as in the case of contraception and late marriages, or positive, as in the case of abortion and infanticide. As is clear, preventive checks reduce fertility, while positive checks lower life expectancy. When such internal checks are lacking, external checks come into play, checks virtually always positive in nature, which can be, for example, disease or famine. Both internal and external checks may well be operative even in such cases as when the size of the population is increasing. Another check to population size, which is external to a society, but internal to humankind, is war. With the accelerated population growth resulting from the horticultural revolution, when the previous internal checks of the hunter-gatherer period were no longer in play, warfare became one way in which the size of the population was restrained in its rate of growth.[2] As the horticultural period advanced, and populations and population pressure grew, so did the amount of warfare.

As has been pointed out by a number of authors, warfare was virtually impossible for hunter-gatherers, not only because of their small numbers but also because of their being unable to accumulate sufficient food to see them through such engagements. Thus, only with the horticultural era, when food could be stored, either as, for example, grain or livestock, did warfare bocame possible. Furthermore, it was the existence of property, which hunter-gatherers lacked, that constituted the immediate cause of war, as well as being a prerequisite for commerce.

Apart from the direct loss of life resultant upon such conflicts, warfare also functioned as a check on population size through its giving rise to female infanticide. By reducing the number of girls in a society, the group could devote its resources to the care and nurture of its boys.

---

2. The idea that overpopulation leads to war is at least as old as Plato. See *Republic*, 2.372c and 2.373c–374a. For a description of this mechanism in the case of the modern-day horticulturalists of Papua, New Guinea, see Reader 1988, 42–44.

A survey of studies of 609 "primitive" societies found that the sex ratio among the young was most imbalanced in those societies in which warfare was current at the time of the study and most nearly normal in those societies in which warfare had not occurred for more than 25 years. In the former, boys outnumbered girls by a ratio of 7 to 5 on the average, indicating that nearly 30 per cent of the females born in these societies had died as a result of female infanticide or neglect. (Lenski et al. 1995, 152)

The Agricultural Revolution

In the vicious circle principle, as is in keeping with the archaeological and historical record, the most important cultural development after the beginning of the use of horticultural methods was the invention and use of the plow. The continuing tendency of the human population to grow beyond what could be supported by existent techniques meant that the only way that the eightfold increase in population could be sustained was by finding a way of exploiting the environment more thoroughly, and the plow was the primary means for accomplishing this end. The vicious circle of population growth, technological innovation, and resource depletion would be repeated on a massive scale.

At first, farmers moved into thinly forested regions with light soils, especially along river valleys. Later, as these soils became depleted and populations continued to grow, the farmers cleared forests, creating both farm and growing land. In the process, they caused accelerated leaching of nutrients and soil erosion, which altered vegetation and soils. Worldwide, where conditions were suitable, seed cultivation expanded at the expense of horticulture, even though these crops depleted soils more quickly than the products of horticulture (Hole 1992, 376).

Once again, technological advance was not a result of a seeking after a better life, but the response to need imposed by increasing numbers of people. Though the average age at death did not change notably in the transition to the agrarian period, remaining at about twenty years, such phenomena as the drought and flooding resulting from changing weather were more widespread in their effects. Similarly, the spread of infectious diseases had a greater impact owing to increased population and greater interaction between groups coupled with worsening hygiene, the most devastating instance being the Black

Death in the middle of the fourteenth century, which killed between a quarter and a half of the population of Europe. And just as the human work load grew with the move to horticulture, it grew again with the move to agriculture. Though oxen were eventually used to plow fields, at the beginning of the agrarian era it was humans who drew the plows. Large areas of land became the property of kings, and almost all of the population worked as peasants or slaves to produce the foodstuffs that constituted the king's wealth, or to create the monuments that would stand as everlasting tributes to the king's greatness, or to fight in the king's wars. In this latter regard it may be mentioned that the period after the harvest was in came to be known as "the season when kings go forth to war." With the amassing of greater amounts of property, society became more stratified, there was a greater division of labor, and the distance between the rich and the poor constantly increased.

While standard of living declined, so too did the quality of the land. The removal of trees—with the aid of iron axes—to allow the creation of fields led to soil erosion, a process accelerated by the exposure of the topsoil to wind and rain by the use of the plow. In areas too hilly or deficient in nutrients for agriculture, goats were let roam, effectually exterminating all but the hardiest bushes. The results of these activities remain with us today, and can be seen, for example, over the whole Mediterranean area. The use of irrigation to supply water to fields in areas that were otherwise too dry to support agriculture led to salinization, leaving the soil unusable for cultivation for thousands of years—as may be witnessed today in the Tigris-Euphrates valley. Wastelands developed around cities, where the area was picked clean of fuel and building materials, and vegetation disappeared owing to the passage of many feet. The increase in the numbers of people not only made the move to agriculture necessary but also made its ecologically disastrous effects more widespread. "Agriculture created serious and irreversible changes when farmers began to plough the soil, clear forests to create fields, move rivers to irrigate wheat or rice, and burn forests to gain a few extra years of agricultural productivity from nutrient-deficient soils. Erosion and the alteration of the balance of species became inevitable" (Hole 1992, 379).

As for other species, the spread of agriculture and the human population forced many from their natural habitats; and some, such as the wild ox, were hunted to extinction.

Where at the beginning of the human revolution adaptation to the environment was cultural change rather than biologic change, with the evolution of commerce and warfare much of that cultural change consisted in adapting to the activities of other human beings rather than to nature. Human beings needed no longer to fear other predators, and mostly had a dependable source of food through the domestication of plants and animals. Major successes and failures consisted in the results of exchanges on the market or on the battlefield, rather than in the results of the hunt. "Nature became less the 'habitat' for the farmer than a set of economic resources to be managed and manipulated by the controlling group. This was particularly true of cultures where the dominant class was urban-based, as in Graeco-Roman antiquity" (Roberts, 1989, 128–29). With the continual distancing of nature from humankind came a gradual change in conception of the world, with reality increasingly being thought of in other people and their actions.

As human population grew because of a paucity of internal checks coupled with the increased productivity of the soil through the use of the plow, warfare also increased. In this regard the availability of bronze weapons, as intimated earlier, played a key role. "The emergence of urban centers was largely the result of the military success of villages that had one important advantage: bronze weapons." For the first time in history, people found that the conquest of other people could be a profitable alternative to the conquest of nature. Thus, beginning in advanced horticultural societies and continuing in agrarian, we find almost as much energy expended in war as in the more basic struggle for subsistence. One might say that bronze was to the conquest of people what plant cultivation was to the conquest of nature: both were decisive turning points in sociocultural evolution (Lenski et al. 1995, 157).

As in the horticultural period, apart from war and disease, one of the constraints on population growth in the agrarian era was infanticide. When crops failed and famine was imminent, families often abandoned their newborn by the roadside or left them at the door of a church or monastery in the hope that someone else might raise them. Sometimes even older children would be abandoned by their parents. In some districts in China as many as a quarter of the female infants were killed at birth—signs were sometimes erected near ponds: "Girls may not be drowned here" (Lenski et al. 1995, 126).

The length of the agrarian period was extended by the discovery of America, which also allowed a continuing increase in the size of the human population, first through emigration from Europe. At the same time, however, population also increased in Europe, giving rise to needs that were eventually met by the technological innovations of the industrial revolution.

The Industrial Revolution

With the industrial revolution began the largest of all turns around the vicious circle, giving rise to the use of vast quantities of fossil fuels, which have indirectly sustained almost an eightfold increase in world population since 1750. The increasing population in Britain about that time led to a shortage of both land and wood, which was used both as a building material and a fuel. The possibility of using coal as a substitute for wood led to the development first of the Newcomen engine and then Watt's steam engine, to pump water out of coal mines.

Coal is an inferior substitute for wood, a fact that required the invention of other devices and processes, such as the use of coke (derived from coal) as a substitute for wood-charcoal in iron-smelting, and later the invention of the coal-fired blast furnace to replace the traditional forge.

With these changes and the implementation of Watt's engine, the use of coal increased tremendously, a result of the vicious circle moving from need—of an energy source for heating and manufacturing—to innovation—the invention of the steam engine, among other devices—and on to resource depletion—through the extraction and use of coal.

The next phase in the vicious circle followed directly, namely, greater economic activity spurred by the profit motive of capitalists, and with it increased use of energy and production of waste. Because of the existence of coal only in isolated areas, it was necessary that a means of distribution be found. This means—again involving innovation—consisted in the construction of railways and canals and the development of hard surfaces for roads. All this construction activity demanded the expenditure of energy and constituted economic growth; at the same time it involved changes in the landscape and increasing pollution, changes that would not have been necessary if population pressure had not in the first place led to a failure to husband wood resources. As expressed by Wilkinson: "Once again it appears that a formidable group of innovations should not be regarded as the fruits of a society's search for progress, but as the outcome of a valiant struggle of a society with its back to the ecological wall (Wilkinson 1973, 126).

Here we have an excellent example indicating why economic growth, the goal of so many of today's decision makers, ought perhaps rather be seen as a measure of the failure of human beings to live in ecological equilibrium with their environment. The overconsumption of a renewable resource such as wood makes it necessary to expend more energy to procure a nonrenewable substitute such as coal; and because in this case the substitute is not widespread, to expend yet more energy to distribute it—all of this activity constituting economic growth. As expressed by Ellul: "History shows that every technical application from its beginnings presents certain unforeseeable secondary effects which are much more disastrous than the lack of the technique would have been" (Ellul 1964, 105). In history each major technological advance has made possible our digging deeper into the barrel of natural resources, and it is only a matter of time, as long as we follow this procedure, until we will be scraping the bottom of the barrel.

The industrial revolution also brought with it a further decrease in the standard of living of the common people. Instead of working out of doors or in cottages and enjoying the many holidays in the medieval calendar, people had no alternative but to work in mines or factories for longer hours at even more specialized tasks and with virtually no holidays. Child labor also increased, children being used, for example, in mines, where they could squeeze into spaces too small for adults. The quality of clothing also became lower, cotton largely replacing linen, wool, and leather.

It should perhaps be emphasized that in this process change did not come about immediately upon the discovery of new technology, but that the new technology was implemented only when there was an experience of need. As has been shown by Wilkinson, the transition to steam power and the use of coal as a fuel did not take place in the United States, even though steam and coal were well known there, until local wood scarcities and shortages of sources of waterpower made their implementation worthwhile.

The Americans chose not to use existing technology. The strength of the thesis that development is not chosen in preference to traditional methods but is a response to ecological pressures seems to be confirmed. "When they could, they chose to clothe themselves in furs and leather rather than woven cloth; they used wood rather than coal, water power rather than steam, primitive extensive agricultural methods rather than the more intensive European ones they were familiar with. They went on using the older established methods and resources long after they need have done, when they were fully aware of the alternatives." (Wilkinson 1973, 161, 171–72)

As Wilkinson suggests, the implementation of new technologies throughout human history has almost always meant a transition to a more onerous life-style. The move from the hunting-gathering life-style to the horticultural meant increased work, as did the transition from the horticultural to the agricultural, and here we see again an increase in the burden on human beings with the advent of the industrial revolution.

At the same time, however, the vicious circle continues; the newly available sources of energy allow a further increase in population, in this case a truly tremendous increase, and one that is still continuing. But where the population of the world has increased by about a factor of five since the 1850s, the world's consumption of energy, mainly fossil fuels, has increased sixty-fold. For the wealthy 20 percent of the world's population, the industrial revolution has also led to an increase in leisure time, because the fossil fuel energy resources were not only enormous but also unequally distributed. But even now we are seeing a change in this regard as the size of the population continues to grow while the availability of energy decreases. In our parents' generation a household could be supported by only one working person, but now two are required, and the length of the working day and the stress involved in work are both increasing.

What will make the aftermath of the industrial revolution so devastating is the fact that it has led to the use of such huge, yet finite, quantities of fossil fuels, the second of major importance being oil. Where coal began to be used in response to a scarcity of wood, petroleum began to be used in response to a scarcity of whale oil (Wilkinson 1973, 171). At present, 88 percent of the commercial energy used in the world comes from fossil fuels, about 40 percent of the total commercial energy coming from oil (Meadows et al. 1992, 67). Furthermore, oil is used in the making of myriad synthetic products, including most plastics and an ever-increasing proportion of textiles.

Where the members of a family could once clothe themselves in woollens and leather using their own raw materials, we are now dependent for clothing on oil wells, oil tankers, refineries, the chemical industry, textile-machinery manufacturers, and the metal and power industries needed to back them up. The same goes for our food, heating, transport and almost every other item we consume. (Wilkinson 1973, 187)

Just as cotton became a substitute for linen, wool, and leather during the industrial revolution, as the world's cotton harvest decreases we are today witnessing the substitution of oil-based synthetic products for cotton. And all this is occurring at such a rate that it is expected that the world's oil resources will be exhausted within the lifetimes of most people living today.

One might say that virtually the whole of the eightfold increase in the human population since the beginning of the industrial revolution is being maintained by the use of fossil fuels. When these fuels are no longer available, either because of the environmental effects to which their use gives rise or because they become exhausted, or when agricultural production drastically drops because their overuse, the world will be facing a situation in which billions of people will experience real need, a need that there will be no way of satisfying.

What Can We Do?

The above considerations lead to the realization that it is imperative for humankind that we get off the vicious circle. That this is possible is clear from the fact that various societies have existed through the development of humankind who have managed to do so. Their preconditons, however, were better than ours, in that they were invariably less densely populated and had a life-style demanding relatively little from the environment. But given the present situation in the world, when should we attempt to leave the vicious circle, and how?

To answer this question we might best look at the components in the vicious circle again. They include population growth, which leads to resource scarcity, which gives rise to technological innovation, which leads to a more thorough exploitation of the resource base, which increases the production and dissemination of goods and waste products at the same time as it provides the basis for further population growth.

First, it may be noted that, in constituting a circle, this list of factors has no real beginning, and furthermore that, owing to the enormity of the problem, efforts will have to be made to solve it at every possible point. At the same time, however, we see that a key aspect of the circle is population growth. We must drastically reduce the size of the human population, in both industrialized and Third World countries, with the least possible delay.

Of the various practical suggestions as to how this might be done, that of Kenneth Boulding warrants particular consideration owing to its flexibility and relative fairness. Boulding's suggestion, which has received the support of Herman Daly and John Cobb (Cobb 1989, 244–46; Daly 1992, 56–61), concerns the implementation of exchangeable birth licenses. The idea is that each woman in a country is given the right by the state to have a certain number of children. This number is decided based on ecological and other considerations, but it is the same for everyone of a certain age. It could be, for example 1.6 children. In that case, if a woman wanted to have two children, she might buy or receive as a gift four deci-licenses from someone else; or, if she wanted only one child, she could sell or give away her six extra deci-licenses. Such a system would have to be supported by a program of family planning and immigration, and be keyed with statistics regarding the degree of success of their implementation.

Now, one might say that this is too much of a "top-down" procedure, and that a decrease in human fertility ought rather come from insight at the grass-roots level. This is all very well, and we have elsewhere (Dilworth 1994) depicted an ecologically benign worldview (the "systems-ecological perspective") in which such an insight would have a place. The trouble is, however, that humankind cannot afford to wait for the spread of such a worldview. The population is too large now, and it is only getting larger. The possibility of taking purely pragmatic steps on the institutional level is not to be ignored.

Similarly, human consumption of resources is too great now, and it too must be drastically reduced, independently of population reduction. Here one's first response might be to say that this is well and good for the rich 20 percent of the world's population, who consume too much anyway, but what of the poor 80 percent, many of whom do not consume even enough to survive? Our response to this is to suggest that what is needed is a fundamentally different economic system, operative in the Third World as well as in industrialized countries, in which the idea of economic growth is replaced by that of economic conservation.

The ideas that have been developed furthest in this direction are probably those of Herman Daly (1992), who argues for the implementation of a steady-state economy. On Daly's conception of such an economy, the quantity of stocks is held constant, while the output is minimized and the service maximized. Some of the changes required in the present economy to transform it to a steady-state economy, a transition which is to occur gradually, include politically supervising and limiting the size and monopoly power of corporations, setting upper and lower limits on income and upper limits on wealth, implementing quotas for the extraction of natural resources, taxing resources higher than income, charging at least as much for nonrenewables as for their nearest renewable substitutes, stopping the subsidizing of energy production, and setting up tariffs to protect local industries.

One aspect of such a steady-state economy as Daly evisages may be its not allowing the accruing of interest. This topic has been developed by Margrit Kennedy,[3] according to whom a reduction of interest rates lessens the pressure for growth in an economy, zero interest being a precondition for the zero growth of a steady-state economy. For a zero-interest economy also to be an ecologically sustainable one, however, there must be a land reform and a tax reform. The land reform would put ownership of the land in the hands of the local government, from whom it may be leased, thereby removing the threat of land speculation; and the tax reform would be like that recommended by Daly, by which products rather than incomes would be taxed.

There are undoubtedly innumerable other ways in which we should attempt to remove ourselves from the vicious circle, the above ones being mentioned because they concern vital aspects of the circle, namely, population growth and economic growth, as well as having the potential to be wide-ranging in their effects. No matter how "environmental" we might become in our choice of articles to buy or in the sorting of our garbage, efforts of this sort are not sufficient to effect the fundamental change necessary for humankind to cope with the future. If we are to survive on this planet, we must see to it that our sources of energy, food, and materials are constantly being renewed at the same rate as they are being used. For this to happen we must stabilize the human population at a level much lower than the level it is at today, and we must adopt an economic system oriented toward husbanding resources rather than squandering them on economic growth.

3. In Kennedy 1988. Mary Clark (1989, 350–51) points out that Keynes advocated a future economy in which one would have "got rid of many of the objectionable features of capitalism," in particular, interest on accumulated wealth.

8. The Social Impact of Scarcity

The Political Responses of Institutionally Developed Societies

Kurt Finsterbusch

The human species is on an unsustainable course. The four major biosystems on which humans depend have been in serious trouble for decades (Postel 1994). On average the topsoils on the world croplands are thinning and declining in quality (Brown et al. 1990; Dregne 1989; Oldeman, et al. 1991; Rozanov et al. 1990). The quality of the world's grasslands is declining and millions of acres are turning to deserts or wastelands annually. The world's forests are declining and tracts that are managed for high productivity have problems of monoculture vulnerability. The world's fisheries seem to be in difficulty, for the world fish catch has remained fairly stable for a number of years even though the fishing effort has increased with more intensive technologies and the growth of on-land fish farming. Thirteen of the world's seventeen major fisheries are in serious decline (Mathews 1994; see also Swardson 1994). In addition, pollution problems are increasing even though regulations have lowered the concentration of some pollutants in some parts of the world. Two pollution problems currently exciting world concern are global warming and ozone depletion with potentially awful consequences for ecosystems and humans worldwide. Another concern is the depletion of relatively accessible energy and mineral resources.

The litany of problems grows each day, but so do efforts to address these problems. As a result there is much debate about many environmental issues, including whether the current rates of environmental degradation and rates of use of nonrenewable resources will have adverse consequences for future generations. Differing conclusions on these issues result in further debates over how radical should the changes be for addressing these problems. The dominant view is that environmental problems are very serious, and, therefore, strong measures for protecting the environment and developing more sustainable life-styles are justified. Nevertheless, the more optimistic minority view cannot be dismissed. It argues that resources are abundant and human inventiveness and adaptiveness along with market pressures for conservation and efficiency will bring about sustainable development without requiring drastic changes in institutions and life-styles. It can boast that many dire predictions in the past have failed to materialize. Past estimates of resource reserves have usually been revised upward and human beings find ways to solve or manage environmental problems when they have to. On the other hand, this view seems to require excessive faith in technology, believing that it will always come to the rescue in the eleventh hour. Many sought-after inventions, however, have not been achieved, such as relatively cheap desalinization or a cure for cancer, and there is some evidence that the returns to investments in research and development and the benefits to society from new technologies have declined significantly over the past sixty years (Giarini and Louberge 1978; Ophuls and Boyan 1992).

This chapter does not take sides in this debate but examines the probable social changes that would result from both the growth and the limits versions of the future. However, because much more is known about the impacts of economic growth on society than the impacts of scarcity, this chapter will emphasize the impacts of scarcity. It first develops a general theory of social change in nation-states involving the growth dynamic and then contrasts this theory to one involving no growth or an extended period of scarcity. Scarcity is herein defined as a decline (or no growth) in the average material standard of living (per capita material production and consumption).

This chapter builds on and extends two of my earlier papers: "The Sociology of Nation States: Dimensions, Indicators, and Theory" (1973) and "Consequences of Increasing Scarcity on Affluent Countries" (1983). The first develops a general theory of social change for nation-states drawn from the sociological literature. It identifies how prominent macrosociological variables interrelate with one another, but it does not deal with scarcity. This theory and most of the interrelationships of its variables undergirds the analysis provided here. The second identifies the impacts of both socioeconomic development and scarcity on the extent of equality, democracy, conflict, legitimacy, disturbances, repression, and centralization. The identified impacts have subsequently received additional empirical support and thus provide the starting point for this chapter. Here these impacts are much more fully explained, the analysis of societal responses is revised and greatly expanded, and the social and political changes that may be necessary to shift to sustainable societies are identified.

A General Theory of Social Change in Nation-States

Basic to macrosociological theory (generally the unit of analysis in macrosociology is the nation-state) are fifteen dimensions and their subdimensions: five factors in the production function, three dimensions of structure, five processes, population size, and the environment. These factors do not include all the factors in the theory of change of nation-states developed in an earlier work (Finsterbusch 1973), but they include all the most basic ones and the ones that are the most relevant for tracing the impacts of scarcity.

The five factors in the production function are capital, labor, knowledge/technology, resources, and organization. These vary both in quantity and quality. Higher quantities and quality of the five factors make the system (whether a nation-state or an organization) more productive (other things being equal). As used here the organization factor is broad and can include the quality of the institutional framework governing productive activities and the quality of the organizational rules and management practices of the productive organizations. The three structural dimensions are vertical differentiation, horizontal differentiation, and centralization/decentralization. Vertical differentiation is labeled stratification by sociologists and involves inequalities in income, wealth, power, opportunities, social status, rights, and privileges. Horizontal differentiation involves skills, roles, and group identities. A high degree of differentiation in skills and roles marks an advanced division of labor and high societal complexity, which are associated with socioeconomic development. High differentiation in group identities is associated with low societal integration. The third dimension of structure, centralization, deals with the system or geographic level at which activities are coordinated and controlled. This should not be confused with the vertical differentiation of power, because centralized control could be exercised in a participatory democratic structure.

The five processes utilized in our theory are integration, interaction, repression, social control and regulation, and productive labor. Integration can be viewed structurally as the height of group boundaries (or the obstacles to interaction), but more generally it is understood as the degree to which the system components work together in producing collective outputs and system survival. Interaction is measured in both quantity and quality. The quality dimension is normally measured on a cooperation/conflict scale. Repression and social control are alternative methods for discouraging harmful or damaging behavior and for encouraging positive behavior. Productive labor involves both paid and unpaid activities that produce valued goods and services. Population is membership size. Finally, the environment for the nation-state consists of the other nation-states and the system of international institutions. The major dimension in this factor is the degree of threat or danger posed by other nations to the subject nation.

To simplify the above theoretical framework, the fifteen factors can be grouped into three categories: socioeconomic development factors, progressive factors, and contextual factors. Socioeconomic development contains eight of the above factors: the five factors of production (capital, labor, knowledge and technology, resources, and organization), the differentiation of skills and roles, interaction across collective units, and productive labor. The progressive factor contains five of the above factors: the equality dimensions, decentralization, integration (including high legitimacy, low differentiation of identities, and low disturbances), social control in high compliance to collective rules, and low repression. This factor is progressive because it embodies the principles of equality, democracy, the rule of law, normative rather than coercive integration, decisions being proximate to rather than distant from the people, group tolerance, and legitimacy. These are the major categories for the impact analysis of the consequences of scarcity on nation-states and will be the focus of this chapter. The contextual factor includes population and the environment (for some purposes, area could be included), which feed into the issue of scarcity.

Theories of social change have focused on socioeconomic develop-ment, for this is the major source of change in the past four hundred years. At the heart of socioeconomic development are the five factors of production: capital, labor, knowledge/technology, resources, and organization, and the many variables that generate them, such as education, research and development, the division of labor, appropri-ate values, communications, dense networks, high interactions and exchanges, laws for contracts and property rights and their enforce-ment, and so on. As the five factors and their associated variables improve and increase, they increase production but also tend to im-prove and increase one another and thus further increase production. Thus, the socioeconomic development factor is a self-causing and maintaining factor in that it is caused by the variables within it and their causal interactions. Once it builds up some momentum the nation-state "takes off to self sustained growth" (Rostow 1960) until external forces (such as environmental and resource limits) or system disintegration stop it.

There have been endless debates over which variable or variables are the most important to igniting and stimulating this self-causing factor. Marx and many other sociologists have credited technology as the prime mover, while Weber gave more credit to rational legal orga-nization, values that encouraged savings and investments, and the work ethic. More recently social capital is being emphasized. Coleman (1988, 1990), Putnam (1993, 1994), and Drucker (1993) emphasize the role of knowledge and knowledge workers. It is not necessary to settle this debate because it is sufficient for our purposes to recognize the contribution of all these variables to socioeconomic development.

In this chapter we examine the impacts of economic growth (a major component of the socioeconomic development) and scarcity on the progressive factor, drawing upon the social science literature. Our finding is that economic growth enhances the progressive factor and scarcity weakens it. Scarcity tends to decrease equality, integra-tion, normative social control, democracy, and system legitimacy, while increasing conflict, regulation, disturbances, repression, and centralization. What is uncertain, however, is how nation-states will respond to these negative impacts of scarcity. It is conceivable that society's response to scarcity will involve reforms that make it more progressive than ever. More ominous predictions, however, seem more likely.

Impacts of Economic Growth and Scarcity on Inequality

Under current conditions economic growth decreases inequality, and scarcity increases inequality. Economic growth may have had negative effects on equality up to the nineteenth century as most of the people remain at a subsistence level and the new wealth goes mainly to a small elite (Kuznets 1955). Even more recently it has increased inequality during the early stages of technological improvement and industrialization in agricultural societies (Kuznets 1963). As Kuznets points out, however, the fuller impact of economic growth is to increase equality, and much empirical evidence for the past half century demonstrates this (Ahluwalia 1974; Bollen and Jackman 1985; Blumberg 1980; Chan 1989; Gagliani 1987; Jackman 1975; Lecaillon et al. 1984; Lindert and Williamson 1985; Lipset 1978, 1994; Muller 1988; Myrdal 1956; Ophuls and Boyan 1992; Viditch 1980; Ward 1978; Weede 1993; Williamson 1990; Williamson and Lindert 1980). The main explanation why economic growth increases equality as expounded by Lenski (1966; Lenski, Lenski and Nolan 1991) is that economic growth greatly increases the need for knowledge. As a result, elites can command a much smaller percent of the useful knowledge needed to expand production and their wealth, so they must depend on an increasingly knowledgeable and sophisticated labor force. Knowledge requirements lead to the expansion of education (education can be considered a component of socioeconomic development), the middle class, and the professions. Elites highly reward these groups to motivate high performance and greatly increase production, and thereby their wealth. Even though their share of the production thereby decreases, their wealth grows faster than if they tried to retain a greater proportion of the gains in production but thereby slowed its growth.

> In an expanding economy, an elite can make economic concessions in **relative** terms without necessarily suffering any loss in **absolute** terms. In fact, if the concessions are not too large, and the rate of the economy's growth is great enough, relative losses can even be accompanied by **substantial** absolute gains. (Lenski 1966, 314)

Put in economic terms Lenski's thesis is that economic development after some threshold of industrialization results in diminishing and even negative returns to elites for their monopolizing the surplus. He also points out that educated workers are not as vulnerable to exploitation as unskilled workers who must compete with masses of other unskilled workers. Educated workers have a better bargaining position that translates into higher incomes. Finally, he discusses how economic growth facilitates the rise of democratic institutions and these in turn increase the political power of lower groups that usually translates into more favorable policies and economic benefits for them.

The above arguments point to elite concessions for their greater absolute benefit and lower groups wresting benefits from upper groups through democratic mechanisms. Another equalizing force is the diffusion of education (which makes society more productive and makes employers richer). When education is rare, returns to education are very high and incomes very unequal. When education is widespread, the middle class expands greatly and, as Lecaillon and others (1984) argue, there is increased competition among qualified applicants, which reduces the relative incomes of the high-skilled occupations (unless they organize to reduce competition). Another equalizing force that is related to the diffusion of education is the upgrading of the occupational structure so that it no longer is a bottom heavy pyramid but bulges in the middle (Lipset 1978).

The above discussion looks at inequality in changes in the production system. Economic growth also increases equality in changes in the consumption system (Blumberg 1980; Firebaugh and Beck 1994; Lipset 1978). The consumption gap among classes declines as the lower class gets medical care, electricity, indoor plumbing, refrigerators, telephones, television, and possibly even cars. The rich have more and higher quality goods but their life-styles do not differ so markedly as elites and peasants in less developed countries.

Another argument that identifies economic growth with greater equality is provided by Ophuls and Boyan (1992). They observe that the normal condition for human societies is scarcity and this condition makes governments necessary for keeping the peace by regulating property to prevent the war of each against all over scarce goods. In keeping the peace "civilized polities have always institutionalized a large measure of inequality, oppression, and conflict" (189). Exceptions to this rule can occur in times of relative abundance as in the past several centuries, which have "made our societies and our civilization what they are today—relatively open, egalitarian, libertarian, and conflict-free" (190). They predict, therefore, that a return to the more normal conditions of scarcity would replace democracy, freedom, individualism, equality, and domestic peace with inequality, oppression, and conflict. In sum, economic growth increases equality and greatly improves the situation of lower groups under current conditions.

In contrast to the positive effects of economic growth, scarcity has negative effects. There is consensus among scholars that scarcity increases inequality (Blumberg 1980; Finsterbusch 1983; Gurr 1985; Lipset 1978; Ophuls and Boyan 1992; Viditch 1980). Five arguments support this proposition. First, because scarcity is the opposite of economic growth, it should have the opposite effects. Two impacts of scarcity are contained in this argument: scarcity eliminates jobs and income disproportionately for lower groups, and scarcity reduces the willingness of upper groups to support programs and policies that benefit the lower groups.

Economic growth expands jobs and opportunities. This generally allows lower groups choices between jobs and reduces the number who must accept truly exploitive wages. In contrast scarcity shrinks the job market, especially the marginal, unskilled jobs, and greatly increases the competition among the unskilled for the remaining jobs that tend to be offered at depressed wages. Economic growth also provides an expanding pie that can finance concessions of various kinds made to lower groups, including welfare for the needy and training for the unemployed. Scarcity, on the other hand, limits society's ability to address the needs of the needy. In political terms this means that the demands of lower groups for better lives in times of scarcity cannot be satisfied without threatening the favorable circumstances of the upper groups. Because the upper groups have the political power, the demands and needs of the lower groups will not be met. Furthermore, the lack of assistance for the lower groups can be justified by claims that such policies would divert resources from those who would invest in economic growth and harm the lower groups more in the long run (the trickle-down theory). This argument seems to be contradicted by evidence that welfare policies have been instituted in times of hardship, but as Gurr (1985) points out, they were always premised on the depressed times being short-term. He argues that a relatively permanent scarcity would greatly limit welfare policies.

The second explanation for scarcity's negative impact on equality is that scarcity translates into inflation, which more adversely impacts lower groups (Blumberg 1980; Gurr 1985; Stretton 1976; Viditch 1980). They spend a greater percent of their income than do upper groups on consumer goods, which have high resource inputs and will inflate substantially with scarcity. Upper groups buy greater quantities of goods but less proportionally. They also spend more on quality, which increases the value of most goods without using much more resources. Quality goods need not inflate as much from resource scarcity as lower quality goods. Upper groups also buy bigger homes and estates, which will inflate with scarcity, but as owners they will benefit when these appreciate in value. On the other hand, the poor pay rent and will experience a marked decline in their standard of living even if they manage to stay employed.

The third explanation of why scarcity increases inequality is that upper groups can better protect themselves from the negative effects of scarcity (Gurr 1985; Ophuls and Boyan 1992; Streeton 1976). They organize faster and more effectively to advance and protect their interests (see Olson 1965, 1982). The managerial and professional classes and unionized labor have some control over the terms of their remuneration and keep them at the level of inflation, which increases inflation even more for the politically and economically weak.

The fourth explanation of why scarcity increases inequality is that as resources become more scarce they become more unevenly distributed. Midlarsky (1982) presents a sophisticated mathematical argument for increasing inequality with the degree of scarcity of a resource and finds actual distributions closely fitting his mathematical models. He then reports a high cross-national correlation between population increase (which increases scarcity relative to land) and inequality in post-World War II agricultural societies. Other studies show high rates of population growth being correlated with high inequality (see Bollen and Jackman 1985; Kuznets 1955; Simpson 1990; Williamson 1991). Finally, Midlarsky demonstrates scarcity is related to inequality, civil strife, and revolution in agrarian societies (see also Russett 1964; Tanter and Midlarsky 1967).

The fifth explanation of why scarcity increases inequality is that the controllers of resources, who are predominantly the rich, will gain in times of scarcity while the rest of the population suffers. Just as homeowners and renters profit from inflation and scarcity, so do those who control natural resources that are becoming scarce.

Impacts of Economic Growth and Scarcity
on Integration

Economic growth increases integration and scarcity decreases it. Economic growth does not eliminate group identities and intergroup conflict, but it does mitigate the conflict between groups, reduces its violent expression, and channels it into legal political actions and compromisable demands (Finsterbusch 1983; Gurr 1985; Heilbroner 1992; Ophuls and Boyan 1992; Shefrin 1980; Stretton 1976). Ophuls and Boyan (1992) point out that economic growth leads to rising expectations so that each generation expects to become richer than its parents. "Thanks to this expectation of growth, the class conflict and social discontent typical of early nineteenth-century Europe were all but absent in America" (237). Throughout this century, growth continued to be a basis for political solidarity. It allows economic bargaining to replace conflict over political principle and the basic structure of society as illustrated by labor winning bargaining power and subsequent economic gains while dropping its demands for socialism. As long as everyone is improving economically, the demands for equality of income and wealth are weak, especially if upper groups can plausibly claim that the current unequal system is necessary for a productive economy. As Ophuls and Boyan observe, "American political history is but the record of a more or less amicable squabble over the division of the spoils of a growing economy" (238). Economic growth, therefore, tends to legitimate the system of inequality and dampen the conflict that inequality stimulates.

Shefrin (1980) similarly explains the connection between economic growth and low or mitigated conflict by describing how it supports what he calls consensus politics in America (nonpolarized, nonideological, and nonradical). Actual conflict is over limited demands by limited strategies and resulting in limited concessions. People do not demand basic change or deeply resent their subordinate position in the economic hierarchy, because economic growth makes them optimistic about their economic future and makes established means for personal betterment appear appropriate.

Economic growth strengthens integration not only by reducing conflict but also by giving people what they want, muting their protests, supporting a pragmatic bargaining style of politics, forestalling civil strife, and enhancing system legitimacy. Ophuls and Boyan (1992) point out that economic growth provides the basis for pragmatic politics, which controls social conflict, diverting it from basic issues to economic bargaining, which is a matter of a little more or a little less. Because economic growth means that even losers win something and because the bargaining is continuous, even losers support the system because they hope to win more next time. Another way that growth enhances integration is by increasing legitimacy. As Lipset (1960) argues, economic development creates the perception of effectiveness and effectiveness is a major cause of system legitimacy.

The effects of scarcity are the opposite. There is widespread agreement that scarcity is likely to reduce integration even though there is not much empirical evidence to draw upon. Scarcity decreases integration by increasing competition, conflict, and disturbances, and decreasing regime effectiveness and system legitimacy. These impacts in turn tend to increase repression and undermine or weaken democracy (Boulding 1973; Finsterbusch 1983; Gurr 1985; Heilbroner 1992; Lipset 1978, 1994; Ophuls and Boyan 1992; Shefrin 1980; Stretton 1976). Five explanations have been advanced in support of this proposition. First, scarcity negates the positive functions of economic growth for integration. Many analysts argue that scarcity will intensify class conflict (Blumberg 1980; Boulding 1973; Gurr 1985; Heilbroner 1992; Ophuls and Boyan 1992; Shefrin 1980). Boulding's exposition of this point is particularly stark.

> In the stationary state, there is no escape from the rigors of scarcity. If one person or group becomes richer, then the rest of society must become poorer. Unfortunately, this increases the payoffs for successful exploitation—that is, the use of organized threat in order to redistribute income. In progressive societies exploitation pays badly; for almost everybody, increasing their productivity pays better. . . . In the stationary state, unfortunately, investment in exploitation may pay better than investment in progress. Stationary states, therefore, are frequently mafia-type societies in which the government is primarily an instrument for redistributing income toward the powerful and away from the weak. (1973, 95)

Shefrin (1980, 3) expresses this theme thus: "In the absence of growth . . . more income or opportunity for disadvantaged classes necessarily involves attacks upon the possessions and privileges of the economic elite. The stratification system itself must then become the visible reason for relative deprivation and the visible obstacle to advancement."

Scarcity provides conditions that do not lend themselves to pragmatic compromising politics, and issues of basic structure reemerge in the political arena. The expanding pie allowed new demands to be at least partially satisfied without sacrifice by the more powerful. It allowed the government to support business interests at the same time that it provided welfare and defense. A shrinking pie means that more severe choices between these policies have to be made, and, therefore, basic principles come into conflict. Furthermore, environmental policies are matters of principle and are not legitimately framed in economic terms. How much is a life worth? How much increase in future cancers can be justified by costs in millions of dollars? How much employment should be sacrificed for an endangered species? These are not good issues for the bargaining table.

Another problem with a shrinking pie is that the conflict between classes and groups becomes a zero sum game in which someone must lose if someone else gains. When the contest results in big winners and little winners, as with the distribution of the expanding pie, the conflict is not as intense as when it results in winners and losers or big losers and little losers. Scarcity also increases resentment. Most Americans do not complain about the obscene wealth of others when they can have their own piece of the American dream. With scarcity, however, the profligate consumption of the wealthy is likely perceived as using up limited resources and leaving less for others. Rationing or some other type of resource-use planning may be advocated and clashes over principles becomes likely. Furthermore, scarcity removes the justification for inequality, which is that the inequality is needed to produce economic growth. If economic growth is not possible owing to environmental limits, this argument loses force, gross inequality becomes less tolerable, and conflict increases.

The second explanation of why scarcity decreases integration is derived from deprivation theory as developed by Gurr (1970, 1985). Unless scarcity arrives very slowly to allow for gradual adjustments, scarcity will cause strong feelings of deprivation as reality falls far short of expectations. The deprivation-induced anger and collective action may at first be deflected away from political institutions toward competitors or opponents or into self-destructive and antisocial behavior.

One would anticipate intensified labor-management conflict and an increase in hostility toward minorities and politically-unpopular groups. The racist policies of the rightist National Front in Britain are a case in point, and by this interpretation their policies are a form of scapegoating. One might also expect an increase in anomic individual behavior among the most deprived. A horrific model is provided by the black underclass in the United States, a group which has responded to institutionalized poverty during the last two decades with high and rising rates of interpersonal violence, substance abuse, and predatory crime. (1985, 61)

In the long run, however, the anger will be directed toward the polity, the powerful, and the system of inequality, and more radical demands and forms of political action will become more legitimate and prevalent.

The third explanation of why scarcity decreases integration is derived from Tilly's (1978) mobilization theory of collective action as reported by Gurr (1985). In times of economic decline, competition increases and groups that organize to protect or advance their special interests will do far better than individuals or weakly organized groups. Those who act first will gain the most benefits, because scarcity will rapidly deplete the government's ability to confer benefits. Furthermore, governments will increasingly respond to challengers with repression, for it is less costly in the short term than concessions. Collective action, therefore, will become more costly, but the costs of inaction are likely to increase even faster. Scarcity, therefore, spurs interest-group organization and the intensification of conflict among groups. Tilly also uses the cost-benefit logic to argue that scarcity fosters conditions that greatly favor revolutionary conflict, particularly the withering of support for the government and the shifting of the previously uncommitted to support the challengers.

The fourth explanation of why scarcity decreases integration focuses on the legitimacy problems of governments in times of economic decline. The importance of economic growth for legitimacy is a favorite theme of Lipset (1960, 1978, 1994). "Legitimacy is best gained by prolonged effectiveness, effectiveness being the actual performance of the government and the extent to which it satisfies the basic needs of most of the population and key power groups" (1994, 8). Unpopular governments can often stay in power in times of economic growth, but economic failure will likely facilitate a breakdown. Established democracies generally have a reservoir of popular support and may survive economic decline for a while. Over time, however, scarcity erodes legitimacy, making even democracies vulnerable to authoritarian movements as in the 1930s.

Another link between scarcity and eroding legitimacy is the type of government policies that scarcity requires. They will require sacrifice. People will have to bear costs and consume less to protect the environment and adjust to scarcity, and these will be unpopular policies as evidenced by the public's rejection in 1978 of President Carter's five-cent-a-gallon gasoline tax. A likely scenario is that the government will institute many relatively painless policies, which will not deal adequately with the problem and allow the crisis to get worse and more costly to deal with. Its failure will decrease legitimacy.

Our attention has been mainly on the developed democracies. When we consider the Third World, the scarcity-induced declines in integration can lead to government collapse and anarchy. Kaplan (1994) provides vivid images of current anarchic situations in West Africa that make societal breakdown seem a very plausible impact of scarcity in societies with weak institutions.

West Africa is becoming the symbol of worldwide demographic, environmental, and societal stress, in which criminal anarchy emerges as the real "strategic" danger. Disease, overpopulation, unprovoked crime, scarcity of resources, refugee migrations, the increasing erosion of nation-states and international borders, and the empowerment of private armies, security firms, and international drug cartels are now most tellingly demonstrated through a West African prism. (1994, 46)

He describes countries where the government cannot provide law and order over most of the country and not even in many parts of the capital at night. He cites a State Department report that describes a major African country as "becoming increasingly ungovernable." His study echoes what Rashmi Mayur wrote a decade earlier (1985) about the devastating results of the population explosion in the urban areas of India, which included the real possibility in the near future of "mass starvation, widespread misery, and breakdown of the local and even global social fabric" (27) and "social, political, and institutional collapse" (28).

The fifth explanation of why scarcity decreases integration is that it aggravates all fissures in society. The shrinking pie intensifies the class struggle as discussed earlier, but Blumberg (1980, 220) adds that scarcity "will almost inevitably increase the overall level of social nastiness" and aggravate all fissures and cleavages, "creating social conflict amid a general scramble for self-aggrandizement." He goes on to describe how racial, gender, educational, generational, and regional conflicts are likely to intensify in the United States.

Impact of Economic Growth and Scarcity on Democracy

Economic growth strengthens democracy and scarcity threatens it. The positive effects of economic growth on democracy has been a major theme in Lipset's work (Lipset 1960, 1978, 1994; Lipset, Seong, and Torres 1993; Diamond, Linz, and Lipset 1990), and it has strong empirical support (Cutright 1963; Diamond 1992; Bollen 1979; Bollen and Jackman 1985a; Flanigan and Fogelman 1971; Inkeles 1991; Neubauer 1967; Olsen 1968). The explanation, in part, is due to the positive effects of economic growth on equality and integration, which both strengthen democracy. It also expands the middle class, the educated, and the percent of the population that have a stake in the system and would be adversely affected by political instability. With the class pyramid bulging at the middle instead of polarized between a small elite and the poor masses, power holders have much less to fear from losing the reigns of government in an election, for the change in policies would not be very radical. "A large middle class tempers conflict by rewarding moderate and democratic parties and penalizing extremist groups" (Lipset 1960, 51). Economic growth and the expansion of education also increase intermediary organizations and tolerance toward those with different views, both of which are essential to the effective functioning of democracy. Finally, economic growth reduces the intensity of conflict as pointed out above and accommodates the resolving of issues and handling of demands through democratic bargaining (see Kassiola 1990; Ophuls and Boyan 1992).

Many other effects of economic growth directly or indirectly strengthen democracy. Lipset explains some of these.

> The general income level of a nation also affects its receptivity to democratic norms. If there is enough wealth in the country so that it does not make too much difference whether some redistribution takes place, it is easier to accept the idea that it does not matter greatly which side is in power. But if loss of office means serious losses for major power groups, they will seek to retain or secure office by any

means available. A certain amount of national wealth is likewise necessary to ensure a competent civil service. The poorer the country, the greater the emphasis on nepotism—support of kin and friends. And this in turn reduces the opportunity to develop the efficient bureaucracy which a modern democratic state requires. (1960, 52)

There is widespread agreement that scarcity is a threat to democracy. We give five explanations for this view. First, as with equality and integration, scarcity cancels the positive effects of economic growth. However, it does not necessarily produce the opposite effects. For example, it does not necessarily shrink the middle class. On the other hand, it could stimulate radicalism, which a large middle class tends to inhibit. Scarcity also increases inequality and decreases integration, which in turn threaten or weaken democracy. The aggravated conflict and loss of legitimacy that scarcity is likely to cause are particularly troublesome for the survival of democracy.

The second explanation of why scarcity weakens or threatens democracy is that it creates problems and crises that are hard for democracies to solve. Then when a democracy fails and the problems deepen, the public is tempted to jettison democracy for a more decisive, forceful, active, and authoritarian government. The strength of democracy is its responsiveness to the will of the people. This strength becomes a weakness in times of scarcity. Dealing with scarcity problems requires sacrifice, restraint, coercion against enjoyed but ecologically harmful behavior, and coercion enforcing ecologically helpful behavior. These requirements, however, are not popular. Politicians in democracies, therefore, usually do not pass the tough legislation that is needed. For example, the American response to the oil crisis in 1973 was to lower the speed limit to 55 MPH and urge the public to voluntarily lower the thermostat in winter. Later it gave tax deductions for some insulation costs and required better gas mileage for cars with a very leisurely implementation schedule. Great sacrifice, such as an increase of $1.50-per-gallon gasoline tax, was never even considered.

Democracy, laissez-faire, and minimal regulation have together helped create some of the problems of scarcity. The famous "tragedy of the commons," or overexploitation of the environment, is the natural result of unregulated free choice. The democratic answer is mutual coercion mutually agreed upon, but it is hard to get that agreement. Ophuls and Boyan state the problem thus:

Under conditions of ecological scarcity, the individuals, possessing an inalienable right to pursue happiness as they define it and exercising their liberty in a basically laissez-faire system, will inevitably produce the ruin of the commons. Thus the individualistic basis of society, the concept of inalienable rights, the purely self-defined pursuit of happiness, liberty as maximum freedom of action, and the laissez-faire principle itself all become problematic. All require major modification or perhaps even abandonment if we wish to avert inexorable environmental degradation and eventual extinction as a civilization. Certainly, democracy as we know it cannot conceivably survive. (1992, 199–200)

The third explanation of why scarcity weakens democracy is that it generates many technical issues that lend themselves poorly to participatory decision-making procedures. Many important decisions with significant distributional side effects are best handled by experts without much public participation. We would expect, therefore, that some amount of democracy would be sacrificed to technocracy.

Ophuls and Boyan (1992) develop this line of argument at length. Assuming that democracies will call upon technological fixes to solve environmental problems with minimum material sacrifice, they observe:

Numerous other writers of varying persuasions see the same trend: more technology means greater complexity and greater need for knowledge and technical expertise; the average citizen will not be able to make a constructive contribution to decision making, so that "experts" and "authorities" will rule perforce; and because accidents cannot be permitted, much less individual behavior that deviates from technological imperatives, the grip of planning and social control will of necessity become a stranglehold. . . . For these problems will require us to depend on a special class of experts in charge of our survival and well-being: a "priesthood of responsible technologists." (209)

In this way "democracy must give way to elite rule . . . [because] the more closely one's situation resembles a perilous sea voyage, the stronger the rationale for placing power and authority in the hands of the few who know how to run the ship" (209). The resulting state will be "more authoritarian and less democratic" (215).

The fourth explanation of why scarcity weakens democracy is that it can cause fear and potentially even panic, which can undermine the confidence in democratic institutions required for them to function

without a strong show of force. This line of argument is more speculative than the others but still highly plausible. Heilbroner (1992)
observes:

> As the historian of ancient and modern democracies illustrate, the
> pressure of political movement in times of war, civil commotion, or
> general anxiety pushes in the direction of authority, not away from
> it. . . . The passage through the gauntlet ahead may be possible only
> under governments capable of rallying obedience far more effectively
> than would be possible in a democratic setting. If the issue for man-
> kind is survival, such governments may be unavoidable, even neces-
> sary. (132–34)

The fifth explanation of why scarcity threatens democracy is that
lower groups in times of scarcity are ineffective in getting their demands met by peaceful means, so some of them turn to more radical
and even violent means. The state is likely to become more authoritarian and repressive to deal with the dynamics of the resulting civil
conflict (Gurr 1985).

Other Impacts of Economic Growth and Scarcity

Just as economic growth has had nearly an infinite number of impacts
over the past centuries, so will scarcity have a great range of impacts.
These have not been discussed and empirically investigated as much
as scarcity's impacts on equality, integration, and democracy, so we
will not discuss them extensively here. A number of these have already been mentioned in connection with equality, integration, and
democracy. Of special interest is Ophuls and Boyan's speculation that
scarcity makes individualism, liberty, minimum restraints, laissez-faire,
and inalienable rights of individuals dysfunctional. They will lose some
legitimacy relative to competing values, so the practices associated
with individualism could be curtailed.

One structural change that is often mentioned in connection with
scarcity is centralization. Scarcity requires greater planning of the use
and allocation of the limited resources, which requires some centralization of control as in time of war. Ophuls and Boyan (1992) hold out
hopes that polities can be democratic and decentralized in the long
run but not in the short run. "During the transition to any form of
steady state one can envision, it would be imperative to minimize

pollution and use resources as efficiently as possible, and this probably would mean greater centralization and expert control in the short term" (213).

Another common speculation is that war and international conflict will increase greatly under scarcity. For example, Gurr summarizes the record on this impact thus:

> Resource scarcity also has consequences for foreign policy, many of which are conflictual. Historically, warfare has been a common response to ecological constraints and economic decline. Colonial expansion and conquest of weak but resource-rich neighboring states provided many states with new sources of supply, economic opportunities for surplus population, and new markets. Carnciro (1970) proposes that resource scarcity and population pressure together were the primary engines of state formation and imperial expansion throughout history. Choucri and North (1975) have demonstrated [a] historical European association between population pressures, increased resources scarcity, and "lateral pressure" to expand territorially. (1985, 65)

Gurr's exposition focuses on wars by the strong against the weak, but according to Heilbroner (1992) underdeveloped countries or terrorist groups might also war or terrorize rich countries, demanding a greater sharing of world wealth and resources. Nuclear weapons are spreading and nuclear blackmail could occur any day now. As national and subnational identities heighten, they make nonviolent resolution to conflicts less feasible.

If Heilbroner is right, the prospects are terrifying. Nuclear materials have become widely available through leaks from the former Soviet Union (Nelan 1994), and nuclear-bomb making is within the capabilities of many terrorist groups (Begley 1993; Lemonick 1994; Cetron and Davies 1994). Biologic and chemical weapons are even easier to acquire and their results can be far more destructive (Cetron and Davies 1994). Terrorist actions are predicted by experts to increase in number and in destruction even if economic growth continues (Cetron and Davies 1994). With increasing scarcity the developed world will be in great danger. Democracies may have to tread on civil rights and greatly increase police powers to deal with the danger of terrorism. This is likely to move America further toward authoritarianism.

Another dismal prognosis for the impacts of scarcity is societal regression to thoroughly corrupt governments, as "rent seeking" by officials under conditions of scarcity becomes prolific and profitable. Though there is not strong evidence for this proposition, Lipset observes that "corruption . . . is inherent in systems built on poverty" (1994, 3) and Klitgaard (1988, 1991) demonstrates that this is the case. What is uncertain, however, is how likely it is for modern nonnepotistic bureaucracies to regress significantly.

Somewhat arbitrarily we end our review of scarcity's impacts at this point. Overwhelmingly, the literature discusses only impacts that are negative from a progressive point of view. Some comments are optimistic, but they must be regarded as wishes, because they are not supported by analyses that show that they are likely outcomes of scarcity. In sum, we have not come across any good news about the impacts of scarcity.

Societal Response to Scarcity

It goes without saying that predictions about how society will respond to relatively long-term scarcity are speculative. They are contingent upon many factors, including the nature and extent of the crisis, public readiness for change, degree of government autonomy from control by the economic elite, and the idiosyncrasies of the leader(s). Accordingly, we offer the following comments as an initial exploration of the topic for democratic capitalist societies.

We focus on three principal sets of actors as central to the societal response: individuals, business firms, and the government. Their actions will be carried out in perceptions, values, and options. It is important to assess, therefore, the influences on perceptions and values on the one hand, and the constraints and forces that determine options on the other hand. Information and ideas as mediated by the media, opinion leaders, universities, and the scientific community affect perceptions, while the media, educational and religious institutions, and opinion leaders affect values.

The first societal response that we predict is the increased production and diffusion of information on environmental issues with the result that environmental issues will be perceived as getting worse and requiring more collective action. Currently, the media present much information on the deterioration of the environment, the depletion of resources, pollution, ecosystem limits, environmental dangers, and health effects. The media is probably responding to the public's interest in these issues. Surveys of public attitudes toward protecting the environment continue to find strong support (Abramson and Inglehart 1995; Dunlap 1993; Inglehart 1990, 1995; Inglehart and Abramson 1994; Portney 1992). Social scientists were surprised that the environmental movement did not rapidly rise and then rapidly decline in salience. This is the normal pattern for national-issue concerns. Instead, it has remained strong for twenty-five years.

It appears that environmental issues have passed a threshold from being the concern of peripheral groups to being the concern of both peripheral groups and core institutions. At universities, courses, programs, and research on environmental concerns are multiplying as are conferences, journals, articles, and books on these topics. Environmental nonprofit organizations have become strong and have real power in Washington (Brulle 1995; Harper 1996). A growing number of businesses are making good profits on pollution control, waste disposal, and other environmental services, so there is a small but growing pro-environment business interest lobbying on Capitol Hill. Environmental legislation and agency attention to environmental problems have become major concerns at the federal level. All these changes make it safe to predict that information gathering and dissemination on the environment should increase, especially because information gathering faces few obstacles.

The second societal response that we predict is technological innovation to reduce the costs of depleting resources and to protect the environment. Businesses will respond to rising costs of resources by using resource-saving technologies and practices. Market forces should spur the development of new conserving technologies. Other innovations will be directed at protecting the environment in ways that do not threaten current life-styles. Many of the innovations will be stimulated by subsidies or by regulations concerning pollution, recycling, conservation, and hazardous substances. Regulations that are politically feasible are likely to have relatively low costs to industry or be widely perceived as important enough to pass over industry resistance. Regulations often are necessary to make it worthwhile for industry to develop new technologies and practices for protecting the environment or more efficiently use and reuse resources. Another source for new technologies is the academic research community, which is subsidized by government and foundation contracts and grants. As awareness of the crisis increases, it is likely that subsidies for research on relevant environmental issues would increase substantially.

The third response that we predict is a range of minor behavior changes by individuals. Increasingly, the public wants to do something to help solve the problems. They participate in recycling programs, buy "save-the-bay" license plates, and contribute in other relatively costless ways.

The crucial question is whether the above responses will be sufficient to improve the environment and set society on the course of sustainable development. One group of scientists, led by Julian Simon, judges environmental problems as less severe than the view developed here and has immense faith in the inventiveness and adaptiveness of human beings. These scientists think that such actions would go a long way toward solving any problems that do exist. Perhaps a few new governmental policies that are not too disruptive to the economy might be helpful, but no dramatic changes would be needed. They argue that environmental problems are often exaggerated by environmentalists and that there is much scientific uncertainty about their extent and potential impacts. They are sanguine on energy availability because fossil-fuels could provide for the world's energy needs far into the next century and nuclear fusion could provide all the energy that will be needed when fossil fuel production declines. (Davidson, the director of the Princeton Plasma Physics Laboratory, predicts that "an electricity-producing fusion demonstration reactor [will be] operating by 2025—or sooner if America so chooses" [1994]). Though this view is plausible (fueled by reports of four- and five-passenger prototype cars that get 70–120 miles per gallon being tested by European and Japanese auto companies [Mathews 1991, 311]), it is highly speculative and does not convince most people that the environment is not in crisis.

Some analysts view the environmental crisis as far more severe than the above optimists, but prescribe actions for dealing with it that are not too disruptive to the economy and demand only modest behavioral changes from the public. Gore's recommendations in *The Earth in Balance* (1992) are called a "Global Marshall Plan" to indicate how daring it is, but it relies heavily on market adjustments, voluntary actions, and nonradical changes in government policies to remove subsidies for environmentally destructive actions and to provide more incentives for environmentally helpful actions. It also emphasizes information gathering and learning. His program is ambitious and unacceptable to the controllers of Washington today, but does not step hard on anyone's toes. It avoids the really painful actions that will be necessary (except for population control in the Third World). In like manner Brown, Flavin, and Postel (1991) are cautious in their suggestions for saving the planet. Nevertheless, both books are rich in helpful policies and actions for addressing environmental problems.

Other scientists who make up a much larger group do not think as the optimists that new technologies and minor behavior changes will overcome environmental scarcity nor do they think as Gore and Brown/ Flavin/Postel that an ambitious government environmental program that avoids significant costs can do the job. These scientists conclude that more significant changes are needed. Following in this line of thinking, the crucial question is, What additional responses are likely or even feasible? Will people make significant changes in their life-style? Will businesses risk some profits to protect the environment? Will governments pass tough environmental legislation? The dominant answer provided by these analysts to all three questions is "No!" (Gurr 1985; Heilbroner 1992; Ophuls and Boyan 1992; Shefrin 1980; Streeton 1976).

This pessimistic view is based on three arguments: the public-goods/free-rider problem, the business of business is profits, and special interests have the power to resist tough new policies. The public-goods argument is that it is not in the rational self-interest of individuals or nations to voluntarily sacrifice for the good of the environment or for the conserving of nonrenewable resources, because they will lose out to others who continue to exploit the environment or use the scarce resources. People will not voluntarily reduce their travel miles by automobile to preserve petroleum; they must be encouraged to do so by high gasoline taxes or forced to do so by gasoline rationing. Nations will not voluntarily reduce their use of fossil fuel to slow down global warming unless other nations do the same, because they would pay heavy costs without getting any more benefits than those who paid no costs.

The argument that the business of business is profits asserts that solutions to environmental problems will not come from businesses unless government policies change their incentives. On their own they will conserve to save money and invent technologies that help them do more with less, but they will not stop doing harmful things from which they benefit nor will they do rightful things that cost them. They must be made to do these things by government policies, but, according to the third argument, they will prevent the passage of such policies (Schnaiberg and Gould 1994). Most commentators, therefore, are pessimistic about the government's ability to take the necessary actions. They believe, therefore, that environmental problems will worsen until an acute crisis forces a change in direction. At that point democratic societies are predicted to become much more authoritarian. In the remainder of this section, therefore, we will present the arguments from several commentators that current democratic polities will fail to deal adequately with environmental scarcity problems and their failure will likely lead to authoritarian systems.

Heilbroner argues that democracies in the developed world and all but "iron governments" in the underdeveloped world will fail. For the latter he argues that "the torrent of human growth imposes intolerable social strains on the economically backward regions" leading to high unemployment, widespread poverty, and urban disorganization. Such societies probably will be ruled either "by dictatorial governments serving the interests of a small economic and military upper class" or by a socialist "government with dedicated leadership, a well-organized and extensive party structure, and an absence of inhibitions with respect to the exercise of power" (1992, 37, 39).

His analysis of the prospects for the developed countries is less gruesome but runs in the same iron government direction. They will require "the most active use of political power" (124) to respond to threats from the underdeveloped world and to deal with the environmental problems.

Gurr (1985) travels a somewhat different path but reaches the same conclusion. He posits that the governments of developed countries will try to stimulate economic growth, but in a scarcity-induced decline they will fail and precipitate a legitimacy crisis. Thereupon, the politically advantaged groups will "assume increasingly autocratic and repressive control which will protect both their economic policies and positions from democratic challenges" (1985, 65).

Should these governments seek instead to adapt to ecological constraints by reducing consumption, they are likely to be defeated at the polls as the historical record shows. Only in an acute crisis are policies of restraint feasible and at that point they will be very painful and "probably will have sharply inegalitarian effects, and may require autocratic political solutions" (1985, 68). Thus, the outcome of environmental crisis, he predicts, is authoritarianism. His argument merits close attention.

In the worst case of escalating crisis, democratic governments which have lost credibility because of their inability to stimulate promised economic growth will face growing pressures from powerful groups seeking to protect themselves from hardship and will be challenged

Kurt Finsterbusch

simultaneously by protestors and rebels who are increasingly willing to use violent means. It is also likely—in fact, is presently the case in most advanced industrial societies—that governments will be fiscally constrained in attempts to buffer the impact of economic change. These are not circumstances conducive to programmatic political and social reform. The more immediate consequence is paralysis of democratic decision making. . . . In such situations governments lurch along from crisis to crisis while bureaucracy acts as caretaker.

Periods of prolonged crisis often are followed by fundamental change in political institutions, sometimes but not always accomplished by revolutionary means. The path most often taken in the contemporary histories of democratic and quasi-democratic capitalist societies is toward the establishment of authoritarian governments which abandon democratic practices and pretenses in order to resolve the crisis and reestablish a stable social order. (1985, 69)

Shefrin traces yet another path to the same authoritarian end. The title of his book is *The Future of U.S. Politics in an Age of Economic Limits* (1980). He begins with a view of the U.S. government being overwhelmed with demands by many special interest groups. Because the gains for the special interests are at the expense of the general good, he sees the political system as the new commons that is being overexploited. Furthermore, the entrenched pattern of incrementalism and delay in American government does not solve problems but only defers them. Meanwhile, policy failures increase because the increasing complexity of problems leads to unanticipated outcomes. The press of elections makes the U.S. polity very present oriented and ineffective on long-range issues. Finally, corporate power prevents effective environmental regulations. All these features make the U.S. government unsuited for dealing with environmental issues, which get much worse with delay. Hence, the system is likely to fail and become delegitimized. In all probability the growing problem of limits spells the end of consensus politics. At worst it means system collapse. In either case greater authoritarianism is likely.

Ophuls and Boyan (1992) present the most extensive analysis of the likely American response to scarcity, and their conclusions are pessimistic. Their thesis is that "ecological scarcity undercuts the basic laissez-faire, individualistic premises of the American political economy so that current institutions are incapable of meeting the challenges of scarcity" (217). A major problem is that potential solutions will be successfully opposed by powerful interests.

Ophuls and Boyan identify three characteristics of the American polity that have prevented and will prevent it from acting effectively on the problem of scarcity: (1) process politics, (2) incremental decision making, and (3) power fragmentation and administrative inadequacy. They contrast process politics, where outcomes are accepted if they result from legitimate procedures, with systems politics, where means are subordinated to ends. The environment does not have a chance in process politics, because the public wants growth for its jobs, opportunities, and lower prices and sides with for-profit interests against sound environmental policies. Incremental decision making supports short-term self-interest and produces the tragedy of the commons. It has led to the current environmental mess. The fragmentation of government and the numerous checks and balances that create long delays and weaken regulations make needed political action practically impossible. Meanwhile, the problems are growing so fast and are so complex that they create policy overload for the inadequate bureaucracy. Thus they conclude that the American polity has failed to act effectively and cannot. It must be radically changed and the change that they expect is greater authoritarianism.

In my earlier article exploring the consequences of scarcity, I came to conclusions like those presented above but predicted that democracies would institute the changes necessary to transform into a sustainable society and remain democratic if four conditions existed. The first two conditions are fairly high levels of equality and integration at the time of the crisis.

> Interest groups are likely to sacrifice for the common good and work together in addressing the crisis when groups are not very unequal or opposed to each other and when the political system is seen as serving all the people rather than only a segment. In other words, if injustice, inequality, and intergroup hostilities are high to start with, the crisis could pull the country apart. (Finsterbusch 1983, 68)

The other two conditions for successful adaptation by a democracy are the right kind of crisis and a charismatic leader. In a gradual crisis the tendency of democracies to be indecisive, inactive, and focused on the short term will make them likely to fail. Only in an urgent

> crisis are democracies likely to shift from their pattern of incrementalism, temporarily consolidate political power, and act decisively. . . . Finally, the survival of democracy may hinge on the degree of charisma

of the chief of state in the time of crisis. He will have to call for self-sacrifice and acceptance of major changes. Unless belief in him is strong, his program may not succeed or discontent may be explosively high. (Finsterbusch 1983, 69)

To the above four conditions for the survival of democratic institutions in long-term scarcity should be added a degree of government autonomy from special interests. It has to have room to operate free of the constraints of powerful groups to implement a program that serves the public interest and is perceived as just and therefore accepted as legitimate. In times of crisis, such as wartime, people are willing to sacrifice, but only if the burdens are shared fairly. If powerful special interests, especially the rich and the large corporations, protect themselves and bias the program, it will generate resentment and civil strife.

In sum, the societal response to scarcity will include research on the issues, technological innovations, and minor behavioral changes. These responses are likely because they will face little opposition. I also predict (in line with most commentators) that these responses will fail to adequately deal with environmentally induced scarcity with the result that democracies will drift into severe crises and the resulting political struggles will probably, but not inevitably, end in authoritarianism.

Social and Political Changes Required for a Sustainable Democratic Society

The literature on sustainability includes thousands of ideas about changes that would make societies more sustainable. Most of these are technical changes and conserving behavior. Space does not allow me to review them here. Rather I limit my remarks to some radical changes in the political economy of the United States that, in my judgment, might be needed to attain a sustainable democratic society. I recognize that many of these ideas are not likely to be implemented unless society is forced into them by an acute environmental crisis. In this section, however, I am not constrained by realism. The previous section presented what was expected; the present section presents what is recommended.

The first requirement for a sustainable democracy is to increase the ability of government to macromanage the economy to the extent that it needs to be macromanaged. For this purpose I recommend a planning agency. It would be a fourth branch of government designed along the lines described by Pirages and Ehrlich (1974) (which builds on Tugwell's [1970] proposal for a new constitution) or the version of this planning branch presented by Milbrath (1989). It would be charged with the tasks of

1. "formulation and regular revision of five-, ten-, and fifty-year plans for America's future" (Pirages and Ehrlich 1974, 174),

2. providing the research necessary for creating these plans,

3. recommending "legislation directly to Congress to implement new macroconstraints" (175), and

4. reporting "to the people annually on the state of the nation" (175).

At first it might contain

1. an Office of Environmental Protection for environmental planning and recommending environmental legislation,

2. an Office of Natural Resources for evaluating resource reserves and future needs and developing resource utilization plans including resource-depletion quotas,

3. an Office of Social Ecology for planning the social aspect of the transition to the sustainable society,

4. an Office of Economic Priorities for performing the duties of the Council of Economic Advisers and propose legislation for redirecting the economy to sustainability, and

5. an Office of Technology Assessment for evaluating major new technologies and designing research and development priorities.

The major social-design problem for this new branch of government is how to keep it independent from special-interest politics. Both Pirages and Ehrlich and Milbrath provide a number of suggestions for achieving this independence. Their most important recommendations are a constitutional mandate to make it an independent fourth branch of government and putting its governance in the hands of a distinguished board of directors. The directors would be prominent and broadly knowledgeable scientists, appointed by the president, confirmed by the Senate, serving for ten- or twelve-year staggered terms, and removable by impeachment only.

Our proposal for a fourth branch of government for planning sustainable policies would increase the centralization of society. Much of the sustainable society literature, however, presents a far more decentralized sustainable society than we do. Though we agree with the values that guide their vision, we believe that the crisis must be dealt with at the macro level first because of the way that power is structured both in nations and the world. Perhaps after national and global reforms are instituted, localism could flourish.

The second requirement for a sustainable democracy is for the power of major corporations to be brought under some measure of public control. They present the greatest threat to pluralist democracy today and effect the greatest special-interest bias in the government. Presently, they possess unaccountable power. The reform that we recommend is the federal chartering of all corporations that do interstate business and exceed some minimal size. In the beginning of the days of corporations, they were chartered by the states and had to report each year on how they served the public good to get their charter renewed. Then Delaware relaxed the chartering and renewal process to the point of providing no oversight and giving the corporations carte blanche. As a result so many corporations incorporated in Delaware that it did not need to have a personal income tax for a long time and it still does not have a sales tax. Very quickly New Jersey followed suit and also won handsomely in the corporation sweepstakes. Other states had to become similarly lax or lose out in the competition between states to recruit and retain businesses. The resulting unaccountability of corporations can be reversed by federal chartering and making charters contingent upon their demonstration of service to the public. In this way environmental impacts, plant closings, safety records, treatment of workers, and so forth could be monitored and the corporations disciplined more effectively than at present.

Another recommendation directed at the corporations is that corporations larger than some minimum size and conducting interstate business would pay government taxes in stock shares instead of money. This would cause a gradual dilution of its stock until the government owns 50 percent of its shares. Then what is good for General Motors would be good for the United States. The board of directors would be restructured to contain representatives of the government, communities containing its facilities, and other interests. In this way values other than profits would have to be honored, though profits would still be their main goal.

The above recommendations have addressed the capacity and fairness of the political economy but have not included reforms that directly deal with environmental problems. The major recommendations for this have been developed by Daly (1977) and are included here (and in nearly everyone's list of proposals for sustainability). They are:

1. setting of minimum and maximum limits on income and a maximum on wealth to discourage excessive consumption and mitigate inequality,

2. transferable birth licenses allocated 2.1 per woman by the government and marketable to achieve zero population growth, and

3. depletion quotas for all nonrenewable resources, set by the government to regulate the annual consumption of each resource, and auctioned to resource buyers. The quotas would slow depletion and lead to higher prices, which would encourage efficiencies and innovations.

All three procedures provide macroconstraints but do not interfere in the microprocesses that are governed by free markets and individual choices within those constraints.

Because the major natural resource in a country is its land, our final recommendation is a national land-use plan that would synchronize with state land-use plans. Real estate interests would provide formidable opposition to this policy to protect their financial interest in using or selling land for the highest price. Nevertheless, it is necessary to preserve agricultural lands, forests, and complex ecosystems and to deal with a wide range of environmental problems. Zoning is necessary in urban areas and now is necessary in other areas for many of the same principles. A current land-use trend that the plan would try to contain is the increasing dispersion of population to low-density housing, which causes high energy and transportation consumption, infrastructure inefficiencies, and greater ecosystem disruption.

The above seven recommendations are radical by current standards of political change. They could not be enacted except in an acute environmental crisis. Many other changes would also be needed for sustainability, including a major realignment of the culture and value system from an emphasis on material consumption and individualism to an emphasis on environmental vitality, inner development, and connections with others (see Brown 1980, Milbrath 1989). We do not, however, specify further the changes required to attain the sustainable society, because the problem is not a dearth of knowledge about what needs to be done, but the current lack of support for the needed changes.

9. Competition, Expansion, and Reaction

The Foundations of Contemporary Conflict

Joseph A. Tainter

The Social Environment and Reactive Process

We live, in some ways, in fortunate times. In a book that concerns present and future calamities, such a statement may seem incongruous. Yet amid all the present misfortunes we have the opportunity to learn, better than any previous people, the reasons for our problems. Any human event or process is a mere moment of reaction to previous events and processes. It is impossible to predict the future consequences of present events without understanding how the present itself has come to be. Historical knowledge is fundamental to designing a sustainable future. We are fortunate to have more such knowledge than any people who preceded us. We can become the first people to know where we are in history.

History is substantially a chronicle of reactive processes. For most societies and many people, the primary context to which they must adapt is not the natural environment, but other societies and other people. Responding to external pressures determines much of the political behavior of states and the cultural behavior of other types of institutions. The need to maintain a defensive posture, to protect citizens, to preserve territory, or merely to remain competitive drives much consumption of resources, regardless of cost. If the cost of protecting resources for the future is to lose autonomy, territory, or cultural identity today, resource conservation will always be foregone. This may be one of the most predictable regularities of political history. It represents an enduring conflict between surviving today at the expense of tomorrow and providing for tomorrow while accepting extinction today. Not surprisingly, history provides no example of a society that has chosen the latter.

One of history's clearest examples of reactive processes is the formation of what are called secondary states. Although states are costly organizations and require high levels of resources (Tainter 1988), they usually have a competitive advantage over less-complex systems. They also tend to be expansive, so that their less-complex neighbors are always in danger of being dominated or absorbed. Neighbors of states that wish to avoid this fate must develop organizational features that allow them to compete with states. This is secondary state formation. It is a major process by which the world has come to be filled with states. Archaeologists have been able to document only six cases of primary state formation in all of human history.[1] Every other state has formed secondarily, many by reactive processes.

Reactive processes have been responsible both for the formation of much of today's world political system and for what may be its impending dissolution. The world system is showing clear signs of fragmenting, manifested in the intensification of cultural identity, the formation of new cultural groups, the equation of cultural distinctiveness with political autonomy, and the establishment of new, smaller nations. The purpose of this chapter is to clarify the historical reasons behind today's culturally defined conflicts. Those conflicts can be understood in the historical context of competition among European nations, their global expansion and colonization, and the reaction of much of the world to Euramerican domination.[2] Politicians, diplomats, and international workers who confront today's disintegration and violence are working with a great handicap if they do not understand the origins of these problems or their reactive nature. Historical processes

1. These are: Mesopotamia and Egypt, ca. 3500–3000 B.C.; China and the Indus River Valley, ca. 2500 B.C.; and Mexico and Peru in the last few centuries B.C. (Service 1975,5).

2. Because this chapter is primarily historical, I do not discuss the recent cold war, nor its influence on the Third World. That influence was substantial and exacerbated the reactive processes described here.

have shaped contemporary violence and must be understood to comprehend that violence.

Two types of reactive historical processes are pertinent to understanding the many problems that confront the world today and threaten to intensify in the future. The first is the pattern of competition that forms when polities with equivalent military abilities contend for dominance. Borrowing a term from archaeological literature, that process is called *peer polity competition* (Renfrew 1982, 1986; Tainter 1992; see also Price 1977). The second is the pattern by which much of the world has reacted to 500 years of European expansion and 150 years of Euramerican domination. These processes in combination have set the foundation for the disintegrative forces of contemporary world politics.[3]

Peer Polity Competition in European History

For at least the past four thousand years, one of the fundamental historical processes has been competition among societies organized at near-equivalent levels of population, territory, technology, organization, per capita product, and military capability (Tainter 1992, 104–5). Such societies are termed peer polities (Renfrew 1982, 1986). Some examples include the warring states of post-Chou China, the Mycenaean polities, the city-states of classical Greece, the Italian city-states of the ancient, medieval, and Renaissance periods, the southern lowland Maya, medieval and Renaissance Europe, and our current era. It is characteristic of peer polities that their evolution is stimulated, not by reaction to a dominant power, nor by relations between cores and peripheries, but by their interaction.

The relations among peer polities typically involve both trade and competition. Trade does not concern us here; competition is a powerful stimulator of sociocultural change (Tainter 1988, 1992). Where natural or

---

3. This chapter represents a convergence of two lines of research. The first, on peer polity competition, was developed for the conference "Effects of War on Society," organized by Giorgio Ausenda. It was held May 26 to June 1, 1991, under the auspices of the Department of Public Education and Culture, Republic of San Marino (Ausenda 1992). The second, on contemporary culturally defined violence, was stimulated by the conference "The State under Siege: Political Disintegration in the Post–Cold War Era," organized by R. Brian Ferguson. It was held at the New York Academy of Sciences, April 22–24, 1994. I am grateful to Professors Ausenda and Ferguson for the opportunities to participate in these conferences.

fiscal resources are sufficient, peer polities may engage in conflict that stretches over generations or even centuries. Such conflicts may involve endless maneuvering for advantage, forming and dissolving of alliances, and continual striving to expand territory or influence at a neighbor's expense, or prevent the neighbor from doing the same. Peer polity competition selects for growth in the size and complexity of military systems; increases in the scale of warfare; innovations in technology, strategy, tactics, and logistics; and the reorganization of society to support competition (Tainter 1992).

In Europe of the past millennium, peer polity competition and warfare selected inexorably for larger states and greater capabilities for making war.[4] This competition was fundamentally related to the technological innovation that allowed European nations to dominate the globe over the past half millennium (Kennedy 1987; Parker 1988). The challenge to each polity to finance such a system of escalating competition is the key to comprehending how European peer polity competition came to change the world.

Europe before 1815 was almost always at war somewhere; scarcely a decade went by without at least one battle. From the twelfth through the sixteenth centuries France was at war from 47 percent of all years in some centuries to 77 percent in others. For England the range was 48 to 82 percent; for Spain, 47 to 92 percent. Even in the most peaceful centuries these nations were involved in war, on average, nearly every other year. In the entire sixteenth century there was barely a decade when Europe was entirely at peace. The seventeenth century enjoyed only four years of total peace; the eighteenth century, sixteen years (Parker 1988, 1; Rasler and Thompson 1989, 40). History provides few comparable examples of such lengthy peer polity conflict, with so many innovations and such far-reaching consequences (Tainter 1992).

An account of the history of this competition could be initiated almost anywhere. Its foundation was established with the collapse of

---

4. To characterize European states of the past millennium as peer polities is not to downplay the very significant differences in the organization of those societies. In the nineteenth century, for example, European societies ranged from feudal to industrial. Two factors make the peer-polity concept useful for evaluating European history, particularly for western and central Europe. The first is that competition demonstrably spurred lockstep developments in technology, organization, and finance, so that competitive states always tended to have approximately equivalent capabilities. The second is that, although states varied widely in size, population, and natural resources, the formation of alliances has tended to even out these inequities (Tainter 1992, 104).

the western Roman Empire and the formation of smaller successor-states. A starting point closer to the present will suffice, however. The development of siege warfare in the middle centuries of the present millennium is a useful point of reference, for it is directly related to subsequent developments in technology, strategy, and logistics.

The development of siege guns in the fifteenth century ended the advantage of stone-built castles and required changes in the strategies and technology of defense. From the early fifteenth century, fortification builders designed walls that could support defensive cannon. A short time later walls were built that could also withstand bombardment. By 1560 all the elements of the *trace italienne* had been developed: a fortification system of low, thick walls with angled bastions and eventually extensive outworks. It was an effective but expensive method of fortification, requiring much labor to construct. The city of Siena in 1553, for example, found it so expensive to build fortifications in this manner that no money was left for its army or fleet. Siena was, ironically, annexed by Florence, against which its fortifications had been built (Creveld 1989, 101–3; Parker 1988, 7, 9, 12).

The *trace italienne* was effective. To capture a place fortified in this way could take months or years. Offensive tacticians responded with more complicated siege methods, and their costs rose as well. A besieging force of perhaps fifty thousand had to be kept in place for weeks or months. Such a force required 475 tons of food per day, to which must be added ammunition, powder, and building materials. From this time on, local lords could not afford to build and defend an effective fortress, nor to attack one. The resources for war were no longer found in the feudal countryside but in capitalist towns (Creveld 1989, 106–8; Parker 1988, 13).

There were parallel developments in open-field warfare. In the fourteenth and fifteenth centuries two developments made the armored, mounted knight obsolete: massed archers and the pike phalanx. These in turn were gradually superseded by firearms. To make the most effective use of firearms, infantry came to be drawn up in ranks, so that those in the rear could reload while the lead musketeers fired (Creveld 1989, 89–91; Kennedy 1987, 21; Parker 1988, 16–20).

As commanders maneuvered for battlefield advantages, tactics were developed to increase the efficiency and effectiveness of firing. Training and battlefield coordination became more important. Uneducated soldiers had to be familiar with what were history's most advanced weapons. Ranks had to open and close on signal. Victory came to depend on the right combination of infantry, cavalry, firearms, cannon, and reserves. Textbooks of drill sprouted across the continent and tactics became a gentleman's topic of study (Creveld 1989, 92–94; Parker 1988, 18–23).

War came to involve ever-larger segments of society and became correspondingly more burdensome. Several European states saw the sizes of their armies increase tenfold between 1500 and 1700. Louis XIV's army stood at 273,000 in 1691. Five years later it was at 395,000, and nearly one-fourth of all adult Frenchmen were in the military. Between 1560 and 1659 Castile lost about 11 percent of its adult male population in the constant wars (Sundberg et al. 1994, 13). Each day, a field army of 30,000 needed 100,000 pounds of flour, and 1500 sheep or 150 cattle. This was more than was required to feed all but the largest cities of Europe (Creveld 1989, 112–13; Parker 1988, 2, 45–46, 75).

Yet for all these developments, land warfare of the time was largely stalemated. There were few lasting breakthroughs. The new military technologies, and the mercenaries to put them to use, could be purchased by any power with enough money. No nation could gain a lasting technological advantage. Moreover, when a nation such as Spain or France threatened to become dominant, alliances would form to counter its power (Kennedy 1987, 21–22). Major wars of the time were therefore long, and tended to be decided by cumulative small victories and the slow erosion of the enemy's economic base. Defeated nations quickly recovered and were soon ready to fight again. Land warfare had to be augmented by what amounted, in effect, to global flanking operations. European wars turned into contests for power and influence overseas (Parker 1988, 43, 80–82).

The great wealth from the New World was one of the factors that allowed Europeans to minimize the threat from their old enemy, the Ottoman Empire (Lewis 1958). They used this wealth also to sustain their ever-more costly competition among themselves (Kennedy 1987, 24, 27–28, 43, 46–47, 52; Tainter 1992, 110, 124). In 1760 the Duke of Choiseul noted that "in the present state of Europe, it is colonies, trade and in consequence, seapower which must determine the balance of power upon the continent" (Parker 1988, 82). The naval powers of the time were England, the Netherlands, Sweden, Denmark/Norway, France, and Spain. From 1650 to 1680 the five northern powers increased their navies from 140,000 to 400,000 tons. By this time England had to import critical supplies for its fleet, including masts, tar, and pitch from Sweden, and tried to develop a tar industry in its North

American colonies. In the 1630s the Dutch merchant fleet required the building of three hundred to four hundred new ships each year, about half of which were used in trade in the Baltic. Between the 1630s and 1650 the Dutch merchant fleet grew by 533 percent (Sundberg et al. 1994, 38, 42).

This naval strategy also led to problems of increasing complexity and cost. In 1511, for example, James IV of Scotland commissioned the building of the ship *Great Michael*. It took almost one-half of a year's income to build, and 10 percent of his annual budget for seamen's wages. It ended its days rotting in Brest harbor, having been sold to France in 1514 (Parker 1988, 90).

As the sizes of armies continued to grow through the eighteenth and nineteenth centuries, new fields of specialization were needed. There was demand for skills such as surveying and cartography. It was necessary to have accurate clocks and statistical reporting. In the eighteenth century some armies carried their own printing presses. Organization became more complex. Staff and administration were separated. Armies no longer marched as a unit, but could be split into smaller elements that traveled, under instructions, on their own. Battles came to last up to several months. In France, the *levée en masse* (mass conscription) was begun in 1793. In 1812 Napoleon invaded Russia with an army of 600,000, including 1,146 field guns, on a 400-kilometer front (Creveld 1989, 114, 117–22; Parker 1988, 153).

In 1499, as he was embarking on a campaign in Italy, Louis XII asked what was needed to ensure success. He was told that three things alone were required: money, money, and still more money (Sundberg et al. 1994, 10). As all things military grew in size and complexity, the main constraint came to be finance. In the decades before 1630 the cost of putting a soldier in the field increased by 500 percent. The increasing expense of wars meant that nations spent more of their income on them. In 1513, for example, England obligated 90 percent of its budget to military efforts. In 1657 the figure was 92 percent. In 1643 expenditures of the French government, mainly on war, were twice the annual income (Kennedy 1987, 58, 60, 63). In the mid-eighteenth century Frederick the Great also spent 90 percent of his receipts on war. He found it necessary to debase his currency and to extract both contributions and plunder from civilians.

Sweden used its vast forest resources to pay for its wars. Copper, steel, and tar produced by the use of forest resources amounted to 90 percent of Sweden's exports. The money earned in this way was the major basis for Sweden's war efforts. In 1701, 86.5 percent of England's tar came from Sweden. Between 1658 and 1814 England sent twenty fleets to the Baltic to secure the trade in masts and timber (Sundberg et al. 1994, 28–29, 40, 42).

Sweden enjoyed a combination of low population, untapped forest reserves, and markets for its products among the combatants. The major states, lacking such circumstances, came to rely on credit to pay for their wars. Notwithstanding the flow of precious metals from her New World colonies, Spain's debts rose from 6 million ducats in 1556 to 180 million a century later, and bankruptcy often undermined Spanish military operations. The cost of war loans grew from about 18 percent interest in the 1520s to 49 percent in the 1550s. Both France and Spain often had to declare bankruptcy, or force a lowering of the rate of interest. Governments coerced bankers into extending new loans by refusing to make payments on existing debts. From the sixteenth through the eighteenth centuries the Dutch, followed by the English, overcame fiscal constraints by gaining access to reliable short-term and long-term credit. They were careful to pay the interest on loans, and so were granted more favorable terms than other nations. They used this advantage to defeat opponents, France and Spain, that were wealthier but were poor credit risks (Parker 1988, 63–67; Rasler and Thompson 1989, 91, 94, 96, 103).

The wars did not directly augment net national wealth. Sweden's expenditures on wars, calculated as energy, exceeded the return by 240 percent (Sundberg et al. 1994, 25). The wars raised permanently the cost of being a competitive state, and war-induced debt levels persisted long after the fighting ceased. Power always shifts, and victorious nations could never dominate for very long (Kennedy 1987; Rasler and Thompson 1989, 106, 175–76). Many people of the time understood the futility of European wars. William Shakespeare created in *Hamlet* the scene of Fortinbras and his army of twenty thousand who "fight for a plot, Whereon the numbers cannot try the cause, Which is not tomb enough and continent To hide the slain."[5] The image of Fortinbras fighting for a plot of land not large enough for the battle, nor to entomb those killed, was echoed explicitly and eloquently in 1775 by Frederick the Great.

---

5. *Hamlet,* act 5, sc. 4.

The ambitious should consider above all that armaments and military discipline being much the same throughout Europe, and alliances as a rule producing an equality of force between belligerent parties, all that princes can expect from the greatest advantages at present is to acquire, by accumulation of successes, either some small city on the frontier, or some territory which will not pay interest on the expenses of the war, and whose population does not even approach the number of citizens who perished in the campaigns. (quoted in Parker [1988, 149])

Global Consequences of European Wars

European peer polity competition stimulated technological innovation, development of science, political transformation, and global expansion. The development of sea power and acquisition of colonies became aspects of strategy in stalemated European warfare. European war thus ultimately affected and changed the entire world. By 1914 the nations of Europe, and their offshoots, controlled fully 84 percent of the earth's surface (Parker 1988, 5).

For all the growth in size, complexity, and costliness, European wars of this period, as noted, rarely produced decisive results. States grew larger in territory and population, but whenever a power threatened to become dominant, its competitors formed alliances to counter it. A peer polity stalemate evolved over several centuries. At times, such as in the nineteenth and twentieth centuries, this balance of power was even formalized through diplomatic arrangements.

As land warfare in Europe produced no lasting advantages, the expansion of competition to the global arena was a logical consequence. Competition expanded to include trade, the capture of overseas territories, the establishment of colonies, attacking adversaries' colonies, and intercepting the wealth that flowed from them. The Thirty Years War (1618–48) is sometimes called the first global war for this reason. The balance of power in Europe came to rest in part on such matters; overseas resources were needed to sustain European competition. These were societies that, until the nineteenth century, were powered almost completely by solar energy. Sweden's support base in the seventeenth century consisted nearly entirely (87 percent) of renewable resources. Lacking colonies outside its region, almost half of Sweden's forest-based exports went to finance foreign wars (Sundberg et al. 1994, 18, 20). England's wars in the 1540s cost about ten times the crown's income

(Kennedy 1987, 60). For societies powered by solar energy, and using that energy so heavily within the limits of their technology, the main way to increase wealth was to control more of the earth's surface where solar energy falls. It became necessary to secure the produce of foreign lands to subsidize European competition. New forms of energy, and nonlocal resources, were channeled into a very small part of the world. This concentration of global resources allowed European conflict to reach heights of complexity and costliness that could never have been sustained with only European resources (Tainter 1992, 123–25).

European rulers of the time faced unbearable pressure to extract wealth from their colonies. Yet even that wealth could not meet the cost of some campaigns. In 1552 the Hapsburg emperor Charles V spent 2.5 million ducats on a campaign at Metz, an amount equal to ten times his American income. By the 1580s Philip II was receiving 2 million ducats a year from American mines, but the ill-fated armada of 1588 cost 10 million ducats (Kennedy 1987, 46–47). Even with this massive transfer of bullion from the New World, Spain's debt grew 3,000 percent in the century following 1556, and bankruptcy caused Spanish military operations to fail. Clearly, they would have failed much earlier (or not been undertaken) if Spain had not been able to draw upon New World wealth.

Peer polity competition not only forced Europeans to search for foreign lands and resources but it also virtually guaranteed them success in doing so. Such conflict, particularly when it is stalemated in balances of power, selects for continual innovation in technology, organization, strategy, tactics, and logistics. Any power that does not match its competitors in these areas risks defeat and domination. A nation that survives this process will be so proficient at making war that, outside of its group of peers, there may be no other military force that can withstand it. The inexorable pressure on European states to become ever better at making war meant that, when they ventured outside Europe, they often had a competitive advantage over other powers, whether organized as states or not (Kennedy 1987, 16–30). Time and again over the past five hundred years, comparatively tiny European forces have defeated much larger forces in the New World, Africa, and Asia. Nor was this unusual. Such abilities are a common consequence of peer polity competition. The global dominance of Europe in the past half millennium came from the same type of process that once allowed numerically inferior Greek and Macedonian armies to defeat much larger Persian forces, and the Romans to conquer the Mediterranean. A state that survives peer polity competition may find the rest of the world at its command (Tainter 1992, 125).

European expansion as a competitive strategy set the stage for a continuing chain of reactive processes in the rest of the world. Understanding those reactive processes is the second historical ingredient to comprehending the ethnopolitical problems we now face.

Patterns of Reaction to Global European Expansion

An epoch of more than four hundred years of colonial expansion, followed by a century of Western economic and cultural penetration of all parts of the globe, has resulted in a world system in which most people must define themselves partly in reaction to Europe and North America[6] (e.g., Marx 1993, 159; Friedman 1993, 229). It was inevitable that many such peoples would define themselves in opposition to Euramerican dominance. This has led to the development of such movements as Islamic fundamentalism, *Sendero Luminoso*,[7] (the Peruvian Shining Path Maoist group), and some cases of reactive ethnonationalism. What is not always so clear, and in consequence is typically misunderstood, is that European expansion has also caused violence *among* non-Western peoples themselves.

These processes began with the earliest phases of European expansion. Europeans in many areas commented upon the frequency with which indigenous peoples engaged in conflict (against Europeans or among themselves) and the ferocity with which they did so. Classic examples include the Yanomami of the Amazon Basin and the Iroquois of northeastern North America. War by such people led to much social speculation, from Hobbes to the present day, about the nature of war in nonstate societies, about the role of conflict in the development of state institutions, and even about the supposedly

---

6. I have not included in this analysis a discussion of Japan, whose economic development was itself a reaction to European expansion. Japan's economic penetration of the world is comparatively recent, but reactions to it are already building. The development of a global reaction to Japanese commercial expansion will bear watching in coming decades.

7. A violent, rural, Marxist movement in Peru, originally proclaiming millenarian aspirations.

aggressive nature of our species. Contemporary research is showing that this violence has been misunderstood from the beginning.

European expansion transformed indigenous societies from the outset, and often before actual contacts had been made. The immediate consequences of expansion were disease, introduction of new plants and animals, and technological change (Ferguson and Whitehead 1992, 8–11). Such effects often arrived before Europeans themselves, so that even the very first descriptions of indigenous societies were sometimes of people who had already been significantly changed. Among these changes were the formation of pan-tribal confederations and new ethnic groups, where previously these had not existed[8] (Ferguson and Whitehead 1992, 12–13; Whitehead 1992). Both tribes and ethnic groups appear to have formed in response to expanding states, and may not have existed before the state.

It now appears that in the era of European expansion, many episodes of conflict among indigenous peoples, and between them and Europeans, concerned access to European goods (e.g., Abler 1992; Ferguson 1992, 1995a). The circulation of goods beyond state frontiers has long been an element of state—nonstate relations. With its capacity for mass production, European expansion magnified this factor. European goods were valued by indigenous peoples not only for utilitarian reasons but also because they came to be embedded in social relations. Manufactured goods were used to validate claims to status and were intimately involved in wars and alliances. War among indigenous peoples, and between such peoples and Europeans, often had much to do with access to European technology (Ferguson and Whitehead 1992, 10–11). It was an early manifestation of the reactive process.

The Yanomami of the Amazon Basin illustrate these points. Long noted in anthropology for the frequency and severity of their violent behavior, they have been brought to public attention with labels such as "the fierce people" (Chagnon 1968). The Yanomami are depicted as representing the Hobbesian state of anarchic war in which all nonstate peoples supposedly once lived (Chagnon 1968, 1974). Yet, contemporary analysis of the Yanomami case by Brian Ferguson (1992, 1995a)

---

8. This too has been a recurrent reactive process. Along the fringes of the Roman Empire, from the second through the fourth centuries A.D., tribal confederations emerged among people who were often in conflict with Rome, and among themselves. These transformations were a direct reaction to Roman expansion (Tainter 1994).

reveals that nothing is pristine or intrinsic about their violence. To the contrary, every reported incident of Yanomami conflict is, directly or indirectly, about access to or control of manufactured goods. Yanomami with direct access to Western goods try vigorously to monopolize them, which creates tension with outlying villages, and even within villages. The problem of access to goods manifests itself not only through violence but also through a set of conflict-related structural changes. These include changes in kin relations, relocation of villages, population aggregation, village alliances, feasting, economic specialization and exchange, the authority of headmen, and the treatment of the Yanomami as a cultural entity. Manufactured goods so significantly transformed Yanomami society that its recent configuration cannot be considered to represent accurately the precontact society. Ironically, some anthropologists who have taken manufactured goods on their visits to the Yanomami may have inadvertently stimulated episodes of the "pristine" violence that they subsequently described (Ferguson 1992, 1995a, and personal communication 1994).

The Iroquois in colonial North America were a group of independent "nations" often noted for their fierceness and territorial ambitions. Although Iroquois conflicts may have originated in the prehistoric period, in the historic era the Iroquois made war well out of proportion to their disease-reduced numbers. This practice was closely linked to their need for European goods. With the new importance of muskets in warfare, and a reduction in the local supply of beaver pelts, the Iroquois in the seventeenth century faced marginalization and ultimate obliteration. Pelts had to be obtained to trade for muskets. At the same time, losses to European diseases were so high that the Iroquois nations had constantly to replenish their populations with war captives and refugees. The Iroquois took to ambushing canoe fleets in Canada for pelts, and concluded that the solution to the shortage of beaver was to expand their hunting territory. Their wars were ultimately concerned with obtaining European goods (Abler 1992). Thus, the nature and intensity of Iroquoian conflict were transformed by European contact.

As frontier encounters were transformed into colonial administrations, and ultimately into independent states, political and economic processes in much of the world were transformed into the European model of the nation-state. Yet, the fundamental reactive nature of many processes did not change. Many of today's conflicts can trace their origins to the expansion, domination, and meddling of the great powers. Political and territorial arrangements in the areas of former colonies, and in what were the Ottoman, Austro-Hungarian, and Soviet empires, have caused cultural groups to stress their differences as they compete for control of state institutions (Ferguson 1995b). Peoples that have coexisted for centuries now stress the "traditional" nature of their conflicts. New cultural identities are emerging, as among the Maya of Guatemala (LeBaron 1993; Warren 1993) and in contemporary Tâjikistân (Schoeberlein-Engel 1994). Ethnogenesis was apparently a policy of the former Soviet Union (Aklaev 1992; Rudensky 1992; Entessar 1993). On a smaller scale, the role of the state in ethnic formation can be seen in Bedouin resistance to Israeli attempts to assign them an ethnic classification. The principal of a Bedouin school once complained, "[I]f it was not enough what they [the Israeli administration] are doing to us, now they tell us we are an ethnic group" (Jakubowska 1992, 85).

Colonial policies have in many cases exacerbated cultural antagonisms, or even created them. When the British displaced the Moslems as rulers of India, for example, they used Hindus to run the colonial administration, and emphasized the differences between the religions. Hindus were sent to English schools and recruited as minor officials. Moslems largely attended Islamic schools, where the teachings concerned religious orthodoxy rather than secular advancement (Zeldin 1994, 266). In the postcolonial era continued poverty, lack of access to power, and disillusionment with Western-derived models of "modernity" have contributed to the rise of Hindu, Moslem, and Sikh nationalism (Spitz 1993). Throughout south Asia, politicians are exploiting these intensifying cultural differences for personal advancement, provoking recent violent events. In such a situation, an aura of antagonism can be rapidly created by unscrupulous leaders, and manipulated to further political ambitions.

One conflict that has deeply impressed itself on the world's consciousness is the tragedy in Rwanda. The true origins of this conflict are little known to the public. A century ago European colonists (first German, then Belgian) found in what is now Rwanda a centralized kingdom consisting of numerous clans, and three groups largely defined by occupational status. There were no distinct ethnic groups. The European administrators transformed the occupational hierarchy into an imaginary racial classification. The minority Tutsi rulers were proclaimed by Belgian missionaries to have a cultural and racial heritage in Ethiopia—and thus nearer Europe. As the Tutsi converted to Catholicism they adopted this new "history" to legitimize their continued rule. Hutu cultivators were consigned to a life of toil. Such recruitment of the native hierarchy is a common ploy in colonial regimes.

In 1959, on the eve of independence, the Belgians reversed both their policy and the order of Rwandese society. They assisted in eliminating the Tutsi monarchy and in the installation of a Hutu republic. The Hutu have since seized upon the myth that the Tutsis originated elsewhere, condemning them now as foreigners. The fact that Tutsi and Hutu "ethnic" and "racial" identities were recently created by an outside power is now irrelevant. As they persecute each other and fight to control the Rwandan state, Tutsi and Hutu identities have emerged of a kind that never existed before. Survival now demands that they *must be* ethnic groups.

In the 1930s the Belgians issued identity cards, categorizing people as Tutsi, Hutu, or Twa (low-caste hunter-gatherers who do not emerge in today's journalism). Unable to implement their racial typology in practice, the Belgian administrators classified people by the ownership of cattle. Those with ten or more were Tutsi in perpetuity; those with fewer were Hutu. These identity cards still exist, and were used to categorize people in the recent massacres. Upon such a distinction 500,000 people were killed (Wall 1994).

Summary

There has been a persistent pattern of reaction to European expansion. That pattern consists of tribalization and ethnogenesis, intensification of cultural identity, and violence. The reasons for conflict range from control of Western-manufactured goods to control of Western-style governments. These patterns are seen historically among the Iroquois, in recent decades among the Yanomami, and today both in those conflicts that receive public attention and those that do not. In such places as the Balkans, Iran, central Asia, Rwanda, Burundi, Somalia, and Liberia, violence is shaped by cultural and political reactions to external forces. Though the forms of these conflicts differ, the factor that unifies them is that each is in part a response to former colonial, imperial, or other global powers.

Synthesis and Implications:
The Historical Foundations of Contemporary
Violence

There is a significant history behind the contemporary outbreak of violence. Its foundations can be traced to remote events that few people involved in today's conflicts would anticipate. It is understandable primarily as an example of a common historic process—the development of reactive patterns. From secondary-state formation, to core-periphery relations, to peer polity interaction, reactive processes have been a dominant, driving force in history.

With the collapse of the western Roman Empire, Europe found itself with a host of small, successor states. As these increased in size and complexity, their conflicts formed into a peer polity pattern. Alliances were formed and broken, investments were made in more complex ways of making war, and rulers continually looked for more money. As continental warfare was stalemated, Europeans sought subsidies through global expansion—trade and colonization. These too became elements of the competitive spiral. By the eighteenth and nineteenth centuries European powers were acquiring colonies largely to prevent their competitors from doing so.

The expansion of Europe generated global changes that we are still experiencing. All societies that it touched were transformed, but none more so than indigenous, nonstate peoples. With disease, environmental change, and the availability of manufactured goods, such peoples were affected in ways that will never be fully calculated. Through phases of frontier contact, colonialism, and the formation of nation-states, the reactions to European expansion have included tribal formation, ethnogenesis, and violence. Where that violence focused on resisting European or American encroachment, the great powers have found it comprehensible if disagreeable. Yet, much of today's violence has seemed so incomprehensible because it is directed internally. Europeans and Americans have not understood that their own expansion has stimulated much of today's culturally defined conflict. There is a direct line of cause and effect from warfare in medieval and Renaissance Europe, to global expansion and colonialism, to today's events in places like Rwanda, Somalia, and India.

A casual reading of this text might suggest two facile but erroneous inferences. It is worthwhile exposing these and dispensing with them. The first is that European states, and other colonial, imperial, or capitalist powers, are morally responsible for the current state of the world. If today's violence is even in part a reaction to European expansion, some will feel inclined to assign blame for this violence accordingly. Although this might give a measure of psychological satisfaction, it would be a short-sighted use of history. The identification of historical scapegoats too easily becomes an excuse for failures of contemporary action. Moreover, to the extent that European colonial expansion was made likely by previous events and processes, such as peer polity competition, the search for a scapegoat can always be shifted further back in time. A morally neutral approach to history must be adopted or else dialogue reduces to accusations and defensiveness.[9] Historical events are neither good nor bad; they are simply a set of potential understandings. To blame any nation or part of the world for its history does little but guarantee further reactions.[10]

The other facile inference would be that this essay denies to today's peoples and nations the ability to behave other than reactively. Clearly, no sensible historian or social scientist would suggest such a thing. One purpose of international policy making should be to encourage those who perpetrate today's violence to use their faculties of choice, and act more responsibly. Yet, history is filled with examples of reactive processes, and an understanding of today's troubles that ignores their origins is bound to be superficial. People always have the ability to choose, but choice requires information. The main purpose of this chapter is to generate an awareness of the origins of today's behavior. Among the benefits of this awareness is that it allows the actors themselves to decide whether to modify their actions.

The discussion in this chapter suggests two implications that are essential to understanding today's and tomorrow's difficulties. The

9. This is written when the participants in World War II have just finished observing the fiftieth anniversary of the end of that conflict. It is a period filled with demands for apologies, acknowledgments of responsibility, and compensation of victims. With respect for the deep feelings of the participants in that struggle, I suggest that humiliation of any nation guarantees a future reaction, perhaps a violent one. Public demands for apologies are not wise, long-term policy. I do not condone any of the things done in that war, merely suggest that a mature understanding of it requires a dispassionate approach.

10. Consider also the contradiction of blaming Europeans for the consequences of their competitive spiral while admiring the consequences of peer-polity competition in ancient Greece—the defeat of the Persian invasions of 490 and 480 B.C.

first, raised at the very beginning, is the importance of knowing where we are in history (Tainter 1995). Historical patterns may develop over generations or even centuries. Rarely can an individual in a lifetime come to understand fully the origins of an event or a process. Yet, to remain ignorant of the origins of today's problems is to condemn ourselves to manage them ineptly, and to condemn others to the consequences of that mismanagement. As for the future, it is folly to suppose that we can use present conditions to predict the twenty-first century if we do not understand how the present came to be. Managing political and cultural problems requires that we know where we are in history.

The culturally defined conflicts of today cannot be understood except in the context of global European expansion. Western nations that attempt to ameliorate or manage conflicts need to understand how their own histories have stimulated many of these problems. If today's culturally defined conflicts are a response to European political and economic expansion, interference carries the risk of provoking further reactions. On one level this can be seen clearly. Video clips released, for example, by Moslem fundamentalists in Lebanon, by the government of Iraq, and by the Bosnian Serbs are clearly intended for Western news broadcasts. The Tutsi-dominated Rwandan Patriotic Front has legitimized its claim to rule Rwanda by asserting that its struggle is based on social transformation rather than ethnicity, that its troops are well disciplined, and that it has no wish for revenge against Hutus, only justice. These messages are meant for European and American ears (Wall 1994, 4). Beyond these obvious reactions to Western intervention, there is a likelihood of more subtle and far-reaching consequences. These include continuing ethnogenesis, further intensification of existing cultural identities, and the emergence of new culturally defined conflicts. In effect, historical processes will continue.

The point of this discussion is not to suggest that the West (or the United Nations) should abstain from involvement in the rest of the world, merely on the possibility of stimulating unforeseen reactions. In an era of global travel, communication, and economic linkages this is obviously impossible. The point is that those who design interventions in world conflicts must do so with the realization that involvement by dominant nations *always* stimulates unanticipated reactions.

A second implication concerns Western perceptions of cultural conflicts. Many in Western nations (including, unfortunately, journalists) assume that cultural differences are innate, immutable, and lead automatically to violence (Ferguson and Whitehead 1992: 27–28, Ferguson 1995b). Both journalistic and some scholarly reporting tend to "explain" violence as the irrational but inevitable result of "ancient tribal feuds." It is assumed that contemporary expressions of cultural differentiation represent both actual history and the "natural" divisions of our species. Scarcity of land or other resources, in some arguments, interacts with these intrinsic divisions to generate violence (e.g., Homer-Dixon 1994).

Cultural differentiation in today's conflicts is, to the contrary, flexible and shifting, and responds to history, external stimuli, and deliberate manipulation. Current conflicts in central Asia are a clear example, where new cultural identities (such as Özbek) are emerging, stimulated substantially by the involvement of external powers (Schoeberlein-Engel 1994). In places such as the Balkans, "ethnic entrepreneurs"[11] manipulate cultural identity for political mobilization. This manipulation masks the underlying issues, sometimes deliberately. To a casual observer it is easy to suppose that conflicts between cultural groups are conflicts *about* culture. Often the conflicts are about relations to the West, about the relations of local groups to Western-style central governments, or, as in Somalia and Liberia, are about the control of those governments (Ferguson 1995b). In such struggles, appeals to culture raise the moral authority of the political claim and tap profound emotions. This is an effective strategy of political assertion, but observers should understand that the label "cultural conflict" conceals more than it reveals.

If the arguments developed here have merit, the conflicts of today, and those of the twenty-first century, cannot be avoided or managed if we consider only conventional, short-term factors. The present analysis suggests a complex picture, in which reactive historical processes may combine with scarcity, power, politics, and culture to provoke violence, or may operate independently of them. The implications for preventing violence in the next century are complex as well: nothing can be more difficult in the management of conflict than to know that intervention itself may generate further violence. No doubt many who work in the crisis-laden world of international relations will be reluctant to accept the additional burden of gaining a historical perspective. Yet, if we accept the simple premise that problems can rarely be

---

11. A term suggested by Dr. Airat Aklaev of the Russian Academy of Sciences, Moscow.

solved if their causes are not understood, historical knowledge is essential. Diplomats, politicians, and other international workers cannot hope to achieve lasting resolutions to conflicts unless they first understand the importance of knowing where we are in history.[12]

12. I am pleased to express my appreciation to Drian Ferguson for stimulating my thinking about contemporary violence, and to Carol Raish for comments on an earlier draft of this chapter.

PART THREE

Case Studies of Scarcity and Mass Death

Introduction

The tragic violence we have witnessed recently in Bosnia, Somalia, Haiti, and Rwanda have some common roots. Resource scarcity is a necessary precondition that apparently activates group conflict and transforms it into the virulent ethnonationalist violence we are seeing with greater frequency. It may be a precursor of genocidal incidents and tendencies that will only be more pronounced as resource-scarcity problems and population pressures continue to intensify in the coming decades. If current trends continue apace, including a combination of environmental damage, loss of agricultural lands, dwindling fuel resources, and a doubling of population to between 8.5 billion and 9.5 billion by 2025, this will lead to conditions of extreme hardship, even disaster, in many parts of the world. These areas, as Roger Smith, David Smith, and Waltraud Morales point out, are the very places where much of genocide since 1945 has taken place. To forestall what may be likely, if not inevitable, we need major paradigm shifts in values, psychology, politics, and economic organization. The authors in this final section begin to address the threat of proliferating genocides and offer some possible solutions.

10. Scarcity and Genocide

Roger W. Smith

Few scholars have addressed the relationships between scarcity and genocide, and the few who have provide sweeping accounts that distort the facts. Richard Rubenstein, for example, has made the relationships between scarcity and genocide the heart of his explanation of genocide (Rubenstein 1978, 1983). He argues that modernization inherently leads to a "surplus" population, which in turn leads to attempts to eliminate those who are "excess." Rationalism, which fuels modernization, dissolves both community and moral limits; persons become "resources" rather than "human beings"; efficiency becomes the chief value. There are, however, severe problems with his theory. The basic concept of a "surplus" population is never defined. Moreover, the problem of genocide mostly has not been that there are too many people for the resources available, but that those in power decide to eliminate groups that are perceived, not as surplus, but as having the "wrong" characteristics—wrong religion, race, social origin, ethnicity, and so on. Yet, in Rubenstein's grammar of motives, there is only one motive—all behavior is reduced to economic motive. Such a theory, though suggestive, cannot explain any of the cases of genocide in the twentieth century.

Hannah Arendt also has some striking comments about the relationships between scarcity and genocide, but they are brief and not developed (Arendt 1958b, 457–59). She does not, in fact, speak of "scarcity," but of "superfluous man." Humans are becoming "superfluous," and in the future, with an ever-increasing population, will become even more so on an "overcrowded earth" (1958b, 457). They are super-fluous in the sense that they no longer have a meaningful place in society: many are unemployed, many are homeless, they no longer contribute to the functions of society. They are not individuals, but lost in the swell of population; they become the "masses." Given the prevailing utilitarian outlook, such humans are useless, they have no meaning. Arendt thinks that the very perspective involved in utilitarianism—judging in use—leads us into meaninglessness, for one can never come to the end of the ends-means chain: what, she asks, is the use of use? (Arendt 1958a, 154–59). Humans are thus viewed essentially in terms of efficiency and as resources, not in any moral terms: as with other things that become useless, they can be cast aside.

Without being specific, Arendt suggests that "political, social, and economic events" all work toward making "men superfluous" (1958b, 459). She thinks that the masses understand the "temptations" that are embodied in their lack of purpose and place. She also thinks that the Nazis and Stalinists demonstrated in their "factories of annihilation" the "swiftest solution to the problem of over-population, of economically superfluous and socially rootless human masses" (1958b, 459). In Arendt's view, such a demonstration serves not only as a "warning" but also as an "attraction." Her fear is that totalitarian solutions are not a part of the past, but may become part of the present and future. "Totalitarian solutions may well survive the fall of totalitarian regimes in the form of strong temptations which will come up whenever it seems impossible to alleviate political, social, or economic misery in a manner worthy of man" (1958b, 459).

Arendt's vision is breathtaking but it misleads. If the killing she expects begins, it will have as its victims, not "men," but members of groups who are, on noneconomic grounds, being singled out for death. The Nazi attempt to exterminate the Jews was not, contrary to her view, an attempt to solve the problem of overpopulation. Her mistake is that of Rubenstein, but on a larger scale.

Despite false starts, the question of the relationships between scarcity and genocide is important, both in understanding the causes of genocide and in anticipating the prospects for genocide in the next century. If current trends continue, a combination of environmental degradation, loss of agricultural land, depletion of fish stocks, dwindling of fuel resources, and a doubling of population to about 11 billion in the latter part of the twentieth-first century will lead to extreme hardship, even disaster, in many areas of the world (Homer-Dixon

1991, 76–116; 1994, 5–40.) These areas, mainly in the Third World, are the very places where much of the genocide since 1945 has taken place (Fein 1993, 87).

The genocides that have occurred in Bangladesh, Burundi, Cambodia, Indonesia, and Rwanda, however, have not been brought about by material scarcity. Genocide, with some exceptions to be noted later, has seldom been the result of material scarcity, whereas material scarcity has often been a direct result of genocide. Nevertheless, in a world that in the twentieth century has displayed an unparalleled capacity for mass slaughter, it would be surprising if severe shortages would not exacerbate existing tendencies toward resolving social and political problems through the elimination of the groups thought to constitute the problem.

This chapter attempts to clarify "scarcity"; identify the historical relationships between scarcity and genocide; indicate why scarcities could be a more decisive factor in genocide in the future; and outline strategies for preventing genocide, partly through controlling scarcities and partly through political and institutional means.

To point out certain plausible scenarios of genocide, to make explicit the logic of genocide, and to analyze the relationships between scarcity and genocide does not mean that genocide is somehow the inevitable result of scarcity or of any other "cause." Genocide is never inevitable; it is a political choice. But political choices, including genocide, are affected by many different forces, internal and external, to the society in question. If present trends continue, scarcity will increasingly be one of those forces in the not-so-distant future.

Scarcity

"Scarcity" includes both the relative and the absolute. For those used to affluence and abundance, a mild reduction in goods available to them will be perceived as scarcity; similarly, they may feel worse off if other persons improve their material condition while they remain at their previous level (Runciman 1966). Scarcity, in these instances, is not only relative but also psychological: desire is confused with need (Rousseau 1960, 275). Psychological scarcity is an important facet of the "developmental" genocide that indigenous peoples have faced, and, most likely, will face. Scarcity may also be both absolute and material: if one lacks the necessary food and water for a certain period, one simply dies.

Should one consider scarcity only in material goods, resources, or employment, scarcity can take at least two different forms. It is important to highlight these distinctions, which not only indicate different sources of scarcity but also suggest possible solutions to conflict that arises, at least in part, from the effects of "scarcity." First, there may be a scarcity of resources—little usable land, few fish, forests that have been depleted, minerals long ago extracted from the soil. Some of these resources can be renewed, others are simply no longer there. Whether resources are renewable is itself an important dimension of overcoming scarcity and any role it may have in prompting murderous conflict. Second, resources may be scarce because of the size of the population: even if all goods were distributed equally, there would still be generalized poverty. To overcome this kind of scarcity, either the material resources would have to be increased (the green revolution in agriculture, for instance) or the population would have to be decreased. Ominously, in the accounts of Arendt and Rubenstein, population reduction is procured through genocide. What are the other ways in which population can be reduced? Will they be tried and, if so, will they be effective? These are questions that we shall return to when we consider how the links between scarcity and genocide could be removed, leaving open the issue of whether they will be.

Besides psychological scarcity and the material scarcities described, there is a kind of scarcity—political scarcity—that includes material and political deprivation. Some scholars, however, note only the resource deprivation and thus think of this as a third type of material scarcity (Homer-Dixon 1994, 9).

Where political scarcity exists, there may be sufficient resources to meet everyone's needs (though not desires), but the allocation of resources favors certain groups and discriminates against other groups. In practice, there will often be a scarcity of resources and an expanding population, and both may contribute further to policies of unequal distribution of goods (Homer-Dixon 1991, 109–11). Such situations frequently exist in ethnically divided (or "plural") societies and help drive demands for equal treatment, demands that may be met with repression and, if the conflict persists, with an attempt at partial or total genocide.

The political deprivation consists of exclusion from power and from being viewed, and treated, as an inferior group. Each dimension of this deprivation is not only related to but also explains the material deprivation members of the group also experience beyond that of other groups.

There are psychological elements present; however, they are not just matters of desire but of substantial political need—to be assured of a stable, secure, and just place within society and the political system. The lack of this assurance in the plural society is one of the major sources of genocide in the twentieth century (Kuper 1981, 57–83, 93). Under conditions of material scarcity that are likely to worsen in the twenty-first century, such conflicts seem more likely still. But again, the solutions to this type of conflict are suggested by the nature of the scarcity. Power sharing, protection of basic rights, and equality of treatment could go a long way in overcoming the difficulties otherwise exacerbated by deteriorating resources and expansion of population.

Relationships between Genocide and Scarcity: The Basic Patterns

The relationships between genocide and scarcity fall into five broad patterns.

1. Genocide that leads to scarcity. The scarcity is unintended but is the consequence of genocide, committed for any number of reasons, such as ideology or to remove a threat to the regime. Examples include Cambodia and Rwanda.

2. Genocide and direct conflict over resources. Direct conflict over scarce resources is most likely to occur in one of three situations: migration, "development," and some instances of societal fragmentation.

3. Genocide as "advertent omission," where the intent is to take advantage of a natural disaster to reduce the population of a despised group. Here the dominant power does not cause the fatal condition, such as famine or disease, but does not provide the necessary aid to support the afflicted group. An example that comes close would be Britain at the time of the Great Famine in Ireland.

4. Genocide that takes place largely through the creation of scarcity, most commonly by depriving the victims of food. The best modern example of this is Stalin's attempt to force collectivization of agriculture and to suppress nationalism in the Ukraine through the manmade famine of 1932–33.

5. Scarcity as a contributing factor in the decision to resort to genocide. Here "scarcity" includes: degradation and depletion of natural resources, fewer goods per capita owing to population growth, and unequal resource distribution. It also includes the psychological and political scarcities that play a large role in the genocide of indigenous

peoples and minorities in plural societies. Each form of scarcity can contribute to the conditions that make genocide more likely: these include conflict over resources; population displacement and ensuing conflict between groups; allocation of resources along racial, religious, or ethnic lines, resulting in demands for autonomy or independence; weakening of the legitimacy of the state, followed by either revolution, an attempt at secession, or a growing authoritarianism that seeks to resolve social and political problems through force. New ideologies may also spring up with the decline of the state—these are likely to be formulated along lines of ethnicity, but other bases, such as religion, may also occur. In some instances, states may fragment into warring groups, with no group able to achieve dominance. Here a small-scale, but continuing, genocide may be acted out.

Genocide That Leads to Scarcity

Genocide typically produces scarcity: it creates social chaos, disrupts the economy, destroys the lives of hundreds of thousands, even millions, of persons who possess skills and productive abilities, whether in farming, manufacturing, or medicine, and diverts the perpetrators themselves from their role in economic life, turning them into those who destroy rather than produce and create. In extreme cases, such as that of Rwanda, economic production may cease altogether (Block 1994, 3–8). Moreover, in many instances, disease may sweep through the society, facilitated in part by famine, water sources contaminated by the dead, and by lack of sanitation. Where the genocide occurs in the context of war, as in Bosnia, human habitations, production facilities, and the environment itself may all suffer damage, creating additional material scarcities.

If genocide falls most heavily upon the intended victims, the perpetrators are not immune to the scarcities it induces. In Cambodia, for example, hundreds of thousands of those whom the Khmer Rouge tried to turn into the foundation of a peasant society died from malnutrition brought about by its agricultural policies (Martin 1994, 173–78; Becker 1986, 248–53). Although humanitarian aid in the form of food and medicine was available, the Khmer Rouge would not accept it for ideological reasons: its vision was of a self-sufficient peasant society; moreover, if food was scarce, it was due to sabotage by "enemies of the revolution," not any failure of the revolutionary design itself. Similarly, in Rwanda, after the Hutu government had unleashed its militias, resulting in the killing of half a million Tutsi and moderate Hutu within three months, its own army was driven from the country by an invading force of Tutsi refugees, victims of an earlier genocide in Rwanda. Several million Hutu thus fled into neighboring countries, where they were placed in squalid, disease-ridden camps; fearful of returning home, they eke out their existence on meager rations provided by humanitarian aid.

Perpetrators may be so intent upon destroying a group that they fail to calculate the effects that their actions will have on themselves. Or there may be a recognition of this, but the calculus used to assess costs and benefits stresses ideology, revenge, or power rather than the material well-being of the perpetrator group. Put differently, the political economy of genocide has its own logic.

In fact, since 1945 almost all genocides, Bosnia is the major exception, have taken place within the Third World in countries already impoverished; most persons in such societies, with their dense populations, fragile economies, and maldistribution of wealth, were already living amid scarcity. Nevertheless, genocide, except developmental genocide, has frequently brought the societies in which it occurs even closer to collapse. In one type of genocide, however, scarcity falls almost entirely upon the victims. In developmental genocide, the indigenous people's land is taken and their sources of food eliminated. The perpetrators, on the other hand, gain land, gold, timber, or cheap electricity from the hydroelectric projects erected on the indigenous people's territory.

Scarcities that stem from genocide may be either short-term (a temporary shortage of food, for example) or long-lasting (where much of the existing housing is damaged or destroyed, as in Bosnia). In some cases, the damage to the economy will continue for generations: eighty years after the genocide of the Armenians, lands once highly productive lie barren in eastern Turkey. In Rwanda the basic infrastructure (social and physical) of the country under the best of circumstances would take years to rebuild, but more immediate is restoring agricultural production, something hard to do with several million refugees afraid to return, and the continued threat of new wars and genocides as those ousted seek to return to power (Block 1994, 3–8). Rwanda will be almost completely dependent upon outside aid to overcome the impact of the genocide. At some point, however, donor fatigue will set in; how rapid is hard to predict, but for Somalia it took just a little more than a year.

Genocide and Direct Conflict over Resources

There are three situations in which direct conflict over scarce resources is likely to occur and each of these is compatible with genocidal actions. The first is the result of migration into areas already occupied by other groups (Homer-Dixon 1991, 108–9). A well-known example is the Israelite exodus from Egypt, their migration into Canaan, and the ensuing wars over resources that the early books of the Bible invariably depict as wars of extermination. Migration may itself result from lack of adequate resources, but more commonly in the modern world from persecution, war, and genocide. Direct conflict over material resources is also likely where resources held by indigenous peoples are slated for "development" (Arens 1976; Bodley 1982; Burger 1987; Davis 1977; Independent Commission on International Humanitarian Issues 1987). Here traditional uses of the land will be replaced by cattle, timbering, strip mining, and hydoelectric plants. To some extent, development will involve migration, but much of the migration will be of machines and corporate enterprise rather than individuals and groups trying to establish a home for themselves. Moreover, much of the scarcity perceived by those who set development into motion involves a lack of abundance rather than economic hardship.

The second form of scarcity involved is that of a maldistribution of resources, particularly land, within the perpetrators' territory, rather than a lack of resources. One of the reasons that development appeals to political and economic elites is that it offers a kind of safety valve to release the frustrations of the landless and the impoverished without requiring any redistribution of resources held by the elites. The costs of development will be borne instead by those whose lands are taken. Another reason that development is subscribed to is that it rests upon an ideology of progress, one that views an ever-growing economy and a limitless supply of goods as the goal of society (Bodley 1982, Walzer 1980, 23–53). That the encroachment on the territory of indigenous peoples will lead to direct conflict, the destruction of a people's habitat, and the eventual disappearance of such groups is understood by those who pursue development strategies, but they are prepared to accept them in the name of progress and economic growth.

There are currently some 200 million indigenous peoples around the world, most of whom are already vulnerable to existing pressures for greater and more productive utilization of resources (Burger 1987,

11). Given an age of scarcity in the twenty-first century, the future of indigenous peoples appears to be bleak.

The third basis for direct conflict over resources occurs when a state collapses, followed by fragmentation, with no group capable of gaining power or control (Van Creveld 1991). When a state fails, with the consequent breakdown of security for life and property, scarcity can be expected to increase, leading to struggle over basic resources. This struggle will itself lead to further scarcity. Thomas Hobbes (reprint 1960, 82) captures this well in his description in 1651 of a chaotic and violent "state of nature."

> In such condition, there is no place for industry; because the fruit thereof is uncertain: and consequently no culture of the earth; no navigation, nor use of the commodities that may be imported by sea; no commodious building; no instruments of moving and removing, such things as require much force; no knowledge of the face of the earth; no account of time; no art; no letters; no society; and which is worst of all, continual fear, and danger of violent death.

In principle, a dominant group may arise out of the fighting and impose a repressive order. But it is possible that various groups, different perhaps in different areas of the former state, will sustain the low-level conflict for many years, repeated genocidal attacks being made by all sides. In this event, genocide, rather than being exceptional, would have become part of an equilibrium of destruction. Here, "the life of man," as Hobbes put it (reprint 1960, 82), would truly be "poor, nasty, brutish, and short." In this situation, any distinction between war and crime and war and genocide would blur or disappear.

Natural Disaster, Advertent Omission, and Genocide

Ben Whitaker, in his United Nations report on the Genocide Convention (Whitaker 1985) notes that some acts of genocide may not only be carried out by acts of commission but also "may be achieved by conscious acts of advertent omission. In certain cases, calculated neglect or negligence may be sufficient to destroy a designated group wholly or partially through, for instance, famine or disease" (par. 40). He therefore recommends that the United Nations Convention on the Prevention and Punishment of Genocide be amended, adding at the end of Article II (which specifies what acts constitute genocide): "In any of the above conduct, a conscious act or acts of advertent omission may be as culpable as an act of commission" (par. 41).

There seem to be two situations where genocide by omission might be possible: (1) where there are indigenous peoples, or other distinct groups, that live in relative isolation from the dominant population; (2) where there is a colonial relationship through which the people of one state control the lives of those in another society. Today these situations would be possible only where they could be hidden: once there is knowledge by the outside world that an epidemic or famine is decimating a particular group, it is likely that international relief efforts would be made. In this case, the group that wished to take advantage of the natural disaster would either have to yield or move from genocide by omission to genocide by commission. In genocide by commission, it would bar, for example, any relief, or adequate relief, to come into the afflicted areas.

Nevertheless, if we look into the middle-to-latter part of the twenty-first century, the increase of population and the continued loss of crop land, and depletion of fish stocks, will result in malnourishment in many countries. Should famine develop in any of these areas, and particularly several places at once, it seems unlikely that the rest of the world would provide the necessary food for more than a short period. In that case, genocide by omission would turn all wealthy nations into either perpetrators or accomplices.

Although genocide by omission by a colonial power would seem to be possible, even likely, no examples of it are fully convincing. The British government's reaction to the Great Famine in Ireland from 1845 to 1848, however, is suggestive of what such a case might involve (Edwards and Williams 1957; O'Neill 1957, 209–59; MacArthur 1957, 263–315; Woodham-Smith 1962; Rubenstein 1983, chapter 6).

The Irish were a conquered people, ruled from abroad; most of the – land was held by English landlords who rented small plots to tenants who were subject to eviction. Population growth in Ireland was high, and poverty was widespread and often pronounced. Not surprisingly, there were organized Irish political movements that sought the end of British rule.

Most people survived on a single crop—the potato—but in 1845 a blight ruined much of the crop; in 1846 the crop failed almost entirely, and again in 1847. By the time the blight was over, the population had declined by some 2.5 million, almost half of the loss due to emigration and half to starvation and various diseases that accompanied the famine (Woodham-Smith 1962, 411–12).

By all accounts, except that of Charles Trevelyan who was in charge of relief, the British response to the famine was a disaster. It was driven by an ideological commitment to laissez-faire economics even facing mass starvation, by a disdain, if not hostility, toward the Irish peasants, and by an extreme parsimony. Food was exported from Ireland amid famine; starving men unable to pay their rents were driven from the land and their huts demolished; and food in government reserves was made available (at market prices) in only the western part of the country. Medical attention, facing typhus and other diseases, was woefully inadequate, and disease was spread rapidly by concentrating the destitute in workhouses (MacArthur 1957, 263–315).

Despite the enormous loss of life, the British government treated the whole matter as a minor crisis. In all official reports, correspondence, and speeches the term used to refer to the famine was "distress" (O'Neill 1957, 259). As late as 1848, when the enormity of the Irish tragedy should have been clear, Trevelyan still spoke of "local distress" instead of famine (O'Neill 1957, 259).

Still, some relief was either provided or allowed, grudgingly to be sure, but without it many more lives would have been lost. Some food was made available, soup kitchens were finally opened, public employment (mainly building roads) was instituted for portions of the population, and others were taken into workhouses. Then, too, private groups, notably the Quakers, provided relief, importing food and operating their own soup kitchens.

Was the British response to the Irish famine a case of genocide by advertent omission? Not if by "genocide" one means an attempt to eliminate an entire group. But the case for a partial or "managed" genocide, though not conclusive, cannot be easily dismissed. We know from Trevelyan's own words that he was grateful to "an all-wise Providence" for bringing about a sizeable reduction of the population in Ireland, allowing for, in his view, a better balance between population and resources. In October 1846 he wrote to Lord Monteagle: "This [problem] being altogether beyond the power of man, the cure had been applied by the direct stroke of an all-wise Providence in a manner as unexpected and unthought of as it is likely to be effective" (O'Neill 1957, 257).

Whatever may have been the case with others involved in the making and implementation of British policy, the person who was at the center of the government's response to the Irish famine held views that are compatible with partial genocide by advertent omission.

Genocide with Scarcity as a Principal Means

The history of genocide provides many examples of the act being carried out primarily through depriving the victims of food. Ancient warfare was synonymous with genocide, the men being killed and the women and children enslaved. When a walled city offered resistance, the perpetrators would resort to siege warfare, cutting the inhabitants off from fresh supplies of food and drink. Most cities would lay in large quantities of necessities, but sieges could go on for months. When supplies began to dwindle, the leaders within the city would often drive out their own sick, elderly, and young to conserve food for those capable of fighting if the walls were breached. In time, those within the city would starve or they would capitulate and then be killed or enslaved (Jonassohn 1991, 3–10).

In other places, as with the Spanish "conquest" of Mexico, Indians would be forced into submission or would die by starvation when their supplies of food were confiscated and their crops burned. Then, too, the control of food in the ghettos and the camps was a calculated, if sometimes wavering, act by the Nazis to weaken and destroy Jews and others while also extracting labor from them; in the case of the Soviet prisoners, millions were starved to death (Browning 1992, 28–56; Streit 1990, 142–44). Another modern example, but one not well known, will be used to illustrate further the creation of scarcity as the primary means to genocidal ends: the Stalinist manmade famine of 1932–33 in Soviet Ukraine (Conquest 1986; Dolot 1985; Krawchenko 1986, 15–26; Mace, 1986, 1–14; Commission on the Ukrainian Famine 1988).

In 1932–33 the Ukraine suffered a manmade famine that led to the death by starvation of some five million Ukrainians, most of them the very peasants who had produced the grain that was confiscated from them (Conquest 1986, 306). A calculated policy to force peasants into collective agriculture and to crush a rising Ukrainian nationalism led, in two years, to the death of almost 20 percent of the population (Conquest 1986, 306). The means was the setting of impossibly high quotas for grain to be turned over to the Soviet government. When signs of mass death through starvation were everywhere, the Soviets ignored them. People were shot for taking a single ear of wheat or a sugar beet (Mace 1986, 7). Borders were sealed between Russia and the Ukraine to prevent the starving to find food. For the few who did manage to travel into Russia and find food, it was seized on their attempt to return to the Ukraine (Conquest 1986, 327–28).

James Mace summarizes some of the survivors' testimony:

[T]hey tell us of an "entire village population swelling up from star-vation, of the numbers of dead exceeding the capacity to bury them decently so that each day a dead wagon would pick up bodies which would then be dumped in large pits; they tell of whole villages be-coming deserted, of literal armies of homeless children . . . roaming the country in search of a way to survive and of railway stations literally flooded with starving peasants who had to beg lying down because they were too weak to stand." (Mace 1986, 8)

Meanwhile, the Soviet response was to hold back food contained in state reserves in the Ukraine, continue to export grain to buy machin-ery, reject offers of international aid on the grounds that there was no need for it, and ban foreign journalists from the areas affected by famine (Krawchenko 1986, 21; Conquest 1986, 328).

In 1930 Stalin learned the uses of famine for political purposes, and this by accident. When he attempted to force the Kazakhs, who were mainly herdsmen, onto collective farms, they resisted and slaugh-tered most of their livestock rather than turn it over to the state. As Mace (1986, 6–7) observes: "Rather than extend them aid, the regime decided to teach them a lesson by letting them starve. So many died that the 1939 Soviet census shows 21.9% fewer Kazakhs in the USSR than there had been in 1926. But resistance among them ceased. The lesson was obvious. Famine could be a highly effective weapon."

The lesson was applied with thoroughness in the Ukraine, but was also supplemented with executions of intellectuals and by the reassertion of control by Moscow. By 1934 Stalin had achieved his goals in the Ukraine: the peasants were defeated, and the flowering of Ukrainian religious and cultural life had been brought to a halt (Con-quest 1986, 328).

Scarcity as a Contributing Factor in Genocide

Genocide is a calculated act rather than an explosion of passion. Once genocide is set in motion, unless more powerful forces from either within or outside the society can intervene, it runs its course. Barring intervention, which need not always be military intervention, the destruction of the "enemy" will continue until the goals of the perpe-trators are realized. Genocide is resorted to largely because it has so often been successful—undeterred, not punished, later forgotten, and highly effective in achieving its goals of, for example, eliminating any threat to the dominant group's power, creation of a homogeneous society, or enriching the perpetrators at the expense of groups that have assets that the perpetrators covet. Motives for genocide are typically mixed, but in their pure form include conquest, retribution, power, material gain, and, where certain ideologies are involved, a kind of salvation/purification that requires the total remaking of society (Smith 1987, 23–27).

What is striking about the motives for genocide is not that material gain has often been a factor in such destruction. Rather, it is that, from ancient times to the present, initiating genocide to overcome material scarcity, in the absolute sense of maintaining the group's physical existence, has rarely been a factor. There are exceptions, previously mentioned, but mostly, one will come closer to understanding the historical role of scarcity in genocide if one views scarcity in its psychological form—desire rather than need—and in its political form—insecurity and inequality. Thus, to consider the plight of indigenous peoples in the twentieth century is not to focus on some kind of material necessity, but on the psychological and political dynamics of what has come to be called "development."

It is not only a question of understanding the historical relationships between genocide and scarcity but also of finding ways to overcome the psychological and political scarcity that can feed genocide. Later we shall consider measures that can reduce scarcity, helping reduce the pressures that contribute to genocide. First, we consider the possible effects of material scarcity—declining resources and increasing population—on genocide in the future. It is likely that many of the motives and pressures for genocide that have existed up to the present will continue, but there will likely be additional pressures that stem from material scarcities expected to characterize the twenty-first century. What are these pressures? How do they relate to possible decisions to commit genocide? And what can be done about them to lessen the likelihood of genocide, at least that related to the material basis of society?

The possible effects of scarcity in contributing to genocide and other mass violence are many; similarly, circumstances in particular cases can vary greatly. One, thus, can neither predict every outcome nor indicate in full how various forms of material scarcity can contribute to genocide. What is possible, however, is to suggest certain scenarios, illuminate particular tendencies, and point to a logic of atrocity that is furthered by scarcity in societies with particular characteristics.

For example, where the legitimacy of the state or the ruling group in a plural society is challenged, it is likely that the old regime will resort to authoritarian solutions to hold onto power. But in so doing, it will further alienate the minority groups that it has previously excluded from power. This effect will provoke further challenge to the elite's authority, which will be met with greater force, including massacres. This is, in fact, the classic case of what leads to genocide in ethnically divided, plural societies (Kuper 1981, 57–83). If there is also the problem of material scarcity, increasing demands will be made on those in power. These demands, owing to lack of resources, competence, or fairness, will not be met, resulting in further erosion in the legitimacy of rule by the dominant elite (Homer-Dixon 1994, 25–31). In such a situation, the tendency is to crack down on those making the demands, but also to allocate scarce resources even more decidedly along ethnic lines, favoring those of the dominant group. This favoring in part might be called a politics of identity, in which one favors one's own group, but also in part a strategy to reward those thought to be loyal to those in power. The result will be that in times of scarcity, the regime will move from its usual pattern of discrimination to a policy that increases hardship and, at the extreme, leads to destitution. At that point, migration will take place, leading to possible violence from neighboring societies, or the destitute will, if they have the means, resort to counterviolence. This violence will in turn initiate a new spiral of repression, beginning with massacres, which are a way of keeping a group in its place, and possibly ending with genocide, which attempts to eliminate the group itself.

In this scenario, a type of society (plural), a type of regime (authoritarian), a type of policy (unequal allocation of resources), a challenge to that policy (by the group that is viewed as inferior and excluded from power), and material scarcity (whatever its sources) come together in a fatal mix.

Or one might look to examples of state collapse, or being on the verge of collapse, because of, for example, defeat in war, the persistence of internal war, loss of legitimacy, or prolonged ecological crisis. In such cases, one possible outcome is that a new power arises, often buttressed with an ideology that will form the basis for a new legitimacy. Typically, such ideologies will create cleavages between groups that belong to the society ("the people") and those that are perceived as either "the enemy," groups to be eliminated, or groups that are seen as marginal and inferior, but that can have a second-class existence within the society (Melson 1992, 18–19, 267–71). In the case of a second-class status, we are back again to the plural society.

Where resources are available and are distributed in ways that are not equal, but at least meet the needs of the suppressed group, violence might be avoided; where resources are scarce, however, the likelihood of confrontation and repression increases (Gurr 1985, 71). Those in power will fall back upon the ideology to determine who gets what: in a given case, the ideology may make the division along lines of class, race, religion, or ethnicity, but judging from the rise of religious fundamentalism and the power of ethnicity in the post–cold war era, religion and ethnicity seem the most likely bases of ideology in the age of scarcity.

Preventing Genocide

Those who study genocide do so to understand why such extreme violence takes place and why it is directed at particular groups. The quest to understand, however, is not only a desire to know but also to find ways in which that understanding can be used to prevent future acts of genocide. As previously mentioned, nothing is inevitable about genocide; nevertheless, there are certain predisposing elements and the likelihood of preventing genocide is enhanced if these can be overcome. The chapter will conclude with some reflections upon possible means of removing the links between genocide and scarcity.

The means fall into two broad patterns. First, there is the question of how "scarcity" (in all the senses that have been identified) can be dealt with so that it does not put pressure on regimes to commit genocide. Second, there is the more general question of how genocide can be prevented, even if such pressure cannot be wholly removed.

Reducing Scarcities

As we have seen, "scarcity" takes three forms: psychological, political, and material. Let us consider each in turn.

"Desire" and its control were central features of the work of thinkers such as Plato, Rousseau, Tocqueville, and Durkheim. On the other hand, the more modern view, one that underlies ideas of progress and development, is that the expansion of desire and continual efforts to satisfy the expectations thereby created is the principal reason for social existence (Walzer 1980, 23–53). This artificial scarcity, a scarcity created by desire rather than need, largely drives the development projects that have destroyed the lives of indigenous peoples in the name of "progress" (Bodley 1982).

Given the central place that the expectation of ever-increasing material satisfaction plays in the modern worldview, it may be impossible, for example, to curb the destruction of rain forests. But if there is to be a check on such destruction, with the resulting deaths of individuals, peoples, and cultures, there seem to be only two ways in which this could be done. The first would require a reorientation within the modern worldview: instead of attempting to dominate nature, we would respect it and work with it, seeing ourselves as part of nature, and dependent upon it for our very existence. The other approach, which is compatible with the first, would call attention to the fact that cutting down rain forests is not the best use to which they can be put, in part because their ecosystems are extremely fragile and in part because the forests are the lungs of the earth. Moreover, many large-scale development projects in indigenous areas have been failures, but failures at great cost in lives, money, and damage to the environment (Davis 1977, chapter 9). If it is not possible to still the desire to "open up" the Amazon, it is possible for organizations like the World Bank in making loans for development projects to exert much more scrutiny in the viability of proposed schemes and their ecological and human impact.

Deprivation, on the other hand, is the hallmark of political scarcity. It contains three elements: deprivation in power, material well-being, and respect. Plural societies often display these forms of deprivation, prompting challenges to the structure of authority, and leading in turn to repression, renewed demands for equality or autonomy, and, without outside intervention, genocide. In fact, the most frequent source of genocide in the twentieth century has been that which springs from the political scarcity imposed by domination and exclusion (Smith 1987, 25–26). This is a question, however, of not only a divided society but also an authoritarian government. The widely held view that democratic regimes do not commit genocide, while not valid for the nineteenth century, is borne out by the history of genocide in the twentieth century (Fein 1993, 79; Rummel 1994, chapter 1).

The conditions for averting genocide that arises in part from political scarcity are reasonably clear. First, genocide would not occur if the society were homogeneous. Oddly, homogeneity is one of the goals of perpetrators of genocide in plural societies. Second, assuming that the society is divided, some form of power sharing would be necessary. The precise form this would take could vary from society to society, but it might involve, for example, federalism, a degree of autonomy, or certain offices, or a percentage of offices in the military, bureaucracy, or parliament, being reserved for members of the previously subordinate group. Third, it would require justice in the allocation of goods. Finally, it would require some degree of acceptance of the minority group as persons, and the repudiation of stereotypes and prejudices that had served as justifications for exclusion from equal treatment.

The conditions are easily stated, but societies have their own histories, and their social arrangements, including political domination and prejudice, are not accidental, though some of them are of very recent origin. If one gives up on changing the existing arrangements, but still believes that genocide must be prevented in such societies, the only other solution is outside intervention. But the refusal of states to intervene in Rwanda both before the genocide (there was strong evidence that it would take place) and after half a million persons had been killed does not bode well for this approach either (Adelman 1995).

The third form of scarcity is, at once, the most obvious and the most difficult to overcome. Material scarcity has two possible sources: resources are either not available or have been degraded in ways that make them less productive; and there may also be fewer goods per capita because of population expansion. The solutions to resource scarcity and population explosion are technical and political. Further, these two sources of scarcity are so entangled that it is not possible to solve one without the other.

Rapid population growth in an affluent society, with a large resource base and fair allocation of goods, could be accommodated with few adverse effects on the stability of society or material satisfaction of individuals. But high growth rates in population tend to occur precisely in societies that can least afford them, those that are already resource scarce or that allocate resources in ways that favor some groups and deprive others. Given the existing strains in such societies, rapid population growth will lead to increased scarcity, violence, and possible genocide. The spiral of scarcity will increase both because goods now have to be divided among more people and because attempts to increase production (especially of food and shelter) often produce severe ecological damage, undermining further the ability to meet material needs (Homer-Dixon 1994, 15–16). Fish will be taken at a rate that depletes their stock; forests will be denuded of their timber, with major consequences for erosion and silting of rivers; and, with the complex changes in the fragile ecosystem, there will be loss of topsoil and, in some cases, the ability to continue irrigation (Homer-Dixon 1991, 91–97). Those unable to provide for themselves will migrate to the cities, where they will be viewed as a burden, or they will migrate to neighboring states, with prospects of either squalid refugee camps or being turned back by violence (Gurr 1985, 71). On the other hand, if great development projects are begun on the lands of indigenous peoples, these groups will likely face extinction within a few years, as their habitat is destroyed, retributive attacks are made upon them as they defend their territory, and they are brought into contact with diseases from the outside world. Finally, as the society struggles with the effects of a sharp increase in population, the usual cleavages in plural societies may reassert themselves, with a rise in authoritarianism, challenges to the regime, increasing repression, material rewards for those in the dominant group and deprivation for others, and, in the end, if there has been no outside intervention, a distinct possibility of genocide.

Populations in the past have been reduced within a specific territory by migration, disease, famine, war, and genocide. These causes may operate in the future: Hannah Arendt saw genocide as the likely "solution" to a world overcrowed with "superfluous men"; others foresee a global threat from infection from emerging diseases that will kill off billions of people worldwide (Arendt 1958b, 457; Garrett 1994). Less apocalyptic visions, however, are possible, though they are not without their own difficulties in implementation. High birthrates will tend to fall where four conditions are present: a low mortality rate; a relative improvement in earnings; the availability of family planning and birth control; and an equal status for women.

Where there is a low mortality rate, parents do not need to produce many children to improve the odds of having one child survive to look after them in old age. An improvement in economic condition provides an incentive to limit the number of children to live better oneself. Family planning services and birth control provide the technical means for men and women to exercise choice. And an equal status for women has several effects in the number of children: it usually means a later age for marriage and leads to women taking more control over their fertility. Where these conditions are not met, the surge in population will most likely continue, leading both to increasing impoverishment and long-term environmental damage.

Solutions to the problems of resource scarcity are likewise difficult to implement, but some progress can be made if the size of the population can be stabilized. Too often, however, the response to growing population has been to adopt means that may offer some temporary relief, but lead to even more resource scarcity in the future. Thus, fish stocks may be depleted, forests devastated, and soil eroded in the unending quest to provide the necessary resources to care for the expanding population. What is required in part is a more careful assessment of the long-term implications of resource utilization. It may also be possible to use resources more efficiently. Or it may be necessary to reduce utilization of dwindling resources, allowing the standard of living to fall. All of these solutions require bureaucratic and entrepreneurial competence, and many would require a high degree of social discipline. International aid in the form of technical assistance can also be of great help, but in the past, it too often has itself been hitched to programs that end up damaging the environment (Burger 1987, 250–56; Independent Commission on International Humanitarian Issues 1987, 109–31). Finally, in some instances, international aid in the form of food may be necessary on a long-term basis. To say that it is necessary is not, however, to say that it will be provided.

Institutional and Political Means

Scarcities exacerbate the conditions that favor genocidal choices, but they do so within societies already divided along racial, religious, or ethnic lines and governed by authoritarian regimes. We come, then, to the more general question of how genocide can be prevented, even if not all of the pressures exerted by scarcities can be removed (Kuper 1985; 1992, 135–61; Hirsch 1995, 161–216). This question encompasses the cases in which scarcity is the result of genocide, not a source of it; where a perpetrator takes advantage of scarcity to commit genocide, but does not create the scarcity; and where the scarcity, usually famine, is deliberately created for carrying out genocide. This question, in other words, brings us back to the full range of cases involving various relationships between scarcity and genocide.

Numerous steps can be taken to prevent genocide. A carrot-and-stick approach might be adopted by states and international organizations to support social and political transformation in divided and repressive societies. Societies that are likely to resort to genocide can be identified and closely monitored. Early warning systems can be devised to forecast the likelihood of genocide, allowing governments and international bodies time to decide upon appropriate responses. Publicity and the mobilization by nongovernmental organizations of a human rights constituency to pressure governments to act are also important in this context. Efforts can be made to dry up the ready supply of arms that repressive governments turn against their own people.

Not only must international law be strengthened, but there needs to be brought into being a standing, permanent tribunal to judge those who commit war crimes, crimes against humanity, and genocide. Punishment can play only a limited role in deterring genocide, but it would strengthen international norms against mass killing for political ends. Also, the right of humanitarian intervention must both be recognized and made effective (Harff 1991, 146–53). Individual states now have the ability to intervene, and the United Nations can put together a coalition of forces, as in Bosnia and Somalia. But far more effective, and most likely a precondition for preventing genocide, is a permanent, standing international force that can be rapidly deployed. What is also crucial, for it is unlikely that the other steps will be undertaken to any extent without it, is for states to enlarge their definition of national interest to include the prevention of genocide (Smith 1992, 232–33).

Conclusion

Many, if not all, of the strategies for preventing genocide and reducing the scarcities—psychological, political, material— that can contribute to it could be effective, if implemented. The prevention of genocide, however, is less a matter of knowledge than of political will. Two related questions thus hang over the future: Will the states, and international organizations, of the world continue to be bystanders to genocide, looking on and doing little? Or will a human ability to resolve political and social problems in a manner befitting humankind finally assert itself in the next century? The questions are real; the answers uncertain. The consequences of doing nothing, however, are not in doubt.

11. Postcolonial Genocide

Scarcity, Ethnicity, and Mass Death in Rwanda

David Norman Smith

1

The scale and speed of the Rwandan genocide in 1994 took the world by surprise.[1] Well over 500,000 people were killed in just fourteen weeks, capturing the horrified attention of a global audience which, until then, had known little or nothing about Rwanda. Soon, however, surprise yielded to journalistic "explanations" that reduced the complexity of this startling episode to misleading clichés. The problem, we were told, lies with the Rwandan people, whose atavistic hatreds cannot be contained. Primordial antagonisms, whether "tribal" or "ethnic," are said to be the ultimate cause of mass murder.

The implication of this line of reasoning is that genocide, in a sense, is a murderous fact of life, an ineliminable danger as long as societies are ethnically divided. In the Rwandan case, this train of thought has led many people to think that the only hope for a lasting solution lies with forces above or outside the public: international lending agencies, once they learn the "policy lessons" of the genocide; the Rwandan state, duly reformed; and perhaps even a "return to colonialism," if all else fails.

The fatal flaw in this perspective, however, is that it rests on a grave misreading of the causes of the genocide—and finds hope in the

1. For help with this chapter I am grateful to John Nagel, Kevin Anderson, Ken Lohrentz, Scott Kerrihard, Isidor Wallimann, and Michael Dobkowski.

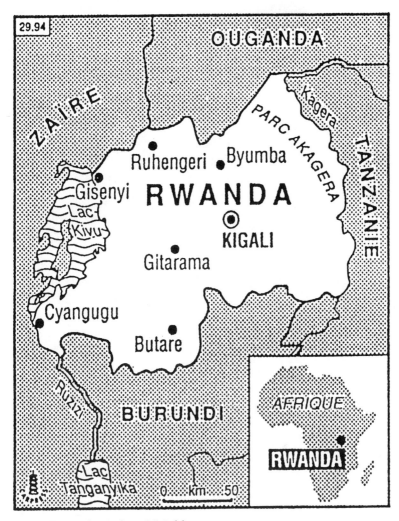

Map 1. Rwanda and Its Neighbors.
From *Rwanda: Histoire d'un Genocide* by Colette Braeckman (Paris: Editions Fayard, 1994).
Courtesy of Fayard © 1994.

very forces that spurred mass death in the first place. In what follows, I will contend that, far from being the singular source of the ills that gave rise to genocide, the Rwandan people are in fact the only force with a realistic chance of curing those ills. Rwanda's problems—political, military, ethnic, demographic and environmental—require popular solutions which existing states and markets are all too likely to oppose.

On the eve of the 1990s, Rwanda seemed to be an "oasis" of order and progress in east central Africa, in striking contrast to neighboring Zaïre, Uganda, and Burundi (Braeckman 1994, 86). The ruling party had been in power uninterruptedly since 1973, and the human rights situation, though "less than perfect," "contrasted favorably" with most other African nations (Reyntjens 1994, 35). So much violence had wracked bordering nations (see map 1) that many schools, missions, and development agencies had sought a safe haven in Rwanda (Newbury 1992, 201).

Rwanda also seemed to be thriving economically. In 1990, though still relying on agriculture for nearly 40 percent of its total GDP, Rwanda had reduced its reliance on farming more since 1965 than any other sub-Saharan country save Lesotho.[2] This shift from agriculture is doubly impressive when we consider that Rwanda also sustained a high level of agricultural productivity. Since 1965, for example, Rwanda had enjoyed more success than any other sub-Saharan nation in turning pasture land into cropland, and in the 1970s, when the ratio of food production to population growth fell for sub-Saharan Africa as a whole, Rwanda enjoyed a modest increase (Pottier 1993, 12). In the mid-1980s, only one other sub-Saharan nation enjoyed a faster growth rate in agricultural exports (Cleaver 1993, tables A-9, A-5), and though Rwanda was hardly unique in its export profile—relying mainly, like many sub-Saharan nations, on coffee production[3]—its marketing system was comparatively so sound that growers in Zaïre, Uganda, and Burundi routinely smuggled in coffee for sale on the world market (Newbury 1992, 201).

2. In 1965 Rwanda was more dependent on peasant labor than any other sub-Saharan country, relying on agriculture for 75 percent of its GDP. By 1990 this percentage had been cut in half, falling to 38 percent—the eleventh highest figure among thirty-four sub-Saharan nations (see Cleaver 1993, table A–2a).

3. World Bank research shows that coffee is by far the most widely produced agricultural export commodity in sub-Saharan Africa (Cleaver 1993, table A–5). Almost half of forty nations listed in a 1992 study specialized in coffee production (19), while more than 25 percent specialized in cotton production (11), and the remaining 25 percent specialized in other products—cocoa, rice, and so on.

Though still extremely poor, Rwanda was clearly on an ascending curve. Once the most impoverished of the five Great Lakes nations, Rwanda was "the least poor" in 1990 (Reyntjens 1994, 35). It was not a great surprise, then, when Rwanda became one of four African nations invited to participate in the Food Strategies program of the European Community in the 1980s (Pottier 1993, 5), or that the World Bank, looking back on nearly a decade of African development, gave Rwanda its highest accolade, calling it an "enabling environment" for private production and trade (1989, 105). Rwanda is a "successful case of adaptation," the World Bank concluded (Newbury 1992, 193).

Few observers in the immediate postindependence period would have predicted so much optimism a quarter of a century later. Rwanda was very poor, very small (about the size of Vermont), and notoriously extreme in many ways—"extremely landlocked," with "an extremely high population density, an extremely high population growth, and an extremely low degree of urbanization" (Braun, de Haen, and Blanken 1991, 15). Of almost no geopolitical significance, Rwanda was almost an afterthought even for its colonial conquerors. Imperial Germany, which ruled Rwanda from 1899 until 1916, was less interested in the Rwandans than in running a transcontinental railroad through Rwanda's hills. Even Belgium, which seized Rwanda and nearby Burundi during World War I, initially hoped to trade "Ruanda-Urundi" to Portugal for territory elsewhere in Africa. When this trade failed to materialize, the new Belgian rulers decided to use Rwanda as a source of food and labor for the Katanga copper mines in the Belgian Congo (now Zaïre). The Congo was vast and thinly populated, with comparatively few resources to support its rapidly growing mining centers. Rwanda, small but dynamic, seemed ideally suited for a supporting role.

Nestled east of the Congo in a fertile part of the Great Rift valley just below the equator, Rwanda was one of the most productive farming regions in all of Africa, rich in bananas, sorghum, and more than two hundred kinds of beans (Gravel 1968). This food had little export value, but it was perfect for Katanga. And although Rwanda as a breadbasket for others placed the Rwandan people at risk for famine, this was a risk, evidently, that the Belgians were willing to take. In the 1920s, Rwanda therefore sent an abundance of food and thousands of laborers to the Congo (while others fled to greener pastures in Uganda). All this changed, however, when the copper market collapsed at the start of the Great Depression. Since Katanga now ceased to be a magnet for food and labor, the Belgians decided to optimize their income from Rwanda itself.

Accordingly, like the British in Uganda, the Belgians in 1931 brought coffee to Rwanda, which they forced the peasants to grow for the world market. The peasants, who paid taxes from the resulting income, were also compelled to perform a great deal of "akazi" (forced labor, corvée). Over time, as Belgian labor exactions grew increasingly onerous, the conditions of life in Rwanda worsened drastically, setting the stage for the spiral of disasters to come.

During the Second World War the peasants were forced to work at redoubled speed, and even amid a long drought "they were forced to sell beans to European middlemen for one franc per kilo" (Newbury 1988, 158; cf. Dorsey 1994). Soon the combined effects of drought, labor corvées, and labor flight to Uganda yielded a famine of epic proportions, in which at least three hundred thousand people died— 10 percent of the population.

Additional misery and tension sprang from the heightened polarization of Rwandan society. Precolonial Rwanda had been divided into two ethnically tinged social classes, the Tutsis (warrior nobles) and a "Hutu" peasantry with roots in a mix of Bantu-speaking farm peoples who were already present when the cattle-rearing Tutsis arrived about five centuries ago (Newman 1995). The key to early Rwanda is that the term "Hutu" refers not to a primordial ethnic group, as journalists assume, but to a servile class drawn from a spectrum of peoples whose shared identity as "Hutus" (literally, "subjects" or "vassals") reflects their common subjection to the Tutsi nobles, who exploited yet also protected them. The Rwandan empire, which soared to prominence in the late precolonial period, was the joint product of both classes. When this empire fell to Europeans, the mutuality of Rwandan class relations declined sharply. The Germans and especially the Belgians recast the Tutsi nobility as a stratum of tax collectors and corvée labor bosses, whose power over the peasants rose as their obligations to them declined.

Hostility to the Tutsis swelled as Belgian exactions increased, reaching a crescendo in the 1950s. A proudly Hutu regime surged into power on a wave of emotion in the early 1960s, leaving thousands of Tutsis dead and many more in exile, the victims of a harsh Hutu nationalism that manifested signs of racism (for many Hutus accepted the Belgian myth that Tutsis are "black Caucasians," racial enemies of the Bantu peoples). The cycle of violence that climaxed in Rwanda in 1994 had begun.

The second act in this classical tragedy unfolded in Burundi (Lemarchand 1994, 174), where Tutsi supremacy had been left intact when Belgium withdrew. Fear of Hutu nationalism, however, and the rise of the extremist "Tutsi-Hima" wing of the ruling minority led to a fateful hardening of Tutsi chauvinism. In 1972 a flicker of Hutu insurgency served as a pretext for a "selective genocide" (Lemarchand and Martin 1974). In short order, the Tutsi military killed at least a hundred thousand Hutus, including every actual or potential leader they could identify. Smaller but similar Burundian massacres that occurred later (most notably in 1988 and 1993) can be understood only in the light of this chilling precedent.

Yet another act in this tragedy took place in strife-torn Uganda, where more than a million Rwandans had fled to escape famine or the pogroms of the 1960s. In 1981 an insurgency backed by many Rwandans provoked a scorched-earth campaign by the Obote government in the Luwero Triangle in central Uganda (Mutibwa 1992). At least three hundred thousand people were killed in this campaign, including about sixty thousand Rwandans (Watson 1991, 11).

After Obote was defeated in 1986, several Tutsis assumed top positions in the new regime—but they, like most Rwandans, were disconnected in Uganda. Bias against them was rife, and memories of the recent slaughter were indelible. When petitions to return from exile were rebuffed by the Rwandan government, Tutsi-led regiments of the new Ugandan military reconstituted themselves as the Rwandan Patriotic Front. In October 1990 RPF troops entered Rwanda to overthrow the one-party Hutu state with a "multi-party, multi-ethnic" regime. In 1994, after Habyarimana and nearly a million other Rwandans perished in a genocidal massacre planned and led by Habyarimana's closest associates, the RPF did indeed come to power.

Rwanda's "enabling environment" had turned into a vast killing field, and the World Bank's talk of "successful adaptation" now sounds like hollow rhetoric. Why? Why did social relations in Rwanda polarize to this extent? What forces plunged Rwanda into this vortex of murder and mass death?

2

As Patrick Chabal points out, it would be easy to conclude that Africa is simply "a continent of violence, perennially on the edge of survival" (1992, 179). Violence is indeed epidemic. Leaving southern Africa aside,

Richard Sandbrook shows that 4.5 million people died in political strife in sub-Saharan Africa from 1960 to 1987—a figure vastly greater than in Latin America or Asia. Almost all of these deaths (nearly 4 million) occurred in civil wars, insurrections, and other internal conflicts (see table). Since 1987 the death toll in Africa has continued to spiral, as Somalia, Liberia, and now Rwanda have been engulfed in deadly strife. The "ultimate reason," Chabal argues (1992, 189), "has more to do with the flaws in the construction of the post-colonial political order than with the inevitability of atavistic hostility."[4] Is this claim accurate? To what extent, we might ask, is the spiral of violence in Rwanda the result of flaws in the political order? And how, if at all, is ethnicity bound up with this disorder?

I have argued elsewhere (Smith 1995) that ethnicity and ethnocentrism remain pivotal to Rwandan society, as they have been for cen-

TABLE

Deaths in Civil Wars in Sub-Saharan Africa, 1960–1987

Country	Opponent	Date	Deaths
Angola	UNITA	1975–1987	213,000
Burundi	Hutu/Tutsi	1972	100,000
Chad	various	1980–1987	7,000
Ethiopia	Eritrea	1974–1987	546,000*
Mozambique	RENAMO	1981–1987	401,000*
Nigeria	Biafra	1967–1970	2,000,000
Sudan	North/South	1963–1972	500,000
Sudan	North/South	1984–1987	10,000
Uganda	various	1981–1987	102,000**
Zaïre	Katanga	1960–1965	100,000
Zimbabwe	Ndebele	1983	2,000
Total			3,981,000

*This figure includes war-induced famine deaths.

**This figure indicates the caution of Sandbrook's estimate, since it omits every death attributable to Idi Amin's regime and—if we are to belive the International Committee of the Red Cross—it understates the deaths in the Luwero Triangle by a factor of three (Watson 1991).

Source: Sandbrook 1993, 51. Reprinted by permission of Cambridge University Press.

4. Writing in 1992, before the latest Rwandan and Burundian slaughter, Chabal listed Rwanda, Burundi, and Uganda as the sites of three of the most "dreadful" civil wars in recent history (189).

turies. Rwandan "ethnicity," however, is so mutable, so much a part of the discourse of genocide, and so fatally entwined with state and class power that it must be analyzed with extraordinary care. Briefly, I would argue that, in the interval from the Belgian withdrawal to the genocide (from 1962 to 1994), the "ethnic" division between Tutsis and Hutus had grown progressively less significant in real terms. Ethnocentric feeling persisted, as the genocide proves—but the object of this hate was an increasingly ephemeral social construct, a memory of oppression more than an actual social division. The new oppressors (a "Hutu" ruling clique from the northwest) sought to exploit residual anger toward the remnants of the former oppressors to legitimate their own predatory rule.

Ethnicity, in other words, increasingly served as an ideological counter in the period that culminated with the genocide. What, formerly, had been a real antagonism turned into a legitimating myth— a myth used to justify murder.

To grasp this point we must turn to the history of Rwandan ethnicity. In the earliest phase, when the Tutsi/Hutu nexus was first established, the division between them was more purely "ethnic" than in any later period. The original "Tutsis" were a mix of the Lwo-speaking peoples who fled the western Nile to escape Dinka raiders. Newly settled in the Great Lakes region, these immigrants soon coalesced into a stratum of cattle-breeding warriors with an ethnic profile very distinct from that of the Bantu-speaking farmers they soon began to dominate (as "Hutus"). In the next phase, however, the terms "Tutsi" and "Hutu" acquired a primary class connotation (Newbury 1992; Vidal 1985; Chrétien 1985; Freedman 1979; Des Forges 1972; d'Hertefelt 1971). Precolonial Rwanda was most fundamentally divided between patrons and clients, who were bound by the labor obligations that clients owed patrons in return for lordly protection (Newbury 1992; Freedman 1974; Vidal 1969; Maquet 1954, 1961). Although the lords were nominally "Tutsis," this had ceased to be a strictly ethnic designation. Wealthy "Hutus," for example, who renounced "Hutuness" (servility) by an act of "kwihutura" were welcomed into the ranks of putative Tutsis. Thus, by the dawn of the colonial period, the Tutsi/ Hutu connection was above all a class affair.

Ironically, at this point, the colonial rulers of Rwanda put a renewed ethnic spin on the old distinction. Convinced that the Tutsis were racially superior to the Hutu masses, the Germans and (after 1916) the Belgians not only forced Tutsi "chiefs" to coerce rising quantities of labor from the Hutu peasants but also justified the many privileges they granted the Tutsis on overtly racial grounds. This racism drove a wedge between the Hutu masses and the newly christened Tutsi "Hamites," simultaneously hardening the class division between them and conferring a new ethnic quality on this division. Accordingly, under Belgian rule, the Tutsis became objects of a passionate hatred among Hutu peasants, who, in turn, became objects of Tutsi disdain. A class division thus became what Fein (1993, 89) rightly calls an "ethnoclass" hatred.

This hatred burst into the open during the anti-Tutsi violence that marked the inaugural period of Rwandan independence. However, in the generation that followed, the Tutsi/Hutu conflict dissipated. The division between the two groups diminished to the vanishing point, as most "Tutsis" became peasants, subject to the depredations of the very same "Hutu" regime that also preyed upon "Hutu" peasants. As the class difference evaporated, only ethnocentrism was left—an ethnocentrism that drew its charge from unhappy colonial-era memories and was nursed by predatory regimes for whom "Hutu" status was a claim to legitimacy (Omaar and De Waal 1994).

To summarize: the Tutsi/Hutu division was originally ethnic; subsequently class-based; acutely and simultaneously ethnic and class-based during the colonial period; and then "ethnic" once again in the postcolonial period, when the Rwandan state found it expedient to promote Hutu chauvinism in lieu of political and economic justice.

Should we conclude, then, that ethnicity is simply a mirage in Rwanda? That "Tutsi" and "Hutu" are simply empty words? I think not. Although the Tutsi/Hutu divide has been reinvented time and again, it remains very real to many Rwandans. Claudine Vidal is right, I think, to resist the temptation to say "that Tutsi and Hutu 'do not exist,' or that they are merely an 'invention' springing from ignorance and colonial Machiavellism" (1991, 24). It is certainly true that modern Rwandan identities are "socially constructed"—yet, they have real consequences. For the Hutu chauvinists of the genocidal regime, Tutsi status was an invitation to murder. The Tutsis in Rwanda are thus what Vidal (echoing Sartre) calls an "objet négatif," for which "it is not enough to establish, from the viewpoint of truth, the mythical aspects of ethnicity" (1991, 24).[5] On the contrary. Ethnicity, once constructed, can be exploited—and it is a vain hope to imagine that pointing to its constructed character will deprive it of its sting.

---

5. Vidal cites Sartre (1960, 344); see the English-language edition (Sartre 1976, 293–307). By the same logic the Hutus in Burundi are equally an "objet négatif."

Ethnicity, then, is a powerful force. Yet as Bayart and Chabal agree, other factors are at least equally influential. In Rwanda in 1994, a four-sided struggle embroiled a predatory state, a popular opposition, a guerrilla army (the RPF), and international lending agencies (mainly the International Monetary Fund [IMF] and World Bank). Tutsi peasants were the focus of racist propaganda in this conflict and they suffered its consequences more horribly than anyone else, but they were not its raison d'être. An authoritarian regime, caught in a vise between the IMF, the RPF (Rwandan Patriotic Front), and domestic *opposants,* lashed out with cold calculation and visceral fury. Their plan was to stay in power by sheer coercive force, to keep a death grip on the means of accumulation, to rule without consent. Hutu racism served this party, but power and profit were its main motives.

My thesis in this chapter is threefold: that the Rwandan genocide was not the "elemental outburst" that the media portrayed, but was, rather, meticulously staged by a state that hoped to profit from the fear and anger of its citizens; that the impetus for this gamble was a grave legitimation crisis; and that the IMF and World Bank played shadowy but pivotal roles in driving the state to the edge of the abyss—and over.

My first proposition, that the genocide was engineered by the state, has been massively documented (Omaar and de Waal 1994; see Human Rights Watch 1992, 1994a, 1994b). The evidence reveals just how coercive the ruling MRND was prepared to be when consent vanished and the IMF/RPF vise tightened.[6] That this ruling party had lost its legitimacy—my second proposition—is the final chapter in a long saga. I will contend that the MRND's legitimation crisis was the terminus of a long process by which power in Rwanda was desacralized and "depatrimonialized." A royal state, which, in the precolonial period, staked its claim to authority on the sacredness and fatherly liberality of its kings, was transformed by colonialism into a predatory bureaucracy, relying less on the loyalty of its subjects than on forced coffee cultivation for the export market.

In the postcolonial period, after toppling the Tutsi king and nobility, the new rulers made a half-hearted effort to leaven their forced-labor agenda with neopatrimonial concessions to the peasantry (most notably

6. MRND (Mouvement Républicain pour le Développement et la Démocratie) is usually pronounced "emerendi." Until falling in 1994, this party ruled Rwanda for nearly two decades.

by forming producer cooperatives). But the main object of these concessions, to mask and rationalize the regime's predatory agenda, became
less compelling in the 1980s, when a sudden influx of international
loans sharply reduced the state's dependence on the world coffee market (and thus on the peasantry). Less worried now about the loyalty of
the coffee producers, the MRND became even more predatory than
before. Hence, when the coffee market collapsed in 1988, it was second
nature for the party to turn the screws on the peasants to recoup its
losses. When the public resisted, and when the IMF/World Bank exerted great pressure on the MRND to relinquish its monopoly on power,
the party leaders felt that they had been backed into a corner. Rather
than gracefully accepting defeat, they chose the most violent alternative
available to them—total war on much of their own public.

Thinly veiled as an eruption of communal violence, the genocide
was a calculated gamble. The hope was that, by eliminating the political opposition, the MRND could stave off the IMF/RPF juggernaut.
The Tutsi peasantry bore the brunt of this genocide for several reasons: a measure of real ethnocentrism on the part of the killers; the
MRND's cynical and desperate wish to exploit residual ethnic hatreds,
in a final bid for a shred of legitimacy; and the assumption that all
Tutsis were naturally *opposants*. But hundreds of thousands of Hutus
were massacred as well, mainly for political reasons. They opposed
the regime. They exposed—and could exploit—the MRND's fatal lack
of legitimacy.

The Rwandan state, desacralized and depatrimonialized, could rely
only on violence to fight its enemies. And yet even violence on the
most appalling scale proved unavailing in the end.

3

Readers familiar with Africanist literature may see parallels between
my argument and related positions—Migdal's theory of "strong states"
dominating "weak societies" (1988), Lonsdale's thesis of the decline of
"political accountability" (1986), Sandbrook's concern about the collapse of consent (1993), Hyden's account of the crisis of "reciprocity"
(1992), and Fatton's analysis of the rise of "predatory rule": "As
quasivoluntary compliance diminishes," Fatton writes, "coercion increases" (1992, 4).

My thesis is, in fact, a variation on Göran Hyden's influential
theme of the "uncaptured peasantry" (1980). Briefly, Hyden says that

although peasants may have less clout than proletarians vis-à-vis the state, they are far from defenseless. Since most African states rely on export taxes for the bulk of their revenues, they have to treat export producers with a degree of diplomacy. If states overtax the coffee, cocoa, and cotton that peasants produce for the export market, they risk driving them back to subsistence farming and away from export crops entirely. This would be tantamount to killing the goose that laid the golden egg. Hence, African states have good fiscal reasons to retain the goodwill of their peasants.

African history is "replete" with episodes that reveal the soundness of Hyden's theory (Isaacman 1993, 239f.). Peasants in many places have uprooted crops, boiled seeds, burned harvests, or turned to the black market. But as many critics point out, Hyden seldom takes complicating or contrary facts into account (Lemarchand 1989). This practice leads some scholars, like Kajsa Ekholm Friedman, to conclude that Hyden's theory is simply "the opposite" of the truth. In the formerly "Marxist-Leninist" Congo, she writes, the state "has disengaged itself from the people. . . . It is not dependent upon ordinary people in any significant way, and it can therefore turn its back to them" (1993, 225).

The truth of this claim vis-à-vis the Congo is not in question (see Mpélé 1993). It is not obvious, however, that Hyden's thesis is irrelevant in cases of the Congolese kind, where the peasantry seems to have been decisively "captured." In Rwanda, too, the state seemed to have captured the peasants. It was able to do this, however, only to the extent that the World Bank freed the MRND from its dependence on the market. Nearly 95 percent of all Rwandans are peasants, and coffee revenues are always crucial. Hence, the state can never be wholly deaf to peasant concerns. But the infusion of foreign aid here, as elsewhere, had a liberating effect on the state. This seems to have been true in Congo, too, since Friedman lists "aid and foreign loans" as two of the state's three main income sources.

In Uganda the parallel is even clearer. This is plain in a study by Stephen Bunker, whose fieldwork initially seemed to confirm the original Hyden thesis. Before the lending boom, the Bugisu coffee cooperative was clearly uncaptured: "I found, however, when I returned to Uganda during the summer of 1983, that [the new] regime was far less susceptible to local political demands than . . . any of the previous national or colonial governments had been" (1987, 228). Instead of courting coffee growers, Obote was preoccupied with foreign loans. From 1981 to 1985 there was "a dramatic increase in external borrowing"

(Mugenyi 1991, 65). Hence, although "still dependent . . . in the long run on peasant crop production," Obote's "more immediate need was to satisfy the demands of these agencies" (Bunker 1987, 229).

In the short run, Obote showed merciless disdain for the Ugandan people. He squeezed the coffee growers, and scourged the Luwero Triangle. It seemed, that is, that the Obote regime was a classically "strong" state; backed by the IMF and World Bank, Obote was free to impose his will on an ever "weaker" society. The 1986 victory of the insurgency against Obote calls this appearance into question. Without legitimacy Obote could not save himself even by slaughtering three hundred thousand people. In Rwanda the numbers differ but the logic is the same.

My stress on the IMF and World Bank parallels a recent current of thought in IMF circles. Prefigured by Sidell (1988) and Nelson (1990), this current is now best represented by Jean-Dominique Lafay. Perturbed that "unexpected violent reactions . . . have accompanied some stabilization or IMF programs," Lafay and his associates scrutinized data on twenty-three African nations (including Rwanda) to find correlations between IMF policies and various forms of political conflict (Lafay, Morrisson, and Dessus 1994, 175–76). The results they obtained are sobering.

In a model that revolves around a trio of "decision-making forces"—the IMF and World Bank, the state, and the public (176), Lafay tracks an arrow of causality that runs from the IMF/WB, acting through the state, to the public, whose protests evoke state reactions.[7] Often, the result is a spiral of violence.

IMF aims are well known, Lafay says (1994, 180–81): cuts in "public expenditures . . . an increase in consumer goods prices . . . more rigorous monetary policy, devaluations, and cuts in public employment." However, the political effects of IMF interventions are seldom studied. It is often said that international lending policies are harsh and unpopular—but Lafay goes further to show that only one of sixteen carefully coded IMF and World Bank interventions is even remotely popular. Spending cuts, rationing tax hikes, and price increases prompt both strikes and demonstrations, often over a long period of time. Wage cuts spur strikes; job cuts, devaluations, and privatizations spark demonstrations (1994, table 9.2).

---

7. From this point on, for ease of reading, I refer to Lafay as the author of the study cited below. It should be kept in mind that Morrisson and Dessus are his coauthors.

There are, in fact, so many correlations between protests and IMF/ World Bank policies that it can hardly be denied, Lafay says, "that economic adjustment is a risky venture" (1994, 182). The magnitude of this risk is manifest when we consider Lafay's finding that African states typically greet protests with violence, arrests, and measures to ban unions and parties, censor the media, forbid rallies, and close schools and universities (1994, table 9.3). Indeed, the "suppression of demonstrations is much more violent than in developed countries" (1994, 183). The African state is so dictatorial and rigid that virtually "any conflict turns into a dispute over the legitimacy of the regime" (1994, 184).

In Rwanda this had not always been true. Indeed, the political process that led to the genocide can be understood as a long-term decline in the legitimacy of a once-"sacred" state. The kings who ruled in the precolonial period were regarded as divine personifications of the highest power, *imaana*, which they showered upon the Rwandan people through royal rituals. This observance, it was believed, ensured the fertility of Rwandan women, cattle, and land (Coupez and d'Hertefelt 1964, 460; see Taylor 1992, Bonte 1991). The kings were also classically "patrimonial" figures in the Weberian sense that they maintained a degree of real reciprocity with the peasants and minor nobles in the pyramid beneath them (see, for example, Weber [1922] 1978, 1010). While relying on the public to fill their granaries and feed their entourages, they also sought to play the role of generous "fathers of the people," granting favors and even opening their granaries during famines (Vanwalle 1982, 73; in Pottier 1986: 222–23).

Toward the end of the precolonial period, the balance of power tilted in favor of the kings, leading to a diminution of reciprocity between the monarchy and the Rwandan people (Des Forges 1972, passim). But the tie that bound them was not severed until the Germans and Belgians entered the scene. A stream of colonial decisions so weakened and humiliated the royal house that, by the end of the colonial era, royalty was no longer sacred in Rwanda. The king had been reduced to a spectral figure, who was relevant in the contemporary setting only as the greatest of the Tutsi lords. When many of the now-hated Tutsis were driven into exile in the early 1960s, the king went with them. State power in Rwanda had been radically desacralized.

Meanwhile, the state was also undergoing "depatrimonialization." Reciprocity between rulers and ruled had declined drastically during the colonial years, as the Belgians, whose power sprang from European sources, effectively "captured" the Hutu peasants. A flicker of hope burst into flame when Hutu nationalists came to power in the postcolonial era, but patrimonial relations were not restored. This became particularly clear during the second decade of the "Second Republic," which was born in a coup in 1973. Reciprocity, it seemed, was not on the agenda. The state was bent on capturing the peasants just as thoroughly as they had been captured by the Belgians.

In the short run, this objective was easily attained, for (until recently) there has been virtually no civil society in Rwanda. Even the capital, Kigali, was a town of just a few thousand as late as 1970, and most Rwandans do not live in towns or even villages, but are dispersed in family farming compounds. Desperately poor, and willing, at first, to give the new "Hutu" regime the benefit of the doubt, the peasants grew increasingly unhappy. Ultimately, the legitimacy of the state fell precipitously, setting the stage for the decidedly postpatrimonial conflict of the present period. To this we now turn.

4

The fall of the Tutsi bureaucracy profoundly changed the political physiognomy of Rwanda. Power now devolved upon circles of Hutu intellectuals (the so-called *evolués*), who had formed two parties in the 1950s to press for independence. Parmehutu, a "Hutu" party with chauvinist impulses, drew its main support from Gitarama, in central Rwanda, and from the northern provinces (Gisenyi, Ruhengeri, and Byumba). Aprosoma, a party based in the southern province of Butare, was multiethnic in ideology and composition.

The regional division here is crucial. The peoples of the northwest—the "Abakiga"—had been the last of the independent Bantuspeaking peoples of the Great Lakes region to be annexed to Rwanda. They had been conquered, in fact, only in the 1920s, and they had never adjusted to the foreign idea that they were "Hutu" pawns in a Belgo-Tutsi chess match. Indeed, as late as the 1970s, many Kigans still considered it an insult to be called a Hutu (Freedman 1979). Nevertheless, in the first decade of independence, avowedly "Hutu" *evolués* from Gitarama (where Tutsi/Hutu relations had prevailed for centuries) joined with anti-Tutsi forces from the Abakigan northwest to forge a common "Hutu" front.

Parmehutu emerged as the leading force in independent Rwanda after a quasi-revolutionary initial phase in which peasant anger, harnessed to the ends of anti-Tutsi nationalism, drove most wealthy Tutsis

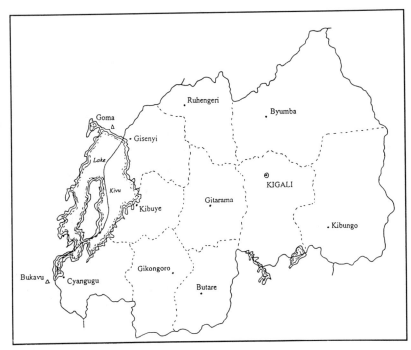

Map 2. Regions of Rwanda.
From *Rwanda: Death, Defiance, and Despair*, 2d ed., by Rukiya Omaar (London: Africa Rights, 1995). Courtesy of the author.

into exile (while many Tutsi peasants stayed in Rwanda, eking out a precarious, almost rightless existence in a setting where everyone was assigned an official ethnic identity, and where most privileges were reserved for "Hutus"). Without reviving forced labor, the new regime nevertheless soon proved to be a worthy heir to the Tutsi bureaucracy. As early as 1965 Parmehutu became the nucleus of a one-party state, and by the late 1960s the "Gitaramistes" in the party had elbowed aside the Abakigan northerners. The inner circle of politicians from Gitarama (grouped around the party leader, Gregoire Kayibanda) soon emerged as a *noblesse d'état*, bent on self-enrichment through the medium of the state.

The main instrument of this quest was the state-run marketing system TRAFIPRO, which channeled export profits to Gitaramiste leaders and businessmen. "The economic power of TRAFIPRO was much feared in the northern prefectures. Controlling 27 shops nationwide and 70 buying-up points for coffee (in 1966) TRAFIPRO was accused by influential Northerners of running a monopoly that strangled other forms of economic enterprise, especially in the North" (Pottier 1993, 11; see Reyntjens 1994, 511f).

The leading northern politicians were incensed not only because they themselves were left out in the cold but also because they saw the Kayibanda regime as an enemy of traditional Abakigan property relations. Unlike the Gitaramistes, for whom the regime itself was the locus classicus of predatory accumulation, the northerners wished to put the state at the service of the *abakonde,* a stratum of Kigan landowners whose wealth and power sprang from *ubukonde* clientship.[8] Although *ubukonde* closely resembled hated forms of Tutsi land tenure that were now banned, it was protected by the Gitaramiste regime as a "Hutu" institution. Hence, when Jim Freedman carried out fieldwork in the north in 1971, he found a way of life very much like the one described in the ethnohistorical records. In particular, "ideas about how social units settle on the land and the principles by which these social units identify themselves, form and fissure, seemed to remain in principle very much the same" (1974, 42). When Freedman returned six years later, he found that the situation had greatly changed. The source of this change was the coup of 1973.

The coup leader, Juvenal Habyarimana, was a military commander from the northwestern province of Gisenyi whose wife belonged to a powerful *abakonde* family. In June, Kayibanda evidently crossed a fatal line when he announced a new bureau, ONACO, which assumed state control over private commerce. For property owners, this may well have been the last straw. In early July, Habyarimana seized power and "suspended" ONACO, which his regime vilified as "communist" (Reyntjens 1985, 505–6).

Quickly showing that he was no populist, Habyarimana took the bold step of reviving corvée labor in 1975. Under the aegis of a system called *umuganda,* all adults were required to participate in labor teams every Saturday under state direction; the penalty for refusal was imprisonment (Omaar and de Waal 1994, 16).[9] In other respects, too,

---

8. Ubukonde was also common in the southwestern region of Kinyaga, which, like Kiga, was incorporated into imperial Rwanda at a very late date. See Newbury 1988, passim.

9. The reactionary daring of this step can be gauged by the fact that *travail-corvée* had been expressly singled out in the revolutionary 1957 "Manifesto of the Bahutu" as a practice "no longer adapted to the situation and psychology of today" (see Newbury 1988, 192). No other single feature of Belgo-Tutsi rule had been more hated.

Habyarimana "greatly intensified" the process of "centralizing and reinforcing the postcolonial state" (Newbury 1992, 198).

The new ruling party, the MRND, was declared the "party of the Rwandan people," and the party slogan, "responsible democracy," was explained in classically Orwellian terms by a spokesman as "the free expression of ideas on condition that they are seen as useful to the collectivity" (Mfizi 1983, 61; cited by Newbury 1992, 198).

The undisguised class and *nordiste* biases of the new regime gave rise to concentric circles of winners and losers. Standing at the very heart of the regime was an inner circle known as the Akazu, "the little hut," which consisted of Habyarimana's intimates, many of whom were Bushiru from Rambura in Gisenyi (Reyntjens 1994, 276). Among the key figures in this group were Habyarimana's wife, Agathe; three of her brothers (Séraphin Rwabukumba, former head of the national bank and director of the Centrale, which enjoyed a near monopoly on food imports; Protais Zigiramyirazo, former prefect of Ruhengeri; and Elie Sagatwa, Habyarimana's secretary); and the former defense minister Theoneste Bagosora, who is widely viewed as the architect of the genocide (Omaar and de Waal 1994, 94–105; Braeckman 1994, 104).

Guarding the inner circle was the elite Presidential Guard, "ninety percent of whom," a former finance minister says, "are from Habyarimana's area, practically from his hill" (interviewed by Omaar and de Waal 1994, 91).

Many other northerners (politicians, landlords, and merchants) orbited the Akazu. So wealthy did this stratum grow that Vidal speaks ironically of a "fourth ethnicity" in Rwanda—the governing rich, defined by their opposition to the peasantry (1991, 88, cited by Reyntgens 1994, 223). "Those in government," Omaar and de Waal conclude, "had a license to print money" (1994, 21).

Habyarimana professed to speak for all Rwandans, but it was self-evident, a former ambassador reports, that "in reality he was only interested in the Bakiga people . . . especially those from Gisenyi" (interviewed by Omaar and de Waal 1994, 40). Gitarama and Kibuye, with 20 percent of the population, received just 1 percent of rural investments (excluding donor funds), while Gisenyi, Ruhengeri, Kigali, and Cyangugu shared almost 90 percent of the total (Guiachaoua 1989a, 173; see Newbury 1992, 203). Analogous disparities were plain elsewhere (Reyntjens 1994, 33).

In a book finished less than two months before the genocide, Reyntjens reported that the Tutsi/Hutu conflict had been "surpassed by a regional conflict" (1994, 34). The north, prospering at the expense of the south, made a mockery of the old rhetoric of "Hutu" unity. Yet, even the north was not free of conflict and class division. When Freedman returned to Kiga in 1977, he found that *ubukonde*, torn from its moorings by an influx of money, had given rise to a sharply divided society. For the Abakiga poor, the "devil word is *amataranga*"—money (1979, 15). The landowners had capitalized on the new money economy to lure peasants into debt, a process leading to the "concentration of land holdings in the hands of a few" (1979, 3; cf. Pottier 1993, 15). An abyss had opened up between the wealthy and the land-poor, the *abakene*, many of whom could no longer support families.

Elsewhere conditions were equally desperate. A 1984 study showed that 42.9 percent of the land was controlled by 16.4 percent of the families (Reyntjens 1994, 223). Average land holdings shrank (Pottier 1993, 12), landlessness became widespread (Jazairy, Mohiuddin, and Pannucio 1992, 50), and peasant incomes fell to levels of "pauperization" well beyond "what is acceptable" (Bézy 1990, 58, cited by Newbury 1992, 203). Overall, Newbury says, Habyarimana's Rwanda revealed "a growing gap between rich and poor as well as a more vigorous assertion of class interests by those in power" (1992, 203).

When the IMF, the RPF and a democratic opposition put this predatory system in question, the *Akazu* decided to take action.

5

"The old is dying and the new cannot be born," Antonio Gramsci once wrote, musing over the miscarriage of capitalism in southern Italy. "In this interregnum a great variety of morbid symptoms appear."

For Rwanda and the many African nations that share its political and economic profile (Sandbrook 1993; Bayart 1993), the twentieth century has been a time of plague and locusts. The old precapitalist ways were irrevocably destroyed, and yet the capitalist millennium never arrived. Corvée labor and coffee exports broke an empire but did not offer emancipation. A multiclass and multiethnic mosaic became a deadly dialectic.

Is there a solution? Is there a path forward for Rwanda and Africa?

The conventional wisdom is that Rwanda has been sabotaged by its own irrepressible past. Primitive hatreds, pulsing beneath the veneer of civilization, have been reawakened. The solution, hence, can only lie outside Rwanda. This is the apparent rationale for a proposal, in *Foreign Affairs,* for a new colonialism: "If anybody is competent to deal sympathetically with these countries, the Europeans are" (Pfaff 1995, 5).[10] This proposal is, at least, imaginative.

A second, equally imaginative way to blame the Rwandan people for the cycle of violence is to focus, not on their "indelible hatreds," but on their soaring birthrate. Population pressure is surely a grave problem for the Rwandan people, yet it is wrong to say, in neo-Malthusian tones, that violence is a simple reflex of "excess" population density. And it is mistaken to imagine that paternalistic birth control campaigns, or anything short of genuine progress in the welfare of Rwandan families, will permanently ease population pressures. This becomes quite clear when we review the demographic facts.

The gravity of the population crisis in Rwanda is plain. Since the turn of the century, the population has risen nearly ninefold, from about a million when the Germans arrived (Des Forges 1986, 313) to three million at the start of the 1943–44 famine (Omaar and de Waal, 14) to a pregenocide total of close to nine million. The Rwandan birthrate, meanwhile, is extraordinarily high, whether measured by African or by global standards. Of all sub-Saharan African countries, Rwanda has the highest total fertility rate—8.3 children per woman.[11] In 1985 each hectare of land supported 5.5 "adult-equivalent persons," yielding a population density seven times greater, for example, than that of Uganda (Braun, de Haen, and Blanken 1991, 12). And pregenocide projections showed that this total would double, at least, by 2005.

Considering how often Rwanda has been afflicted by famine, it is plain that concerns about population pressure are definitely warranted. But why exactly is this so?

Isidor Wallimann goes straight to the heart of the matter when he observes that "the more vulnerable people become economically . . . the

---

10. Equal amnesia, if less hope, was revealed by a former British ambassador, who lamented that Belgian charity had failed, alas, to pull up "Rwanda's bloody roots" long ago. It is "chastening," he says, to think that "bringing Rwanda peacefully to independence as a democratic society [may have been] beyond human ingenuity and statesmanship" (*New York Times,* Murray 1994, A–19). Enlightened opinion, in other words, is divided about the likelihood that well-meaning Belgians can solve Rwanda's problems.

11. The total fertility rate, Kevin Cleaver explains (1993, table A-1), "is the average number of children who would be born alive to a woman . . . during her lifetime if she were to pass through her childbearing years confirming [sic] to the age-specific fertility rates of a given year." No other sub-Saharan nation has a TFR above 8.0, and only three exceed 7.0. Burundi is one step removed at 6.8.

more they are inclined to maintain birth rates that enhance population growth" (1994, 45). Far from being "irrational," this is an illustration of the kind of peasant rationality that Alexander Chayanov clarified long ago. In a peasant economy—where, as Freedman notes, "birth is nearly the only form of labor recruitment" (1984, 76)—prosperity and progeny are practically synonymous.

This comes as no surprise to Rwandans, for whom fertility has long been a veritable obsession (Taylor 1992). Indeed, the very idea of well-being is tied to female fertility in the Rwandan language: "the verb 'to be fertile,' for a woman, is most accurately rendered by the verb which describes a general state of well being. This is *kwera*," a term that (with an implication of purification or "whitening") designates "good fortune in the reproduction of children, animals, and the productivity of fields" (Freedman 1974, 144, 147). The customary term for a home, meanwhile, is *urugo,* which also means a pregnant body. And the circular outline of a home under construction "is explicitly identified with the womb" (Freedman 1974, 136, 85).

It is hence no wonder that, in Rwanda, prosperity and progeny are quite literally synonymous. "Poverty and existence without a family . . . are rendered by the same Rwandan noun: *ubukene*" (Freedman 1979, 6).

Are the peasants wrong to make this connection? Not at all. Soaring birthrates are undoubtedly a danger in the long run, but in the short run, for each family, children are still the most precious of resources. "Contrary to [our] study hypothesis," Braun and others reported in 1991, "an increased household size is found in this sample in northwest Rwanda to be positively related to nutritional improvement and significantly so for the long-term" (94). The solution to the population problem in Rwanda, then, lies not in isolated measures to curb birthrates, but in efforts to raise living standards. Not until children cease to be an economic necessity will birthrates stabilize.

The prospect of raising living standards, meanwhile, is far from hopeless. In 1990, though the Rwandan population was far greater than it had been during the colonial era, "hunger was less pervasive" (Omaar and de Waal 1994, 17). And although the Habyarimana regime cynically used the rhetoric of "overpopulation" to keep Rwandan exiles in Uganda, the data suggest that, as crowded as Rwanda has been, the saturation point has not yet been reached. Most nations in Asia "have to sustain populations which are infinitely larger in absolute and relative terms than they are anywhere on the African continent," as Chabal observes. "Despite a widespread belief to the contrary, Africa is not overpopulated in the sense in which these Asian countries are" (1992, 184).

Braun, de Haen, and Blanken report "the interesting finding . . . that increased land scarcity [in Rwanda] can still be substantially compensated for by intensification of labor and capital input per unit of land" (1991, 12). Scarcity in Rwanda is not, it appears, primarily a result of insuperable environmental barriers, but of policy limitations. Pottier (1993, 1986), for example, reports that, besides forcing the peasants to devote scarce time and land to badly paid coffee production, Habyarimana's state imposed restrictions on cultivation that kept subsistence production well below optimum levels. And by forcing farmers to specialize in particular crops, the state created a situation of artificial scarcity in which it profited by selling farmers staples that it prevented them from producing.

The solution, plainly, is to abolish forced labor, establish democratic control over coffee production (and revenues), improve farming methods and technology while encouraging cooperative production and distribution.

This is not, unfortunately, the path taken by the IMF and World Bank. It was, in fact, precisely Habyarimana's success in organizing forced labor that first attracted the attention of international lenders in the 1970s (Pottier 1993, 5). This remained true thereafter: "In the eyes of the U.S. government and other donors, Rwanda before the [genocide] was a model of development efficiency. Every Rwandan citizen had to participate in collective labor on Saturdays.

The system was harsh but effective—roads were built, trees planted. During the 1980s, the U.S. provided the Rwandan government with significant development aid" (Hilsum 1994, 16; see World Bank 1989, 58).

Other donors were also impressed, and many were generous. From 1980 to 1986, Rwanda received at least $200 million in new aid commitments every year except one. In 1987 the total soared to $340 million. The result, as Catharine Newbury observed in 1992, is that "Rwanda depends, to an extraordinary degree, on foreign assistance" (199).

This made the Habyarimana regime all the more vulnerable when the coffee market collapsed in 1988 and export earnings fell 50 percent by 1991 (Chossudovsky 1995). Rwanda was compelled to seek assistance from the IMF for the first time, agreeing to a Structural Adjustment Program with stringent "conditionalities." This was a very inauspicious time to start a SAP, since the IMF had just decided to demand rigorous compliance with far stricter requirements. And the collapse of the Soviet Union gave the IMF a freer hand to push for the decentralization of states that blocked the free action of the market. Authoritarian allies of the West were no longer automatically exempt from the pressure to "democratize"; and the IMF, which had been preaching the gospel of laissez faire since the early Reagan/Thatcher years, began to push Rwanda as hard as anyone (Omaar and de Waal 1994; Chossudovsky 1995).

The Habyarimana regime was soon in great difficulty. In October 1990, the RPF invaded from Uganda. The early invasion was repulsed (with French help), but the RPF and its battle-tested leaders remained dangerous. On the domestic front, after reluctantly bowing to Western pressure to begin a process that would lead to full "multipartyism" in a few years, the Habyarimana forces witnessed a proliferation of *opposant* parties and papers. Old Gitaramiste forces sprang from the woodwork, to be joined by a plethora of others, including, for example, the Parti des écologistes, the Rassemblement travailliste pour la démocratie, the Mouvement des femmes et du baspeuple (Reyntjens 1994, 135). In 1992, suffering the consequences of the coffee crisis doubly and trebly as the state intensified its exactions—and refusing to be wholly "captured"—peasants uprooted three hundred thousand coffee trees (Chossudovsky 1995). This was an act of defiance and desperation, and strictly illegal (Pottier and Nkundabashaka 1991, 151).

In 1993, after further fighting with the RPF and increased pressure from the IMF and its allies, Habyarimana signed the Arusha Accords, committing the regime to carry reform through to completion. This apparently convinced the Akazu extremists (organized as "Network Zero") that they would have to fight the RPF and the democratization of Rwanda with or without Habyarimana. Bagosora, on leaving the Arusha meetings, told colleagues that he was going home "to prepare the Apocalypse" (Omaar and de Waal 1994, 79). Death squads, thousands strong, had been in training since the early 1990s. Open threats of genocide became common, and it was well known that oppositionists were in danger. Many were assassinated.

The signal for the start of the genocide was Habyarimana's death in a plane crash on April 6, 1994. In the ensuing days the regime's death squads, aided by the military, fanned across Rwanda, killing as many actual and potential oppositionists as possible, many of whom had been marked for death ahead of time. Peasants on many hills and in many prefectures were bribed, coerced, and cajoled to participate in the slaughter; many did, and many did not.

In barely three months, a shower of death rained on the Rwandan people, leaving as many as 750,000 dead (Omaar and de Waal 1995). The genocide came to an abrupt halt in July, when the RPF captured Kigali. Since then the situation has remained pregnant with danger. Burundi is profoundly volatile, and the remnants of the genocidal Akazu regime dominated the refugee camps in Zaïre until the camps dissolved in late 1996. The cycle of conflict and mass death, in other words, is not necessarily at an end. Nor is concord truly likely until the underlying factors that promote conflict are resolved.

As long as Rwanda remains at the mercy of the world market, it is always in danger of reconstituting forced-labor. Tellingly, the genocidal death squads were known as *interahamwe*—a name formerly reserved for the teams organized to perform corvée labor. And the slang term for murder itself is "work" (Omaar and de Waal 1994, 70). The distance from forced labor to forced murder is evidently not as great as it might seem. And whenever power rests with a forced-labor state, there is a prospect of resistance—greeted, in normal cases, by repression.

In late 1994 the Rwandan human rights activist Monique Mujawamariya was asked, "What happened in your country?" "The people," she said, "revolted against a well-armed dictatorial regime and they are paying a high price for their attempt to install democracy. . . . The dictator's clan knew that, as a result of international pressure and the mobilization of the people, it would have to share power. People had massively joined opposition parties; this threw the regime into a fever. So it decided to crush the moderate opposition, to eliminate the intellectuals, to kill everybody who could have laid claim to power. It is a revolution, within which a genocide has taken place" (Saint-Jean 1994, 13).

The comparative calm in the first year after the genocide gives us reason to hope that new episodes of mass death can be avoided. But as long as Rwanda remains an orphan in the world economy, with few resources and fewer genuine friends, conflict will remain a permanent danger. Western banks and governments may express their "concern." But "it is one thing," as David Keen reminds us, "to condemn violence; it is another, and more useful, exercise to sponsor a pattern of development that makes violence less likely" (1994, 445).

Only the Rwandan people, and others who share their plight, can take the steps needed to avert mass death in the future. Unless this happens, Rwanda will likely remain adrift in the postcolonial twilight.

> Wandering between two worlds,
>   one dead,
> The other powerless to be born.[12]

Powerless to be born? Only time will tell.

---

12. Matthew Arnold, "Stanzas from the Grande Chartreuse"

12. Intrastate Conflict and Sustainable Development

Lessons from Bosnia, Somalia, and Haiti

Waltraud Queiser Morales

The Scarcity Connection

> *A community, alas, cannot be built on the unrelenting degradation of its inhabitants.*
>
> —Gerald Early
> "Super Fly Meets Our Daily Bread"

Theoretical and philosophical literature on social revolution and societal instability have long isolated the central role of scarcity in provoking violence. Marxian and neo-Marxian theories of class struggle have emphasized the effects of oppression, exploitation, and emiseration of a subservient economic class. Liberal and neoliberal explanations have focused on the individual's political and economic deprivations and personal injustice. On the other hand, recent nationalist perspectives suggest a more ambivalent and secondary role for economic scarcity as a facilitator of violence. Culturalist theories, as many nationalist ones often are, point to social fragmentation, or what some have termed "balkanization," as the major cause of conflict within states. However, this explanation begs the question of *why and when* balkanization triggers violence. Ironically, despite, or perhaps because of, contemporary attention to multiculturalism and diversity, internal violence may be facilitated by a postmodern climate. Questions such as what kind of diversity, how much diversity, and the historical timing and political and socioeconomic context of diversity have become extremely significant. The global spread of democratization, and the consequent changes in ethos, values, and sociopolitical structures, may be instrumental in the spread of ethnic and nationalistic violence. And radical and rapid shifts in the structure of minority-majority relations, especially under conditions of actual or perceived scarcity and deprivation, may encourage intrastate conflict and political instability.[1]

Scarcity-induced ethnic or racial violence is everywhere, not just in the Balkans, Somalia, or Haiti, but even in the United States. No society is immune. Explanations of increased violence in Florida draw upon the classic 1949 study of the political scientist, V. O. Key, Jr. The theory suggests that Florida's historical fragmentation impeded the development of a workable political structure, and that its physical geography created "a significant impediment to unity." Recent waves of emigration from the Caribbean and Central America have further exacerbated "the state's internal divisions" (Colburn 1993, G-3). Rootlessness and the absence of a shared culture and a sense of shared community are additional important causes of ethnic and racial conflict. These factors are further aggravated by the heightened political opportunism of political leaders, especially those who may manipulate xenophobia and the fear of outsiders. Without enlightened leadership Florida's people, not unlike others around the world, will continue to succumb "to the social and geographic pressures that isolate them," leaving few to believe in "a common heritage and similar needs" (Colburn 1993, G-3).

An important causal element, often only implied in these theories but which facilitates racial, ethnic, and nationalistic intrastate conflict, is economic scarcity. Although theoretical explanations may ignore or downplay the critical ingredient of scarcity—whether actual or perceived, or primarily economic, sociocultural, or a mixture of these—scarcity activates "balkanization." Both the "objective" and "subjective" increase in socioeconomic competition for scarce state resources is an

---

1. Intrastate conflict is defined as violence between or among one or more advantaged or disadvantaged minority or majority groups, and one or more of these groups and the political/juridical state, to gain either a greater share of limited resources or control or autonomy or both over the territorial state. Violence may take on ethnonationalist, indigenist, or religious dynamics.

essential (but not necessarily sufficient) precondition of intrastate violence. Scarcity establishes, triggers, and heightens the "us" versus "them" polarization of society. Therefore, explanations close to home isolate many of the same structural and cultural preconditions of intrastate conflict found in our three case studies and other similar cases around the world. The central argument of my analysis does not suppose that socioeconomic scarcity represents a unicausal explanation for global wars, ethnic violence and civil unrest within states (or between and among states). However, it does assert that the important conditioning and motivating role of scarcity may be obscured by overemphasis on cultural, ethnic, and nationality factors alone.[2] Analysis of intrastate violence in Somalia, Bosnia, and Haiti will attempt to support this interpretation.

Theories of Intrastate Conflict

> *Invidious discrimination is an engine of oppression, subjugating a disfavored group to enhance or maintain the power of the majority.*
> —William H. Chafe
> "Providing Guarantees of Equal Opportunity"

Contemporary theories of intrastate conflict reinterpret both classical and contemporary theories of revolution and civil violence; indeed, the well-known social scientist Harry Eckstein presciently termed such conflict "internal war," and recently Ted Robert Gurr's theory of "why men rebel" has been revisited as "why minorities rebel" (Morales 1973–74; Eckstein 1964; Gurr 1970, 1993a, 1993b, 14: 161–201; Johnson 1966; Davies 1971; Tilly 1978; Skocpol 1979). Moreover, the convergence of theories of revolution, war, and violence with both classical and current studies of nationalism, ethnonationalism, and racial and indigenous resurgences has revitalized interdisciplinary theoretical and policy investigations (Wickham-Crowley 1991; Kellas 1991; Smith 1986; Shaw 1987, 31: 5–31; Gurr 1993b). Nor does the substantive overlap

---

2. For example, Colombia has long been characterized as one of the world's most violent countries and as the "murder capital of the world" with eight times the murder rate of the United States. Sociologists have blamed this violence on a history of violence, proliferation of weapons, weak law enforcement and adjudication, drug wars, and decades of guerrilla warfare. However, a triggering factor or essential precondition would seem to be the economic inequality and scarcity endemic to the society. For recent statistics see the *Orlando Sentinel* (1995, A-14).

and theoretical cross-fertilization stop here. The precarious narrow line between internal and external conditions of strife, or domestic and international dimensions of conflict, has also been compromised. Nationalism and ethnopolitics pose major domestic as well as international and global challenges (Midlarsky 1992; Gurr 1990, 1: 82–98). With this convergence in mind, Joseph Rothschild's term, "politicized ethnicity," includes "all types of nationalism in international relations" and explains both intrastate and interstate conflict (quoted in Kellas 1991, 147). Rothschild asserts that "politicised ethnicity has become the most keen and potent edge of intrastate and interstate conflict, displacing class and ideological conflict, and it asserts itself today, dialectically, as the leading legitimator or delegitimating challenger of political authority" (quoted in Kellas 1991, 147; Rothschild 1981). Indeed, "real world" conflict management and many academic discplines (comparative politics, comparative sociology, and international relations) are in turmoil because of extensive cross-penetration of internal and external violence in the post–cold war period. Decision makers have had to reassess their bag of "how-to's" and scholars their conceptual orthodoxies. Although the war in Bosnia is an example of the unprecedented substantive and theoretical overlap that confounds the conditions of war and revolution, and interstate and intrastate conflict, the multilateral interventions and peacekeeping operations in Somalia and Haiti also demonstrate significant deterioration in state boundaries, authority, and sovereignty. For this reason, despite the emphasis on intrastate conflict in this chapter, the potential for a violent spillover into the international arena remains a constant threat, activated by many of the same forces that trigger outbreaks of internal strife.

James Kellas, in his impressive effort to provide an "integrated theory of the politics of nationalism and ethnicity," has also provided useful theoretical directions for a theory of intrastate conflict. Not unlike the more quantitative recent study of Ted Gurr on ethnic violence and minorities, Kellas meticulously differentiates among nationalism, ethnic politics, and racism (1991; Gurr 1993a).[3] Common to both theoreti-

---

3. Although all of these careful distinctions (nation, nationalism, ethnic group, race, racism, ethnocentrism, and ethnicity) are not critical here, for my purposes, Kellas defines a nation as "a group of people who feel themselves to be a community bound together by ties of history, culture, and common ancestry," and share both objective (territory, language, religion) and subjective characteristics (awareness and affection for one's nationality). He further distinguishes among an "ethnic nation," composed of one ethnic group; a "social nation," or several ethnic groups in one nation; and an "official

cal approaches is the significance of the timing, place, and context of minority-group relations with a dominant majority, and the mechanisms (economic, social, psychological, and cultural) that create or intensify ingroup (the common ethnic group, nation, or race) and outgroup perceptions, attitudes, and behavior (peaceful and violent). Both theorists agree that an important indicator of the potential for intrastate conflict is whether the ethnic, racial, or nationality groups aspire to revolutionary political or territorial claims or both.

In his theory Kellas differentiates between necessary and sufficient conditions—an important logical distinction, which is also useful to explain internal violence. Regarding the current debate on the role of human nature and sociobiology in group conflict, Kellas concludes that "identity and behaviour are partly genetic, but they are also shaped by context and choice. In politics they are resources waiting to be used by politicians and their supporters for their own advantage. Human nature provides the 'necessary' condition for ethnocentric behavior, but politics converts this into the 'sufficient conditions' for nationalism" (1991, 19). Although Gurr also emphasizes the political dimension, his concept of "politicized communal groups" relies on the socioeconomic condition of discrimination and deprivation: "Treat a group differently, by denial or privilege, and its members become more self-conscious about their common bonds and interests" (1993a, 3). To be "politically salient," Gurr believes that politicized communal groups must experience one or both of two key criteria: economic or political discrimination and political activism on behalf of collective interests (1993a, 5–6). Discrimination and deprivation, with or without collective mobilization are, therefore, essential and "sufficient conditions" for potential conflict.

Another important theoretical perspective attempts to link ethnic mobilization for warfare to human evolution and genetic predisposition. Theorists Paul Shaw and Yuwa Wong propose "that kin selection

---

nation," or the nationalism created by the state. An ethnic group is smaller, exclusive, or ascriptive, and more clearly based on common ancestry and shared inborn characteristics; it may refer to a "quasi-national kind of 'minority group' within the state which has not achieved the status of a 'nation.'" Race is distinguished from these as referring to predominantly biological, phenotypical, and genetic distinctions (1991, 2–4). Gurr focuses on "politicized communal groups," divided into two main types and respective subtypes: (1) "national peoples," or ethnonationalists and indigenous peoples; and (2) "minority peoples," or ethnoclasses, militant sects, and communal contenders—either disadvantaged or advantaged (1993a, 15–23).

has interacted with environmental forces over evolutionary time to predispose genetically related individuals to band together in groups, oriented for conflict" (Shaw 1987, 31: 5). In other words, their research seeks to determine the "ultimate causes" or underlying reasons ("inclusive fitness" considerations) for warlike behavior, in distinction to the "emergent proximate causes" of human behavior, such as nepotism, xenophobia, and altruism (Shaw 1987, 31: 8–9).[4] By combining kin selection theory and its axiom of "inclusive fitness" with cost-benefit analysis, they identify certain behaviors (intergroup conflict and warfare) as functional to reproductive fitness and survival of close relatives. Neither further elaboration of their complex and preliminary theory nor its acceptance is central to Shaw and Wang's essay. What is essential, however, is the importance they place on certain environmental, structural, and socioeconomic conditions in triggering violent behavior.

Despite distinct and even competing approaches to nationalism and ethnopolitics, the three theories considered so far identify socioeconomic mechanisms (scarcity, deprivation, competition, and economic discrimination) as instrumental in the intensification of ingroup versus outgroup conflict. Several other theories of ethnonationalism (reviewed by Kellas) focus more exclusively on economic causes; two are of particular interest. First, Michael Hechter's theory of "internal colonialism" posits that modernization, and the economic inequalities (or localized and discrimination-based scarcity) that it engenders, will increase the conflict between ethnic groups within a state and between these groups and the state (1975). Hechter's related theory of the "cultural division of labour" asserts that internal colonialism will cause the "social stratification of ethnic or cultural groups, with the core group occupying the best class positions and the peripheral groups the inferior positions" (quoted in Kellas 1991, 39–40). Second, Ernest Gellner's economic theory proposes that the development of industrial society necessitated the modern state system and a homogenous

---

4. "Inclusive fitness" is a central theorem of behavioral and evolutionary biology and a more controversial proposition in sociobiology. It refers to an individual's expected prospects for genetic survival or reproductive success (classical fitness), combined with the reproductive fitness-enhancing effects (including health, power, beauty, or other physical traits) of an individual's actions on the survival of his or her affected kin (inclusive fitness). Shaw and Wong define kin as "nucleus ethnicity," or one's "immediate relatives who share a high degree of genetic relatedness," and "number a few hundred individuals at most" (Shaw 1987, 31, 8–9).

society and nation to maximize industrial production; thus, the hybrid nation-state was formed. Where the result was the repression of other cultures, nationalist unrest grew (Kellas 1991, 41–44). Gellner further argues that the volatile combination for conflict was the correspondence of nationality or cultural differences with class divisions: "Classes, however oppressed and exploited, did not overturn the political system when they could not define themselves 'ethnically.' Only when a nation became a class . . . did it become politically conscious and activist. . . . Neither nations nor classes seem to be political catalysts: only nation-classes or class-nations are such" (quoted in Kellas 1991, 43).

Whether the ultimate causes of ethnonationalistic violence are biological, cultural, or economic, reputable theorists generally agree on the importance of changing environmental and contextual conditions—particularly competition over scarce resources. Specifically, this sampling of theorists—as well as others (not discussed here) who emphasize conditions of unequal economic development and incongruity between economic status and power resources—strongly suggests that conditions of unequal distribution and discrimination, and "absolute" or "relative" (or both) deprivation and scarcity of resources have a critical relationship to group violence. On this point, Ted Gurr is quite explicit: "By assumption, any communal group or minority that has been subject to political or material discrimination is at risk of collective adversity" (1993a, 6). Material deprivation (often extreme impoverishment) and systematic discrimination (by dominant groups and advantaged minorities) may threaten the group's physical survival. In this sense, resource scarcity (both broadly or narrowly defined) is a necessary precondition that activates group conflict and transforms it into intrastate and ethnonationalist violence.[5] Perhaps this convergence of grievances is what Gellner meant by his intriguing terms "nation-classes" and "class-nations."

The most forceful presentation of the contributing role of scarcity and deprivation is found in Shaw and Wong. The biological process underlying human cooperation and aggression, they variously argue, "would be exacerbated under conditions of scarce resources or stress";

5. Intrastate violence is defined as physical conflict between advantaged or disadvantaged minority or majority groups and the political/juridical state, or among the groups themselves, to gain either a greater share of limited resources or autonomy or control over the territorial state. This violence may take on ethnonationalist, indigenist, or religious dynamics.

that "membership in an expanded group would have increased each individual's access to scarce resources"; and that in the past "an increasing proportion of man's 'hostile environment' has been other nucleus ethnic groups engaged in resource competition" (1987, 31: 6–7). They unequivocally affirm the hypothesis of competition and "conflict in an environment of scarce resources," over the idea of resource sharing and conflict avoidance. The cooperative scenario would be likely only "when resources were abundant," because if resources were really limited, "sharing would be unlikely." An extensive quote best sums up their theory.

> We propose that inclusive fitness considerations (an ultimate cause), have combined with competition over scarce resources (environment), intergroup conflict and weapon development (changing environment), to (1) reinforce humanity's propensity to band together in groups of genetically related individuals, (2) predispose group members to act in concert for their own well-being, first and foremost, and (3) promote xenophobia, fear and antagonism among genetically related individuals towards strangers. We interpret these responses as "emerging" or reinforcing proximate causes which shaped the structure of social behavior in hunter/gatherer groups for 99 percent of humanity's existence. (1987, 31: 11)

In conclusion, this limited review of current theories of intrastate conflict indicates that conditions of regional, and most especially, global scarcity are potentially devastating for the future of human cooperation and the delicate calculus between war and peace. Indeed, at no time in human history does it seem more vital that both civil and global society function as a "collective survival enterprise," organized for peaceful competition and cooperation. Perhaps the combination of human "egoistic cooperation," social learning, and a frank and calculated assessment of survival consequences can help forge awareness of, and a strategy to navigate, the difficult global future ahead.[6] Certainly, a most viable choice, especially if we assume that the more difficult task would be to drastically alter human nature, is to facilitate a supportive environment and context for human behavior by reducing or eliminating the dehumanizing conditions of resource scarcity, inequality, and discrimination at all levels of social organization. In-

---

6. "Collective survival enterprise" and "egoistic cooperation" are quoted in Shaw (1987, 31: 26–27) from P. A. Corning (1993).

deed, a global policy of authentically sustainable development represents a necessary step toward a comprehensive solution to global scarcity and intrastate conflict.

Sustainable Development and Collective Survival

> *The twenty-first century began with a North-South war. It will continue with a battle fought by all human kind for the collective survival of the planet. To stop this battle of all human kind for itself from turning once more into a North-South war, an alternative development is needed, in North and South. . . . Today, choosing peace implies choosing a new, alternative, social and ecological model."*
>
> —Walden Bello

The cold war represented a long hiatus from the pressing global work at hand: the intractable problems of poverty, scarcity, overpopulation, and chronic underdevelopment. Activists in the development field have tended to assume that with the end of the cold war ideologized "developmentalism" would give way to rational and environmentally sound development policies. However, misguided orthodox developmentalism persists as free market (neoliberal) models and technological growth ideologies. Intolerance of alternative economic and social organizing models, whether nationalistic, socialistic, or mixed, has increased. Instead a "new cold war," directed against the Third World and its radical development agenda, is being waged. Walden Bello, of the Institute for Food and Development Policy (Food First), has termed this northern process "structural resubordination" and argued: "Regarding the South as the principal enemy has since been institutionalized in US defense planning. In what was billed as the first detailed military planning for the post-Cold War era, the Pentagon in the early 1990s prepared seven scenarios of conflict—five of which saw US troops intervening in Third World countries" (1994, 109). Despite the policy rhetoric of governments, the goals of democratization, nation building, and sustainable development remain elusive, and if seriously implemented will complicate global interstate and intrastate politics in the short term and revolutionize them in the long term. Indeed, there may be no dedicated political will for this task, which will surely necessitate serious global redistribution and sharing of scarce resources. Early in the cold war, George Kennan, fittingly known as the "father of containment," warned in a top secret State Department briefing paper that because "we have about 50% of the world's wealth but only 6.3% of its population . . . [o]ur real task in the coming period is to devise a pattern of relationships which will permit us to maintain this position of disparity without positive detriment to our national security" (cited in Etzold 1978, 227). Can this egoistic development of global resources be replaced by a communal model?

A viable alternative is the new development model known as sustainable development. What is meant by sustainable development? Can an authentic sustainable development model resolve the global scarcity crisis and create an equitable and peaceful new world economic order? One Third World development expert has broadly defined sustainable development as "meeting the needs of the present without destroying resources that will be needed in the future" (Fisher 1988, xi). Another, more specific, definition, based on the 1987 Brundtland Commission's report, asserts that "sustainable development therefore means, in essence, sustainable industrial development"; or minimally an annual 3 percent global per capita GDP growth rate (Chatterjee 1994, 21).[7] A third definition argues that "sustained development depends on the existence of a viable middle class made up of people with education, technical know-how, and adequate facilities. . . ." (Fisher 1988, 137). Consider the similar terminology and assumptions in the 1950s Millikan-Rostow foreign aid request "that the United States employ its resources to create and encourage conditions for self-sustaining economic growth in the underdeveloped countries . . . [that] would lead to the evolution of politically stable and viable democratic societies that could not easily be victimized by Communist promises or intimidation" (Millikan 1957 cited in Stoessinger 1979, 240). By comparison with the earlier cold war document, one can see that the Brundtland report, despite popularization of sustainable development and environmentalism, largely reasserted a traditional development paradigm of technological and industrialized growth.

Moreover, even the more recent 1992 Rio Summit (or Earth Summit), the ambitious United Nations–sponsored conference on environment and development, was ultimately coopted by traditional

7. The Brundtland Commission refers to the World Commission on Environment and Development created by the United Nations and headed by the former premier of Norway, Ms. Gro Harlem Brundtland with the mandate to report on the condition of the planet. The official title of the 1987 Brundtland report is *Our Common Future* (World Commission 1987).

developmentalism and the global development establishment. In their book, scholars Pratap Chatterjee and Matthias Finger term this powerful planetary development elite "the Earth Brokers" (1994). They quote a frank admission by Maurice Strong, the influential secretary-general of the Earth Summit, that "the pattern of production and consumption that gave rise to so many of the global risks [*sic*] we are dealing with are still in place" (1994, 60). And, although Strong founded the Earth Council (a group of independent experts) in 1992 to promote "people power" and planetary awareness, and sought to ally "brassroots" business, financial, and scientific constituencies with "grassroots" developmentalist nongovernmental organizations (NGOs), Greenpeace International (one such NGO) dismissed these efforts as an institutionalized "greenwash" of powerful global corporations (Chatterjee 1994, 160–61).

Because of an obsession with growth over equitable distribution and environmentally sustainable modes of production, traditional developmentalism has perpetuated and aggravated the conditions of global scarcity. The "old development myth" relied on established stages of growth: the first stage depends on society's natural resource base to create the intellectual, economic, and technological capacity to fuel the second stage of growth, which establishes independence from the natural resource base. Brundtland and Rio basically reformulated "the myth of unlimited industrial development" and increased technological efficiency as primary solutions to scarcity and underdevelopment. Despite defining sustainable development as "development that meets the needs of the present without compromising the ability of future generations to meet their own needs," in application, sustainable development contradicted this goal with a process based on society's "techno-economic capacities, rather than on the natural resource base" (Chatterjee 1994, 21, 27). This hybrid model compromised "limits to growth." Within its rubric, sustainable development meant inputs of "financial and human capital, technology, and organizational capacity," which were all assumed to be independent of the planet's natural and environmental limits (Chatterjee 1994, 27). From this perspective, inadequate technology and not natural-resource scarcity impeded planetary growth.

The fallacious promise implied in the Rio model is that all societies can achieve sustainable development with standards of living comparable to the industrial and postindustrial north. In short, "coopted" sustainable development seemed virtually indistinguishable from modernity (Chatterjee 1994, 28). The "greening" of traditional developmentalism (under the guise of sustainable development) and slogans of "green business is good business" served as revamped vehicles for growth-based and market-based development strategies. The exclusive focus on environmentally friendly development encouraged the popular myopia that "clean growth," or growth that minimizes environmental and ecological damage, and growth that is technologically and organizationally efficient holds the solution. The "eco-efficiency" approach, by asserting that efficient growth provides the solution to problems of environmental destruction, scarcity, and economic inequality, deftly evaded the more fundamental and devastating impending crisis of limits to growth.

The critical analysis of Chatterjee and Finger further demonstrates that the "politically green" environmental and developmental NGOs were tricked by easy access to the United Nations Conference on the Environment and Development (UNCED) in Rio, unaware that the sessions and agenda were purposely structured to favor governments and business and industry partners. Small grassroots NGOs had little meaningful impact on the substance of the official agreements reached and were basically coopted by complex lobbying. The big winners at Rio were the financially powerful, especially the transnational corporations (TNCs), responsible for major global pollution, unsustainable depletion of habitats and resources, and other irreparable environmental damage. The Earth Summit legitimated TNCs as major global actors in sustainable development and made them appear less part of the problem and more part of "the solutions to the kind of problems for which they were at least partly responsible" (Chatterjee 1994, 107). Both the TNCs and the more powerful and mainstream NGOs have realized that environmentalism can be a profitable enterprise, especially when it stimulates more lucrative development projects. Chatterjee and Finger persuasively argue that as long as sustainable development is defined by "unsustainable development models" that fail to question the traditional assumptions of growth and further industrial development, the real crisis and the real solutions will be missed. Only a new vision of global ecology that affirms limits to growth, fosters downscaled consumption patterns, and challenges the roles of powerful nation-states and TNCs will truly foster sustainable development (1994, 173).

If in the development field the proponents of NGO-populism and the empowerment of grassroots people's movements found themselves upstaged by a so-called new global order run by a global managerial elite, a similar scenario has unfolded on the stage of global power politics managed by the U.S.-led international security elite. Many of the same actors are involved: nation-states and governments of north and south, transnational corporations, the United Nations system, and the United States. In global politics, as in sustainable development, the role and efficacy of the nation-state was also suspect and under attack, largely because of its inability and unwillingness to define and resolve global crises appropriately. In both arenas the fixation on technocratic crisis management became part of the problem. And whether dealing with the crises of global poverty, resource scarcity, and environmental destruction, or with the crises of global "disorder" and ethnic, tribal, and religious warfare, the tendency has been the same: to blame the victims. In both arenas the persistence of dominant, but irrelevant, traditional paradigms has impeded the implementation of real solutions. Finally, not only is the structure of global crises of underdevelopment, ecological destruction, and warfare the same in many fundamental respects, but all of these crises are integrally related. Perhaps, as with the rhetoric of the Earth Summit, the political rhetoric of the so-called new world order has also distracted many from the sure realization "that the only answer to the global crisis lay in profound structural changes, accompanied by deindustrialization and demilitarization" (Chatterjee 1994, 142).

Intrastate Wars: Why Bosnia, Somalia, and Haiti?

> To the extent that the exploited classes, poor peoples, and despised ethnic groups have been raising their consciousness of the oppression they have suffered for centuries, they have created a new historical situation. . . . [I]t is a situation charged with promise—a promise that the lords of this world see rather as a menace.
>
> —Gutiérrez

What do Bosnia, Somalia, and Haiti, three contemporary cases of intrastate conflict, have in common? The peoples, languages, cultures, histories, governments, and religions (in part) are distinct. Yet, the violence in these countries from three different and distant regions of the world may suggest similar causal roots. First, these societies share, in various forms and degrees, internal economic, social, cultural, and political oppression and exploitation. Second, parallel histories of colonialism, neocolonialism, and dependent development in the periphery perpetuated chronic underdevelopment and the "development of underdevelopment." Third, unsustainable development models have created and increased resource scarcity, poverty, and ecological and environmental devastation. Fourth, activist racial, ethnic, religious, and nationalist identities have combined with socioeconomic differentials to intensify out-group discrimination. Fifth, the context and balance of minority/majority group relations and the role or condition of the state has recently and radically changed. Sixth, potential conflict and instability threatens neighboring spheres of prosperity. As the theorist Jacques Attali eloquently observed: "If the people in the emerging spheres of prosperity knew how to think in the long term, they would watch carefully the peripheries at their doors. In the coming world order, there will be winners and there will be losers. The losers will outnumber the winners by an unimaginable factor" (Attali 1991 cited in Bello 1994).

In summary, the three cases exhibit the environmental, structural, and socioeconomic preconditions of intrastate violence that have been identified by selected theorists. Bosnia, Somalia, and Haiti contain societies torn by the uncertainty and stress of resource competition and discrimination-based scarcity and deprivation; they have become "nation-classes" or "class-nations." In response to extreme collective adversity and violent threats to the physical survival of minority and majority groups in Bosnia, Somalia, and Haiti, intrastate conflict has escalated into war and revolution.

Bosnia: Rich Man's War

> When Tito died, leaving a Yugoslavia too decentralized for any ethnic group to dominate, it became inevitable that a Serbian nationalist would rise up to redress the perceived wrongs dealt his people.
>
> —Warren Zimmermann
> "The Last Ambassador"

United Nations secretary-general Boutros Boutros-Ghali lashed out at the world community in mid-1992 for its apparently racist preoccupation with the "rich man's war" in Bosnia while thousands starved in Somalia. The United States, nevertheless, assumed a direct role in Somalia but not in Bosnia, where its interests were more confused, but greater, perhaps because intervention in the Balkans looked costly and militarily not very "do-able." Several North American concerns were clear: the sanctity of international borders; the proliferation of a Balkan war; the swell of war refugees; and the global spread of ethnic warfare (ABC 1993). Despite the world press coverage of "ethnic cleansing" and genocide, power politics has largely kept the United States from direct involvement in the Balkans. Experts were divided: was this an intrastate or interstate conflict; a civil war, interethnic war, religious war, or international aggression? In a sense, Bosnia was all of these. In Bosnia by the summer of 1995, as the United Nations peacekeeping forces were themselves being held hostage, multilateral diplomacy and conflict management were too little, too late. As Robert Oakley observed regarding both Somalia and Bosnia, "once a crisis has gone beyond preventive diplomacy or small-scale conventional peacekeeping, the distinction between peacekeeping and peace enforcement cannot easily be maintained" (Hirsch 1995, 162). What were some of the critical causes behind this most gruesome intrastate conflict?

The crisis began in early 1991. The former republic of Yugoslavia, a multiethnic state of six component republics or regions (Bosnia, Croatia, Macedonia, Montenegro, Serbia, and Slovenia) under Titoist communism, disintegrated largely because the Greater Serbian nationalism of Slobodan Milosevic raised the ethnic consciousness and fears of other minorities. Between 1987 and 1989, Milosevic's attempts to make Greater Serbia the new postcommunist Yugoslavia precipitated the secession of Slovenia and Croatia in 1991. Serbia (or the new Yugoslav army) attacked, but both Slovenia and Croatia won independence. In Croatia, local Serbs rebelled against the new Croatian government and hoped to reunite their Serbian Krajina republic (some 30 percent of Croatian territory) with Serbia (Kinzer 1993, 4). In 1992 Bosnian Moslem leaders also voted for secession; but the Bosnian Serbs (about one-third of the population) boycotted the referendum. The United States and European Community recognized the newly independent state of Bosnia-Herzegovina in April 1992. Serbia's leader, Milosevic, then armed local Bosnian Serbs and began a wider war (Haass 1994, 37–43).

In February 1992 a United Nations peacekeeping force was dispatched to Croatia and by November 1992 some six thousand peacekeeping troops were also sent to Bosnia, eventually some twenty-five thousand peacekeepers, largely from Western European countries, to protect "safe havens" and prevent "ethnic cleansing." To date, the three-way, intrastate and interstate conflict has resulted in hundreds of thousands of deaths and some 3 million refugees. And after more than three years of negotiations, violated cease-fires, Western bombing of

Serbian military targets, and on-and-off-again Western threats to lift the arms embargo on the Bosnian Muslims, the Balkan war continued.

Armed violence and "ethnic cleansing" by Bosnia's internal Serbian minority, allied with the Serbian/Yugoslav army, created conditions of comprehensive oppression, which provoked further ethnic conflict and, finally, the intervention of United Nations' forces. Before the outbreak of war in Bosnia, the Moslem majority (about 44 percent of the population) faced the prospect of being a disadvantaged minority group in Serbia, subject to various degrees of economic, social, cultural, and political oppression. After Bosnian independence the Bosnian Serb minority (about 31 percent of the population) feared that they would become a disadvantaged minority instead of an advantaged majority group in Serbia. And unless reunited with independent Croatia, the Catholic Bosnian Croats (17 percent) would be a minority in either state. Regime change or the dissolution of the communist system in Yugoslavia (which had kept firm authoritarian control over separatist nationalist aspirations) and the consequent severe weakening of the central state created the destabilizing precondition that potentially reopened minority/majority group relations. The 1990 multiparty elections represented an important regime change, or alteration in the condition and status of the state and its relationship to minority groups. The elections allowed noncommunist, nationalist governments to be elected in Slovenia and Croatia, which led to the independence of these republics (Kellas 1991, 116). Further, with the demise of communist ideology and the death of Tito, "the power of the centre to resist these nationalisms" became particularly weak, James Kellas explains, because there was "little in the way of 'official nationalism,'" and no really charismatic leader (1991, 116). Ironically, democracy in the former Eastern Europe advantaged all the region's ethnic and minority groups, but also made it almost impossible for the state government to reassert central control and a state-nationalist unity.

The economic preconditions of the Balkan crisis also suggest that some ethnic groups were economically disadvantaged more than others, and that uneven economic development and internal colonialism favored certain regions over others. These regional disparities in income, employment, and industrial production (and the resulting ethnic group inequalities) became more severe with the failures in the Yugoslav economy in the 1980s (Lydall 1989, 4; Hall 1994). The economic downturn in the post-Tito period had a greater impact in Kosovo, one of the poorest parts of the country, and less on Slovenia and Croatia, two of the richest provinces, and also the first to become independent after 1990. Although not extreme compared to European standards, the major regions of the former Yugoslavia could easily be divided into the northern developed (Croatia, Slovenia, Serbia, and Vojvodina) and southern lesser-developed regions (Bosnia-Herzegovina, Montenegro, Macedonia, and Kosovo).

On the other hand, the southern areas possessed many of the country's important natural resources (coal, bauxite, iron, chrome) (Hall 1994, 130–32, 142–43). Economic decentralization in 1974 increased the importance of nationalistic considerations, so that ethnic strife became played out more and more in economic terms, with richer republics complaining that development assistance was squandered by the poorer regions, and the poorer regions complaining of exploitation by the richer north (Hall 1994, 136–37). Finally, critics of the Yugoslav economy argue that misconceived development models and an emphasis on industrialization resulted in the waste of needed resources, high rates of inflation, unemployment, price controls, IMF-imposed austerity (1988), and economic stagnation. As Gregory Hall concludes, "essentially, Yugoslavia's citizens had become increasingly impoverished in the 1980s, and the government . . . found it increasingly difficult to meet peoples' needs" (Hall 1994, 138–39).

When the Balkan conflict first erupted, the Western European nations responded halfheartedly, and have continued to reject more forceful action by the United Nations forces, NATO, or the United States. With peacekeepers on the ground and subject to death and mass hostage taking, their main concern remains containment of the crisis in Bosnia. And although the destructive intrastate conflict in Bosnia threatens the neighboring spheres of prosperity in Europe and the region, the threat is not yet great enough to risk greater intervention.

Somalia: A Failed Humanitarian Intervention

But it seems likely that, as environmental degradation proceeds, not only will the size of the potential social disruption increase, but the capacity to intervene to prevent this disruption will decrease.

—Thomas Homer-Dixon
"Global Environmental Change and International Security"

The immediate problem in Somalia was starvation, but the underlying problem was intrastate violence among some fifteen warring clans, engaged in a protracted urban guerrilla conflict. The warring in 1992 seemed a phase in the broader historical struggle for national liberation from foreign rule and repressive internal dictatorship. A United Nations trusteeship between 1949 and 1960 ended formal colonial rule by Italy in southern Somalia and Britain in the north (Rinehart 1982, 27–35). And after only a decade of independence came a brutal twenty-year dictatorship, which a coalition of clans finally toppled in 1991. Interposing itself into these complicated political events, the 1992 United States–United Nations humanitarian rescue mission ("Operation Restore Hope") rapidly escalated into a nasty policing operation against the relentless violence among the forces of the warlord, Gen. Mohammed Farah Aidid and rival warlords and clans who still supported the former president-dictator.

President Mohamed Siad Barre's Socialist-Islamic dictatorship, which seized power in a 1969 coup, had forcefully repressed rival clan loyalties (sought to control fundamentalist Islamic leaders) and imposed a state-sponsored nationalism on the country.[8] Although a people largely homogeneous ethnically, Siad Barre's imposition of an artificial nationhood activated and intensified the tribal and, to some extent, religious differences (fundamentalism versus a scientific socialist version of Islam) among the Somalis. Nevertheless, Siad Barre tended to favor his own minority Marehan clan, and in the last years of dictatorship, he manipulated clan politics to remain in power, undermining the foundations of the state-nationalist identity he had tried to build. Moreover, colonialism had left Somali minorities in the neighboring countries of Ethiopia, Kenya, and Djibouti, and a cultural and economic divide between the south and the north of the country. Irredentism and Pan-Somali nationalism touched off repeated border fighting and a major regional war (Somali-Ethiopian War in the Ogaden in 1977–78). These conflicts and a protracted civil war (1988–91) interrupted farming and herding, devastated the land, created a massive refugee crisis (there were some 1.3 million in camps in 1981), and reinforced a cycle of mass famine.

By July 1992 a famine had been raging for over eight months and two hundred thousand Somalis had already starved to death; another 2 million were at risk, and fighting continued over access to, and hoarding of, private food and medical aid. In times of extreme scarcity

8. Siad Barre and his revolutionary government hoped to eliminate "clan particularism" or "tribalism," which he saw as the pernicious disease afflicting the Third World and obstructing national development (Rinehart 1982, 46–49).

(as well as in the best of times), food and resources were divided up along tribal and clan lines, with the dominant clans discriminating against the outgroups.[9] Thus, in Somalia, once tribal identities were reinforced by wide socioeconomic differentials and further aggravated by scarcity and famine, several key preconditions of intrastate conflict were in place. Finally, the civil war, which deposed Siad Barre, overturned the established balance of minority and majority group relations in Somalia, and simultaneously created a political vacuum that radically undermined the legal status and authority of the official state. Both the polity and society disintegrated into chaos.

Siad Barre's model of economic development (if one may call it that) had turned Somalia into an economic and military client of both superpowers (Bryden 1995, 94: 145–51). Jeremy Harding notes that Siad Barre received some "$600 million in US military aid, which he used to enforce a new but no less ruinous form of totalitarian rule in Somalia. After almost twenty years of tyranny, his country simply fell apart" (Harding 1993, 265). Somalia, like Haiti, is one of the world's poorest countries, chronically dependent on food imports, and with scarce arable land, subject to misuse by farmers, overgrazing by nomadic herdsmen, and, ultimately, desertification. The economy (as in most of Africa, and again as in Haiti) relied upon cash crop–primary exports (livestock, hides, bananas, and some cotton—whose earnings have steadily declined) and import-intensive and capital-intensive development. This situation resulted in a severe trade imbalance, with imports greatly exceeding exports, and a $2 billion foreign debt. When the government attempted IMF structural adjustment measures, riots broke out in 1987. In addition, dependence on United States economic aid (Somalia with the Sudan, Zaïre, Kenya, and Liberia—all "police states"—received half of all the total aid for sub-Saharan Africa in 1985) did solve local needs, and in the case of food aid, undermined local farm prices and agricultural productivity. Northern focus on "growth" areas for development assistance ignored the importance of

9. Although space does not permit further elaboration here, the Somali case appears to mesh well with the theory of ethnic conflict developed by Shaw and Wong. Culturally, conditions reinforced the environmental, inclusive fitness, and cost-benefit aspects of their model. Traditionally, Somali society is a warrior society that extolls aggression because "force or the potential to use force often decided who prevailed in the harsh environment." Also, warfare was important in the relations among Somali clans and outsiders. "Antagonists in intra-Somali conflicts generally belonged to groups bound by their commitment to pay or receive *dia* (blood compensation)." The entire group was responsible for this compensation, calculated as either a loss or a gain (Ehrenreich 1982, 237).

sustainable development and left the poorest of the poor few alternatives other than humanitarian assistance or more anthropogenic destruction of their habitat (Timberlake 1986).

At the time of the U.S.-UN intervention, Presidents Bush and Clinton insisted that no North American security interests were involved; however, Clinton justified the U.S. military presence as one of superpower credibility and keeping faith with commitments made to the United Nations and the world community. There was little public analysis of U.S. regional, Middle Eastern, and African interests—such as insulating oil-rich sheikdoms, especially Saudi Arabia, and the Sudan and Egypt from the tribal instability in the Horn of Africa, a geostrategic access point to the Suez Canal and Red Sea. As one reporter argued: "How Somalia is put together is likely to have implications for other African nations. The kind of political system created here could fuel or snuff aspirations in other regions" (Schemo 1993, 3). In short, intrastate conflict in Somalia posed a potential threat to the neighboring spheres of prosperity in the region.

Somalia (not unlike Bosnia and Haiti) was a hapless victim of both cold war and post–cold war intervention and a shortsighted and exploitative northern model of unsustainable development. Despite statistics of thousands of lives saved, the claims of success for the 1992–93 humanitarian intervention ring hollow because little was done to deal with the endemic causes of hunger, scarcity, and conflict. In June 1995 the French organization, International Action Against Hunger, reported steadily worsening conditions of hunger. Since the pullout of North American troops in March 1994 and the United Nations in March 1995, unemployment had greatly increased; there was a scarcity of clean drinking water, and one child in four was starving. Although the capital of Mogadishu seemed calm, some 500 kilometers to the north the fighting between the supporters of Mohammed Farah Aidid and those of Mohamed Siad Barre continued unabated. The cost of the United Nations' humanitarian operation ranged from $3 to $4 billion.

Haiti: The Black Slave Revolution

In Haiti, the peasantry is the nation.

—Trouillot

If the Haitians don't sell their blood, what do you want them to do with it?

—Saint-Gérard

The Haitian recent and historical experience reflects comprehensive oppression and exploitation, which has been compounded by cumulative resource scarcity in the twentieth century. Not unlike the fantastic but true story of former Nicaraguan dictator Anastasio Somoza's lucrative trade in blood to the United States by his company, Plasmaférica, in Haiti, Hemo-Caribbean and Company, financed by North American and international capital and with the blessing of dictator-president François Duvalier and even facilitated by his notorious *macoutes,* sold plasma to the United States (Farmer 1994, 49–50). This brutal image of "blood sucking" the people dry starkly captures the depths of Haiti's exploitation by internal and external colonialism. Before and since independence, the country's history of political instability can be attributed to foreign and class exploitation. After the original Indian inhabitants had been exterminated, Spanish and French colonizers imported black African slave labor to mine the riches of the island paradise. First a mercantilist plantation system and later export-based dependent development reduced today's Haiti, one of France's most prosperous colonies, into the poorest country in the Western Hemisphere. After independence in 1804 the black nation was isolated and shunned by a "white world" of racist and slave-owning states, like the United States, which withheld recognition until 1862. In 1915 the United States Marines intervened, occupied Haiti (after a series of eight revolutions in four years) and made the country a United States protectorate. When they withdrew in 1934, their experiment in nation building left behind a Caribbean pattern of repressive dictatorship, agro-export plantations, and cheap-labor assembly platforms.

An unsustainable development model relied on the export of primary commodities (sugar, rum, cotton, woods, cocoa, and coffee) and assembly products (apparel, toys, and baseballs) to the United States and global market, and on aid from the United States (USAID). As dictator Papa Doc bragged to Nelson Rockefeller in 1969, "Haiti could be a vast reservoir of man-power for Americans establishing re-exportation industries closer, safer, and more convenient than Hong Kong" (quoted in Farmer 1994, 115). In this model, U.S. industries enjoyed a cheap (the minimum hourly wage is less than fifteen cents), subservient, nonunionized labor force, no customs taxes, and full repatriation of profits. This model contributed to an absolute poverty level in 1986 of $60 per capita income per year, with 60 percent of all Haitians at this level (Farmer 1994, 117; Chomsky 1994,

12).[10] Describing Haiti as the rising "Taiwan of the Caribbean," Noam Chomsky writes that the effect of this development strategy was "to shift 30 percent of cultivated land from food for local consumption to export crops" (1994, 13). Desperation to survive forced starving peasants to denude the island of trees for cheap fuel, and to exhaust sparse arable land to eke out a small food crop. Already by the time Baby Doc came to power in 1971, Haiti's soil and resource depletion portended a major environmental and ecological disaster. Extreme resource depletion, brutal deprivation and inequality, and decades of dictatorship spurred the thousands of Haitian "boat people" since the 1970s until more than a million and a half Haitians lived abroad, despite a vigorous and forceful return policy by the U.S. Coast Guard (Stepick 1992). Paul Farmer poignantly writes that Haiti had become "a country increasingly immiserated even as the false 'industrialization' of offshore assembly grew; a country governed by one iron-fisted family; and a country increasingly inhospitable to its own people" (1994, 119).

Internal and external developments in Haiti were accompanied by racial discrimination. As the first sovereign black republic under the self-rule of free African slaves, Haiti was a threatening anomaly and symbol to neighboring centers of prosperity. A powerful mulatto elite (which comprised the commercial and political sectors, the military, and to an extent the Catholic Church) controlled the land and economic wealth of Haiti and maintained the darker peasantry as wage slaves. The rise of François (Papa Doc) Duvalier broke the hold of the creole and mulatto elite in favor of his personal palace guard, the dark-skinned Haitian Guard, and the hated and feared paramilitary national security forces, the Tontons Macoutes. A scholar of Haitian culture, Duvalier mobilized personal and political support for his dictatorship with a racist doctrine of African negritude and anti-American Haitian nationalism (Morales 1995, 38: 29). But by the time his nineteen-year-old son Jean Claude (Baby Doc) Duvalier, succeeded as president for life, relations with the lighter-skilled creole elite and the United States defined a cozy dependency: the U.S. Pentagon supported and trained the Haitian military, and the Agency for International Development (USAID) virtually dictated the Haitian economy through economic assistance and development planning. Thus, when revolution

10. Farmer cites 1976 World Bank data, which note a per capita income of $140 per year, with 75 percent of all Haitians at this level (1994, 117).

erupted in 1986, the lines of struggle were determined by racism, nationalism, and class.

The 1986 revolution was preceded by some of the worst violations of human rights and genocide in Haitian history. Amnesty International documented the violence, torture, and killings by the state's military and security forces against the peasantry, youth movement, and the Christian Base Communities of Haiti's popular church led by Rev. Jean-Bertrand Aristide. Between 1986 and Aristide's landslide election in 1990, and again after Aristide's overthrow by the military in 1991 and his restoration to the presidency in October 1994 by the North American intervention, a form of "Duvalierism without Duvalier" gripped the island. Successive military juntas (the most recent headed by Gen. Raúl Cédras) brutalized the people and made a mockery of democracy and free elections. This period represented a major shift in the balance of power and the traditionally subservient relationship between the minority ruling class and the peasant majority. The state machinery and leadership were under daily attack; the 1986 revolution represented a radical sea change. It became clear to all that "in Haiti, the peasantry is the nation," and any long term solution would have to deal with this fact. The United States' response, therefore, was to intervene in September 1994 and contain the threatening intrastate conflict off its shores before thousands more boat people invaded its sphere of prosperity. Aristide was to be the instrument of this "structural resubordination" and containment.

Conclusion

> One possible alternative explanation for the rise in hostilities during past years is the cumulative effect of decades of unsustainable development, the consequences and pressures of which have begun to undermine the well-being and security of many countries.
>
> —Hal Kane
> "The Hour of Departure"

Perhaps the passing of the cold war will not have as great an effect on the potential for global war and peace and intrastate conflict as many policy makers have feared. More global conflicts appear to be rooted in the convergence of resource scarcity, environmental depletion, human degradation and deprivation, minority/majority group relations, and ethnopolitical and religious discrimination. If this is the case, it will become necessary to redefine human security in a more humane manner and to systematically investigate and address the causes behind the conditions and preconditions of intrastate conflict. The 1994 United Nations Development Report asserts that global interdependence means that the world's crises of famine, disease, environmental degradation, and ethnic strife are no longer isolated or confined within national borders (United Nations 1995, 94: 229). This portends a future of immense challenge in which either truly sustainable development, equitable resource consumption, and the elimination of poverty and scarcity will help liberate the body and soul of man or in which resource wars and ethnopolitical conflicts will proliferate. I share the view of Fred Riggs that "the rise of inter-nationality conflict in recent years should forewarn us of much worse to come. Unless radical solutions are found, the massive death-tolls of the 20th century may appear trivial by contrast with what is yet to come" (1994, 15: 585).

13. Scarcity, Genocide, and the Postmodern Individual

Leon Rappoport

If Walliman and Dobkowski's thesis (chapter 1) is nearly correct, and future scarcities create a global condition characterized by increasing conflict and "a great potential for mass death and even genocide," how are people likely to react? More specifically, what sort of psycho-social and behavioral responses may be anticipated from persons who have grown up in a postmodern cultural/technological environment? That is, the high-tech, media-saturated environment already well established in North America and Western Europe and beginning to emerge in urban centers throughout much of the rest of the world with the penetration of MTV, McDonald's, the Internet, Disney Worlds, and so on. To examine this question, this chapter is organized in three sections dealing first with the various forms of genocidal events that seem probable in future conditions of scarcity, second with the general issue of postmodern culture and personality—those personality attributes many social scientists and culture critics already perceive to be characteristic of youth in postmodern environments—and third with the potential reactions of such postmodern individuals to genocidal events.

Scarcity and Genocidal Events

In an article titled "The Coming Anarchy: How Scarcity, Crime, Over-population, Tribalism, and Disease Are Rapidly Destroying the Social

Fabric of Our Planet," journalist Robert Kaplan (1994) provides a remarkably powerful, documented argument directly supportive of Walliman's thesis on scarcity. Kaplan suggests that facing increasing scarcity, a condition he has observed in West Africa and Eastern Europe, systematic campaigns of rationalized mass killing as exemplified by the Holocaust or the Cambodian genocide are very unlikely because they require dedicated cadres under the command of a strong central government. Scarcity, however, tends to erode the power of central governing authorities. Lacking the material resources to implement or impose their policies in an orderly fashion, governments become ineffective, corrupt, and decay toward anarchic tribalism. Yet, if this situation precludes massive genocide programs, it makes a broad range of smaller-scale genocidal events not only more likely but also, according to Kaplan, virtually inevitable.

It takes no great leap of the imagination to understand the connection between scarcity and a convergent manifold of deadly events that can ultimately (and almost as quickly) kill as many people as perished in Auschwitz. Over the past decade, for example, famines brought on by warfare or natural disasters or both have killed millions in Ethiopia, Somalia, and other parts of Africa. Besides the continuing political instability and ethnic conflicts, soil erosion, water shortages, and overpopulation are all predicted to make famines more frequent in the future. Moreover, the international relief efforts that have mitigated famines in the past appear destined to decline as the resources available for relief, as well as the will to provide it, become reduced under conditions of global scarcity.

A similar dynamic applies to outbreaks of epidemic diseases. Scarcity already limits what is being done to control AIDS in the poorer countries and in the poorer segments of the richer countries. As the AIDS epidemic spreads, and as new and relatively untreatable diseases emerge (for example, the Ebola virus, cerebral malaria, variations of tuberculosis), the demand for biomedical relief will be increasing at the same time as the resources available to provide it will be decreasing.

Another domain of genocidal events is war. Appealing to Martin van Creveld's analysis of post–cold war warfare, Kaplan points out that as scarcity undermines the authority of central governments, organized warfare conducted by national armies is being replaced by varieties of tribal, ethnic, and religious wars. Recent and current examples include the struggles in the former Yugoslavia, the Russo-

Chechin war, the tribal war in Rwanda, and lesser conflicts or rebellions in Afghanistan, Sri Lanka, Peru, and Northern Ireland. Kaplan further notes that scarcity makes participation in such forms of warfare an attractive alternative for many young men: "As anybody who has had experience with Chetniks in Serbia, 'technicals' in Somalia, Tontons Macoutes in Haiti, or soldiers in Sierra Leone can tell you, in places where the Western Enlightenment has not penetrated and where there has always been mass poverty, people find liberation in violence" (1994, 72).

This point clearly applies equally well to the growth of urban gang violence in the United States and the attractiveness of guns for youth in general, not to mention the middle-aged wearing camouflage and playing with guns on weekends. It is also suggested that low-intensity armed conflicts shade directly into terrorism and the illegal traffic in weapons and drugs. The Afghan tribal armies, for example, substantially support themselves by exporting opium; the Shining Path guerrillas in Peru receive support from cocaine producers, and U.S. motorcycle gangs transport drugs. In this connection, it deserves emphasis that powerful nations such as the United States are not immune to the domestic violence associated with scarcity. The social dislocations produced as the United States makes a transition toward a postindustrial economy appears directly or indirectly linked to the rise of armed religious cults, private militias, and gang violence. If the death toll thus far from gangs, cults, suicidal paranoids, or terrorist bombers is still relatively small, it may well show a dramatic increase under the impact of serious scarcity.

Finally, no discussion of the potential genocidal events associated with scarcity would be complete without mention of the terrorist or rogue nation-state nuclear-weapon scenario. The theme is that the political and economic pressures created by scarcity will increase the likelihood that nuclear weapons or the means to produce them will be offered for sale to any high bidder. And the same sorts of pressures are likely to make terrorists or rogue nations more anxious to acquire, and eventually use, such weapons.

Postmodern Culture and Personality

Although detailed discussion of the end of the modern and beginning of the postmodern era is beyond the scope of this chapter, some brief perspectives on the issue may be cited. Rappoport and Kren (1995) argue that the modernity ideal died at Auschwitz and Hiroshima. That is, the underlying assumption of modernity, that human progress toward a better world could be achieved through increased rationality, technological efficiency, and social control, has been, on the evidence of the Nazi death camps and the nuclear bombing of Japan, shown to be false. Nothing in modern science, law, or religion forestalled or seriously mitigated the mass genocides of this century.

Another perspective on the end of modernity was suggested by the architecture critic Charles Jencks (1978). He claims that modernity lost its credibility when the Pruitt-Igoe public housing project in St. Louis was demolished in 1972. Designed according to the rationally efficient, functional criteria of modernity, this low-income housing complex was finally seen to be unfit for human habitation.

A broader historical view relevant to the end of modernity can be found in a recent review of Hobsbawm's history of the twentieth century: "In short, Eric Hobsbawm's history of the twentieth century is the story of the decline of a civilization, the history of a world which has both brought to full flowering the material and cultural potential of the nineteenth century and betrayed its promise" (Judt 1995, 20).

One way to epitomize the postmodern era as opposed to the modern is by appeal to a series of antinomies between them. Marshak (1995), for example, lists the following as intrinsic to modernity: gunpowder, the printing press, mechanical clocks, national markets, sequential technologies, and independent relationships. Intrinsic to postmodernity are: atomic weapons, television, electronic clocks, global markets, simultaneous technologies, and interdependent relationships. He further contrasts modern management with postmodern management principles as follows: stable versus flexible operations, structured channels versus fluid flows, hindsight versus foresight, and hierarchies versus networks.

Comparative lists of this sort are oversimplifications postulating dichotomies where there are often underlying continuities, but they provide a useful sense of the quantum leap many commentators perceive to be characteristic of the movement beyond modernity. This view can be seen clearly in Stanley's (1993) economics-oriented description of the "principles underlying postmodernization," which include "the appeal to unadorned market relations, the erosion of the state as a source of dependence, the weakening of workplace solidarities and the elevation of the private over the public in matters of cultural and social provision" (30).

Kvale (1992, 2) provides a broader philosophical and cultural statement.

> Postmodernity refers to an age which has lost the Enlightenment belief in emancipation and progress through more knowledge and scientific research. Postmodern society consists less of totalities to be ruled by preconceived models than by decentralization to heterogeneous local contexts characterized by flexibility and change. There is a change from a mechanical . . . to an information industry, and from production to consumption as the main focus of the economy. It is an age in which the multiple perspectives of new media tend to dissolve any sharp line between reality and fantasy.

He also notes as definitive of postmodern culture: art as collage, Las Vegas architecture, rock videos, and the novels of Umberto Ecco. I would add certain films, such as *Bagdad Cafe* and *Pulp Fiction*.

Films and television have an important status in postmodern culture because they allow persons to evade domination by established, prosaic realities and encourage awareness of alternative, possible worlds. It has been suggested, moreover, that in some respects postmodern electronic technologies have advanced to where their simulations/representations can become, if not an independent reality, at least a criterion of the given reality. "Thus, signs may attain the same status as the objects they signify in societies that are increasingly immersed in media imagery, and the categorization of persons, objects or events will vary not with their intrinsic properties but with the sign qualities these properties evoke when presented in the media" (Baumgardner and Rappoport 1995, 14).

Given the truism among social scientists that personality is grounded upon, and reflective of, culture, whereas culture is understood to be an expression of the "collective personality" of society, it is not surprising that over the past decade an increasing number of personality theorists (for example, Lifton 1993; Gergen 1991; Cushman 1990; Secord 1990; Rowan 1990; Sampson 1989; Baumeister 1987) have begun to discuss the psychosocial significance of the socioeconomic and cultural changes noted above under the heading of postmodernism. Most of this burgeoning literature follows the culture-personality logic laid out by Geertz (1973), namely, that culture is the ultimate source of the individual's core sense of self or identity, because it provides the systems of meaning—roles, norms, values, and language—through which individuals conduct their lives and sense of self. (Parenthetically, although the terms *self-concept* or *self-image* refer to both self as object and subject, while identity is usually described as the core structure of self as subject, no such fine distinctions are made in the following text.) Writing in more concrete terms, Berger, Berger, and Kellner (1974, 12) stipulate that "the consciousness of everyday life is the web of meanings that allow the individual to navigate his way through the ordinary events and encounters of his life with others." It is also considered axiomatic that major changes in a culture will be accompanied by major changes in the self-concepts of its inhabitants. Frequently cited as exemplary are the changing self-concepts of women in American society.

How do such changes come about? What are the mechanisms of identity formation or change or both? In premodern and early modern societies, this was not considered problematic. The individual's self-concept or identity was seen to be largely determined by the cultural meanings attached to their gender, status in the family (first or later born), and the position of the family in society (as often indicated by the family name: Baker, Smith, Hunter, Taylor, and so on). In modern industrial societies, and even moreso in postindustrial, that is, postmodern societies, however, identity and the self have become profoundly problematic because the family-based and societal mechanisms no longer apply.

Some of the reasons for this are obvious. At the level of the family, it is simply that stable intact families able to transmit a strong sense of independent selfhood to their children are becoming the exception rather than the rule. Even where such families exist, they can hardly succeed in this task, because the culture meanings carried by, and embodied in, parents and elders are often irrelevant to the situations challenging young people in the postmodern environment. It is no mere irony that America today resounds with discourses on the "family values" that have become yet another kind of scarce resource.

At the level of society, identity has become more and more problematic because structural and process changes now occur so rapidly as to offer only an amorphous, constantly shifting basis for identity formation. One need only mention here the gender role changes (for example, women become astronauts and drive trucks; men become nurses and grade-school teachers), the corporate takeovers, downsizing of the white- and blue-collar labor force, and relocations of industries that have become commonplace.

More significantly, however, at the level of popular culture, the formation of personal identity and construction of a firm self-concept has for many youths gone beyond the problematic and, like the manual typewriter or rotary telephone, taken on the quality of a curious historical artifact. Thus, as may be seen on MTV, the models of personality popular among young people emphasize flexibility, diversity, and multiple identities. For example, a music video by Madonna was reportedly criticized by a middle-aged columnist for being "chaotic" because of her changing personas: seductress, naive innocent, aggressive dominator. But the same report quoted one of her young fans as saying it was wonderful because "Madonna is always herself."

The ideal of a variable, multidimensional rather than unitary self was also modeled in the recent television series *Quantum Leap*. The series centered on a protagonist who took over the minds and bodies of people to rescue them from difficult situations. Similarly, in the series *Highway to Heaven*, the lead characters were angels who created novel identities for themselves as they went about aiding people in distress. The underlying attraction of these and other popular culture models of a pluralistic self or diversified personal identity is their representation of exciting tranformational possibilities. On the one hand, they dramatize the rich potentials that may emerge when the social construction of reality principle is applied to personality development, and on the other, they present a glamorous alternative to the mundane effort required to build a single, unitary identity. In sum, for young people in the postmodern environment of rapid socioeconomic changes and a 50 percent divorce rate, the modern ideal of a unitary identity based on singular loyalties to a specific career and intimate psychosexual relationship—the classic foundations of integrated identity postulated by Erik Erikson (1950)—may simply appear to be a bygone romantic myth.

Besides the popular culture models encouraging a pluralistic self-concept, human potential psychologists also contribute to this trend by warning against entrapment in a fixed sense of self that can inhibit further personal growth. A number of self-transformational therapies are available to save people from such a situation. Moreover, by taking advantage of readily available body-work facilities and cosmetic surgery, the body itself may be harnessed to the task of self-transformation (see Finkelstein 1991 for a detailed treatment of the body issue).

Some therapists consider that cultural pressures toward pluralistic self-concepts signal a dangerous slide into psychopathology. The current American Psychiatric Association diagnostic manual (DSM-111) defines as an identity "disorder" the "inability to integrate aspects of the self." And a recent survey reported a significant rise in the number of persons diagnosed with such disorders (Ross 1991). However, some clinical theorists do not see any danger here. DeBerry (1993) suggests that a "schizoid consciousness" is adaptive to contemporary life conditions, and Rowan (1990) considers that "subpersonalities" are a normal "semi-permanent and semi-autonomous region of the personality."

Empirical support for the more-positive viewpoint is growing. Markus and Nurius (1986) described evidence showing that normal college students represent their various developmental possibilities as a range of different "possible selves." These authors concluded that it is a mistake to believe in a single self "to which one can be true." Linville (1985, 1987) found that persons with complex or pluralistic self-concepts could better cope with stress, the premise being that if a failure or loss of self-esteem occurs in one self-domain, it can be offset by success in another. A current study, moreover, indicates that persons with high scores on a measure of personality multiplicity show higher levels of creativity than others (Boone 1995).

Theoretical discussions of postmodern personality qualities are more variable. Lifton (1993) acknowledges the multiplicity imposed by postmodern culture while suggesting that an "integrative proteanism" can hold disparate aspects of the self loosely together. Hermans, Kempen, and Van Loon (1992), however, argue that personality should be understood as centering on a "dialogical self" in which the "I" may fluctuate through various positions and thus facilitate dialogical relations between those positions. Gergen (1991) characterizes the postmodern self as being "saturated," that is, overstimulated and thus fragmented by exposure to the plethora of postmodern communication technologies. He suggests that this condition may eventually yield persons with a new and beneficial "global consciousness."

In sharp contrast to Gergen's saturated self, Cushman (1990) postulates an "empty self" brought about by the fragmentation and absence of stable values in postmodern society. He maintains that postmodern individuals have become relentless consumers who smother their interior emptiness with material goods. Writing on the theme of "how the self became a problem," Baumeister (1987) sees contemporary individuals caught in a double bind, on the one hand having to define their life meanings and purposes for themselves, yet on the other still being bound up in society. In this situation, many come to define themselves by how others see them; hence their concern with style statements and consumption. Finally, Sampson (1985) attributes the problems of contemporary selfhood to the obsolescence of the American ideal of "self-contained individualism." In the emerging globally linked world system, the postmodern individual can no longer find much meaning in assertive independence, but must find it through relationships and integration with a larger community. Sampson conceives the postmodern self to be "a decentralized, nonequilibrium structure, a pantheon of selves, within a single body." A similar view has been adopted by Fiske and Taylor (1991), who describe the self as "an unordered, non-hierarchical collection of features."

As might be expected when any fundamental culture change relevant to the theoretical focus of a field or discipline sets in, interpretations of its meaning will vary a good deal; this has certainly been the case insofar as postmodern culture and personality are concerned. But underlying the diverse formulations of theorists, therapists, and researchers is a generally agreed-upon conclusion that as compared with moderns, postmodern individuals tend to have multiple self-concepts, or multifaceted identities or both. Taken together, the burden of evidence emerging from analyses of popular culture as well as empirical research and theoretical discourse clearly points to multiplicity as the defining quality of postmodern personality. Particularly noteworthy are the apparent parallels between the features of postmodern culture—collage, networks, fluidity, decentralization—and the personality qualities suggested as characteristic of postmodern individuals—schizoid consciousness, subpersonalities, possible selves, dialogical self, saturated self, and empty self.

It also seems clear that the hierarchical structure of personality idealized in modern psychology, that is, a vertically integrated, centrally organized system in which lower-order impulses and emotions are supposed to be controlled by higher-order cognitive (ego) processes, is no longer viable. It appears destined to be replaced by a horizontally integrated, decentralized system—one in which the cognitive and emotional sides are seen as interpenetrating rather than opposed, and the model for consciousness becomes a conversation of equals rather than a struggle for power.

Viewed in this perspective, the modern idea that personal morality can be understood as residing in a unitary "superego" or conscience that wrestles with our basic instincts while trying to enforce obedience to internalized moral values seems not only irrelevant but also reminiscent of a Victorian steam engine. A postmodern approach, by contrast, would conceptualize personal morality as a manifold of context-dependent evaluative possibilities. In a valuable comprehensive review of postmodern morality, Hill (1995, 7) concludes: "Instead of moral universals, the postmodern self acknowledges the multiplicity of moral choices and seeks to understand morality in terms of our relations to others and community." It is further suggested that this is a highly relativistic and relational type of morality that transcends rationality. The postmodern culture recognizes a plurality of rationalities, and for any given situation it may offer such a broad range of possible values and actions as to reduce the exercise of moral choice to an arbitrary act of will—a "leap of faith."

Postmodern's Reactions to Genocidal Events

To explore the question of how postmoderns may respond to genocidal events, it will be helpful to first mention a few general disclaimers—theoretical "points of order." Thus, if one wished to address the question in a genuinely postmodern voice, there would be an immediate appeal to the principles of contextualism and the social construction of meaning. One would question the question: where is it coming from, who is asking it, what sort of genocidal events are concerned, and what is the range of meanings that might plausibly be attributed to these events? In short, one might easily fall into an endless discursive textual analysis postmodern thinkers call deconstruction, and the likely bottom line would simply be "it all depends."

It should also be stipulated that, like moderns, postmoderns come in different varieties. Ambiguous as traditional socioeconomic and class distinctions may be, for example, they are, nevertheless, still applicable to postmoderns. Indeed, at least metaphorically, the contemporary two-class society distinction fits quite well. There are the postmodern proletarians who service and maintain the information highway versus the plutocrats who cruise on it. And there appear to be "lumpen" postmoderns—homeless surfers of cyberspace forever seeking a new electronic fix versus the avant-garde of artists and professionals pushing the limits of global linkage.

But though the significance of the foregoing considerations must be acknowledged as undoubtedly useful in various contexts, they will be set aside here in favor of a more conventional type of comparative analysis: how do the salient features of postmodern culture and personality relate to knowledge about individual responses to genocidal events?

In their analysis of "the genocidal mentality" Lifton and Markusen (1990) provide a detailed discussion of the psychosocial adjustment they found to be characteristic of persons able to accept and participate in genocidal activities. Called "doubling," the process involves a type of psychic splitting analogous to the Freudian ego defense mechanism of compartmentalization. Doubling, however, is defined as a form of dissociation by which the individual's self is divided into "two functioning wholes, so that a part-self acts as an entire self" (Lifton and Markusen, 106). This phenomenon was identified by Lifton (1986) as a particularly strong personality factor enabling Nazi physicians to carry out their work in the death camps. A less intense but very similar type of doubling was also found by Lifton and Markusen to be typical of American nuclear-warfare planners and atomic-weapons scientists.

Insofar as doubling is a valid formulation of the way persons can accommodate themselves to genocidal events, and insofar as doubling would seem to be a specific variant of the general multiplicity (if not "schizoid consciousness") typical of postmoderns, it follows that postmoderns would probably not find it very difficult to tolerate genocidal events. They are, from this standpoint, already geared up to carry out the appropriate psychosocial adjustment.

Language and imagery are another source of the genocidal mentality. Lifton and Markusen refer to a "language of nonfeeling," noting that nuclear strategists very frequently speak in a language of euphemisms, acronyms, and metaphors, which allow them to distance themselves or dissociate from the realities of human destruction intrinsic to their work. Here too, there is a direct parallel with the semiotics of postmodern culture, in that much of contemporary language and imagery is manifestly "nonfeeling." One need only consider the rapid collage imagery, metaphors, and language of music videos and video games, computer screen icons, passwords, PIN numbers, and the trivialization of violence on television.

Immersion in such a semiotic environment may not produce full-blown dissociation but can hardly fail to facilitate a degree of nonfeeling or desensitization toward genocidal events. And this process would seem particularly relevant to situations in which victims lack the sign qualities that can evoke empathy among "viewers." In a rudimentary form, perhaps such desensitization is already apparent from the way postmoderns can navigate through the homeless people cluttering urban centers, either treating them as invisible or dropping a handout without breaking stride.

The empathy issue deserves further emphasis, because it is generally viewed as the key psychological factor determining individual behavior in problematic social situations, and has, accordingly, been heavily researched. Drawing on this research for his analysis of major genocides of the twentieth century, Staub (1989) concluded that at least two general conditions militate against empathy. One is material scarcity, which drives people toward preoccupation with personal needs and reduces their sense of connection with others. This was the case in Weimar Germany, and presently in the former Soviet Union. The other condition is an inner-psychic state Staub describes as typified by a weak ego or poorly articulated self-concept. It tends to be characteristic of people who have been traumatized during childhood by an abusive family, or by the chaotic deprivation occurring in war zones, or by any number of other conditions, including family breakups owing to divorce.

Such people are likely to deal with anxiety and stress by using paranoid projection mechanisms, that is, by perceiving others to be the source of their difficulties. A "popular" paranoid scenario related to genocidal events throughout the modern era has centered on the idea of an international Jewish conspiracy to rule the world. A more recent one often mentioned by Americans in private militias is that gun control laws are part of a government conspiracy (probably instigated by Jews) to turn the United States over to the United Nations.

Although there is no substantial evidence indicating that the multiplicity characterizing postmoderns inclines them toward paranoid defense mechanisms, the implications of Staub's analysis are obvious. The postmodern "empty," "saturated," or "dialogical" self may not directly equate to a weak modern ego, but there is enough similarity between these formulations to suggest parallel psychodynamic reactions to scarcity-induced stress. Something along the line of a "blaming the victim" dynamic would certainly fit the free market orientation of postmodern culture.

Turning from psychodynamic theory to a more general level of discussion, however, the final issue demanding consideration concerns differences between modern and postmodern morality. It will be recalled that in contrast to the modern ideal of universal moral values, postmodern moral values were described as "context-dependent evaluative possibilities." The reactions of postmoderns to genocidal events, therefore, are likely to be complex and variable depending upon the range of possible moral interpretations associated with those events.

The point in question here is nicely illustrated by certain films drama-tizing the postmodern mindset toward moral values. In *Pulp Fiction* and *Apocalypse Now*, for example, modern moral values are deliber-ately confounded by situating characters in amoral contexts and thereby forcing viewers away from any simplistic moral interpretation. The modern films made by John Ford and John Wayne impose straightfor-ward, "predigested" moral values, whereas the moral values in films by Quentin Tarantino and Harvey Keitel are confabulated. The mod-ern films could succeed as popular entertainments because they pro-vided assurances of moral certainties; the postmodern succeed today because they provide assurances of moral ambiguities. A relevant citation—life imitating art?—might be the way the O. J. Simpson mur-der trial has become a major media entertainment.

Other aspects of postmodern culture also promote complex, rela-tivistic moral perspectives. During the Gulf war with Iraq, television news often presented near-simultaneous reports from both sides of the conflict, and viewers could find themselves being encouraged to cheer for the bombers while almost at the same being encouraged to sympathize with the bombees. Even the abhorrent rationality un-derlying genocidal acts of terrorism is now widely understood to be a facet of postmodern culture. Thus, terrorism has its logic: when anyone can become a victim, governments are shown to be impotent; when terror attacks generate wide media coverage, they become a public-relations tactic; and when everyone can be defined as a direct or indirect participant in the current world system, there are no inno-cent bystanders. This is not to say that the logic of terrorism is ac-cepted as legitimate. What *is* accepted, however, is that as soon as yesterday's terrorist group (for example, the PLO, the IRA) agrees to renounce violence, it becomes a legitimate participant in the world system.

In general, therefore, and in the light of the increasing climate of moral ambiguity indicated above, postmoderns are not likely to make knee-jerk, moralistic responses to genocidal events. On the contrary, the postmodern response is likely to be tentative, inquisitive, and multifaceted. Or in circumstances when the events and victims are remote, apathetic. Insofar as recent American government policies may be taken as prototypical, the tentative, multifaceted response pattern can be seen in the negotiated invasion of Haiti, or the drawn-out, variable efforts to reduce or contain civil warfare in the former Yugo-slavia. The apathetic pattern can be seen in the ritual condemnations but relative indifference that followed the massacre of Chinese students in Tiananmen Square, or the withdrawal of American forces from Somalia. The operative principle of postmodern policy responses to genocidal events may sum up to something like this: "If you can't wait them out, talk them out, or buy them out, then blow them up, but only if the cost-benefit ratio is very favorable."

Conclusion: A Koan for the Twenty-first Century

The views developed in this chapter about how postmodern individuals will respond to genocidal events must be taken with a large grain of salt. They are, at best, speculations on the future informed by a present body of fallible knowledge that may not apply. If it does apply, however, it would seem that postmoderns will generally be tolerant, and perhaps indifferent to genocidal events. There is no other plausible conclusion to be drawn from our present knowledge of postmodern culture and personality. All of the relevant cultural factors—the language, imagery, and climate of moral ambiguity—suggest that a growing desensitization is at work. And all of the relevant personality theory and research suggest that the multiplicity characterizing postmoderns facilitates the adoption of desensitizing stress-coping or defense mechanisms.

What this may mean for the future of civilization is the great koan of the twenty-first century. Does it portend a new Dark Age in which a privileged postmodern minority becomes smugly detached from the chaotic genocidal events afflicting everyone else? Or does it portend movement toward a new Enlightenment, in which a privileged postmodern minority will find the means, however slowly and tentatively, to save what can be saved while expanding the world culture base for a liberating multiplicity? Stay tuned . . .

14. Critical Reflections on the Doomsday, Apocalyptic Vision

Craig A. Rimmerman

What kind of culture is it, when some serious analysis appears and is almost at once placed as another installment of "doom and gloom"? What kind of culture is it which pushes distraction, in its ordinary selection even of news, to the point where there is hardly any sustained discussion of the central and interlocking issues of human survival?

—Raymond Williams
The Year 2000

Over the past twenty years, the doomsday, apocalyptic perspective has characterized much of the environmental literature. At its most extreme, this literature warns, in the words of Bill McKibben, that we are witnessing "the end of nature" as we know it. The metaphor of "the apocalypse" has captured much attention. As Lawrence Buell points out, "apocalypse is the single most powerful master metaphor that the contemporary environmental imagination has at its disposal" (Buell 1995, 285).[1]

Underlying this perspective is a belief in resource scarcity. Resource scarcity generally manifests itself in two ways. At the broadest level, resource scarcity refers to a scarcity of planetary resources, including clean water, air, and energy sources at affordable prices. At a more

1. My thanks to Steven Lee and David Ost for their thoughtful suggestions in response to an earlier draft of this chapter.

narrow level, resource scarcity indicates the kind of budgetary scarcity that has transformed American politics over the past fifteen years. As deficits mounted throughout the late 1970s and 1980s, politicians from both parties were forced to confront the reality of declining resources to pay for myriad social and economic programs, especially given the American public's aversion to raising taxes. This has increasingly led to a political and social environment that the economist Lester Thurow has identified as a "zero-sum society," where there are clear winners and losers in the distribution of scarce resources (Thurow 1980). It is this zero sum dilemma that underlies much of the doomsday, apocalyptic literature, though much of the focus is on the broader conception of resource scarcity.

This chapter provides a critical evaluation of the doomsday, apocalyptic literature regarding the future of the planet, with a specific focus on energy and environmental concerns. In doing so, several questions are addressed: What is the purpose of this literature? To what extent does the doomsday, apocalyptic perspective undermine possible meaningful political and policy responses addressing resource scarcity issues? In what ways does the doomsday perspective prevent serious grassroots mobilizing efforts in response to the distribution of energy and environmental resources? In other words, if the future is so bleak, why do anything at all? How useful is it to frame a discussion of the future of the planet within the broader context of resource scarcity? How should one teach the doomsday, apocalyptic perspective in the classroom? In addressing these questions, I argue that there is value in teaching the doomsday perspective and its critique. Students are forced to confront serious questions regarding values underlying our political and economic order as well as how various analysts on the left and the right have attempted to interrogate questions that should be at the center of our public discourse. Before these issues can be addressed adequately, however, we must first outline the central tenets of the doomsday, apocalyptic perspective.

The Doomsday Perspective: An Overview

At the core of the doomsday view is a belief that "the economic and social development of the United States over the last two centuries might better be characterized as extraordinary, fortuitous, and nonsustainable" (Miles 1976, 1). Recognizing the limits to economic growth is of the utmost importance if we are to survive as a planet over the long term. The emphasis here is on long-term planetary survival and what we can and should be doing to provide for ecological sustainability and stability.

Most doomsday theorists also embrace a Hobbesian conception of humanity, positing that only a centralized state, one that embraces some form of government coercion, can adequately provide for societal stability in both the short and long term, because heightened inequalities in a time of increased resource scarcity will foster class conflict and ultimately threaten the stability of the political and economic order. Doomsday theorists also believe that the environmental problems we face are so severe that those in power must respond to them in a decisive and timely manner. If the goal is planetary survival, such decisions cannot possibly be made through the kind of democratic procedures associated with liberal democracy. For analysis I have chosen the work of William Ophuls and Stephen Boyan, Jr., and Robert Heilbroner as representative of the doomsday perspective.

Like almost all doomsday theorists, Ophuls and Boyan have a Hobbesian conception of humanity. They raise this question: How do we protect or advance the interests of the collective, when the individuals that comprise it behave in a selfish, greedy, and quarrelsome fashion? Their solution is government coercion, as government must give way to elite rule. They offer this justification for what many would regard as an extreme solution: "It is simply not true that, once they are aware of the general gravity of the situation, men will naturally moderate their demands on the environment" (Ophuls and Boyan 1992, 202). Like the other doomsday theorists, Ophuls and Boyan's primary concern is to provide collective stability for the long term.

Robert Heilbroner frames his doomsday analysis by posing this question: "Is there hope for man?" (Heilbroner 1991, 20).[2] In answering his query, Heilbroner offers a bleak analysis: "The outlook for man is painful, desperate, and the hope that can be held out for his future seems to be very slim indeed" (Heilbroner 1991, 20). He identifies two basic reasons for his grim prognosis—mankind's struggle for individual

---

2. Like all other doomsday authors whom I have met, Heilbroner is insensitive to gender in his use of language. When discussing the doomsday perspective, I have adopted the doomsday authors' use of "mankind," rather than the more acceptable, more inclusive, and gender-neutral "humankind."

achievement and man's inherent self-centeredness. The second, in particular, is a human nature argument. Heilbroner embraces a Hobbesian conception of humanity when he raises these concerns.

> When men can generally acquiesce in, even relish, the destruction of their living contemporaries, when they can regard with indifference or irritation the fate of those who live in slums, rot in prison, or starve in lands that have meaning only insofar as they are vacation resorts, why should they be expected to take the painful actions needed to prevent the destruction of future generations whose faces they will never live to see? Worse yet, will they not curse these future generations whose claims to life can be honored only by sacrificing present enjoyments; and will they not, if it comes to a choice, condemn them to nonexistence by choosing the present over the future? (Heilbroner 1991, 169)

Like Ophuls and Boyan, Heilbroner rejects the notion that citizens can and will sacrifice now to promote long-term planetary stability.

What are some of the specific global problems according to the doomsday perspective? As one representative of this view, Heilbroner identifies four external challenges to the human prospect that warrant immediate attention if the doomsday scenario is to be avoided—overpopulation, the threat of nuclear war, the greenhouse effect, and science and technology. For Heilbroner the demographic trends over the next two to three generations suggest that the planet will not be able to adjust to the consequences of overpopulation. Heilbroner contends, for example, that "in one century, the underdeveloped world[,] which today totals 2.5 billion, will have to support something like 40 billion by that date if it continues to double its numbers approximately every quarter century" (Heilbroner 1991, 33). Indeed, overpopulation will lead to serious environmental problems. What factors might check the overpopulation problem? Heilbroner recognizes that the ability of overpopulated areas to introduce effective and stringent birth control programs might begin to address overpopulation. In the second edition to his book, he points out that China has begun to make progress through these sorts of measures (Heilbroner 1980), but he is not optimistic that such measures will deal adequately with the full gravity of the problem. Instead, Heilbroner grimly concludes that "the eventual rise of iron governments" that practice "government coercion" may be the only way to halt "the descent into hell." For Heilbroner and the other doomsday theorists, "hell" is the fundamental instability that will arise as members of an overpopulated planet compete for increasingly scarce resources.

A second external challenge is the threat of nuclear war. In addressing this challenge, Heilbroner raises this question: Will the twenty-first century be an era of annihilation? His chief concern here is that poor nations might use the threat of nuclear power as blackmail of rich nations for food and other resources in a time of heightened scarcity.

The greenhouse effect is Heilbroner's third external challenge. He worries that we are already "encroaching on the environment beyond its ability to support the demands made on it" (Heilbroner 1991, 47). For Heilbroner "the inescapable need to limit industrial growth" and prevent the heating up of the earth's atmosphere deserves immediate global attention, as does the depletion of the ozone layer (Heilbroner 1991, 54). His analysis thoughtfully addresses the capability of both capitalist and socialist societies' abilities to curb the growth imperative. Not surprisingly, Heilbroner concludes that both systems will have difficulty limiting growth over the long term, though socialist societies will do a better job in the short term. Indeed, both systems will have to address environmental problems, such as the greenhouse effect and air pollution, over the long term.

Heilbroner cites science and technology as a fourth challenge that must be confronted. He recognizes that many skeptics have invoked science and technology to address the challenges facing the human prospect. For Heilbroner and other doomsday theorists, however, science and technology provide society with a false sense of security, a security that is not warranted given the intractability and seriousness of the external challenges that he outlines throughout his book.

William Ophuls and A. Stephen Boyan, Jr., elucidate several additional components of the doomsday analysis. Like Heilbroner, they raise serious questions about the capability of liberal democratic societies to address larger resource-scarcity issues. They contend that the political implications of heightened scarcity include greater inequality and conflict among classes, conflict that poses a serious threat to system stability. Furthermore, they believe that the unpleasant reality of heightened scarcity is that "the golden age of individualism and liberty is all but over" (Ophuls and Boyan 1992, 192).

Their most significant contribution to the doomsday perspective is their claim that the American political and economic system will not be able to make the sweeping changes needed to deal with the challenges of scarcity. This inability is due to a larger political culture that embraces radical individualism as the hallmark of liberal democracy. They also worry that our Madisonian system of checks and balances and separate political institutions sharing power is far too fragmented and dispersed to arrive at the kind of timely consensus needed to address the challenges to the human prospect that Heilbroner describes. They cite two additional problems—disjointed incrementalism and policy decision making that inevitably lags far behind events (Ophuls and Boyan 1992, 247–48). For Ophuls and Boyan "the external reality of ecological scarcity has cut the ground out from under our own political system, making merely reformist policies of ecological management all but useless" (Ophuls and Boyan 1992, 3). Working within the broader structure of the American political and economic system as we know it constrains our ability to respond in a meaningful way.

In the end, they believe that mankind's political, economic, and social life must once again become thoroughly rooted in the realities of diminished planetary resources. This imperative cannot be met under a system that adheres to liberal democratic values. As a result, democracy must give way to elite rule and a society where state coercion is the norm. Ophuls and Boyan are not alone in arguing that government coercion is the only vehicle for promoting global stability over the long term. Heilbroner, for example, believes that "the most successful governments may be governments capable of rallying obedience far more effectively than would be possible in a democratic setting. If the issue for mankind is survival, such governments may be unavoidable, even necessary" (Heilbroner 1991, 134).

Clearly, the doomsday, apocalyptic perspective provides a grim analysis of the future and the capability of governments to respond to global challenges, but there are occasional glimpses of hope. For example, in the most recent edition of his book (updated in 1991), Heilbroner finds "it hopeful that we know we live in difficult times— a necessary state of mind if we are to appraise the prospect before us with clear eyes" (Heilbroner 1991, 30). He points out that ecology is now a household word and believes that the 1990s might "become a 'turnaround decade'—not in the actual extent of environmental deterioration, but in taking action to prevent further deterioration" (Heilbroner 1991, 76). In the end, Heilbroner is hopeful that a "survivalist ethic," sown in the nature of humankind, will prompt us to confront the external challenges to the human prospect with mean-ing and force.

As might be expected, the doomsday critique has provoked an array of critical responses. Those on the Right who criticize the doomsday perspective from a modern conservative[3] vantage point find that it ex-aggerates our global dilemma and ignores reasons to believe that progress can be achieved working within existing political and economic institu-tions. On the Left, critics point to the serious problems with embracing the paradigm of resource scarcity associated with the doomsday per-spective. Leftist scholars also criticize the doomsday perspective for failing to confront global inequalities in the distribution of property, wealth, and resources. To feminist leftist critics, a central flaw of the doomsday perspective is its failure to confront global gender inequities. To a discussion of these perspectives we now turn.

The Critique of the Doomsday Approach

One vocal conservative critic of the doomsday approach is Julian Simon, whose ideas are well articulated in his 1981 book, *The Ultimate Re-source*. To Simon, the doomsday scenario can be avoided if we adhere to the following four principles rooted in neoclassical economics:

1. the federal government should play a limited role in the energy development arena;

2. the economic marketplace, through Adam Smith's notion of the law of supply and demand, can and will deal with resource-scarcity concerns;

3. an increase in demand for energy resources will lead to an increase in new discoveries of such resources;

4. our present use of resources has little negative effect upon fu-ture generations, because current prices make an automatic allowance for future generations (Simon 1981).

Embracing the principles of neoclassical economics, Simon believes that market forces and present prices already take into account expected future developments, thus automatically conserving scarce resources for future consumption. Hence, he rejects calls for shared sacrifice and

3. I use "modern conservative" to refer to thinkers who embrace the free-market principles associated with neoclassic economics. Modern conservative thought is dis-tinct from the organic conservatism associated with Edmund Burke and Michael Oakeshott.

extreme conservation measures. In the end, Simon is optimistic that the doomsday scenario can be avoided, especially if we rely on the science, technology, and human ingenuity that Heilbroner believes provide a false sense of security against serious external challenges to the human prospect. Simon concludes optimistically by suggesting that "the ultimate resource is people—skilled, spirited, and hopeful people who will exert their wills and imaginations for their own benefit, and so, invariably, for the benefit of us all" (Simon 1981, 348).

Like Simon, Ronald Bailey embraces a conservative perspective when he identifies serious weaknesses in the doomsday perspective and criticizes the culture that devotes much attention to such faulty analyses. Bailey singles out books such as Rachel Carson's *Silent Spring* (1962), Paul and Ann Ehrlich's *The Population Bomb* (1968), and the Club of Rome's *The Limits to Growth* (1972) for describing the future in hopelessly bleak terms. These books have had negative consequences, not the least of which is affecting public policy in ways that led to the slowing of economic growth, thus unnecessarily increasing human misery. Unlike the doomsday theorists, Simon and Bailey believe that economic growth is the hallmark of a vital and stable society.

Bailey also contends that the doomsday theorists (whom he identifies as "environmental alarmists") "must be held accountable for their faulty analyses, their wildly inaccurate predictions, and their heedless politicization of science" (Bailey 1993, xi–xii). To Bailey the world faces some real problems, but they do not call for the draconian measures embraced by the doomsday theorists. He is particularly critical of the media for focusing on the doom-and-gloom analyses warning of ecological collapse, which he believes have motivated voters and policy makers to adopt "environmentalist policies." Like Simon's work, Bailey's analysis is rooted in a sense of hope and optimism that the American political system can tackle virtually any problems now and in the future. He suggests that "human history shows that our energy and creativity will surmount whatever difficulties we encounter" (Bailey 1993, xii).

For those who embrace the critique from the Left, the doomsday, apocalyptic perspective is misguided to the extent that it fails to confront global gender inequities and inequalities in the distribution of property, wealth, and resources. This critique manifests itself in the response to overpopulation concerns. For example, Joni Seager believes that what is needed is a "feminist rethinking of population/environment issues." She supports her belief in this way:

Women want access to reproductive planning services; they do not want to be instruments of population control. Global population growth may well be a "problem," but not in the ways that most of us are encouraged to believe. . . . There is good reason to be concerned about the environmental pressures exerted by population growth, just as there are good humanitarian and feminist reasons to promote programs that provide women everywhere with access to reproductive planning services. What is disturbing, though, is the manner in which men have framed the public environmental debate on population, and the extent to which women's lives are, once again, made invisible within the debate. (Seager 1993, 217).

Seager perceptively recognizes that it is easier for doomsday theorists to call for strict birth control measures than confront the social and economic structures that perpetuate global inequality. The next section argues that Seager's critique is useful for pedagogical purposes because it asks students to explore global inequities and how they intersect with power and gender concerns. To more fully understand the critique from the Left, we turn to John Bellamy Foster's critique and explore how to incorporate his perspective in the classroom.

Reflections on Teaching the Doomsday View

If the doomsday, apocalyptic perspective contains serious weaknesses, does it deserve serious consideration in the classroom? The short answer is yes, as there is much value in asking students to evaluate this perspective. To engage this perspective effectively, however, it is crucial to explicate its basic tenets and then offer a critique from different vantage points. I have been doing so for the past fourteen years at the college level, in my American political system, environmental policy, and public policy courses.

If this perspective is to be taught, it seems to me that it should be in ways that enable students to make important connections to the broader values of radical individualism, equality of opportunity, acquisition of private property, and emphasis on procedural democracy, all of which underlie liberal democratic systems. Indeed, I cannot think of a better way to ask students to evaluate the consequences of adhering to radical individualistic impulses, such as material acquisition associated with an emphasis on economic growth. Just what are the consequences of adhering to such values for the collective in the short and long term? In a recent essay,[4] John Bellamy Foster provides a useful metaphor for engaging the doomsday view and the values associated with liberal democracy.

> What is all too often overlooked in such calls for moral transformation is the central institutional fact of our society: what might be called the global "treadmill of production. . . ." A defining trait of the system is that it is a kind of giant squirrel cage. Everyone, or nearly everyone, is part of this treadmill and is unable or unwilling to get off. Investors and managers are driven by the need to accumulate wealth and to expand the scale of their operations in order to prosper within a globally competitive milieu. For the vast majority the commitment to the treadmill is more limited and indirect: they simply need to obtain jobs at liveable wages. (Foster 1995, 2).

Foster's analysis provides an excellent vehicle for responding to the doomsday perspective in the classroom, as it forces students to recognize that the global problems that we currently face are hardly worthy of mere individual responses. Indeed, "our wants are conditioned by the kind of society in which we live." The central enemy of the environment, then, "is not individuals acting in accordance with their own innate desires, but rather the treadmill of production on which we are all placed" (Foster 1995, 3). Foster's analysis is important because it enables instructors to raise important questions about the relationship between the individual and the collective. It also affords students the opportunity to challenge the underlying Hobbesian conception of human nature underlying the doomsday perspective. Virtually all of the doomsday theorists embrace a deductive analysis, much like Hobbes uses in *Leviathan*. This deductive analysis begins with negative assumptions about human nature and links these assumptions to the importance of maintaining system stability. Students need an opportunity to examine the core assumptions underlying an array of perspectives regarding the future of the planet, and the doomsday view provides a particularly useful opportunity for doing so.

I have found, as well, that the institutional analysis offered by Ophuls and Boyan raises compelling questions concerning the capability of the American political system to respond to the zero sum environment of resource scarcity. Before raising such questions, I devote much attention to explaining the basic principles of Madisonian

---

4. I am grateful to Christopher Gunn for bringing Foster's essay to my attention.

democracy as outlined by James Madison in "Federalist 10." It is then possible to explore the ability of an incremental policy characterized by separate institutions sharing power to respond with the sweeping changes needed to address energy and environmental concerns. Can a political and economic system that was created more than two hundred years ago in a time of relative plenty respond to the demands of heightened scarcity? What institutional changes might allow the system to respond in a more timely and effective manner? For example, would it be useful to adopt changes that would move our system of government in a more parliamentary direction? And what are the criteria for policy "effectiveness"? These are just some of the questions that might be addressed as we explore broader questions of change that might be occasioned by the doomsday analysis.

Much of the analysis here has suggested that the doomsday perspective is useful for teaching because it enables the instructor and students to raise broad considerations regarding the political and economic system and the cultural values emanating from that system regarding the relationship between the individual to the larger society. Students also see that scholars from the political Left and Right are exploring questions that should be at the core of public discourse today. At the same time, the doomsday approach asks the citizenry to confront its own responsibilities vis-à-vis the planet.

It is useful to ask students to recognize that much of what is associated with the doomsday view embraces a top-down approach to the world, one that lodges many decision-making responsibilities with a small group of policy elites who hold power. Indeed, note that Heilbroner and Ophuls and Boyan all suggest (albeit reluctantly and unhappily) that democracy must give way to elite rule if the interests of the collective are to be protected over the long term. To what extent is such a view compatible with democratic principles? And does the doomsday analysis suggest, unequivocally, that participatory democratic opportunities are destined for failure? Can we envision a participatory democratic society that links individual interests with the interests of the collective in routine decision making? If so, what might such a society look like in practice? These questions can also be engaged by discussing the doomsday perspective and its critics.

Those who worry that the doomsday perspective paralyzes citizens who might otherwise mobilize politically have a legitimate point. We should not forget that in the early 1980s the Brown University student body voted to have cyanide tablets in every student's dormitory in case of a nuclear holocaust. Much was made at the time regarding the resignation, futility, and passivity associated with the Brown student body's response. The reasons for this passive response need to be engaged in the classroom as a part of any discussion of the doomsday perspective.

The response to the doomsday view need not be resignation, futility, or passivity. C. B. Macpherson, for one, believes that environmental awareness and concern about the future of the planet may well inspire the larger citizenry to get more involved politically, especially at the grass roots. In this way, environmental problems may well inspire a more participatory democratic society. Writing in the late 1970s, Macpherson contends that more people are recognizing the deleterious environmental consequences associated with economic growth, such as pollution, "the depletion of natural resources and the likelihood of irreversible ecological damage" (Macpherson 1977, 102). To Macpherson recognizing that these problems are associated with economic growth is one of several conditions that must be met if a more participatory democratic society is to be achieved.

Macpherson's analysis is important and worthwhile to share with students for several reasons. It allows students to connect the broader values of Western society with environmental policy making and citizenship. In doing so, students will be forced to confront their roles as global citizens as well as their responsibilities as citizens within the American political system. Finally, Macpherson's analysis enables important connections to be made between democratic theory and environmental policy. The following questions might be addressed: Who makes global environmental policy? Who *should* make global environmental policy? Who makes environmental policy in the United States? Who should have the most say in formulating U.S. environmental policy? Should the citizenry be more active in environmental policy making and in policy implementation? If so, how? What are the barriers to citizen participation in environmental decision making and policy implementation? Can the barriers be overcome? If so, how? What are the arguments against having citizens be more active in environmental decision making? What are concrete examples of environmental organizations at the grass roots that adhere to participatory democratic principles? These are just some of the rich questions that I have asked students to consider as they respond to the doomsday, apocalyptic perspective.

Much attention should be focused, as well, on global inequities in the distribution of property, wealth, and resources and how these inequities structure and affect people's lives. As we know, the dooms-day perspective largely ignores these concerns. To the extent that it does, it neglects an element of the global condition. Instead, the dooms-day view merely embraces the language of scarcity. Students should be given an opportunity to break out of the scarcity paradigm and explore ways to redistribute the world's resources in a more equitable manner.

Finally, it seems to me that students should confront a paradox, one that is not unique to America, but one that is surely prominent in the United States. Lawrence Buell describes the paradox.

> For more than a century the United States has been at once a nature-loving and resource consuming-nation.... The earth's most suburbanized citizens, we like being surrounded by greenery but ig-nore our reliance on toxic substances that increase the comfort of our surroundings until waste disposal becomes a local issue—whereupon we are relieved when the incinerator gets built in the less affluent and politically weaker county fifty miles downwind. (Buell 1995, 4)

A discussion of this paradox is important because it enables students to address important questions pertaining to the sources of American attitudes and values regarding the environment as well as compelling issues of environmental justice. They can then interrogate broader values growing out of the American political culture and connect these values to political, social, and economic change affecting our plan-etary future. I have found, as well, that discussion of the paradox enables students to reflect upon their lives critically as they confront their relationships to the planet.

In the end, the most valuable response that educators can have to the doomsday, apocalyptic perspective is our daily work in the class-room and in curriculum development. In the past twenty years, we have made progress at all levels of education in asking the young to confront the true meaning of economic growth, the sources of our belief that "human domination is good," and the notion that material acquisition and progress is crucial for a productive society (Orr 1994, 32). But we still have much work to do as we ask our students to challenge the underlying assumptions of the doomsday, apocalyptic perspective. In doing so, we will ask students to challenge years of political socialization and ultimately focus their attention on what it truly means to be a citizen.

Works Cited
Index

Works Cited

ABC News. 1993. U.S. Department of State news conference. Feb. 10.

Abernethy, V. 1979. *Population Pressure and Cultural Adjustment.* N.Y.: Human Sciences Press (Plenum Press).

———. 1993. *Population Politics: The Choices That Shape Our Future.* N.Y.: Plenum Press/Insight Books.

———. December 1994a. "Optimism and Overpopulation." *Atlantic Monthly* (Dec.): 84–91.

———. 1994b. "Asclepian Perspective on Immigration: First Do No Harm." *National Geographic Research and Exploration* 10, no. 4: 379–83.

Abler, Thomas A. 1992. "Beavers and Muskets: Iroquois Military Fortunes in the Face of European Colonization." In *War in the Tribal Zone: Expanding States and Indigenous Warfare,* edited by R. Brian Ferguson and Neil L. Whitehead, 151–74. Sante Fe: School of American Research Press.

Abramson, Paul R., and Ronald Inglehart. 1995. *Value Change in Global Perspective.* Ann Arbor: Univ. of Michigan Press.

Adelman, Howard. 1995. "Preventing Genocide: The Case of Rwanda." Paper presented to the first meeting, Association of Genocide Scholars, Williamsburg, Va., June 14–16.

Ahlburg, D. A., and J. W. Vaupel. 1990. "Alternative Projections of the U.S. Population." *Demography* 27, no. 4: 639–47.

Ahluwalia, Montek S. 1976. "Income Distribution and Development: Some Stylized Facts." *American Economic Review* 66: 128–35.

Aklaev, Airat. 1992. "War and Social Stress and Their Effects on the Nationalities in the U.S.S.R." In *Effects of War on Society,* edited by G. Ausenda, 194–210. San Marino: Center for Interdisciplinary Research on Social Stress.

American Psychiatric Association. 1987. *Diagnostic and Statistical Manual of Mental Disorders.* 3d ed. Washington, D.C.

Arendt, Hannah. 1958a. *The Human Condition.* Chicago: Univ. of Chicago Press.

———. 1958b. *The Origins of Totalitarianism.* Cleveland: The World Publishing Company.

Arens, Richard, ed. 1976. *Genocide in Paraguay.* Philadelphia: Temple Univ. Press.

Arrow, Kenneth, Bert Bolin, Robert Costanza, Partha Dasqupta, Carl Folke, C. S. Holling, Bengt-Owe Jansson, Simon Levin, Karl-Göran Maler, Charles Perrings, and David Pimentel. 1995. "Economic Growth, Carrying Capacity, and the Environment." *Science* 268: 520–21.

Ashley, R. 1980. *The Political Economy of War and Peace.* London: Pinter Nichols.

Attali, Jacques. 1991. *Millennium: Winners and Losers in the Coming World Order.* New York: Random House.

Ausenda, G., ed. 1992. *Effects of War on Society.* San Marino: Center for Interdisciplinary Research on Social Stress.

Averitt, P. 1969. *Coal Measures of the United States.* Washington, D.C.: U.S. Geological Survey Bulletin 1275.

Baer, G. 1964. *Population and Society in the Arab East.* New York: Praeger.

Bahn, Paul, and John Flenley. 1992. *Easter Island, Earth Island.* New York: Thames and Hudson.

Bailey, Ronald. 1993. *Eco-Scam: The False Prophets of Ecological Apocalypse.* New York: St. Martin's Press.

Barnet, Richard, and John Cavanagh. 1994. *Global Dreams: Imperial Corporations and the New World Order.* New York: Simon and Schuster.

Bartlet, Albert, and Edward P. Lytwak. 1995. "Zero Growth of the Population of the United States." In *Population and Environment* 16, no. 5: 415–28.

Baumeister, R. 1987. "How the Self Became a Problem." *Journal of Personality and Social Psychology* 52: 163–76.

Baumgardner, S., and L. Rappoport. 1994. "Is There a Postmodern Personality?" Unpublished manuscript.

Bayart, Jean-François. 1993. *The State in Africa.* Translated by Mary Harper, Christopher and Elizabeth Harrison. London: Longman.

Becker, Elizabeth. 1986. *When the War Was Over: Cambodia's Revolution and the Voices of Its People.* New York: Simon and Schuster.

Begley, Sharon. 1993. "Chain Reaction." *Newsweek* (July 12): 50–51.

Bello, Walden, with Shea Cunningham and Bill Rau. 1994. *Dark Victory: The United States, Structural Adjustment, and Global Poverty.* London: Pluto Press, for Institute for Food and Development Policy, or Food First.

Berger, P., B. Berger, and H. Kellner. 1974. *The Homeless Mind.* New York: Vintage Books.

Bernstein, Aaron. 1994. "Inequality: How the Gap Between Rich and Poor Hurts the Economy." *Business Week* (Aug. 15): 78–83.

Bézy, Fernand. 1990. *Rwanda. Bilan Socio-Économique d'un Régime, 1962–1989.* Louvain-la-Neuve, France: Institut d'Étude des Pays en Développement.

Block, Robert. 1994. "The Tragedy of Rwanda." *New York Review of Books* 41, no. 17: 3–8.

Blumberg, Paul. 1980. *Inequality in an Age of Decline.* New York: Oxford Univ. Press.

Bodley, John H. 1982. *Victims of Progress.* 2d ed. Palo Alto, Calif.: Mayfield Publishing Company.

Bokris, J. 1975 *Energy: The Solar Hydrogen Alternative.* Sydney, Australia: ANZ Book Co.

Bollen, Kenneth A. 1979. "Political Democracy and the Timing of Development." *American Sociological Review* 44: 572–87.

Bollen, Kenneth A., and Robert W. Jackman. 1985a. "Economic and Noneconomic Determinants of Political Democracy in the 1960s." *Research in Political Sociology* 1: 27–48.

———. 1985b. "Political Democracy and the Size Distribution of Income." *American Sociological Review* 50: 438–57.

Bonar, J. 1966. *Malthus and His Work.* 1924. Reprint. London: Frank Cass and Co.

———. 1992. *Theories of Population from Raleigh to Arthur Young.* 1931. Reprint. Bristol, England: Thoemmes Press.

Bonte, Pierre. 1991. " 'To Increase Cows, God Created the King': The Function of Cattle in Intralacustrine Societies." In *Herders, Warriors, and Traders,* edited by John G. Galaty and Pierre Bonte. Boulder, Colo.: Westview.

Boone, G. 1995. "Personality Multiplicity: Developmental Antecedents and Behavioral Implications." Doctoral thesis, Kansas State Univ.

Borjas, George. 1995. "Know the Flow." *National Review* (Apr. 17): 44–49.

Borjas, George, and R. B. Freeman. 1992. *The Economic Effects of Immigration in Source and Receiving Countries.* Chicago: Univ. of Chicago Press.

Bouvier, Leon. 1995. "More African Famines in the Future: Lessons for the U.S." *Bulletin* 5, no. 2: 1–3. Washington, D.C.: Carrying Capacity Network.

Bradsher, Keith. 1995. "U.S. Ranks First in Economic Inequality." *International Herald Tribune* (Apr. 18): 1.

Braeckman, Colette. 1994. *Rwanda: Histoire d'un Génocide.* Paris: Fayard.

Braun, Joachim von, Hartwig de Haen, and Jürgen Blanken. 1991. *Commercialization of Agriculture under Population Pressure: Effects on Production, Consumption, and Nutrition in Rwanda.* International Food Policy Research Institute: Research Report 85.

Breyman, Steve. 1993. "Knowledge as Power: Ecology Movements and Global Environmental Problems." In *The State and Social Power* in *Global Environmental Politics,* edited by Ronnie Lipschultz and Ken Conca. New York: Columbia Univ. Press.

Briggs, V. M., Jr. 1990. "Testimony Before the U.S. House of Representatives Judiciary Committee Subcommittee on Immigration, Refugees, and International Law." *Congressional Record* (Mar. 13).

———. 1992. *Mass Migration and the National Interest.* Armonk, N.Y.: M. E. Sharpe, Inc.

Brittain, Victoria. 1994. "The Continent That Lost Its Way." In *Global Issues,* edited by Robert M. Jackson 150–52. Guilford, Conn.: Dushkin Publishing.

Brown, Lester R. 1980. *Building a Sustainable Society.* New York: W. W. Norton.

———. 1990, 1991. *The State of the World.* Washington, DC: Worldwatch Institute.

———. "Nature's Limits." 1995. In *State of the World,* edited by Lester Brown et al., 3–20. New York: W. W. Norton.

Brown, Lester R., Christopher Flavin, and Sandra Postel. 1991. *Saving the Planet: How to Shape an Environmentally Sustainable Global Economy.* New York: W. W. Norton.

Brown, Lester R., et al. 1990. *State of the World.* New York: W. W. Norton.

Brown, Lester R., and Hal Kane. 1994. *Full House: Reassessing the Earth's Population Carrying Capacity.* New York: W. W. Norton.

Browne, Albert N. 1995. "Letters." *Dollars and Sense.* Bureau of the Census 1995. U.S. Population Projections. Washington, D.C.: Government Printing Office.

Browning, Christopher. 1992. "Nazi Ghettoization Policy in Poland, 1939–1941." In *The Path to Genocide: Essays on Launching the Final Solution.* Cambridge: Cambridge Univ. Press.

Brulle, Robert J. 1995. *Agency, Democracy, and the Environment: An Examination of U.S. Environmental Movement Organizations from the Perspective of Critical theory.* Ph.D. diss., George Washington Univ.

Bryden, Matthew. 1995. "Somalia: The Wages of Failure." *Current History* 94, no. 591 (Apr.): 145–51.

Buell, Lawrence. 1995. *The Environmental Imagination: Thoreau, Nature Writing, and the Formation of American Culture.* Cambridge, Mass.: Harvard Univ. Press.

Bunker, Stephen G. 1987. *Peasants Against the State.* Urbana: Univ. of Illinois Press.

Bureau of the Census. 1995. U.S. Population Projections. Washington, D.C.: Government Printing Office.

Cetron, Marvin J., and Owen Davies. 1994. "The Future Face of Terrorism." *The Futurist* (Nov./Dec.): 10–15.

Chabal, Patrick. 1992. *Power in Africa.* New York: St. Martin's Press.

Chafe, William H. 1995. "Providing Guarantees of Equal Opportunity." *The Chronicle of Higher Education* (June 30): B1.

Chagnon, Napoleon. 1968. *Yanomamö: The Fierce People.* New York: Holt, Rinehart and Winston.

———. 1974. *Studying the Yanomamö.* New York: Holt, Rinehart and Winston.

Chan, Steve. 1989. "Income Inequality among LDCs: A Comparative Analysis of Alternative Perspectives." *International Studies Quarterly* 33: 45–65.

Chapman, P. 1976. *Fuel's Paradise*. Harmondsworth, England: Penguin.

Chapman, P., and F. Roberts. 1983. *Metal Resources and Energy*. London: Butterworths.

Chase-Dunn, D. 1980. *Global Formation*. Cambridge, England: Blackwell.

Chatterjee, Pratap, and Matthias Finger. 1994. *The Earth Brokers: Power, Politics, and World Development*. New York: Routledge.

———. 1994. "The Tragedy of Haiti." In *The Haiti Files: Decoding the Crisis*, edited by James Ridgeway, 5–15. Washington, D.C.: Essential Books.

Chomsky, Noam. 1994. *World Orders Old and New*. New York: Columbia Univ. Press.

Chossudovsky, Michel. 1995. "IMF–World Bank Policies and the Rwandan Holocaust." Published on-line by Third World Network Features, Malaysia. E-mail: twn@igc.apc.org. Jan. 28.

Chrétien, Jean-Pierre. 1985. "Hutu et Tutsi au Rwanda et au Burundi." In *Au Cour de l'Ethnie: Ethnies, Tribalisme et État en Afrique*, edited by Jean-Loup Amselle and Elikia M'bokolo. Paris: Éditions la Découverte.

Clark, M. E. 1989. *Ariadne's Thread*. New York: St. Martin's Press.

Cleaver, Kevin M. 1993. "A Strategy to Develop Agriculture in sub-Saharan Africa and a Focus for the World Bank." Washington, D.C.: The World Bank. World Bank Technical Paper no. 203, Africa Technical Department Series.

Colburn, David R. 1993. " 'Cincinnati Factor' vs. Florida Identity." *Orlando Sentinel* (May 2): G-3.

Coleman, James S. 1988. "Social Capital in the Creation of Human Capital." *American Journal of Sociology* 94: 95–120.

———. 1990. *Foundations of Social Theory*. Cambridge, Mass.: Harvard Univ. Press.

Connelly, Matthew, and Paul Kennedy. 1994. "Must It Be the Rest Against the West?" In *Atlantic Monthly* 274 (Dec.): 61–83.

Conquest, Robert. 1986. *The Harvest of Sorrow: Soviet Collectivization and the Terror-Famine*. New York: Oxford Univ. Press.

Corning, P. A. 1993. *The Synergism Hypothesis*. New York: McGraw-Hill.

Coupez, André, and Marcel d'Hertefelt. 1964. *La Royauté Sacrée de l'Ancien Rwanda: Texte, Traduction, et Commentaire de Son Rituel*. Tervuren: Musée Royal de l'Afrique Centrale.

Creveld, Martin van. 1991. *The Transformation of War*. New York: The Free Press.

Crossette, Barbara. 1995. "U.N. Parley Ponders Ways to Stretch Scarce Aid Funds." *New York Times* (Mar. 7): A6.

Cushman, P. 1990. "Why the Self is Empty: Towards a Historically Situated Psychology." *American Psychologist* 45: 599–611.

Cutright, Phillips. 1963. "National Political Development: Measurement and Analysis." *American Sociological Review* 28: 253–64.

Cypher, J. M. 1981. "The Basic Economics of Rearming America." *Monthly Review* (Nov): 16–18.

Daly, Herman E. 1977. *Steady State Economics: The Economics of Biophysical Equilibrium and Moral Growth.* San Francisco: Freeman.

———. 1992. *Steady-State Economics.* 2d ed., London: Earthscan.

Daly, Herman, and J. Cobb. 1989. *For the Common Good.* London: Greenprint.

Dasgupta, Partha. 1995. "Population, Poverty, and the Local Environment." *Scientific American* 272: 40–45.

Davidson, Ronald C. 1994. "Fusion Dreams: Plugging in the Planet." *Washington Post* (May 10).

Davies, James C., ed. 1971. *When Men Revolt and Why.* New York: The Free Press.

Davis, Shelton H. 1977. *Victims of the Miracle: Development and the Indians of Brazil.* Cambridge: Cambridge Univ. Press.

Davis, K. 1951. *The Population of India and Pakistan.* Princeton, N.J.: Princeton Univ. Press.

DeBerry, S. T. 1993. *Quantum Psychology: Steps to a Postmodern Ecology of Being.* Westport, Conn.: Praeger.

Des Forges, Alison L. 1972. *Defeat Is the Only Bad News: Rwanda under Musiinga, 1896–1931.* Ph.D. diss., Yale Univ.

———. 1986. " 'The Drum Is Greater Than the Shout': The 1912 Rebellion in Northern Rwanda." In *Banditry, Rebellion, and Social Protest in Africa,* edited by Donald Crummey, 311–31.

Diamond, Larry. 1992. "Economic Development and Democracy Reconsidered." In *Reexamining Democracy: Essays in Honor of Seymour Martin Lipset,* edited by G. Marks and Larry Diamond, 93–139. Newbury, Calif.: Sage.

Diamond, Larry, Juan Linz, and Seymour Martin Lipset, eds. 1990. *Politics in Developing Countries: Comparing Experiences with Democracy.* Boulder, Colo.: Lynne Rienner.

Dicksinson, William B. 1995. "Twin Specters: Population and Displaced People." *Newsletter* (Feb. 1). Lawrence, Kans.

Dilworth, C. 1994. "Two Perspectives on Sustainable Development." *Population and Environment* 15: 441–67. Also published as Appendix 6 in *Scientific Progress* by C. Dilworth. 3d ed. Dordrecht, Netherlands: Kluwer.

———. 1995. *The Metaphysics of Science.* Dordrecht, Netherlands: Kluwer.

Dolot, Miron. 1985. *Execution by Hunger: The Hidden Holocaust.* New York: W. W. Norton and Company.

Dorsey, Learthen. 1994. *Historical Dictionary of Rwanda.* Metuchen, N.J.: The Scarecrow Press.

Douthwaite, R. 1992. *The Growth Illusion.* Devon, England. Green Books.

Dregne, Harold. 1989. *World Agriculture Situation and Outlook Report.* Washington, D.C.: U.S. Department of Agriculture, Economic Research Service.

Drucker, Peter. 1993. *Post-Capitalist Society*. New York: Harper.

Duchin, Faye, and Glen-Marie Lange. 1994. *The Economy and the Environment*. New York: Oxford Univ. Press.

Duncan, J., and R. Swanson. 1965. *Organic-Rich Shale of the US World Land Areas*. U.S. Geological Survey Circular 523. Washington, D.C.

Dunlap, Riley. 1993. "Global Concern for the Environment." *Environment, Technology, and Society*. no. 70 (winter): 1–11.

Early, Gerald. 1995. "Super Fly Meets Our Daily Bread." *Hungry Mind Review*. no. 33 (spring): 7.

Easterlin, R. 1976. "Does Money Buy Happiness?" In *Current Issues in the American Economy*, edited by R. C. Puth. Lexington, Mass., Health.

Eckstein, Harry, ed. 1964. *Internal War*. New York: The Free Press.

Edwards, R. Dudley, and T. Desmond Williams, eds. 1957. *The Great Famine: Studies in Irish History 1845–52*. New York: New York Univ. Press.

Ehrenfeld, David. 1978. *The Arrogance of Humanism*. New York: Oxford Univ. Press.

Ehrenreich, Frederick. 1982. "National Security." In *Somalia: A Country Study*, edited by Harold D. Nelson, 229–75. Washington, D.C.: Area Handbook Series.

Ehrlich, Paul, and Ann Ehrlich. 1981. *Extinction: The Causes and Consequences of the Disappearance of Species*. New York: Random House.

———. 1990. *The Population Explosion*. New York: Touchstone.

Elliot, Gil. 1972. *Twentieth Century Book of the Dead*. New York: Scribners.

Elliott, D. L., L. L. Wendell, and G. L. Gower. 1991. *An Assessment of the Available Windy Land Area and Wind Energy Potential in the Contiguous United States*. Washington: Pacific Northwest Laboratory.

Ellul, J. 1964. *The Technological Society*. New York: Random House/Vintage Books.

Entessar, Nader. 1993. "Azeri Nationalism in the Former Soviet Union and Iran." In *The Rising Tide of Cultural Pluralism: The Nation-State at Bay?*, edited by Crawford Young, 116–37. Madison: Univ. of Wisconsin Press.

Enzensberger, Hans Magnus. 1993. *Civil Wars: From Los Angeles to Bosnia*. New York: The New Press.

Erikson, E. 1950. *Childhood and Society*. New York: W. W. Norton.

Escobar, Arturo. 1995. *Encountering Development: The Making and Unmaking of the Third World*. Princeton, N.J.: Princeton Univ. Press.

Esman, Milton J. 1994. *Ethnic Politics*. Cornell, N.Y.: Cornell Univ. Press.

Estrada, R. 1990. "Less Immigration Helps Hispanics." *The Miami Herald* (July 24): 13A.

———. 1991. "The Impact of Immigration on Hispanic Americans." *Chronicles* (July): 24–28.

Etzold, Thomas H., and John Lewis Gaddis, eds. 1978. *Containment: Documents on American Policy and Strategy, II 1945–1950*. New York: Columbia Univ. Press.

Farmer, Paul. 1994. *The Uses of Haiti*. Monroe, Maine: Common Courage Press.

Fatton, Robert, Jr. 1992. *Predatory Rule: State and Civil Society in Africa*. Boulder, Colo.: Lynne Rienner Publishers.

Fein, Helen. 1993. "Accounting for Genocide after 1945: Theories and Some Findings." *International Journal on Group Rights* 1: 79–106.

———. 1993. *Genocide: A Sociological Study*. London: Sage Publications.

Ferguson, R. Brian. 1992. "A Savage Encounter: Western Contact and the Yanomami War Complex." In *War in the Tribal Zone: Expanding States and Indigenous Warfare*, edited by R. Brian Ferguson and Neil L. Whitehead, 199–227. Santa Fe: School of American Research Press.

———. 1995a. *Yanomami Warfare: A Political History*. Sante Fe: School of American Research Press.

———. 1995b. "(Mis)understanding Resource Scarcity and Cultural Difference in Contemporary Conflict." *Anthropology Newsletter* 36, no. 8 (in press).

Ferguson, R. Brian, and Neil L. Whitehead. 1992. "The Violent Edge of Empire." In *War in the Tribal Zone: Expanding States and Indigenous Warfare*, edited by R. Brian Ferguson and Neil L. Whitehead, 1–30. Santa Fe: School of American Research Press.

Fettweis, G. B. 1979. *World Coal Resources*. New York: Elservier.

Finkelstein, J. 1991. *The Fashioned Self*. Philadelphia: Temple Univ. Press.

Finsterbusch, Kurt. 1973. "The Sociology of Nation States: Dimensions, Indicators, and Theory." In *Comparative Social Research: Methodological Problems and Strategies*, edited by Michael Armer and Allen Grimshaw, 417–66. New York: John Wiley and Son.

———. 1983. "Consequences of Increasing Scarcity on Affluent Countries." *Technological Forecasting and Social Change* 23: 59–73.

Firebaugh, Glenn, and Frank D. Beck. 1994. "Does Economic Growth Benefit the Masses." *American Sociological Review* 59, no. 5: 631–53.

Fisher, Glen. 1988. *Mindsets: The Role of Culture and Perception in International Relations*. Yarmouth, Maine: Intercultural Press.

Fiske, S. T. and S. E. Taylor. 1991. *Social Cognition*. New York: McGraw Hill.

Flanigan, William H., and Edwin Fogelman. 1971. "Patterns of Political Development and Democratization: A Quantitative Analysis." In *Macro-Quantitative Analysis: Conflict Development, and Democratization*, edited by J. Gillespie and B. Nesvold. Beverly Hills, Calif.: Sage.

Foley, G. 1976. *The Energy Question*. Harmondsworth, England: Penguin.

Foster, John Bellamy. 1995. "Global Ecology and the Common Good." *Monthly Review* 46, no. 9 (Feb.): 1–10.

———. 1995. "The Self-Organization Approach in Economics." In *Economics and Thermodynamics: New Perspectives on Economic Analysis*, edited by Peter Burley and John Foster. Boston: Kluwer Academic Press.

Frey, William. 1994. *White and Black "Flight" from High Immigration Metro Areas: Evidence from the 1990 Census*. #94-319. Population Studies Center, Univ. of Michigan.

———. 1995. "Immigration and Internal Migration "Flight": A California Case Study." *Population and Environment* 16, no. 4: 353–75.

Freedman, James M. 1974. "Principles of Relationship in Rwandan Kiga Society." Ph.D diss., Princeton Univ.

———. 1979. "East African Peasants and Capitalist Development." In *Challenging Anthropology*, edited by David H. Turner and Gavin A. Smith, 245–60. Toronto: McGraw-Hill.

———. 1984. *Nyabingi: The Social History of an African Divinity*. Tervuren: Musée Royal de l'Afrique Centrale.

French, Hillary. 1995. "Forging a New Global Partnership." In *State of the World 1995*, edited by Lester Brown et al., 170–90. New York: W. W. Norton.

Friedman, Edward. 1993. "Ethnic Identity and De-Nationalism and Democratization of Leninist States." In *The Rising Tide of Cultural Pluralism: The Nation-State at Bay?*, edited by Crawford Young, 222–41. Madison: Univ. of Wisconsin Press.

Friedman, Kajsa Ekholm. 1993. "Afro-Marxism and Its Disastrous Effects on the Economy." In *Economic Crisis in Africa*, edited by Magnus Blomström and Mats Lundahl, 219–45. London: Routledge.

Gagliani, Giorgio. 1987. "Income Inequality and Economic Development." *Annual Review of Sociology* 13: 313–34.

Gardels, Nathan. 1995. "Tide of Globalization." In *New Perspectives Quarterly*, 12 (winter): 2–3.

Garrett, Laurie. 1994. *The Coming Plague: Newly Emerging Diseases in a World Out of Balance*. New York: Farrar, Straus and Giroux.

Geertz, C. 1973. *The Interpretation of Cultures*. New York: Basic Books.

Georgescu-Roegen, Nicholas. 1971. *The Entropy Law and the Economic Process*. Cambridge, Mass.: Harvard Univ. Press.

———. 1976. *Energy and Economic Myths*. New York: Pergamon Press.

Gergen, K. J. 1991. *The Saturated Self*. New York: Basic Books.

Gever, J., A. Kaufman, D. Skole, and C. Vorosmarty. 1986. *Beyond Oil: The Threat to Food and Fuel in the Coming Decades*. Cambridge: Ballinger.

Giarina, Orio, and Henri Louberge. 1978. *The Diminishing Returns of Technology*. Oxford: Pergamon.

Goldin, Claudia. 1993. *The Political Economy of Immigration Restriction in the United States, 1890 to 1921*. NBER Working Paper 4345. Harvard Univ.

Goldsmith, Edward. 1985. "Is Development the Solution or the Problem?" *The Ecologist* 15: 215.

Gore, Al. 1992. *The Earth in Balance: Ecology and the Human Spirit*. Boston: Houghton Mifflin.

Gowdy, John. 1994. *Coevolutionary Economics: Economy, Society, and Environment*. Boston: Kluwer Academic Press.

Gowlett, J. A. J. 1992. *Ascent to Civilization: The Archaeology of Early Humans*. 2d ed. New York: McGraw-Hill.

Grant, Lindsey. 1992. "What We Can Learn from the Missing Airline Passengers." *The NPG Forum.* Teaneck, N.J.: Negative Population Growth.

Gravel, Pierre Bettez. 1968. *Remera: A Community in Eastern Ruanda.* Paris: Mouton.

Gruhn, Isebill. "Collapsed States in Africa." Paper given at the 1995 Meeting of the American Society for Environmental History in Las Vegas.

Guiachaoua, André. 1989. *Destins Paysans et Politiques Agraires en Afrique Centrale.* Vol. 1. Paris: Harmattan.

Gurr, Ted. 1970. *Why Men Rebel.* Princeton, N.J.: Princeton Univ. Press.

———. 1985. "On the Political Consequences of Scarcity and Economic Decline." *International Studies Quarterly* 29: 51–75.

Gutiérrez, Gustavo. 1983. *The Power of the Poor in History.* Translated by Robert Barr. Maryknoll, N.Y.: Orbis.

Haass, Richard N. 1994. *Intervention: The Use of American Military Force in the Post–Cold War World.* Washington, D.C.: Carnegie Endowment.

Hall, D. C., and J. V. Hall. 1984. "Concepts and Measures of Natural Resource Scarcity with a Summary of Recent Trends." *Journal of Environmental Economic Management* 11: 363–79.

———. 1990. "Ethnic Warfare and the Changing Priorities of Global Security." *Mediterranean Quarterly* 1, no. 1: 82–98.

———. 1993a. *Minorities at Risk: A Global View of Ethnopolitical Conflict.* Washington, D.C.: United States Institute of Peace.

———. 1993b. "Why Minorities Rebel: A Global Analysis of Communal Mobilization and Conflict since 1945." *International Political Science Review* 14, no. 2 (April): 161–201.

Hall, Gregory O. 1994. "Ethnic Conflict, Economics, and the Fall of Yugoslavia." *Mediterranean Quarterly* 5, no. 3 (summer): 123–43.

Hardin, G. 1974. "Lifeboat Ethics." In *Environmental Ethics: Readings in Theory and Application,* edited by L. P. Pojman, 283–90.

Harding, Jeremy. 1993. *The Fate of Africa: Trial by Fire.* New York: Simon and Schuster.

Harff, Barbara. 1991. "Humanitarian Intervention in Genocidal Situations." In *Genocide: A Critical Bibliographic Review.* vol. 2, edited by Israel W. Charny, 146–53. New York: Facts on File.

Harper, Charles L. 1996. *Environment and Society: Human Perspectives on Environmental Issues.* Upper Saddle River, N.J.: Prentice Hall.

Hauchler, Ingomar, and Paul Kennedy, eds. 1994. *Global Trends: The World Almanac of Development and Peace.* New York: Continuum Publishing.

Hechter, Michael. 1975. *Internal Colonialism: The Celtic Fringe in British National Development, 1536–1966.* London: Routledge.

Heilbroner, Robert L. 1981. *An Inquiry into the Human Prospect: Updated and Reconsidered for the 1980s.* New York: W. W. Norton.

———. 1991. *An Inquiry into the Human Prospect: Looked at Again for the 1990s.* New York: W. W. Norton.

Hermans, J. M., J. G. Kempen, and R. J. P. Van Loon. 1992. "The Dialogical Self: Beyond Individualism and Rationalism." *American Psychologist* 47: 23–45.

Hill, D. B. 1995. "The Postmodern Reconstruction of Self." Paper presented to the International Society for Theory in Psychology meeting in Ottowa, Canada, May 25.

Hilsum, Lindsey. 1994. "Settling Scores." In *Africa Report* 39, no. 3: 13–17.

Hirsch, Herbert. 1995. *Genocide and the Politics of Memory: Studying Death to Preserve Life.* Chapel Hill, N.C.: Univ. of North Carolina Press.

Hirsch, John L., and Robert B. Oakley. 1995. *Somalia and Operation Restore Hope: Reflections on Peacemaking and Peacekeeping.* Washington, D.C.: United States Institute of Peace.

Hobbes, Thomas. 1960. *Leviathan or the Matter, Form, and Power of a Commonwealth Ecclesiastical and Civil* Reprint. 1651. Oxford: Blackwell.

Holdren, John P. 1991. "Population and the Energy Problem." *Population and Environment* 12, no. 3: 231–56.

Hole, F. 1992. "Origins of Agriculture." In *The Cambridge Encyclopedia of Human Evolution,* edited by S. Jones et al., 373–79.

Homer-Dixon, Thomas F. 1987. *Indigenous Peoples: A Global Quest for Justice.* London: Zed Books Ltd.

———. 1991. "On the Threshold: Environmental Changes as Causes of Acute Conflict." *International Security* 16: 76–116.

———. 1993. "Global Environmental Change and International Security." In *Building a New Global Order: Emerging Trends in International Security,* edited by David Dewitt, David Haglund, and John Kirton, 185–228. New York: Oxford Univ. Press.

———. 1994. "Environmental Scarcities and Violent Conflict: Evidence from Cases." *International Security* 19: 5–40. Independent Commission on International Humanitarian Issues.

Homer-Dixon, Thomas F., Jeffery Boutwell, and George Rathjens. 1993. "Environmental Change and Violent Conflict." *Scientific American* (Feb.): 33–45.

Honan, William. 1995. "Maya: Ecological Doom?" *International Herald Tribune* (Apr. 13): 9.

Hubbert, M. K. 1976. "Outlook for Fuel Resources." In *Encyclopedia of Energy,* edited by D. N. Lapedes. New York: McGraw Hill.

Huddle, D. L. 1992. *Immigration, Jobs, and Wages: The Misuses of Econometrics.* Teaneck, N.J.: Negative Population Growth.

———. 1993. "Dirty Work: Are Immigrants Taking Jobs That the Native Underclass Do Not Want?" *Population and Environment* 14, no. 6: 515–38.

Human Rights Watch. 1992. *Rwanda: Talking Peace and Waging War—Human Rights since the October 1990 Invasion.* New York: Human Rights Watch/Africa, vol. 4, no. 3 (Feb.).

———. 1994a. *Arming Rwanda: The Arms Trade and Human Rights Abuses in the Rwandan War.* New York: Human Rights Watch Arms Project, vol. 6, no. 1. (Jan).

———. 1994b. *Genocide in Rwanda: April–May 1994.* New York: Human Rights Watch/Africa, vol. 6, no. 4 (May).

Hyden, Göran. 1980. *Beyond Ujaama in Tanzania.* Berkeley: Univ. of California Press.

———. 1992. "Governance and the Study of Politics." In *Governance and Politics in Africa,* edited by Göran Hyden and Michael Bratton, 1–26. Boulder, Colo.: Lynne Rienner Publishers.

Ihonvbere, Julius O. 1992. "The Third World and the New World Order." In *Developing World,* edited by Robert J. Griffiths, 6–16. Guilford, Conn.: Dushkin Publishing.

In Context Institute. 1991. *Ecovillage and Sustainable Communities.* Seattle.

Inglehart, Ronald. 1990. *Culture Shift in Advanced Industrial Society.* Princeton, N.J.: Princeton Univ. Press.

———. 1995. "Public Support for Environmental Protection: Objective Problems and Subjective Values in 43 Societies." *PS: Political Science and Politics* 28, no. 1: 57–72.

Inglehart, Ronald, and Paul R. Abramson. 1994. "Economic Security and Value Change." *American Political Science Review* 88, no. 2: 336–54.

Inkeles, Alex, ed. 1991. *On Measuring Democracy: Its Consequences and Concomitants.* New Brunswick, N.J.: Transaction.

Intergovernmental Panel on Climate Change. 1990. *Climate Change: The IPCC Scientific Assessment.* London: Cambridge Univ. Press.

Isaacman, Allen F. 1993. "Peasants and Rural Social Protest in Africa." In *Confronting Historical Paradigms,* 205–317. Madison: Univ. of Wisconsin Press.

Jackman, Robert W. 1975. *Politics and Social Equality.* New York: John Wiley and Sons.

Jakubowska, Longina. 1992. "Resisting 'Ethnicity': The Israeli State and Bedouin Identity." In *The Paths to Domination, Resistance, and Terror,* edited by Carolyn Nordstrom and JoAnn Martin, 85–105. Berkeley: Univ. of California Press.

Jazairy, Idriss, Mohiuddin Alamgir, and Theresa Pannucio. 1992. *The State of World Rural Poverty.* New York: New York Univ. Press.

Jencks, C. 1978. *The Language of Postmodern Architecture.* London: Academy Editions.

Johnson, Chalmers. 1966. *Revolutionary Change.* Boston: Little, Brown.

Johnson, S. P. 1994. *World Population—Turning the Tide.* London: Kluwer.

Jonassohn, Kurt. 1991. "Hunger as a Low Technology Weapon: With Special Reference to Genocide." Montreal: Montreal Institute for Genocide Studies.

Jones, S., et al., eds. 1992. *The Cambridge Encyclopedia of Human Evolution.* Cambridge: Cambridge Univ. Press.

Judt, T. 1995. "Downhill All the Way." *New York Review of Books* (May 25): 20–25.

Kane, Hal. 1995. "The Hour of Departure: Forces That Create Refugees and Migrants." *World Watch Paper* 125 (June): 5–56.

Kaplan, R. D. 1994. "The Coming Anarchy." *Atlantic Monthly* (Feb.): 44–76.

Kassiola, Joel Jay. 1990. *The Death of Industrial Civilization: The Limits to Economic Growth and the Repoliticization of Advanced Industrial Society.* Albany: State Univ. of New York Press.

Kates, Robert, Billie L. Turner II, and William Clark. 1990. "The Great Transformation." In *The Earth as Transformed by Human Action,* edited by Billie Turner et al., 1–18. New York: Cambridge Univ. Press.

Keen, David. 1994. *The Benefits of Famine.* Princeton, N.J.: Princeton Univ. Press.

Kellas, James G. 1991. *The Politics of Nationalism and Ethnicity.* New York: St. Martin's Press.

Kennan, George F. 1993. *Around the Cragged Hill: A Personal and Political Philosophy.* New York: W. W. Norton.

———. 1995. "On American Principles." *Foreign Affairs* 74, no. 2: 116–25.

Kennedy, M. 1988. *Interest- and Inflation-Free Money.* Permaculture.

Kennedy, Paul. 1987. *The Rise and Fall of the Great Powers: Economic Change and Military Conflict from 1500 to 20000.* New York: Random House.

———. 1993. *Preparing for the Twenty-first Century.* New York: Vintage.

Kiely, J. R. 1978. *World Energy: Looking Ahead to 2020,* London: IPC Science and Technology Press.

Kinzer, Stephen. 1993. "Croatia: The Once and Future Battleground?" *New York Times* (Oct. 10): sec. 4.

Kleinman, Arthur, et. al. 1995. *World Mental Health: Problems and Priorities in Low-Income Countries.* New York: Oxford Univ. Press.

Klitgaard, Robert. 1988. *Controlling Corruption.* Berkeley: Univ. of California Press.

———. 1991. *Adjusting to Reality: Beyond State Versus Market in Economic Development.* San Francisco: ICS Press.

Korten, D. C. 1990. *Getting to the Twenty-first Century.* West Hartford, Conn.: Kumarian Press.

Kottak, C. P. 1994. *Anthropology: The Exploration of Human Diversity.* 6th ed. New York: McGraw-Hill.

Kraushaar, J. J., and R. A. Ristinen. 1993. In *Energy and Problems of a Technological Society.* 2d ed. New York: John Wiley and Sons.

Krawchenko, Bohdan. 1986. "The Man-Made Famine of 1932–1933 and Collectivization in Soviet Ukraine." In *Famine in Ukraine, 1932–1933,* edited by Roman Serbyn and Bohdan Krawchenko, 15–25. Edmonton, Alberta: Canadian Institute of Ukrainian Studies, Univ. of Alberta.

Kuper, Leo. 1981. *Genocide: Its Political Use in the Twentieth Century.* New Haven, Conn.: Yale Univ. Press.

———. 1985. *The Prevention of Genocide.* New Haven, Conn.: Yale Univ. Press.

———. 1992. "Reflections on the Prevention of Genocide." In *Genocide Watch,* edited by Helen Fein, 135–61. New Haven, Conn.: Yale Univ. Press.

Kuznets, Simon. 1955. "Economic Growth and Income Inequality." *American Economic Review* 45: 1–28.

———. 1965. "Qualitative Aspects of the Economic Growth of Nations, VIII: Distribution of Income by Size." *Economic Development and Cultural Change* 11, no. 2 (part 2): 1–80.

Kvale, S. 1992. *Psychology and Postmodernism.* California: Sage Publications.

Lafay, Jean-Dominique, Christian Morrisson, and Sébastien Dessus. 1994. "Adjustment Programmes and Politico-Economic Interactions in Developing Countries: Lessons from an Empirical Analysis of Africa in the 1980s." In *From Adjustment to Development in Africa,* edited by Giovanni Andrea Cornia and Gerald K. Helleiner, 174–91. New York: St. Martin's Press.

Lane, Robert E. 1993. "Does Money Buy Happiness?" *The Public Interest* (fall): 56–65.

Laqueur, T. 1993. "Sex and Desire in the Industrial Revolution." In *The Industrial Revolution and British Society,* edited by P. O'Brien and R. Quinault, 100–23.

Latino National Political Survey. 1992. New York: Ford Foundation Program for Governance and Public Policy (Dec. 15).

LeBaron, Alan. 1993. "The Creation of the Modern Maya." In *The Rising Tide of Cultural Pluralism: The Nation-State at Bay?,* edited by Crawford Young, 265–84. Madison: Univ. of Wisconsin Press.

Lecaillon, Jacques, et al. 1984. *Income Distribution and Economic Development: An Analytical Survey.* Geneva: International Labor Office.

Lee, Ronald D. 1980. "A Historical Perspective on Economic Aspects of the Population Explosion: The Case of Preindustrial England." In *Population and Economic Change in Developing Countries,* edited by R. E. Easterlin, 517–56. Chicago: Univ. of Chicago Press.

———. 1987. "Population Dynamics of Humans and Other Animals." *Demography* 24, no. 4 (Nov.): 443–65.

Lemarchand, René, and David Martin. 1974. *Selective Genocide in Burundi.* London: Minority Rights Group.

———. 1989. "African Peasantries, Reciprocity, and the Market." In *Cahiers d'Études Africaines* 29 (1), no. 113: 33–67.

————. 1994. *Burundi: Ethnocide as Discourse and Practice*. Cambridge: Cambridge Univ. Press.

Lemonick, Michael D. 1994. "Could a Free-lancer Build a Bomb?" *Time* (Aug. 29): 48–49.

Lenski, Gerhard. 1966. *Power and Privilege: A Theory of Social Stratification*. Chapel Hill: Univ. of North Carolina Press.

Lenski, Gerhard, Jean Lenski, and Patrick D. Nolan. 1991. *Human Societies: An Introduction to Macrosociology*. 6th ed. New York: McGraw-Hill.

————. 1995. *Human Societies*. 7th ed. New York: McGraw-Hill.

Levi, Primo. 1989. *The Mirror Maker*. New York: Schocken.

Lewis, Bernard. 1958. "Some Reflections on the Decline of the Ottoman Empire." *Studia Islamica* 9: 111–27.

Lifton, R. J. 1986. *The Nazi Doctors: Medical Killing and the Psychology of Genocide*. New York: Basic Books.

————. 1993. *The Protean Self*. New York: Basic Books.

Lifton, R. J., and E. Markusen. 1990. *The Genocidal Mentality*. New York: Basic Books.

Lindert, Peter H., and Jeffrey G. Williamson. 1985. "Growth Equity and History." *Explorations in Economic History* 22: 341–77.

Ling-Ling, Yeh. 1995. "U.S. Can't Handle Today's Tide of Immigrants." *Christian Science Monitor* (Mar. 23): 19.

Linville, P. W. 1985. "Self-Complexity and Affective Extremity." *Social Cognition* 3: 94–120.

————. 1987. "Self-Complexity as a Cognitive Buffer Against Stress-Related Illnesses and Depression." *Journal of Personality and Social Psychology* 52: 663–76.

Lipieta, Alain. 1992. *Towards a New Economic Order: Post-Fordism, Ecology, and Democracy*. New York: Oxford Univ. Press.

Lipset, Seymour Martin. 1960. *Political Man*. New York: Doubleday.

————. 1978. "Growth, Affluence, and the Limits of Futurology." In *From Abundance to Scarcity: Implications for the American Tradition*, by Kenneth E. Boulding, Michael Kammen, and Seymour Martin Lipset. Columbus: Ohio State Univ. Press.

————. 1994. "The Social Requisites of Democracy Revisited." *American Sociological Review* 59, no. 1: 1–22.

Lipset, Seymour Martin, Kyoung-Ryung Seong, and John Charles Torres. 1993. "A Comparative Analysis of the Social Requisites of Democracy." *International Social Science Journal* 45: 155–75.

Lonsdale, John. 1986. "Political Accountability in African History." In *Political Domination in Africa: Reflections on the Limits of Power*, edited by Patrick Chabal, 126–57. Cambridge: Cambridge Univ. Press.

Lovins, A. M. 1975. *Soft Energy Paths*. Cambridge, Mass.: Ballinger.

Lydall, Harold. 1989. *Yugoslavia in Crisis*. Oxford: Oxford Univ. Press.

MacArthur, Sir William P. 1957. "Medical History of the Famine." In *The Great Famine: Studies on Irish History 1845–52,* edited by R. Dudley Edwards and T. Desmond Williams, 263–315. New York: New York Univ. Press.

Mace, James E. 1986. "The Man-Made Famine of 1933 in Soviet Ukraine." In *Famine in Ukraine, 1932–1933,* edited by Roman Serbyn and Bohdan Krawchenko, 1–14. Edmonton, Alberta: Canadian Institute of Ukrainian Studies, Univ. of Alberta.

Macpherson, C. B. 1977. *The Life and Times of Liberal Democracy.* Oxford: Oxford Univ. Press.

Malcolm, Noel. 1995. "The Case Against 'Europe'." *Foreign Affairs* 74, no. 2: 52–61.

Malthus, T. R. 1970. *An Essay on the Principle of Population and a Summary View of the Principle of Population.* 1798. Reprint. Harmondsworth, England: Penguin Books.

Manabe, Syukuro, and Ronald Stouffer. 1993. "Century-Scale Effects of Increased Atmospheric CO_2 on the Ocean-Atmosphere System." *Nature* 364: 215–18.

Maquet, Jacques J. 1954. *Le Système des Relations Sociales dans le Ruanda Ancien.* Tervuren: Annales du Musée Royal du Congo Belge.

Maquet, Jacques J. 1961. *The Premise of Inequality in Ruanda.* London: Oxford Univ. Press.

Markus, H., and P. Nurius. 1986. "Possible Selves." *American Psychologist* 41: 954–69.

Marshak, R. J. 1995. "Managing in Chaotic Times." In *Managing in the Age of Change,* edited by R. A. Ritro and A. H. Litwin, 58–66. New York: NTL Institute.

Marshall, Jonathan. 1995. "How Immigrants Affect the Economy." *San Francisco Chronicle* (Jan. 9): B3.

Martin, Marie Alexander. 1994. *Cambodia: A Shattered Society.* Berkeley: Univ. of California Press.

Marx, Anthony W. 1993. "Contested Images and Implications of South African Nationhood." In *The Violence Within: Cultural and Political Opposition in Divided Nations,* edited by Kay B. Warren, 157–79. Boulder, Colo.: Westview.

Mathews, Jessica Tuchman. 1991. "The Implications for U.S. Policy." In *Preserving the Global Environment,* edited by Jessica Tuchman Mathews. New York: W. W. Norton.

———. 1994. "Today's Catch—and Tomorrow's." *Washington Post* (Mar. 13).

Mayumi, Kozo. 1993. "Development, Ecological Degradation, and North-South Trade." Proceedings of the International Conference: Training of Experts for European Cooperation on Protection of the Environment and Promotion of Sustainable Development. Krakow, Poland: University of Mining and Metallurgy.

Mayur, Rashmi. 1985. "Supercities: The Growing Crisis." *The Futurist* (Aug.): 27–30.

McCracken, P. W. 1991. "The Big Domestic Issue: Slow Growth." *Wall Street Journal* (Oct. 4): A14.

McKibben, Bill. 1989. *The End of Nature*. New York: Random House.

Meadows, Dennis H., and J. Randers. 1972. *The Limits to Growth*. London: Earth Island.

Meadows, D. H., et al. 1992. *Beyond the Limits: Global Collapse or a Sustainable Future*. London: Earthscan.

Melson, Robert F. 1992. *Revolution and Genocide: On the Origins of the Armenian Genocide and the Holocaust*. Chicago: Univ. of Chicago Press.

Meyer, R. F., ed. 1977. *The Future Supply of Nature Made Petroleum and Gas*. New York: Pergamon.

Midlarsky, Manus I. 1982. "Scarcity and Inequality: Prologue to the Onset of Mass Revolution." *Journal of Conflict Resolution* 26, no. 1: 3–38.

———, ed. 1992. *The Internationalization of Communal Strife*. London: Routledge.

Migdal, Joel. 1988. *Strong Societies and Weak States*. Princeton, N.J.: Princeton Univ. Press.

Milbrath, Lester W. 1989. *Envisioning a Sustainable Society: Learning Our Way Out*. Albany: State Univ. of New York Press.

Miles, Jack. 1992. "Blacks vs. Browns." *Atlantic Monthly* (Oct.): 41–68.

Miles, Rufus E., Jr. 1976. *Awakening from the American Dream: The Social and Political Limits to Growth*. New York: Universe Books.

Millikan, Max F., and Walt W. Rostow. 1957. *A Proposal*. New York: Harper.

Mishel, Laurence, and Jared Bernstein. 1995. *The State of Working America*. Washington, D.C.: Economic Policy Institute.

Morales, Waltraud Q. 1973–74. *Social Revolution: Theory and Historical Application*. Denver: Univ. of Denver Monograph Series in World Affairs 11, no. 1.

———. 1995. "Caribbean Intervention—Then and Now: The Case of Haiti." *South Eastern Latin Americanist* 38, no. 3 (winter): 25–40.

Morris, E. 1990. "Testimony Before the U.S. House of Representatives Judiciary Committee Subcommittee on Immigration, Refugees, and International Law." *Congressional Record* (Mar. 13).

Morris, Frank L., Jr. 1995. "Illegal Immigration and African American Opportunities. Testimony Before the U.S. House of Representatives Judiciary Committee Subcommittee on Immigration and Claims." *Congressional Record* (Apr. 5).

Mpélé, Jean P. E. 1993. "High Stakes in Brazzaville." In *International Viewpoint* no. 246 (June): 33–35.

Mugenyi, Joshua B. 1991. "IMF Conditionality and Structural Adjustment under the National Resistance Movement." In *Changing Uganda*, edited by Holger Bernt Hansen and Michael Twaddle, 61–77. London: James Currey.

Muller, Edward N. 1988. "Democracy, Economic Development, and Income Inequality." *American Sociological Review*. 53, no. 1: 50–68.

Mumford, L. 1967. *The Myth of the Machine, Vol. 1: Technics and Human Development.* San Diego: Harcourt Brace Jovanovich.

Murdock, Steve H. 1995. *America Challenged: Population Change and the Future of the United States.* Austin: Univ. of Texas Press.

Murray, Sir James. 1994. "Rwanda's Bloody Roots." *New York Times* (Sept. 3).

Mutibwa, Phares. 1992. *Uganda since Independence: A Story of Unfulfilled Hopes.* Trenton, N.J.: Africa World Press.

Myrdal, Gunnar. 1956. *An International Economy.* London: Routledge.

Nelan, Bruce W. 1994. "Formula for Terror." *Time* (Aug. 29): 46–51.

Nelson, Gene. 1994. "How Has Science and Engineering Been Ruined as a Career?" *American Engineer* 4, no. 4.

Nelson, Harold D., ed. 1982. *Somalia: A Country Study.* Washington, D.C.: Area Handbook Series.

Nelson, Joan M. 1990. *Economic Crisis and Policy Choice.* Princeton, N.J.: Princeton Univ. Press.

Nettleship, R. A. 1975. *War: Its Causes and Correlates.* The Hague: Mouton.

Neubauer, Deane. 1967. "Some Conditions of Democracy." *American Sociological Review* 61: 1002–9.

Newbury, Catharine. 1988. *The Cohesion of Oppression: Clientship and Ethnicity in Rwanda, 1860–1960.* New York: Columbia Univ. Press.

———. 1992. "Rwanda: Recent Debates over Governance and Rural Development." In *Governance and Politics in Africa,* edited by Göran Hyden and Michael Bratton, 193–220. Boulder, Colo.: Lynne Rienner Publishers.

Newman, James L. 1995. *The Peopling of Africa: A Geographic Interpretation.* New Haven, Conn.: Yale Univ. Press.

Norgaard, Richard B. 1994. *Development Betrayed.* New York: Routledge.

O'Brien, P., and R. Quinault, eds. 1993. *The Industrial Revolution and British Society.* Cambridge: Cambridge Univ. Press.

O'Connor, James. 1994. "Is Sustainable Capitalism Possible?" In *Is Capitalism Sustainable,* edited by Martin O'Connor, 152–75. New York: The Guilford Press.

Oldeman, L. R., et al. 1991. *World Map of the Status of Human-Induced Soil Degradation.* Wageningen, Netherlands: United Nations Environment Programme and International Soil Reference and Information Centre.

Olsen, Marvin E. 1968. "Multivariate Analysis of National Political Development." *American Sociological Review* 33: 699–712.

Olson, Mancur. 1965. *The Logic of Collective Action: Public Goods and the Theory of Groups.* Cambridge, Mass.: Harvard Univ. Press.

———. 1982. *The Rise and Decline of Nations.* New Haven, Conn.: Yale Univ. Press.

Omaar, Rakiya, and Alex de Waal. 1994. *Rwanda: Death, Despair, and Defiance.* London: African Rights.

———. 1995. "The Genocide in Rwanda and the International Response." In *Current History* 95, no. 591 (Apr.): 156–61.

O'Neill, Thomas P. 1957. "Organization and Administration of Relief, 1845–52." In *The Great Famine: Studies in Irish History 1845–52,* edited by R. Dudley Edwards and T. Desmond Williams, 209–59. New York: New York Univ. Press.

Ophuls, William. 1977. *Ecology and the Politics of Scarcity.* New York: W. H. Freeman.

Ophuls William, and A. Stephen Boyan, Jr. 1992. *Ecology and the Politics of Scarcity Revisited: The Unraveling of the American Dream.* New York: W. H. Freeman and Company.

Orlando Sentinel. 1995. Apr. 21, A-14.

Orr, David. 1994. *Earth in Mind.* Washington, D.C.: Island Press.

Parker, Geoffrey. 1988. *The Military Revolution: Military Innovation and the Rise of the West, 1500–1800.* Cambridge: Cambridge Univ. Press.

Perrings, Charles. 1995. "Conservation of Mass and the Time Behavior of Ecological-Economic Systems." In *Economics and Thermodynamics: New Perspectives on Economic Analysis,* edited by Peter Burley and John Foster. Boston: Kluwer Academic Press.

Petrella, Ricardo. 1995. "A Global Agora vs. Gated City-Regions." In *New Perspectives Quarterly* 12 (winter).

Pfaff, William. 1995. "A New Colonialism?" In *Foreign Affairs* 74, no. 1 (Jan./Feb.): 2–6.

Pimentel, David C. Harvey, P. Resosudarmo, K. Sinclair, D. Kurz, M. McNair, S. Crist, I. Shpritz, L. Fitton, R. Saffouri, and R. Blair. 1995. "Environmental and Economic Costs of Soil Erosion and Conservation Benefits." *Science* 267 (Feb.24): 1117–23.

———. 1994. "Natural Resources and an Optimum Human Population." *Population and Environment* 15, no. 5 (May).

Pirages, Dennis C., and Paul R. Ehrlich. 1974. *Ark II: Social Response to Environmental Imperatives.* San Francisco: W. H. Freeman.

Pojman, L. P., ed. 1994. *Environmental Ethics: Readings in Theory and Application.* Boston: Jones and Bartlett.

Ponting, Clive. 1991. *A Green History of the World: The Environment and the Collapse of Great Civilizations.* New York: St. Martin's Press.

Portney, Kent E. 1992. *Controversial Issues in Environmental Policy: Science vs. Economics vs. Politics.* Newbury Park, Calif.: Sage.

Postel, Sandra. 1994. "Carrying Capacity: Earth's Bottom Line." *Challenge* (Mar.–Apr.): 4–12.

Potter, David. 1954. *People of Plenty.* Chicago: Univ. of Chicago Press.

Pottier, Johan P. 1986. "The Politics of Famine Prevention: Ecology, Regional Production, and Food Complementarity in Western Rwanda." In *African Affairs* 85: 207–37.

———. 1989. "Debating Styles in a Rwandan Co-operative." In *Social Anthropology and the Politics of Language,* edited by Ralph Grillo, 41–60. London: Routledge.

———. 1993. "Taking Stock: Food Marketing Reform in Rwanda, 1982–89." In *African Affairs* 92: 5–30.

Pottier, Johan P., and Augustin Nkundabashaka. 1991. "Intolerable Environments." In *Bush Base: Forest Farm,* edited by Elisabeth Croll and David Parkin. London: Routledge.

Price, Barbara. 1977. "Shifts of Production and Organization: A Cluster Interaction Model." *Current Anthropology* 18: 209–34.

Putnam, Robert D. 1993. *Making Democracy Work: Civic Traditions in Modern Italy.* Princeton, N.J.: Princeton Univ. Press.

———. 1994. "The Prosperous Community: Social Capital and Public Life." *The American Prospect.*

Pyle, A., ed. 1994. *Population: Contemporary Responses to Thomas Malthus.* Bristol, England: Thoemmes Press.

Rappoport, L., and G. Kren. 1995. "The Holocaust and the Postmodern Trend in Human Science." Paper presented to the International Society for Theory in Psychology meeting. May 23. Ottowa, Canada.

Rasler, Karen, and William R. Thompson. 1989. *War and State Making: The Shaping of the Global Powers.* Boston: Unwin Hyman.

Reader, J. 1988. *Man on Earth.* London: Penguin.

Redclift, Michael. 1987. *Sustainable Development: Exploring the Contradictions.* New York: Routledge.

Rees, W. R. 1992. "Appropriated Carrying Capacity: What Urban Economies Leave Out." *Environment and Urbanization* (Oct.)

Renfrew, Colin. 1982. "Polity and Power: Interaction, Intensification, and Exploitation." In *An Island Polity: The Archaeology of Exploitation on Melos,* edited by Colin Renfrew and Malcolm Wagstaff, 264–90. Cambridge: Cambridge Univ. Press.

———. 1986. "Introduction: Peer Polity Interaction and Socio-Political Change." In *Peer Polity Interaction and Socio-Political Change,* edited by Colin Renfrew and John F. Cherry, 1–18. Cambridge: Cambridge Univ. Press.

Reyntjens, Filip. 1985. *Pouvoir et Droit au Rwanda: Droit Public et Evolution Politique, 1916–1973.* Tervuren: Musée Royal de l'Afrique Centrale.

———. 1994. *L'Afrique des Grands Lacs en Crise: Rwanda, Burundi, 1988–1994.* Paris: Karthala.

Ridgeway, James, ed. 1994. *The Haiti Files: Decoding the Crisis.* Washington, D.C.: Essential Books.

Rielly, John E. 1995. "Leaders vs. the Public: Foreign Policy Preferences." *The Polling Report* 11, no. 6 (Mar. 20): 2.

Riggs, Fred W. 1994. "Ethnonationalism, Idustrialism, and the Modern State." *Third World Quarterly* 15, no. 4 (Dec.): 583–611.

Rinehart, Robert. 1982. "Historical Setting." In *Somalia: A Country Study*, edited by Harold D. Nelson, 1–63. Washington, D.C.: Area Handbook Series.

Roberts, N. 1989. *The Holocene: An Environmental History*. Oxford: Basil Blackwell.

Roberts, Paul Craig, and Lawrence M. Stratton, Jr. 1995. "Color Code." *National Review* (Mar. 20): 36–50.

Ross, C. A. 1991. "Epidemiology of Multiple Personality Disorder and Dissociation." *Psychiatric Clinics of North America* 14: 503–17.

Rostow, Walter W. 1960. *The Stages of Economic Growth: A Non-Communist Manifesto*. New York: Cambridge Univ. Press.

Rothschild, Joseph. 1981. *Ethnopolitics: A Conceptual Framework*. New York: Columbia Univ. Press.

Rousseau, Jean-Jacques. 1950. "A Discourse on the Origin of Inequality." In *The Social Contract and Discourses*, edited by G. D. H. Cole. New York: E. P. Dutton and Company.

Rowan, J. 1990. *Subpersonalities: The People Inside Us*. New York: Rutledge.

Rozanov, Boris G., Viktor Targulian, and D. S. Orlov. 1990. "Soils." In *The Earth as Transformed by Human Activity*, edited by B. L. Turner II et al., 203–14. Cambridge: Cambridge Univ. Press.

Rubenstein, Edward. 1995. "Missing the Point." *National Review* (Feb. 20): 16.

Rubenstein, Richard. 1978. *The Cunning of History*. New York: Harper and Row.

———1983. *The Age of Triage: Fear and Hope in an Over-crowded World*. Boston: Beacon Press.

Rudensky, Nikolai. 1992. "War as a Factor of Ethnic Conflict and Stability in the U.S.S.R." In *Effects of War on Society*, edited by G. Ausenda. San Marino: Center for Interdisciplinary Research on Social Stress.

Rummel, R. J. 1994. *Death By Government*. New Brunswick, N.J.: Transaction Publishers.

Runciman, W. G. 1966. *Relative Deprivation and Social Justice*. Berkeley: Univ. of California Press.

Runnels, Curtis. 1995. "Environmental Degradation in Ancient Greece." *Scientific American* 272: 96–99.

Russett, Bruce M. 1964. "Inequality and Instability: The Relation of Land Tenure to Politics." *World Politics* 16: 442–54.

Sachs, Wolfgang. 1995. "Global Economy and the Shadow of 'Development'." In *Deep Ecology for the Twenty-first Century*, edited by George Sessions. Boston: Shambhala Press.

Saint-Gérard, Yves. 1984. *L'État de Mal: Haïti*. Toulouse, France: Eche.

Saint-Jean, Armande. 1994. "Rwanda: An Activist Reflects on Her Nation's Trauma and Recovery." In *Ms* 5, no. 3 (Nov.–Dec.): 10–14.

Sampson, E. E. 1985. "The Decentralization of Identity." *American Psychologist* 40: 1203–11.

———. 1989. "The Challenge of Social Change for Psychology: Globalization and Psychology's Theory of the Person." *American Psychologist* 44: 914–21.

Sandbrook, Richard. 1993. *The Politics of Africa's Economic Recovery.* Cambridge: Cambridge Univ. Press.

Sartre, Jean-Paul. 1960. *Critique de la Raison Dialectique.* Paris: Gallimard.

———. 1976. *Critique of Dialectical Reason,* translated by Alan Sheridan-Smith. London: New Left Books.

Schemo, D. J. 1993. "Nearly Everything in Somalia Is Now Up for Grabs." *New York Times* (Feb. 22): 3.

Schipper, L., and S. Meyers. 1992. *Energy Efficiency and Human Activity,* Cambridge: Cambridge Univ. Press.

Schnaiberg, Allan, and Kenneth Alan Gould. 1994. *Environment and Society: The Enduring Conflict.* New York: St Martin's Press.

Schor, Julia. 1991. *The Overworked American.* New York: Basic Books.

Schumpteter, J. 1955. *Imperialism and Social Classes.* New York, Meridian.

Schwarz, Benjamin. 1995. "The Diversity Myth: America's Leading Export." In *Atlantic Monthly* 275 (May 1995): 57–67.

Seager, Joni. 1993. *Earth Follies.* New York: Routledge.

Secord, P.F. 1990. "Explaining Social Behaviors." *Theoretican and Philosophical Psychology* 10: 25–38.

Service, Elman R. 1975. *Origins of the State and Civilization: The Process of Cultural Evolution.* New York: W. W. Norton.

Shaw, R. Paul, and Yuwa Wong. 1987. "Ethnic Mobilization and the Seeds of Warfare: An Evolutionary Perspective." *International Studies Quarterly* 31, no. 1 (Mar.): 5–31.

Sharpe, Rochelle. 1993. "In Latest Recession, Only Blacks Suffered Net Employment Loss." *Wall Street Journal* (Sept. 14): 1.

Shefrin, Bruce M. 1980. *The Future of U.S. Politics in an Age of Economic Limits.* Boulder, Col.: Westview Press.

Sidell, Scott R. 1988. *The IMF and Third-World Political Instability: Is There a Connection?* London: Macmillan.

Simon, Julian. 1981. *The Ultimate Resource.* Princeton, N.J.: Princeton Univ. Press.

Simpson, Miles. 1990. "Political Rights and Income Inequality: A Cross-National Text." *American Sociological Review* 55: 682–93.

Sitarz, Daniel, ed. 1994. *Agenda 21: The Earth Summit Strategy to Save Our Planet.* Boulder, Colo.: Earthpress.

Skchoeberlein-Engel, John. 1994. "Toppling the Balance: The Creation of 'Inter-Ethnic' War in Tâjikistân." Paper presented at the conference "The State under Siege: Political Disintegration in the Post-Cold War Era," organized by R. Brian Ferguson. New York: New York Academy of Sciences. Apr. 22–24.

Skinner, B. J. 1987. "Supplies of Geochemically Scarce Metals." In *Resources and World Development,* edited by B. J. Skinner and D. J. McClaren. Dahlem Workshop Reports. New York: Wiley.

Skocpol, Theda. 1979. *States and Social Revolution.* New York: Cambridge Univ. Press.

Smil, Vaclav. 1993. *China's Environmental Crisis: An Inquiry into the Limits of National Development.* New York: M. E. Sharpe.

Smith, Anthony D. 1986. *The Ethnic Origin of Nations.* Oxford: Basil Blackwell.

Smith, David Norman. 1995. "The Genesis of Genocide in Rwanda: The Fatal Dialectic of Class and Ethnicity." In *Humanity and Society* 19, no. 4 (Nov.).

Smith, Roger W. 1987. "Human Destructiveness and Politics: The Twentieth Century as an Age of Genocide." In *Genocide and the Modern Age: Etiology and Case Studies of Mass Death,* edited by Isidor Wallimann and Michael N. Dobkowski, 21–39. Westport, Conn.: Greenwood Press.

———. 1992. "Exploring the United States' Thirty-five-Year Reluctance to Ratify the Genocide Convention." *Harvard Human Rights Journal* 5: 227–33.

Smith, V. L. 1992. "Economic Principles in the Emergence of Humankind." *Economic Inquiry* 30: 1–13.

Sorokin, Pitirim. 1962. "Social and Cultural Dynamics." Vol. 3. *Fluctuations of Social Relations, War, and Revolution.* New York: Bedminister Press.

Speth, James Gustave. 1992. "A Post-Rio Compact." In *Foreign Policy* (fall): 145–61.

Spitz, Douglas. 1993. "Cultural Pluralism, Revivalism, and Modernity in South Asia: The Rashtriya Swayamsevak Sangh." In *The Rising Tide of Cultural Pluralism: The Nation-State at Bay?,* edited by Crawford Young, 242–64. Madison: Univ. of Wisconsin Press.

Stanley, C. 1993. "Repression and Resistance: Problems of Regulation in Contemporary Urban Culture." *International Journal of the Sociology of Law* 21: 23–47.

Staub, E. 1989. *The Roots of Evil.* New York: Cambridge Univ. Press.

Steadman, David W. 1995. "Prehistoric Extinctions of Pacific Island Birds: Biodiversity Meets Zooarchaeology." *Science* 267 (Feb. 24): 1123–27.

Stein, P. L., and B. M. Rowe. 1995. *Physical Anthropology: The Core.* New York: McGraw-Hill.

Steiner, Stan. 1976. *The Vanishing White Man.* Norman: Univ. of Oklahoma Press.

Stepick, Alex. 1992. "Unintended Consequences: Rejecting Haitian Boat People and Destabilizing Duvalier." In *Western Hemisphere Immigration and United States Foreign Policy,* edited by Christopher Mitchell, 125–55. University Park: Pennsylvania State Univ. Press.

Stevens, William K. 1995. "Entire Ecosystems on Endangered List." *San Francisco Chronicle* (Feb. 14): 2.

Stevenson, J. 1993. "Social Aspects of the Industrial Revolution." In *The Industrial Revolution and British Society,* edited by P. O'Brien and R. Quinault, 229–53.

Stoessinger, John G. 1979. *The Might of Nations.* New York: Random House.

Streit, Christian. 1990. "The Fate of the Soviet Prisoners of War." In *A Mosaic of Victims: Non-Jews Persecuted and Murdered by the Nazis,* edited by Michael Berenbaum, 142–49. New York: New York Univ. Press.

Stretton, Hugh. 1976. *Capitalism, Socialism, and the Environment.* Cambridge: Cambridge Univ. Press.

Stycos, J. Mayone. 1995. "Population, Projections, and Policy: A Cautionary Perspective." *Population and Environment* 16, no. 3: 205–20.

Sundberg, Ulf, Jan Lindegren, Howard T. Odum, and Steven Doherty. 1994. "Forest EMERGY Basis for Swedish Power in the Seventeenth Century." *Scandinavian Journal of Forest Research,* Supp. 1.

Swardson, Anne. 1994. "Net Losses: Fishing Decimating Oceans' 'Unlimited' Bounty." *Washington Post* (Aug. 14).

Tainter, Joseph. 1988. *The Collapse of Complex Societies.* New York: Cambridge Univ. Press.

———. 1992. "Evolutionary Consequences of War." In *Effects of War on Society,* edited by G. Ausenda, 103–30. San Marino: Center for Interdisciplinary Research on Social Stress.

———. 1994. "La Fine Dell'Amministrazione Centrale: Il Collaso Dell'Impero Romano in Occidente." In *Storia d'Europa, Volume Secondo: Preistoriae Antichià,* edited by Jean Guilaine and Salvatore Settis, 1207–55. Turin: Einaudi.

———. 1995. "Sustainability of Complex Societies." *Futures* 27: 397–407.

Tanter, Robert, and Manus I. Midlarsky. 1967. "A Theory of Revolution." *Journal of Conflict Resolution* 11: 264–80.

Taylor, Christopher C. 1992. *Milk, Honey, and Money: Changing Concepts in Rwandan Healing.* Washington: Smithsonian Institution Press.

Teo, Peggy. 1995. "Population Planning and Change in Singapore." *Population and Environment* 16, no. 3: 237–52.

Thurow, Lester. 1980. *The Zero Sum Society.* New York: Penguin.

Tilly, Charles. 1978. *From Mobilization to Revolution.* Reading, Mass.: Addison-Wesley.

Timberlake, Lloyd. 1986. *Africa in Crisis: The Causes, the Cures of Environmental Bankruptcy.* Philadelphia: New Society Publishers.

Trainer, F. E. 1985. *Abandon Affluence!* London: Zed.

———. 1989. *Developed to Death.* London: Greenprint.

———. 1995a. *The Conserver Society: Alternatives for Sustainability.* London: Zed Books.

———. 1995b. *Towards a Sustainable Economy.* Sydney, Australia: Envirobooks.

———. 1994c. *There Are Alternatives.* London: Zed Books.

———. Forthcoming. "How Long Will Resources Last?"

Trouillot, Michel-Rolph. 1990. *Haiti: State Against Nation—The Origins and Legacy of Duvalierism.* New York: Monthly Review Press.

Tugwell, Rexford. 1970. *Model for a New Constitution.* Palo Alto: James E. Freel.

Turner, Billie L. II, et al., eds. 1990. *The Earth as Transformed by Human Action: Global and Regional Changes in the Biosphere over the Past Three Hundred Years.* New York: Cambridge Univ. Press.

United Nations Development Program. 1995. "Redefining Security: The Human Dimension." *Current History* 94, no. 592 (May): 229–36.

United States Bureau of Mines. 1985. *Mineral Facts and Problems.* World Scientists Warning Briefing Book. Cambridge, Mass.: Union of Concerned Scientists.

United States Department of the Interior World Bank. 1990. *World Development Report.* Washington, D.C.

Van Creveld, Martin L. 1991. *The Transformation of War.* New York: The Free Press.

van der Merwe, N. J. 1992. "Reconstructing Prehistoric Diet." In *The Cambridge Encyclopedia of Human Evolution,* edited by S. Jones et al., 369–72.

Vanwalle, Rita. 1982. "Aspecten van Staatsvorming in West-Ruanda." In *Africa-Tervuren* 28.

Vidal, Claudine. 1969. "Le Rwanda des Anthropologues ou le Fétichisme de la Vache." In *Cahiers d'Études Africaines* 9: 389–400.

———. 1985. "Situations Ethniques au Rwanda." In *Au Cour de l'Ethnie: Ethnies, Tribalisme, et État en Afrique,* edited by Jean-Loup Amselle and Elikia M'bokolo. Paris: Découverte.

———. 1991. *Sociologie des Passions (Côte d'Ivoire, Rwanda).* Paris: Karthala.

Viditch, Arthur J. 1980. "Inflation and Social Structure: The United States in an Epoch of Declining Abundance." *Social Problems* 27, no. 5: 636–49.

Vitousek, Peter, Paul Ehrlich, Anne Ehrlich, and Peter Matson. 1986. "Human Appropriation of the Products of Photosynthesis." *BioScience* 36: 368–73.

Wall. Alex de. 1994. "The Genocidal State: Hutu Extremism and the Origins of the 'Final Solution' in Rwanda." *Times Literary Supplement* 4761 (July 1): 3–4.

Wallimann, Isidor. 1994. "Can the World Industrialization Project Be Sustained?" In *Monthly Review* (Mar.): 41–51.

Walzer, Michael. 1980. "Dissatisfaction in the Welfare State." In *Radical Principles,* by Michael Walzer, 23–53. New York: Basic Books.

Ward, M. D. 1978. *The Political Economy of Distribution: Equality Versus Inequality.* New York: Elsevier.

Warren, Kay B. 1993. "Interpreting la Violencia in Guatemala: Shapes of Mayan Silence and Resistance." In *The Violence Within: Cultural and Political Opposition in Divided Nations,* edited by Kay B. Warren, 25–56. Boulder, Colo.: Westview.

Watson, Catharine. 1991. *Exile from Rwanda: Background to an Invasion.* Washington, D.C.: The U.S. Committee for Refugees, Issue Paper (Feb.).

Weatherford, Jack. 1994. *Savages and Civilization: Who Will Survive.* New York: Crown Publishers.

Weede, Erich. 1993. "The Impact of Democracy or Repressiveness on the Quality of Life, Income Distribution, and Economic Growth Rates." *International Sociology* 8: 177–95.

Weiskel, Timothy. 1989. "The Ecological Lessons of the Past: An Anthropology of Environmental Decline." *The Ecologist* 19: 104–9.

Weiss, H., M.-A. Courty, W. Wetterstrom, F. Guichard, L. Senior, R. Meadow, and A. Currow. 1993. "The Genesis and Collapse of Third Millennium North Mesopotamian Civilization." *Science* 261: 995–1004.

Whitaker, Ben. 1985. *Revised and Updated Report on the Question of the Prevention and Punishment of the Crime of Genocide.* New York: United Nations Document, E/CN.4 Sub. 2/1985/6. July 2.

Whitehead, Neil L. 1992. "Tribes Make States and States Make Tribes: Warfare and the Creation of Colonial Tribes and States in Northeastern South America." In *War in the Tribal Zone: Expanding States and Indigenous Warfare,* edited by R. Brian Ferguson and Neil L. Whitehead, 127–50. Santa Fe: School of American Research Press.

Whitmore, R. 1992. "When Living and Wages Don't Meet." *The Tennessean* (Jan.5): 1, 4E.

Wiarda, Ieda Siqueira, and Howard D. Wiarda. 1986. *Population, Internal Unrest, and U.S. Security.* Amherst: Univ. of Massachusetts Internal Area Studies.

Wickham-Crowley, Timothy P. 1991. *Exploring Revolution: Essays on Latin American Insurgency and Revolutionary Theory.* Armonk, N.Y.: M. E. Sharpe.

Wilkinson, R. G. 1973. *Poverty and Progress: An Ecological Perspective on Economic Development.* New York: Praeger.

Willey, David. 1994. "UK Round Table on Sustainable Development." Response to Department of the Environment "Further Government Proposals," Oct. 24, 1994. London. Nov. 16.

Williams, Raymond. 1983. *The Year 2000.* New York: Pantheon.

Williamson, Jeffrey G. 1991. *Inequality, Poverty, and History.* Cambridge, Mass.: Basil Blackwell.

Williamson, Jeffrey G., and Peter Lindert. 1980. *American Inequality: A Macroeconomic History.* New York: Academic.

Wilson, Edward O. 1992. *The Diversity of Life.* Cambridge, Mass.: Harvard Univ. Press.

Woodburn, James. 1978. "Sex Roles and the Division of Labour in Hunting and Gathering Societies." Paper presented at the First International Conference on Hunting and Gathering Societies. Paris. June.

————. 1982. "Egalitarian Societies." *Man* 17: 431–51.

Woodham-Smith, Cecil. 1962. *The Great Hunger: Ireland 1845–1849.* New York: Harper and Row.

World Bank. 1989. *Sub-Saharan Africa: From Crisis to Sustainable Growth.* Washington, D.C.: The World Bank.

World Commission on Environment and Development. 1987. *Our Common Future.* Oxford: Oxford Univ. Press.

Young, John. *Sustaining the Earth.* Cambridge, Mass.: Harvard Univ. Press, 1990.

Zeldin, Theodore. 1994. *An Intimate History of Humanity.* New York: Harper Collins.

Zimmermann, Warren. 1995. "The Last Ambassador: A Memoir of the Collapse of Yugoslavia." *Foreign Affairs* 74, no. 2 (Mar./Apr.): 4.

Index

Syracuse Studies on Peace and Conflict Resolution
Harriet Hyman Alonso, Charles Chatfield, and Louis Kriesberg, *Series Editors*

Other titles in the series include:

CUMBERLAND COLLEGE LIBRARY
PO BOX 517
VINELAND, NJ 08362-0517